**THE BOSPHORUS**
*Pages 136–149*

**EXCURSIONS**
*Pages 150–171*

**BEYOĞLU**
*Pages 100–107*

*Beyoğlu*

B O S P H O R U S

**SERAGLIO POINT**
*Pages 50–67*

**SULTANAHMET**
*Pages 68–83*

*Seraglio
Point*

0 meters          500

0 yards          500

EYEWITNESS *TRAVEL GUIDES*

# ISTANBUL

# EYEWITNESS *TRAVEL GUIDES*

# ISTANBUL

DK PUBLISHING, INC.

# A DK PUBLISHING BOOK

PROJECT EDITOR Nick Inman
ART EDITOR Kate Poole
EDITORS Claire Folkard, Jane Oliver, Christine Stroyan
US EDITORS Mary Sutherland, Michael Wise
DESIGNERS Jo Doran, Paul Jackson
VISUALIZER Joy FitzSimmons
MAP CO-ORDINATORS Emily Green, David Pugh
RESEARCHERS Didem Mersin Alıcı, Hasan Kelepir

MANAGING EDITOR Georgina Matthews
MANAGING ART EDITOR Annette Jacobs
SENIOR MANAGING EDITOR Vivien Crump
DEPUTY ART DIRECTOR Gillian Allan

PRODUCTION Anna Pauletti, David Proffit
PICTURE RESEARCH Ellen Root
DTP Cooling Brown
DTP DESIGNER Lee Redmond

MAIN CONTRIBUTORS
Rosie Ayliffe, Rose Baring, Barnaby Rogerson, Canan Sılay

MAPS
Paul Bates, Anne Rayski, Glyn Rozier (ESR Cartography Ltd)
Neil Cook, Maria Donnelly, Ewan Watson
(Colourmap Scanning Ltd)

PHOTOGRAPHERS
Anthony Souter, Linda Whitwam, Francesca Yorke

ILLUSTRATORS
Richard Bonson, Stephen Conlin, Gary Cross, Richard Draper,
Paul Guest, Maltings Partnership, Chris Orr & Associates,
Paul Weston, John Woodcock
•
Text film output by Graphical Innovations (London)
Reproduced by Colourscan (Singapore)
Printed and bound in China by L.Rex Printing Co., Ltd.

First American Edition, 1998
2 4 6 8 10 9 7 5 3

Published in the United States by
DK Publishing, Inc.,
95 Madison Avenue, New York, New York 10016

Copyright © 1997 Dorling Kindersley Limited, London
Visit us on the World Wide Web at http://www.dk.com

Library of Congress Cataloging-in-Publication Data
Istanbul. -- 1st American ed.
   p.     cm. -- (Eyewitness travel guides)
Includes index.
ISBN 0-7894-2751-6
1. Istanbul (Turkey)-- Guidebooks.   I. Series.
DR718.I76  1998                              97-35005
914.961'80439 -- dc21                        CIP
•
Every effort has been made to ensure that the information in this
book is as up-to-date as possible at the time of going to press.
However, details such as telephone numbers, opening hours, prices,
gallery hanging arrangements, and travel information are liable to
change. The publishers cannot accept responsibility
for any consequences arising from the use of this book.

We would be delighted to receive any corrections and
suggestions for incorporation in the next edition. Please write to:
Senior Editor, Eyewitness Travel Guides,
DK Publishing, Inc., 95 Madison Avenue, New York, New York 10016.

# CONTENTS

Madonna mosaic in the Church of
St. Savior in Chora

## INTRODUCING ISTANBUL

Tile panel in the Paired Pavilions
of Topkapı Palace's Harem

◁ The Blue Mosque and the church of Hagia Sophia, dominating Sultanahmet Square

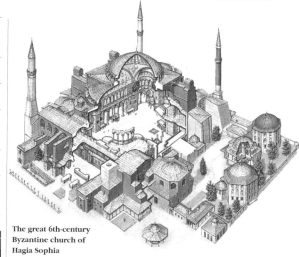

The great 6th-century Byzantine church of Hagia Sophia

Men smoking bubble pipes in Çorlulu Ali Paşa Courtyard

*Simit* seller

Ferry passing the waterfront of Karaköy below the Galata Tower

Dolmabahçe Mosque with the skyline of Sultanahmet in the distance

# HOW TO USE THIS GUIDE

THIS GUIDE helps you to get the most from your stay in Istanbul. It provides both expert recommendations and detailed practical advice. Introducing Istanbul locates the city geographically, sets Istanbul in its historical and cultural context, and gives an overview of the main attractions. Istanbul Area by Area is the main sightseeing section, giving detailed information on all the major sights, with photographs, maps, and illustrations. Greater Istanbul looks at sights outside the city center, The Bosphorus guides you through a trip up the straits, and Excursions from Istanbul explores other places within easy reach of the city. Carefully researched suggestions for restaurants, hotels, entertainment, and shopping are found in Travelers' Needs, while the Survival Guide contains useful advice on everything from changing money to traveling by tram.

## FINDING YOUR WAY AROUND ISTANBUL

The center of Istanbul has been divided into four sightseeing areas, each with its own chapter, color-coded for easy reference. All sights are numbered and plotted on an area map for each chapter. The major sights are covered in more detail.

**1 Area Introduction**
*This describes the history and character of the area and has a map on which the sights have been plotted. Other key information is also given.*

**Each area** has color-coded thumb tabs

**Locator Map**

**The area shaded pink** is shown in greater detail on the Street-by-Street map on the following pages.

**2 Street-by-Street map**
*This gives a bird's-eye view of the heart of each sightseeing area. Interesting features are labeled. There is also a list of "star sights" that no visitor should miss.*

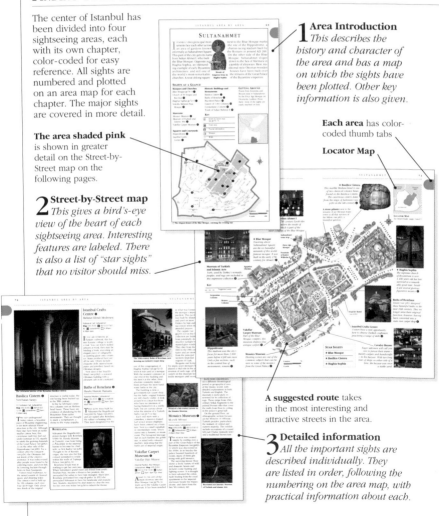

**A suggested route** takes in the most interesting and attractive streets in the area.

**3 Detailed information**
*All the important sights are described individually. They are listed in order, following the numbering on the area map, with practical information about each.*

## ISTANBUL AREA MAP

THE COLORED areas shown on this map (inside the front cover) are the four main sightseeing areas used in this guide. Each is covered in a full chapter in *Istanbul Area by Area (pp48–107)*. They are highlighted on other maps throughout the book. In *Istanbul at a Glance (see pp32–43)*, they help you to locate the top sights. The introduction to the Street Finder *(see pp238–255)* shows on which detailed street map you will find each area.

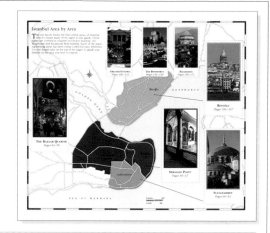

**Introductory text** gives an overview of the main sights in the Greater Istanbul area.

**A map** of the city shows Greater Istanbul and the areas covered in the chapter's sub-divisions.

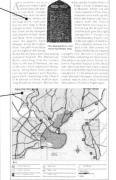

**4 Introduction to Greater Istanbul**
*Greater Istanbul has its own introduction, outlining what the city suburbs have to offer the sightseer. It is divided into five districts, shown on a map.*

**Practical information** is provided in an information block. The key to the symbols used is on the back flap.

**5 Introduction to Greater Istanbul areas**
*An introduction places the area in its historical context and provides a map showing the numbered sights.*

**The Visitors Checklist** provides detailed practical information

**6 The major sights**
*These are given two or more full pages. Historic buildings are dissected to reveal their interiors. Where necessary, sights are color-coded to help you locate the most interesting areas.*

# INTRODUCING ISTANBUL

# Putting Istanbul on the Map

ISTANBUL STANDS AT the straits of the Bosphorus, straddling the European and Asian parts of Turkey and bordered to the south by the Sea of Marmara. The city is divided not only by the Bosphorus but also by the Golden Horn, an inlet forming a natural harbor. Although no longer the capital of Turkey (*see p29*), Istanbul is still the country's largest and most monumental city.

**Satellite view of Greater Istanbul**

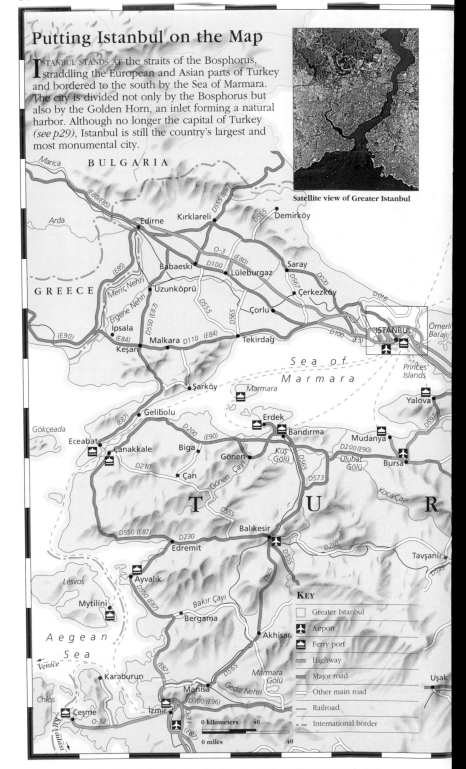

**KEY**

| | |
|---|---|
| ☐ | Greater Istanbul |
| ✈ | Airport |
| ⛴ | Ferry port |
| ═══ | Highway |
| ─── | Major road |
| ─── | Other main road |
| ─── | Railroad |
| ─·─ | International border |

0 kilometers    40

0 miles    40

◁ **Miniature depicting the lavish festivities staged for the circumcision of Ahmet III's sons in 1720**

**Istanbul and its Environs**
*The sights in central Istanbul are covered in detail on pages 48–107, and a Street Finder is provided on pages 238–55. Sights outside the center are covered on pages 108–49. Places of interest on the Bosphorus and farther afield, still within easy reach of the city, are explored on pages 134–71.*

Odessa

GREATER ISTANBUL AND ENVIRONS

Haraçci

D020

D016

Kemerburgaz

Beykoz

D 3 (E80)

Halkalı

(E80)

D020

O-4 (E80)

D100

D100 (E5)

0 kilometers    7

0 miles    4

See next page

*Black Sea*

Samsun
Trabzon

Zonguldak

D010

D75.5

Ereğli

Devrek

D030

Şile

D020

Kandıra

D 020

Karabük

Yenice Irmağı

Karasu

D010

Akçakoca

D655

D750

Kocaeli
(İzmit)

O-4 (E80)

Sakarya
(Adapazarı)

D100

Düzce

D100 (E80)

D100

D130

D100

(E80)

Gerede Çayı

Sapanca
Gölü

D140

D160

Bolu

D650

D 150

İznik
Gölü

İznik

D17.0

D140

D750

O-4 (E80)

Bilecik

D200 (E90)

Sakarya Nehri

Nallıhan

Beypazarı

Kirmir Çayı

D140

ANKARA

D595

D650

K          E          Y

Sarıyar
Barajı

D200
(E90)

Eskişehir

Milhallıçcık

D200 (E96)

D230

EUROPE AND THE MEDITERRANEAN REGION

ESTONIA

SWEDEN

DENMARK

LATVIA

LITHUANIA

RUSSIAN
FEDERATION

UNITED
REP. OF   KINGDOM
IRELAND

NETHERLANDS

BELORUSSIA

BELGIUM

GERMANY

POLAND

LUXEMBOURG

CZECH REP.

UKRAINE

SLOVAKIA

FRANCE

AUSTRIA

HUNGARY

MOLDOVA

SWITZERLAND

SLOVENIA

CROATIA

ROMANIA

BOSNIA-
HERZ.

ITALY

YUGOSLAVIA

BULGARIA

GEORGIA

PORTUGAL

SPAIN

MACEDONIA
ALBANIA

Istanbul

GREECE

TURKEY

D715

Tuz
Gölü

TUNISIA

LEBANON

SYRIA

IRAQ

MOROCCO

ALGERIA

ISRAEL
JORDAN

SAUDI
ARABIA

D625

LIBYA

EGYPT

# Greater Istanbul

THE EXPANDING METROPOLIS of Istanbul spreads along the Bosphorus to the north, beyond the airport to the west, and inland from the Asian shore in the east. Its official population is put at a little over 7 million, but the actual population is probably much higher. A new, integrated transportation system is being built to make getting around this vast urban area easier. Most visitors, however, stay in the historical central parts where the major sights are located.

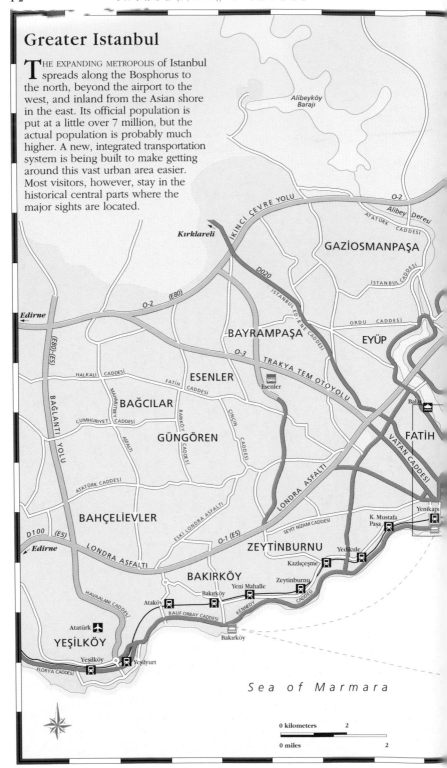

Sea of Marmara

0 kilometers    2

0 miles    2

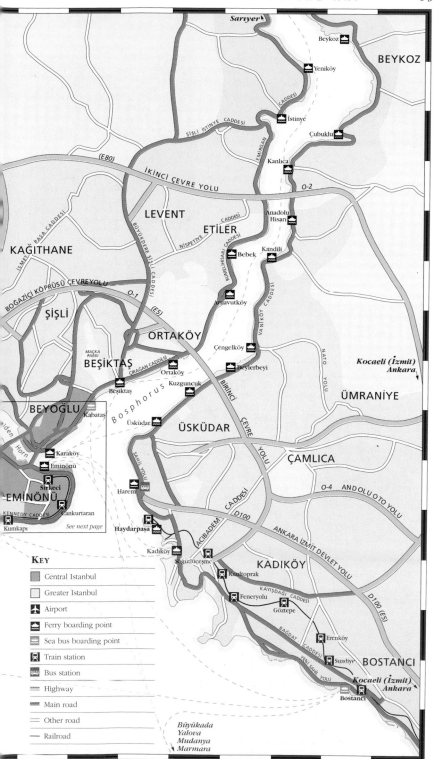

Sarıyer

Beykoz

BEYKOZ

Yeniköy

İstinye

Çubuklu

ŞİŞLİ İSTİNYE CADDESİ

Kanlıca

EMİRGAN CADDESİ

(E80)

İKİNCİ ÇEVRE YOLU

O-2

LEVENT

Anadolu Hisarı

ETİLER

CADDESİ

KAĞITHANE

NİSPETİYE

RUMELİ HİSARI CADDESİ

BÜYÜKDERE ŞİŞLİ CADDESİ

İSMET PAŞA CADDESİ

Bebek

Kandili

Arnavutköy

VANİKÖY CADDESİ

BOĞAZİÇİ KÖPRÜSÜ ÇEVREYOLU

O-1

(E5)

ORTAKÖY

ŞİŞLİ

Çengelköy

MAÇKA PARKI

BEŞİKTAŞ

ÇIRAĞAN CADDESİ

Ortaköy

Beylerbeyi

Kocaeli (İzmit) Ankara

Beşiktaş

Kuzguncuk

BİRİNCİ

Bosphorus

NATO YOLU

ÜMRANİYE

BEYOĞLU

Kabataş

Üsküdar

ÜSKÜDAR

ÇEVRE YOLU

Karaköy

Eminönü

ÇAMLICA

SAHİL YOLU

Sirkeci

Harem

O-4

ANDOLU OTO YOLU

EMİNÖNÜ

Cankurtaran

CADDESİ

KENNEDY CADDESİ

D100

Kumkapı

See next page

Haydarpaşa

ANKARA İZMİT DEVLET YOLU

Kadıköy

ACIBADEM

Söğütlüçeşme

KADIKÖY

D100 (E5)

Kızıltoprak

KAYIŞDAĞI CADDESİ

Feneryolu

Göztepe

BAĞDAT CADDESİ

Erenköy

Suadiye

BOSTANCI

Kocaeli (İzmit) Ankara

YENİ SAHİL YOLU

Bostancı

Büyükada
Yalova
Mudanya
Marmara

# Central Istanbul

**Shoe shine man outside the New Mosque**

THIS GUIDE divides central Istanbul into four distinct areas, each with its own chapter. Three areas lie on the southern side of the Golden Horn. Seraglio Point is a raised promontory on which stands the sumptuous Topkapı Palace. Two architectural masterpieces, Hagia Sophia and the Blue Mosque, dominate the area of Sultanahmet. The pace of life is quite different in the Bazaar Quarter, a maze of narrow streets filled with frenetic commerce. North of the Golden Horn is Beyoğlu, which for centuries was the preferred place of residence of Istanbul's foreign communities, and is still markedly cosmopolitan in atmosphere.

**İstiklal Caddesi, Beyoğlu**
*Old-fashioned trams shuttle up and down the pedestrian street that forms the backbone of this area (see pp100–7).*

**The Grand Bazaar, in the Bazaar Quarter**
*This quaint former coffeehouse stands at a junction in the labyrinthine old shopping complex at the heart of the city's Bazaar Quarter (see pp84–99).*

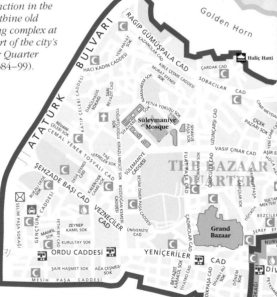

## KEY

| | |
|---|---|
| ▪ | Major sight |
| ⚓ | Ferry boarding point |
| 🚉 | Train station |
| Ⓜ | Metro or Tünel station |
| 🚋 | Tram stop |
| ℹ | Tourist information |
| 👮 | Police station |
| 🛁 | Turkish bath |
| C | Mosque |
| ✝ | Church |
| ✉ | Post office |

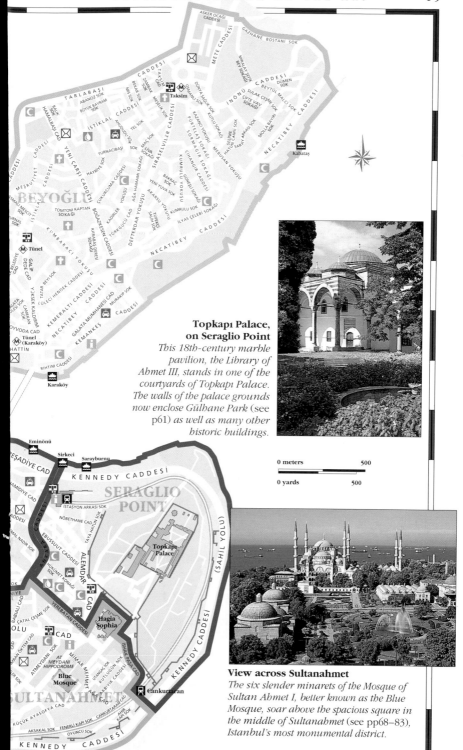

**Topkapı Palace,
on Seraglio Point**
*This 18th-century marble
pavilion, the Library of
Ahmet III, stands in one of the
courtyards of Topkapı Palace.
The walls of the palace grounds
now enclose Gülhane Park (see
p61) as well as many other
historic buildings.*

| 0 meters | 500 |
| --- | --- |
| 0 yards | 500 |

**View across Sultanahmet**
*The six slender minarets of the Mosque of
Sultan Ahmet I, better known as the Blue
Mosque, soar above the spacious square in
the middle of Sultanahmet (see pp68–83),
Istanbul's most monumental district.*

# THE HISTORY OF ISTANBUL

ISTANBUL WAS FOUNDED *in the 7th century BC on a naturally defensive site from which trade along the Bosphorus could be controlled. For 16 centuries it was a great imperial capital, first of the Byzantine Empire and then of the Ottoman sultans. Some knowledge of the histories of these two civilizations helps the visitor to appreciate the magnificent monuments found throughout the city.*

The topography of Istanbul was formed at the end of the last Ice Age, when meltwaters created the Bosphorus. The Stone Age cultures in the area were replaced by Copper Age villages and walled Bronze Age towns (notably Troy, *see p171*). The Bosphorus was an important trade route in the ancient world, along which ships carried wine and olive oil north from the Mediterranean, and grain, skins, wool, lumber, wax, honey, salted meat, and salted fish south from regions around the Black Sea.

Septimius Severus, who devastated the city in the 2nd century AD

The area around the Bosphorus was subjugated by a series of peoples, starting with the Mycenaeans (1400–1200 BC). Between 800 and 680 BC, the region was controlled by the kingdom of Phrygia. Later, in 676 BC, Greek expeditionaries founded the city of Chalcedon, on the site where modern Kadıköy now stands.

### THE FOUNDATION OF BYZANTION

The foundation of Istanbul is usually dated to 667 BC. According to legend, a Greek colonist, Byzas, led an expedition from the overcrowded cities of Athens and Megara to establish a colony on the European side of the Bosphorus. This colony, known as Byzantion, grew to be a successful independent city-state, or *polis*, one of the 40 most important such states throughout the Ancient Greek world. During the next few centuries, Byzantion worked in partnership with Chalcedon, using the same coinage and sharing the tolls exacted from passing sea trade.

But Byzantion had to struggle to maintain its independence in the mercurial politics of the ancient world. It endured Lydian (560–546 BC), Persian (546–478 BC), Athenian (478–411 BC), and Macedonian (334–281 BC) rule before briefly regaining its autonomy. In 64 BC it was subsumed into the Roman Empire as Byzantium. The city was almost destroyed in AD 195 by Septimius Severus because of its support for his rival for the imperial throne, Pescennius Niger. It survived the Goths' devastation of Chalcedon in AD 258, but trade in the region dramatically declined in the following years.

## TIMELINE

**c.676 BC** Chalcedon, a Greek settlement, founded on Asian shore

**340 BC** Philip II of Macedonia unsuccessfully besieges city

*Alexander the Great*

**AD 195** Roman emperor Septimius Severus destroys Byzantium but later rebuilds it, laying out the Hippodrome

| 600 BC | 400 BC | 200 BC | AD 1 | AD 200 |
|---|---|---|---|---|

**c.667 BC** Byzantion reputedly founded by Greek colonists from Athens and Megara, led by Byzas

**334 BC** Alexander the Great crosses the Hellespont (Dardanelles) and conquers Anatolia

**64 BC** Pompey brings Byzantion into the Roman Empire, renaming it Byzantium

**AD 258** Goths destroy Chalcedon

◁ **The Byzantine emperor Justinian the Great shown with one of his prefects in a mosaic**

## CONSTANTINE THE GREAT

In AD 324, after defeating his co-emperor Licinius, Constantine the Great (324–37) became sole ruler of the Roman Empire. One of his greatest achievements was to move the capital of the empire from Rome to Byzantium. Initially, Constantine preferred the site of Troy *(see p171)* for his capital, but was persuaded by advisers that Byzantium held a superior position for both defense and trade. Constantine's city was officially styled the "New Rome" but became widely known as Constantinople. The emperor quickly started on an ambitious program of construction work, which included the Great Palace *(see pp82–3)* and various public buildings.

**Gold aureus of Constantine**

Constantine was also instrumental in the spread of Christianity. According to legend, he saw a vision of the cross before a battle in 312. Although not actually baptized until just before his death, he worked hard to create a coherent system of Christian belief out of the variant practices of the day. All the early church councils took place in the city or nearby, the first being held in Nicaea, (modern-day İznik, *see p160),* and the second in Constantinople itself.

A successor of Constantine, Theodosius I (379–95), divided the Empire between his two sons, Honorius and Arcadius. When the Latin-speaking Western Empire fell to barbarian armies during the 5th century, the Greek-speaking Eastern Empire, thereafter known as the Byzantine Empire, survived.

## THE AGE OF JUSTINIAN

The 6th century was dominated by the extraordinary genius of Justinian (527–65), who developed Constantinople into a thriving city and almost succeeded in reconquering the lost provinces of the Western Empire from the barbarians. At the time of his death the empire had expanded to its greatest size, and covered Syria, Palestine, Asia Minor, Greece, the Balkans, Italy, southern Spain, and many territories in northern Africa, including Egypt.

**Empress Theodora, wife of Justinian**

Justinian's formidable wife, the ex-courtesan Theodora, had a great deal of influence over him. In 532 she persuaded the emperor to use mercenaries to put down an angry mob in the most notorious event of his reign, the Nika Revolt. In the carnage that followed 30,000 were killed inside the Hippodrome *(see p80).*

Justinian was also responsible for much of the city's great architecture, including Hagia Sophia *(see pp72–5),* Hagia Eirene *(see p60),* and parts of the Great Palace.

**Relief from the Egyptian Obelisk *(see p80),* showing Theodosius I and his courtiers**

## TIMELINE

| 300 | | 400 | | 500 | 600 | 700 |
|---|---|---|---|---|---|---|
| **324** Constantine becomes sole ruler of the Roman Empire | **330** Inauguration of Constantinople | **395** On the death of Theodosius I, the empire is divided in two | **476** The Western Roman Empire falls to barbarians | **532** Nika Revolt is put down by mercenaries; 30,000 are killed | | **674** Five-year-long siege of Constantinople initiated by the Saracens |
| **325** First church council meets at Nicaea | **337** Constantine is baptized a Christian on his deathbed | **412** Construction work begins on the Walls of Theodosius II *(see p20)* | | **537** Emperor Justinian dedicates the new Hagia Sophia | **726** Leo III issues a decree denouncing idolatry, and many icons are destroyed | |

*Walls of Theodosius II*

## THE BYZANTINES AT WAR

The Byzantine Empire never again attained the splendor of the reign of Justinian, but throughout the first millennium it remained rich and powerful. During the early Middle Ages, Constantinople was an oasis of learning, law, art, and culture at a time when Europe was plunged into a

"Greek fire," used by the Byzantines against the Arabs

dark age of ignorance and illiteracy. Considering themselves to be the leaders of Christianity, the Byzantine rulers dispatched missionaries to spread their religion and culture among the Slavic nations, especially Russia.

During this period, Constantinople produced some capable emperors, in particular Heraclius (610–41), Basil the Macedonian (867–86), Leo the Wise (886–912), and Basil the Bulgar-Slayer (976–1025). Between them these rulers contributed a number of buildings to the city and recaptured lost provinces.

Never without enemies greedy for a share of the prodigious riches that had been amassed in the city, Constantinople was besieged by Slavs, Arabs, Avars, Bulgars, Persians, and Russians, all without success because of the protection of the land walls. The surrounding seas, meanwhile, were under the control of Constantinople's powerful navy. Its main ship was the *dromon*, an oared vessel that could ram another ship but above all deliver the dreaded "Greek fire," an early napalm-like weapon.

A 6th-century ivory carving of a Byzantine emperor, possibly Anastasius I (491–518)

In 1059 Constantine X, the first of the Dukas dynasty of emperors, ascended to the throne. The state over which the dynasty presided was a weakened one, divided between the overprivileged bureaucracy in the capital and the feudal landlords of the provinces. At the same time increasing dependency on foreign mercenaries placed the empire's defense in the hands of its most aggressive neighbors. These included the Normans from southern Italy, the Venetians, and Turkic nomads from the east.

The Byzantine imperial army was totally destroyed at the Battle of Manzikert (1071) and again, a century later, at the Battle of Myriocephalon (1176) by the Seljuk Turks from the east. These losses effectively ended Byzantine rule of Anatolia, which had for so long been the backbone of the empire. The remarkable Comnenus dynasty (1081–1185) ruled for a century after the Dukas emperors, between these two defeats. Their main achievement was to succeed in holding the rest of the empire together.

| | | | |
|---|---|---|---|
| **843** Icons are permitted again by seventh church council at Hagia Sophia | **1071** The Byzantine army is destroyed by the Seljuk Turks at the Battle of Manzikert. Emperor Romanus Diogenes is disgraced and deposed | **1138** John II Comnenus recovers Serbia | **1176** The Seljuk Turks defeat the Byzantine forces at the Battle of Myriocephalon |
| 800 | 900  1000 | 1100 | 1200 |

*Hagia Sophia mosaic*

**1054** The Orthodox and Catholic churches break away from each other because of differences over dogma

**1096** The armies of the First Crusade pass through Constantinople and assist Alexius I Comnenus to retake the Anatolian seaboard from the Seljuk Turks

# The City of Constantinople

**Mosaic of the Virgin, St. Savior in Chora**

FOR ALMOST a thousand years Constantinople was the richest city in Christendom. It radiated out from three great buildings: the church of Hagia Sophia *(see pp 72–5)*, the Hippodrome *(see p80)*, and the Great Palace *(see pp82–3)*. The city also had a great many other fine churches and palaces, filled with exquisite works of art. Daily life for the populace centered on the four market squares, or *fora*. Meanwhile, their need for fresh water was met by an advanced network of aqueducts and underground water cisterns.

**Walls of Theodosius**
*Theodosius II's great chain of land walls* (see p114) *withstood countless sieges until the Ottoman conquest of the city in 1453* (see p24).

## THE CITY IN 1200

At its height, the magnificent city of Constantinople probably had about 400,000 inhabitants. The population density was relatively low, though, and there was space within the city walls for fields and orchards.

**Mocius Cistern**

**The Golden Gate** was a ceremonial gate through the city's ramparts.

**Church of St. John of Studius** *(see p116)*

**Walls of Constantine (now totally destroyed)**

**Forum of Arcadius**

**Harbor of Theodosius**

## BYZANTINE CHURCH ARCHITECTURE

Early Byzantine churches were either basilical (like St. John of Studius) or built to a centralized plan (as in SS. Sergius and Bacchus). From the 9th century, churches, like the typical example shown here, were built around four corner piers, or columns. Exteriors were mostly unadorned brickwork, but interiors were lavishly decorated with golden mosaics. Although the Ottomans converted Constantinople's churches into mosques after their conquest of the city, many original features are clearly discernible today.

**TYPICAL LATE BYZANTINE CHURCH**

**A central apse** is flanked by two smaller side apses.

**Four columns** support the dome.

**Brickwork** may alternate with layers of stone.

**The narthex**, a covered porch, forms the entrance to the church.

**Golden mosaics** cover the ceilings and upper walls.

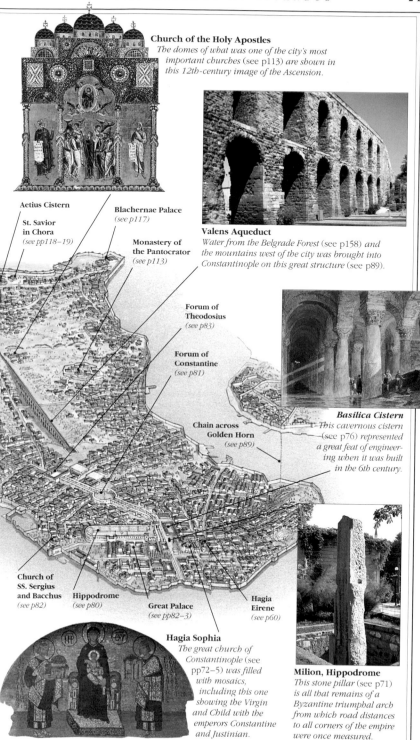

**Church of the Holy Apostles**
*The domes of what was one of the city's most important churches (see p113) are shown in this 12th-century image of the Ascension.*

**Valens Aqueduct**
*Water from the Belgrade Forest (see p158) and the mountains west of the city was brought into Constantinople on this great structure (see p89).*

Aetius Cistern

**St. Savior in Chora**
*(see pp118–19)*

**Blachernae Palace**
*(see p117)*

**Monastery of the Pantocrator**
*(see p113)*

**Forum of Theodosius**
*(see p83)*

**Forum of Constantine**
*(see p81)*

**Chain across Golden Horn**
*(see p89)*

**Basilica Cistern**
*This cavernous cistern (see p76) represented a great feat of engineering when it was built in the 6th century.*

**Church of SS. Sergius and Bacchus**
*(see p82)*

**Hippodrome**
*(see p80)*

**Great Palace**
*(see pp82–3)*

**Hagia Eirene**
*(see p60)*

**Hagia Sophia**
*The great church of Constantinople (see pp72–5) was filled with mosaics, including this one showing the Virgin and Child with the emperors Constantine and Justinian.*

**Milion, Hippodrome**
*This stone pillar (see p71) is all that remains of a Byzantine triumphal arch from which road distances to all corners of the empire were once measured.*

The capture of Constantinople during the Fourth Crusade of 1202–4

## THE FOURTH CRUSADE

In 1202, an army of 34,000 responded to an appeal from Pope Innocent III for a new crusade to the Holy Land. This unruly force of Christians lacked the funds to get beyond Venice, where it needed ships. Consequently, it fell under the influence of Enrico Dandolo, the manipulative Doge of Venice. With his backing, the crusaders were soon diverted to Constantinople where they helped the young Alexius IV take the throne.

However, six months later, when they realized they were unlikely to receive their promised financial reward from the emperor, the crusaders lost patience and launched a new attack, ousting Alexius in favor

Icon of St. Michael, now in Venice, an example of the fine Byzantine art plundered by the Venetians during the Fourth Crusade

of one their own, Baldwin I, Count of Flanders. Through the dark years that followed, known as the Latin Empire, the once great city was reduced by pillage, misrule, and emigration to a scattering of disconnected villages grouped behind the city walls. Outside Constantinople, the exiled Byzantine emperors survived the turmoil, biding their time as the rulers of the Empire of Nicaea, just to the south, which included modern-day İznik (see p160).

## CONSTANTINOPLE IN DECLINE

In 1261, Constantinople was recaptured for Byzantium by Michael VIII Paleologus (1258–82), who met almost no resistance in the process. He did this with the aid

## TIMELINE

**1202** An army assembles in Venice to launch the Fourth Crusade

**1204** Alexius IV is deposed and Baldwin I is crowned emperor of a new Latin Empire

**1261** Michael VIII Paleologus recaptures Constantinople from the Venetians

**1331** Ottomans capture Nicaea (modern İznik)

**1326** Prusa (Bursa) is taken and becomes Ottoman capital

| 1200 | 1225 | 1250 | 1275 | 1300 | 1325 |
|------|------|------|------|------|------|

**1203** Dandolo, Doge of Venice, diverts the Fourth Crusade to Constantinople. He cuts the chain across the Golden Horn (see p21) and storms the city

**1301** Osman I founds the Ottoman Empire

*Bronze horses taken by Dandolo from the Hippodrome (see p80) to Venice*

**1321** Outbreak of disastrous 33-year-long Byzantine civil war

of the Italian city of Genoa, which was naturally disposed to fight against her rival Venice. Yet she still exacted a crippling price for her assistance. The Genoese established the colony of Pera across the Golden Horn from Constantinople and effectively took control of the city's trade.

Constantinople's recapture and reconstruction caused a flowering of scholarship and artistic activity, known as the Paleologue Renaissance after the family of emperors. An example of the many beautiful buildings dating from this period is the Church of St. Savior in Chora *(see pp118–19)*.

During this period the double-headed eagle was adopted as the imperial crest, with the two heads symbolizing the western and eastern halves of the empire. Yet, within a few decades there was further discord in Constantinople, when a quarrel arose

**Two-headed Byzantine eagle**

between Andronicus II (1282–1328) and his grandson Andronicus III (1328–41) over the succession. This led to the disastrous civil war of 1321–54.

## THE RISE OF THE OTTOMANS

The Ottoman state was born in 1301 when Osman I, a leader of warriors who were fighting for the Muslim faith on the eastern frontier of the Byzantine Empire, declared his independence. The new state quickly expanded and in 1326 captured Prusa (modern-day Bursa, *see pp162–8*), which became its capital. The judicious piety of the Ottomans soon won them the support of the general population of their territories, and even of some Christian brotherhoods. Meanwhile, a professional core of Janissaries *(see p127)* was created to add stability to an army that was otherwise too dependent on Turkic and renegade volunteer cavalry.

By 1362, with the Ottoman capture of Adrianople (Edirne, *see pp154–7*), Byzantium had been reduced to the city-state of Constantinople and a few minor outposts, isolated within Ottoman domains. Only a Mongol incursion in 1402 delayed the Ottoman invasion of Constantinople itself. In 1422 the Ottoman army made its first attack on the city's colossal land walls. As the threat increased, the Byzantine emperor made a last ditch effort to win the support of the Latin West in 1439. The Hungarians alone answered his call for help, forming a 25,000-strong crusade. However, in 1444 they were defeated en route by the Ottomans at the Battle of Varna on the Black Sea.

**Mosaic of the Virgin and Child in St. Savior in Chora**

## THE CONQUEST OF CONSTANTINOPLE

On May 29, 1453, Sultan Mehmet II (1451–81), known as "the Conqueror," entered Constantinople after a 54-day siege during which his cannon had torn a huge hole in the Walls of Theodosius II *(see p114)*. Mehmet's first task was to rebuild the wrecked city, which would later become known as Istanbul. The Grand Bazaar *(see pp98–9)* and Topkapı Palace *(see pp54–7)* were erected in the years following the Muslim conquest. Religious foundations were endowed to fund the building of mosques such as the Fatih *(see p113)* and their associated schools and baths *(see pp36–7)*. The city had to be repopulated by a mixture of force and encouragement. People from all over the empire moved to Istanbul, and Jews, Christians, and Muslims lived together in a cosmopolitan society.

Sultan Mehmet II, "the Conqueror"

Mehmet and his successors pushed the frontiers of the empire across the Middle East and into Europe. In the early 16th century, Selim I (1512–20) conquered Egypt and assumed the title of caliph *(see p27)*, as well as establishing the Ottomans as a sea power. He is also notorious for killing all his male relatives bar one son, to ensure that there were no rivals for the succession.

### SÜLEYMAN THE MAGNIFICENT

Selim's one surviving son was Süleyman I, "the Magnificent" (1520–66), under whose rule the Ottoman Empire reached its maximum extent. At the time of his death the empire stretched from Algiers to the Caspian Sea and from Hungary to the Persian Gulf. Much of Western Europe only just escaped conquest when an Ottoman army was driven back from the gates of Vienna in 1529. Süleyman's

**OTTOMAN EMPIRE**
■ *Maximum extent (1566)*

reign was a time of great artistic and architectural achievements. The architect Sinan *(see p91)* designed many mosques and other great buildings in the city, while the Ottoman arts of ceramics *(see p161)* and calligraphy *(see p95)* also flourished.

**Depiction of the unsuccessful siege of Vienna**

## TIMELINE

| | | | | |
|---|---|---|---|---|
| **1453** Mehmet the Conqueror enters Constantinople on May 29 | **1456** The Ottomans occupy Athens<br><br>**1461** Trebizond on the Black Sea, the last part of the Byzantine Empire, is conquered | **1536** Grand Vizier İbrahim Paşa is killed on the orders of Süleyman's wife, Roxelana *(see p76)* | **1561** Süleyman executes his son Beyazıt on suspicion of treason | **1571** Defeat of the Ottoman navy at the Battle of Lepanto |

| 1450 | 1475 | 1500 | 1525 | 1550 | |
|---|---|---|---|---|---|

| | | | | |
|---|---|---|---|---|
| **1455** Yedikule Castle *(see p115)* is built and work begins on the Grand Bazaar | **1478** Topkapı Palace completed<br><br>**1470** Fatih Mosque is built over the Church of the Holy Apostles | **1533** Hayrettin Paşa, better known as Barbarossa, is appointed grand admiral | **1556** Inauguration of Sinan's Süleymaniye Mosque *(see pp90–91)* |  *Süleyman I* |

## THE SULTANATE OF WOMEN

Süleyman's son Selim II (1566–74), "the Sot," was not a very capable ruler, although he added Cyprus to the empire. The defeat of his navy by the Venetians at the Battle of Lepanto was a heavy blow to Ottoman ambitions to be a seafaring power. This era was also

The Battle of Lepanto, a defeat for the Ottoman navy

the start of the so-called "Sultanate of Women," when Selim's mother (the valide sultan, *see p26*) and Nur Banu, his principal wife (the first *kadın*), effectively took over power and exercised it for their own ends. Corruption and intrigue became endemic, and after Selim's death Nur Banu kept her son, Murat III (1574–95), distracted by the women of the harem so that she could maintain her control over imperial affairs.

Osman II (1618–22) was the first sultan to try to reverse the decline of the empire. But when the Janissaries *(see p127)* learned of his plans to abolish their corps, they started a revolt which eventually led to his assassination. Murat IV (1623–40) enjoyed more success in his attempts at reform and significantly reduced corruption

Osman II, who failed to halt Ottoman decline

during his stable period of rule.

The late 17th century saw many years of capable government by a succession of grand viziers from the Albanian Köprülü family. Yet their efforts were not sufficient to stem the decline in imperial fortunes, symbolized by a failed attempt to capture Vienna in 1683. The Treaty of Karlowitz in 1699 marked the start of the Ottoman withdrawal from Europe.

## THE TULIP PERIOD

Ahmet III (1703–30), on his succession to the throne, left power in the hands of his capable grand vizier, İbrahim Paşa. The sultan preferred pleasure to politics. During his reign, beautiful Baroque palaces, such as Aynalı Kavak Palace *(see p127)*, fountains, mosques, and yalis *(see p139)* were built. Formal gardens were laid out and filled with tulips, Ahmet's favorite flower, which lent their name to the period of his rule. The sultan even ordered tulips to be scattered over the floor at the lavish festivals and entertainments that he staged for the Ottoman elite. He also sent an ambassador, Mehmet Çelebi, to France to investigate Western civilization and culture. On his return, Western clothes and costumes became not only acceptable for the first time but fashionable.

**1616** The Blue Mosque *(see pp78–9)* is finished after eight years of construction work by the architect Mehmet Ağa

**1699** The loss of Hungary under the Treaty of Karlowitz marks the Ottomans' retreat from Europe

1600 | 1625 | 1650 | 1700 | 1725

**1622** Revolt of the Janissaries. They murder Osman II in Yedikule Castle, the Prison of the Seven Towers

*Domes of the Blue Mosque*

**1729** The first Ottoman printing press is set up in Istanbul and begins to print texts in Turkish

# Ottoman Society

**B**ENEATH THE SULTAN, Ottoman society was divided into a privileged ruling class (the *askeri*, which included the religious hierarchy, or *ulema*) and a tax-paying subject population (*reaya*). Rank and honor, however, were not hereditary but could be gained through education or service in the army or administration. This social structure was modified during the reforms of the 19th century (*see p28*), but Ottoman titles were finally abolished only in 1924 after the Turkish Republic was created (*see p29*).

*The sultan* was at the apex of the social order, and everyone owed allegiance to him. He lived a life of ease and luxury, as seen in this portrait of Mahmut I (1730–54). The Ottoman (Osmanlı in Turkish) sultans were always succeeded by one of their sons but not automatically by the oldest.

*The grand vizier,* the prime minister, was the sultan's right-hand man.

**BAYRAM RECEPTION** (*c.1800*)
In this painting by Konstantin Kapidagi, Selim III (1789–1807, *see p28*) presides over a parade of high-ranking officials during the celebration of a religious festival (*see p47*) at Topkapı Palace.

**Ağa of the Janissaries** / **Minister of the Interior** / **Şeyhülislam (Grand Mufti)** / **Chief executioner**

*Men of high rank* could be recognized by their different uniforms, above all their large and distinctive headgear, as seen in this portrait of four Ottoman officials. The turban was abolished by Mahmut II (see p28) in 1829 in favor of the more egalitarian fez.

## THE WOMEN OF THE HAREM

Like all other Ottoman institutions, the harem was hierarchical. It was presided over by the sultan's mother, the valide sultan. Next in order of importance came the sultan's daughters. Immediately below them were the four *kadıns*, the official wives or favorites. Then came the *gözdes* (girls who had recently caught the sultan's eye), and the *ikbals* (women with whom he had already slept). Apart from the sultan's family members, all these women had entered the harem as slaves. They were kept under a watchful eye by a powerful stewardess, the *kahya kadın*.

**One of the sultan's favorites as depicted in a 19th-century engraving**

Black eunuchs

Sword bearer to the sultan

**The Gate of Felicity** (see p54), in the second courtyard of Topkapı Palace, was used for such ceremonial occasions.

The sultan is surrounded by his courtiers. He is the only seated figure.

Şeyhülislam (Grand Mufti)

Chief lackey (footman)

Chief of the sultan's bodyguard

Black eunuch

Dancing women

Valide sultan

Dwarf

*The valide sultan, the most powerful woman in the harem, is the center of attention in this festive scene. The picture was commissioned c.1689 by Madame Giradin, wife of the French ambassador.*

## OTTOMAN TITLES

**Ağa**: leader of an organization. The most influential *ağas* were the commander of the Janissary corps, the sultan's elite troops (see p127), and the Ağa of the Abode of Felicity, or chief black eunuch, who was in charge of the harem (see pp58–9).

Chief black eunuch

**Bey**: governor of a district or province. The word is now used simply to mean "Mr."

**Caliph**: spiritual ruler of the Islamic world. The title was assumed by the Ottoman sultans, beginning with Selim the Grim in 1517.

**Gazi**: honorary title given to a victorious Islamic warrior.

**Kadi**: judge charged with interpreting Islamic law and Ottoman administrative codes.

**Khedive**: viceroy of Egypt under Ottoman rule (1867–1914). The autonomous khedives acknowledged the religious leadership of the Ottoman Empire.

**Paşa**: title bestowed on a senior civil servant or high-ranking army officer. According to his rank, a *paşa* was entitled to display one, two, or three horsetails on his standard (see p56).

**Sultan**: political and religious ruler of the empire.

**Şeyhülislam** (Grand Mufti): head of the *ulema*, a religious institution that was made up of "learned men" responsible for interpreting and enforcing Islamic law (sharia).

**Valide sultan**: mother of the ruling sultan.

**Vizier**: minister of state. The four most senior ministers were called "viziers of the dome" because they attended cabinet meetings in the domed hall of the divan in Topkapı Palace (see pp54–9). From the 16th century, the divan was presided over by the immensely powerful grand vizier (the prime minister).

Grand vizier

A Janissary leaps to his death in a German painting of the Auspicious Event of 1826

### THE REFORMING SULTANS

Abdül Hamit I (1774–89) resumed the work of reform and was succeeded by Selim III, who instituted a wide range of changes to the military and Ottoman society. He was deposed by a Janissary mutiny in 1807. Mahmut II (1808–39) realized that the Janissary corps *(see p127)* could not be reformed, so he replaced them with a modern army, but the Janissaries rebelled and were massacred on June 15, 1826 in the "Auspicious Event." Soon after, in 1829, the sultan introduced further modernizing measures including changes in the dress code.

Later in his reign, Mahmut reorganized central government so that a regulated bureaucracy replaced the old system of rule by military and religious powers. By doing this he paved the way for his sons Abdül Mecit (1839–61) and Abdül Aziz (1861–76) to oversee the Tanzimat (Reordering), a series of legislative reforms. Functionaries were given salaries to deter them from taking bribes, and the grand vizier's post was replaced by that of prime minister.

A constitution was declared in 1876, creating parliamentary government. However, the Russian-Turkish War of 1877–88 led to Abdül Hamit II's suspending it and ruling alone for the next 30 years. In 1908 a bloodless revolution by a collection of educated men – the so-called Young Turks – finally forced the sultan to recall parliament.

### ATATÜRK AND WESTERNIZATION

Throughout the 19th- and early 20th-centuries, the Ottoman Empire steadily lost territory through wars with Russia and Austria and to emerging Balkan nation-states such as Serbia, Greece, and Bulgaria. Then, in World War I, despite famously winning the battle for Gallipoli in a valiant defense of the Dardanelles *(see p170)*, the Ottoman Empire found itself on the losing side. Istanbul was occupied by victorious French and British troops and much of Anatolia by Greek forces. The peace

Turkish artillery in action at Gallipoli

### TIMELINE

*Dolmabahçe clock tower*

| | | | | | |
|---|---|---|---|---|---|
| **1807** Much of the city is destroyed during a Janissary revolt against Mahmut II | | **1845** First (wooden) Galata Bridge is built over the Golden Horn | **1870** Schliemann begins excavation of Troy *(see p171)* | **1888** Train link with Paris leads to first run of the Orient Express *(see p66)* | |
| 1800 | 1825 | 1850 | 1875 | 1900 |
| **1826** Mahmut II finally destroys the Janissaries in their own barracks in the "Auspicious Event" | **1856** Abdül Mecit I abandons Topkapı Palace for the new Dolmabahçe Palace *(see pp128–9)* | | *Orient Express poster* | |
| | **1875** The Tünel subway system, the third built in the world, opens in Galata | | | |

treaties that followed rewarded the victors with Ottoman territory and as a result stimulated Turkish nationalists to take over power from the sultan.

A portrait of Ataturk

The history of modern Turkey is dominated by the figure of Mustafa Kemal Paşa (1881–1938), a military hero turned politician, universally known as Atatürk, or "Father of the Turks." It was at his instigation that the Turkish War of Independence was fought to regain territory lost to the Allies and, in particular, Greece. At the conclusion of this war, the present territorial limits of Turkey were established. Atatürk then set in motion an ambitious program of political and social change. The sultanate was abolished in 1922, and religion and state were formally separated when the country was declared a secular republic in the following year. His reforms included replacing the Arabic alphabet with a Roman one, allowing women greater social and political rights, encouraging Western dress (the fez was banned), and obliging all Turks to choose a last name.

## MODERN ISTANBUL

Another part of this process was to move the institutions of state from the old Ottoman city of Istanbul to the more centrally located Ankara, which became the capital of Turkey in 1923. Since then, Istanbul has undergone a dramatic transformation into a modern city. As migrants

Modern tram *(see p232)*

from Anatolia have poured in, the population has increased, and although small communities of Jews, Arabs, Armenians, and Christians remain within the city, they are now vastly outnumbered by Turks.

A booming economy has led to the building of new highways and bridges, and the public transit network has been revolutionized by the introduction of modern trams, light rail, and fast catamaran sea buses *(see p235)*. Meanwhile Istanbul has geared itself up for tourism; its ancient monuments have been restored, and many new hotels and restaurants have opened in recent years to accommodate increasing numbers of visitors.

But, like Turkey as a whole, Istanbul is forever wrestling with a divided half-Asian, half-European identity. The influences of these contrasting cultures remain widely evident today and create the city's unique atmosphere.

Suspension bridge spanning the Bosphorus

**1915** Allied forces land at Gallipoli but are beaten back by Turks

**1919–22** British and French occupy Istanbul

**1922** Sultanate finally ends

**1928** *Istanbul* becomes the city's official name

**1936** Hagia Sophia becomes a museum. Restoration starts

**1938** Atatürk dies in Dolmabahçe Palace at 9.05am on November 10 *(see p129)*

*Turkish flag*

**1966** The city's old trams are taken out of service. A few are later reintroduced *(see p233)*

**1973** A suspension bridge is built across the Bosphorus *(see p138),* linking east and west Turkey

**1993** The Islamicist Welfare Party takes control of the Greater Istanbul Municipality

**1996** The United Nations Conference on Human Settlement (Habitat II) is held in Istanbul

| 1925 | 1950 | 1975 | 2000 |
|------|------|------|------|

# The Ottoman Sultans

THE FIRST OTTOMANS were the leaders of warlike tribes living on the borders of the Byzantine Empire. From the 13th century on, however, the dynasty established itself at the head of a large empire. In their heyday, having captured Istanbul in 1453 *(see p24)*, the Ottoman sultans were admired and feared for their military strength and ruthlessness toward opponents and rival pretenders to the throne. Later sultans often led a decadent lifestyle while power was exercised by their viziers *(see p27)*.

**Murat III**
(1574–95), whose *tuğra (see p95)* is shown above, fathers over 100 children

**Selim II,** "the Sot" (1566–74), prefers drinking and harem life to the affairs of state

**Selim I,** "the Grim" (1512  20), seen here at his coronation, assumes the title of caliph after his conquest of Egypt

**Osman Gazi**
(1280–1324), a tribal chieftain, establishes the Ottoman dynasty

**Murat I**
(1360–89)

**Memhet I**
(1413–21)

**Beyazıt II**
(1481–1512)

| 1250 | 1300 | 1350 | 1400 | 1450 | 1500 | 1550 |
|------|------|------|------|------|------|------|

| 1250 | 1300 | 1350 | 1400 | 1450 | 1500 | 1550 |
|------|------|------|------|------|------|------|

**Orhan Gazi**
(1324–59) is the first Ottoman to bear the title of sultan

**Beyazıt I** (1389–1402) is nicknamed "the Thunderbolt" because of the speed at which he makes strategic decisions and moves his troops from one place to another

**Period of Interregnum**
(1402–13) while Beyazıt's sons fight each other over the succession

**Süleyman I,** "the Magnificent" (1520–66), expands the empire and fosters a golden age of artistic achievement

**Murat II**
(1421–51), the greatest of the warrior sultans, gains notable victories against the Crusaders

**Mehmet II,** "the Conqueror" (1451–81), captures Constantinople in 1453. He then rebuilds the city, transforming it into the new capital of the empire

**Mehmet III** (1595–1603) succeeds to the throne after his mother has all but one of his 19 brothers strangled

**Mustafa I** (1617–18 and 1622–3), a weak and incompetent ruler, reigns for two short periods and is deposed twice

**Abdül Mecit I** (1839–61) presides over the reforms of the Tanzimat (see p28)

**Mehmet VI** (1918–22), the last Ottoman sultan, is forced into exile by the declaration of the Turkish Republic (see p29)

**İbrahim**, "the Mad" (1640–48), much despised, goes insane at the end of his short and disastrous reign

**Mahmut II**, "the Reformer" (1808–39), finally defeats the Janissaries (see p127)

**Mehmet V** (1909–18)

**Mahmut I** (1730–54)

**Mustafa II** (1695–1703)

**Murat V** (1876)

**Süleyman II** (1687–91)

**Mustafa III** (1757–74)

| 1650 | 1700 | 1750 | 1800 | 1850 | 1900 |
|---|---|---|---|---|---|

| 1650 | 1700 | 1750 | 1800 | 1850 | 1900 |
|---|---|---|---|---|---|

**Osman III** (1754–7)

**Abdül Mecit II** (1922–3) is caliph only, the sultanate having been abolished in 1922 (see p29)

**Abdül Aziz** (1861–76)

**Mehmet IV** (1648–87)

**Abdül Hamit I** (1774–89)

**Murat IV** (1623–40)

**Mustafa IV** 1807–08

**Ahmet III** (1703–30) presides over a cultural flowering known as the Tulip Period (see p25)

**Osman II** (1618–22)

**Abdül Hamit II** (1876–1909) suspends parliament for 30 years and rules an autocratic police state until toppled from power by the Young Turk movement

**Ahmet I** (1603–17) has the Blue Mosque (see pp78–9) constructed in the center of Istanbul.

**Selim III** (1789–1807) attempts Western-style reforms but is overthrown by a revolt of the Janissaries

# ISTANBUL AT A GLANCE

ORE THAN 100 places worth visiting in Istanbul are described in the *Area by Area* section of this book, which covers the sights of central Istanbul as well as those a short way out of the city center. They range from mosques, churches, palaces, and museums to bazaars, Turkish baths, and parks. For a breathtaking view across Istanbul, you can climb the Galata Tower *(see p105)*, or take a ride on a ferry *(see pp234–5)* to the city's Asian shore. A selection of the sights you should not miss is given below. If you are short on time you will probably want to concentrate on the most famous monuments, namely Topkapı Palace, Hagia Sophia, and the Blue Mosque, all of which are all located close to one another.

## ISTANBUL'S TOP TEN SIGHTS

**Topkapı Palace**
*See pp54–7*

**Archaeological Museum**
*See pp62–5*

**Blue Mosque**
*See pp78–9*

**Dolmabahçe Palace**
*See pp128–9*

**Hagia Sophia**
*See pp72–5*

**Basilica Cistern**
*See p76*

**Süleymaniye Mosque**
*See pp90–91*

**The Bosphorus Trip**
*See pp144–9*

**Grand Bazaar**
*See pp98–9*

**Church of St. Savior in Chora**
*See pp118–19*

◁ View of Hagia Sophia, a great Byzantine church later converted into a mosque, in central Sultanahmet

# Istanbul's Best: Mosques and Churches

MOST VISITORS TO ISTANBUL will immediately be struck by the quantity of mosques, from the imposing domed buildings dominating the skyline to the small neighborhood mosques, which would pass unnoticed were it not for their minarets. Several mosques were built as churches but converted for Islamic worship after the Ottoman conquest *(see p24)*. Some of the most outstanding of them have since become national monuments but no longer serve a religious function.

**St. Savior in Chora**
*The Dormition of the Virgin is one of many beautiful mosaics that fill this Byzantine church (see pp118–19).*

**Eyüp Mosque**
*The holiest mosque in Istanbul stands beside the tomb of Eyüp Ensari, a companion of the Prophet Mohammed (see p120).*

**Church of the Pammakaristos**
*An image of Christ Pantocrator gazes down from the main dome of what was one of the most important churches in the city (see p113).*

GOLDEN HORN

**Fatih Mosque**
*Rebuilt after an earthquake, this mosque was founded by Mehmet the Conqueror after his conquest of the city (see p24). The inner courtyard is especially fine (see p113).*

**Süleymaniye Mosque**
*Sinan, the greatest Ottoman imperial architect, built this mosque in honor of his patron, Süleyman the Magnificent (see p24). He placed ablution taps in the side arches of the mosque to serve a large number of worshipers (see pp90–91).*

**Atik Valide Mosque**
*The last major work of Sinan (see p91), this mosque was built in 1583 for the wife of Selim II. Its mihrab (niche indicating the direction of Mecca) is surrounded by İznik tiles (see p131).*

**Rüstem Paşa Mosque**
*The fine tiles decorating this mosque date from the mid-16th century, the greatest period of İznik tile (see p161) production (see p88).*

**Hagia Sophia**
*One of the world's greatest feats of architecture, Hagia Sophia dates from AD 537. The calligraphic roundels were added in the 19th century (see pp72–5).*

BOSPHORUS

BEYOĞLU

ASIAN SIDE

**Blue Mosque**
*Istanbul's most famous landmark was built by some of the same stonemasons who later helped construct the Taj Mahal in India (see pp78–9).*

SERAGLIO POINT

THE BAZAAR QUARTER

SULTANAHMET

**Church of SS. Sergius and Bacchus**
*An intricate frieze with a Greek inscription honoring the two dedicatees of this former church has survived for 1,400 years (see p82).*

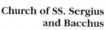

0 meters 500

0 yards 500

# Exploring Mosques

**F**IVE TIMES A DAY throughout Istanbul a chant is broadcast over loudspeakers set high in the city's minarets to call the faithful to prayer. Over 99 percent of the population is Muslim, though the Turkish state is officially secular. Most belong to the Sunni branch of Islam, but there are also a few Shiites. Both follow the teachings of the Koran, the sacred book of Islam, and the Prophet Mohammed (c.570–632), but Shiites accept, in addition, the authority of a line of 12 imams directly descended from Mohammed. Islamic mystics are known as Sufis *(see p104)*.

**Overview of the Süleymaniye Mosque complex**

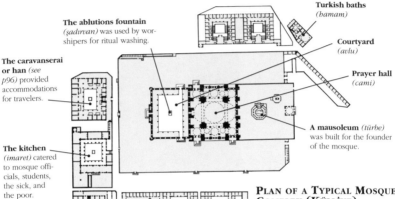

**The ablutions fountain** *(şadırvan)* was used by worshipers for ritual washing.

**Turkish baths** *(hamam)*

**Courtyard** *(avlu)*

**The caravanserai or han** *(see p96)* provided accommodations for travelers.

**Prayer hall** *(cami)*

**A mausoleum** *(türbe)* was built for the founder of the mosque.

**The kitchen** *(imaret)* catered to mosque officials, students, the sick, and the poor.

**Hospital** *(darüşşifa)*

**Colleges** *(medreses)* for general and theological education were built adjacent to the mosque. Most now serve other uses.

## PLAN OF A TYPICAL MOSQUE COMPLEX (KÜLLİYE)

A large complex such as the Süleymaniye Mosque *(see pp90–91)*, shown here, was built as a charitable foundation as well as a place of worship. It would typically include a hospital, school, Islamic study halls, caravanserai (lodgings for travelers), public kitchen for the poor, and bathhouse. Today most such buildings no longer fulfill their original functions.

## INSIDE A MOSQUE

Visitors will experience a soaring sense of space on entering the prayer hall of one of Istanbul's great mosques. Islam forbids images of living things (human or animal) inside a mosque, so there are never any statues or figurative paintings; but the geometric and abstract architectural details of the interior can be exquisite. Men and women pray separately. Women often use a screened-off area or a balcony.

**The müezzin mahfili** *is a raised platform found in large mosques. The muezzin (mosque official) stands on this when chanting responses to the prayers of the imam (head of the mosque).*

**The mihrab,** *an ornate niche in the wall, marks the direction of Mecca. The hall is laid out so that most people can see the niche.*

**The minbar** *is a lofty pulpit to the right of the mihrab. This is used by the imam when he delivers the Friday sermon (khutba).*

## MUSLIM BELIEFS AND PRACTICES

Muslims believe in God (Allah), and the Koran shares many prophets and stories with the Bible. However, where for Christians Jesus is the son of God, Muslims hold that he was just one in a line of prophets – the last being Mohammed, who brought the final revelation of God's truth to mankind. Muslims believe that Allah communicated the sacred texts of the Koran to Mohammed, via the archangel Gabriel.

There are five basic duties for Muslims. The first of these is the profession of faith: "There is no God but God, and Mohammed is his Prophet." Muslims are also enjoined to pray five times a day, give alms to the poor, and fast during the month of Ramazan (see p47). Once in their lifetime, if they can afford it, they should make the pilgrimage (hajj) to Mecca (in Saudi Arabia), the site of the Kaaba, a sacred shrine built by Abraham, and also the birthplace of the Prophet.

### PRAYER TIMES

The five daily prayer times are calculated according to the times of sunrise and sunset, and so change throughout the year. Exact times will be posted up on boards outside large mosques. Those given here are a guide.

| Prayer | Summer | Winter |
|--------|--------|--------|
| Sabah | 5am | 7am |
| Öğle | 1pm | 1pm |
| İkindi | 6pm | 4pm |
| Akşam | 8pm | 6pm |
| Yatsı | 9:30pm | 8pm |

*The call to prayer* used to be given by the muezzin from the balcony of the minaret. Today loudspeakers broadcast the call across the city. Only imperial mosques have more than one minaret.

*Ritual ablutions* must be undertaken before prayer. Worshipers wash their head, hands, and feet either at the fountain in the courtyard or, more usually, at taps set in a discreet wall of the mosque.

*When praying*, Muslims always face the Kaaba in the holy city of Mecca, even if they are not in a mosque, where the mihrab indicates the right direction. Kneeling and lowering the head to the ground are gestures of humility and respect for Allah.

## VISITING A MOSQUE

Visitors are welcome at any mosque in Istanbul, but non-Muslims should avoid visiting at prayer times, especially the main weekly congregation and sermon on Fridays at 1pm. Take off your shoes before entering the prayer hall. Shoulders and knees should be covered. Men must remove their hats. Women need to cover their hair, so take a light scarf when sightseeing. Do not eat, take photographs with a flash, or stand very close to worshipers. A contribution to a donation box or mosque official is courteous.

*The loge* (hünkar mahfili) *provided the sultan with a screened-off balcony where he could pray, safe from would-be assassins.*

*The kürsü, seen in some mosques, is a chair or throne used by the imam while he reads extracts from the Koran.*

**Board outside a mosque giving times of prayer**

# Istanbul's Best: Palaces and Museums

AS THE FORMER CAPITAL of an empire that spanned
from Algeria to Iraq and from Arabia to Hungary,
Istanbul is home to a huge and diverse collection of
treasures. Some, from musical instruments to priceless
jewels, are housed in the beautiful former imperial
palaces of the Ottoman sultans, which are worth visiting
in any case for their architecture and opulent
interiors. Topkapı and Dolmabahçe are the most
famous palaces in Istanbul. The Archaeological
Museum should also be on any itinerary of the
city. This map points out these and other
palaces and museums that are worth visiting
for their splendid buildings or the
exceptional collections they contain.

**Aynalı Kavak Palace**
*This reclusive palace,
with its airy feel and
intimate proportions,
shows subtler aspects of
Ottoman taste. It houses
a collection of Turkish
musical instruments.*

**Archaeological Museum**
*Established in 1896, this
superb museum has exhibits
ranging from prehistory to
the Byzantine era. They
include this classical sculpture of the 2nd-century
Roman Emperor Hadrian.*

**Museum of Calligraphy**
*Some of the texts in Istanbul's
collection of Ottoman calligraphy
(see p95) are by sultans, such as this
panel by Ahmet III (1703–30).*

GOLDEN HORN

BEYOĞLU

THE BAZAAR
QUARTER

SERAGLIO
POINT

SULTANAHMET

**Museum of Turkish
and Islamic Arts**
*This Seljuk example is
one of the many carpets
(see pp210–11) included
in this museum's display
of Turkish heritage. Other
collections include glassware and ceramics.*

**Mosaics Museum**
*Gladiators fighting
a lion are shown in
one of the floors from
the Great Palace (see
pp82–3) displayed in
this small museum.*

## Military Museum
*A highlight of this museum is the famous Mehter Band, which gives regular outdoor concerts of Ottoman military music.*

## Şale Pavilion
*One of a group of pavilions built in leafy Yıldız Park by 19th-century sultans, the Şale Pavilion has around 50 splendid rooms, including the Mother-of-Pearl Hall.*

BOSPHORUS

THE ASIAN SIDE

## Dolmabahçe Palace
*This opulent 19th-century palace is home to such marvels as 2-m (7-ft) high vases, a crystal staircase, and an alabaster bathroom.*

## Beylerbeyi Palace
*Adorning one of the principal atriums of this 19th-century imperial summer palace is this elegant marble fountain. The palace was built to entertain visiting foreign dignitaries.*

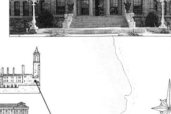

## Topkapı Palace
*This huge palace was used as the official royal residence for 400 years. The treasury contains a myriad of precious objects, such as jewel-encrusted thrones and this ornate ceremonial canteen.*

| 0 meters | 750 |
|---|---|
| 0 yards | 750 |

# Exploring Istanbul's Collections

**E**ACH MUSEUM in Istanbul contributes a piece to the vast cultural jigsaw of this cosmopolitan city. From Ancient Greek remains and early Chinese ceramics, which arrived in the city along the Silk Route, to 16th-century tiles commissioned for the great mosques and modern industrial machinery, each has its place in the history of Istanbul. Many of the larger museums have a wide range of exhibits, so are listed under several of the headings below.

The *saz*, a type of lute

The Sarcophagus of the Mourning Women, Archaeological Museum

## ARCHAEOLOGY

**T**HE ARCHAEOLOGICAL fruits of the expansive Ottoman Empire are displayed in the **Archaeological Museum**, where the exhibits range from monumental 6th-century BC Babylonian friezes to exquisite classical sarcophagi and statues. Classical sculpture fills the ground floor. Upstairs there is a gallery for the archaeology of Syria and Cyprus. Ancient oriental finds are housed in an annex. The **Museum of Turkish and Islamic Arts** features specifically Muslim artifacts, including early Iraqi and Iranian ceramics as well as beautiful displays of glassware, metalwork, and woodwork.

Byzantine mosaic floor in the Mosaics Museum

## BYZANTINE ANTIQUITIES

**A**LTHOUGH Constantinople was the capital of the Byzantine Empire *(see pp18–23)* for over 1,000 years, it can be hard to get a full picture of the city in that period. The best place to start is the **Archaeological Museum**, which has displays illustrating the city's Byzantine history. Its courtyard contains the purple sarcophagi of the Byzantine emperors.

For Byzantine church mosaics, visit the **Church of St. Savior in Chora**, near the city walls, which has some particularly fine examples vividly depicting the lives of Christ and the Virgin Mary. The impressive **Hagia Sophia** has a few brilliant gold mosaics remaining, some dating back to the reign of Justinian *(see p18)*. The galleries and upper walls of the **Church of the Pammakaristos** are covered with mosaics, although public access is restricted.

The **Mosaics Museum** houses mosaic floors and murals from the now-vanished Byzantine Great Palace *(see pp82–3)*. They were discovered by archaeologists in 1935. The **Sadberk Hanım Museum** also houses several Byzantine antiquities, including icons, ceramics, and jewelry.

Mosque lamp from the Archaeological Museum

## THE ARTS OF THE BOOK

**I**N THE DAYS BEFORE the printed word, Ottoman calligraphy *(see p95)* developed into a highly skilled artform, widely used both to ornament religious texts and to lend gravity to legal documents and decrees. The **Museum of Calligraphy** holds a continuous series of temporary exhibitions, while beautiful early Koranic calligraphy can be viewed in both **Topkapı Palace** and the **Museum of Turkish and Islamic Arts**.

## CERAMICS

**E**XPERTS AND AMATEURS come from all over the world to view the collection of Chinese ceramics and porcelain on display in the kitchens of **Topkapı Palace**. The earliest examples provided the inspiration for Turkey's indigenous ceramic production at İznik *(see p161)*. Examples of İznik tiles can be seen on the walls of Topkapı Palace and in the city's mosques. İznik tiles and also pottery are on display in the Çinili Pavilion, an annex of the **Archaeological Museum**, and at the **Sadberk Hanım Museum**. A wider selection of ceramics from all over the Islamic world can be found in the **Museum of Turkish and Islamic Arts**.

## OTTOMAN INTERIORS

**T**HE INTERIORS that can be visited in Istanbul run the gamut from the classical Ottoman styling of the older parts of **Topkapı Palace** to extravagant European-inspired 19th-century decor. In the latter category, the huge **Dolmabahçe Palace** set the style. It was decorated with Bohemian glass and Hereke carpets and has an

The opulent Süfera Salon in Dolmabahçe Palace

ornate central stairway fashioned of crystal and brass. The **Pavilion of the Linden Tree** and the Rococo **Küçüksu Palace**, although more intimate in scale, are equally lavish in their interior style.

## TEXTILES

THE OTTOMANS were justifiably proud of their textile tradition, which can be admired in the huge imperial costume collection at **Topkapı Palace**, begun in 1850. The palace collection houses older materials, including kaftans dating back to the 15th century. The **Sadberk Hanım Museum** houses magnificent, mostly 19th-century pieces on the top floor and some fine examples of embroidery.

On a larger scale, there are huge imperial campaign tents in the **Military Museum**, which also has a collection of miniature Janissary *(see p127)* costumes. Uniforms, nomadic tents, and fine carpets are on display in the **Museum of Turkish and Islamic Arts**. Antique carpets can also be seen in the **Vakıflar Carpet Museum**, housed in an annex of the Blue Mosque. It contains some valuable old carpets that come originally from mosques all over Turkey.

Costume from
Topkapı Palace

## MUSICAL INSTRUMENTS

EXAMPLES OF typical Turkish instruments, such as the *saz* (lute), can be found in a museum devoted to them at **Aynalı Kavak Palace**. Those played by the Whirling Dervishes are on display at the **Mevlevi Monastery**. Instruments can also be seen – and bought – in two stores situated near the entrance to Gülhane Park *(see p61)*. Traditional Turkish military instruments can be seen and heard at the **Military Museum**.

## MILITARIA

THE BEAUTIFUL barges in which the Ottoman sultans were rowed around the Golden Horn and the Bosphorus are among the exhibits at the **Naval Museum**. Its most fascinating collection, however, is of the beautiful maps created by the Ottoman cartographer Piri Reis. Weapons and armor from the 12th to 20th centuries can be found in the **Military Museum**, along with a huge cannon, captured by the Turks during their European campaigns. There is a smaller selection of weaponry in the armory of **Topkapı Palace**. The **Florence Nightingale**

**Museum** (in the Selimiye Barracks on the Asian Side) commemorates the work of the nurse during the Crimean War. It also has some interesting military exhibits.

## PAINTING

CLOSE TO Dolmabahçe Palace is Istanbul's **Museum of Fine Arts**, which offers a collection of largely late 19th- and early 20th-century Turkish paintings. Those interested in more contemporary works of art may also like to visit the changing exhibitions at the **Municipal Art Gallery**.

## SCIENCE AND TECHNOLOGY

LOCATED IN a converted warehouse in the heart of Istanbul's docks is the **Rahmi Koç Museum**. It is home to a selection of mechanical and scientific instruments dating from the early years of the Industrial Revolution, as well as an entire reconstructed bridge taken from an early 20th-century ship.

# Celebrated Visitors and Residents

THE CITY OF ISTANBUL has attracted foreign visitors since time immemorial. As reports of its beauty, its architecture, and the opulence of its court circulated, it came to be included on the extended Grand Tour route of the 19th century, undertaken by those seeking a little exotic pleasure while broadening their education. Because of Istanbul's pivotal geographic position, the ambassadors of the great powers of Europe were important figures, rubbing shoulders with the sultans. Other visitors were brought here by war, as either participants or refugees.

**Lord Byron**
*The itinerant British poet stayed in Pera in 1810–11. During this time, he swam the Dardanelles (see p170) and met Sultan Mahmut II in Topkapı Palace (see pp54–9).*

GOLDEN HORN

**Pierre Loti**
*The Café Pierre Loti (see p120) in Eyüp is named after the 19th-century French romantic writer who spent much time there.*

**Gurdjieff**
*A refugee of the Russian Revolution, the mystic, wily businessman, and sometime spy was a frequent visitor to the Mevlevi Monastery (see p104) in 1920–21.*

THE BAZAAR QUARTER

**Le Corbusier**
*During his visit to Istanbul in 1911, the French modern architect made drawings of mosques, among them the Süleymaniye (see pp72–5), houses, and boats.*

**Agatha Christie**
*Room 411 of the Pera Palas Hotel (see p104) preserves the memory of the thriller writer whose* Murder on the Orient Express *was inspired by her journeys on the train (see p66) in the 1920s–30s.*

### Adam Mickiewicz

*The Polish national poet came to Istanbul from Paris in 1855, during the Crimean War. He hoped to quell factional squabbles in the Polish military forces, but caught typhus soon after his arrival and died the same year.*

### Kaiser Wilhelm II

*The last Kaiser of Germany visited Istanbul in 1889 and 1898. The Şale Pavilion at Yıldız Palace (see pp124–5) and the fountain in the Hippodrome (see p80) were built in his honor.*

BEYOĞLU

BOSPHORUS

### Ernest Hemingway

*Sent to Istanbul from Paris in 1922 by his newspaper, to cover the war between Greece and Turkey, Hemingway stayed at the Hotel de Londres (see p182).*

### Florence Nightingale

*Modern nursing methods were pioneered by Florence Nightingale in 1855–6, during the Crimean War, as she tended the injured in the Selimiye Barracks (see p132).*

SERAGLIO
POINT

### Lady Wortley Montagu

*As wife of the British Ambassador, Lady Mary Wortley Montagu was in Istanbul from 1718. Her letters give an intimate and appreciative insight into the workings of Ottoman society, from the sultan and his harem downward.*

THE ASIAN SIDE

| 0 meters | 500 |
| 0 yards | 500 |

# ISTANBUL THROUGH THE YEAR

ISTANBUL is at its best in late May and early September, when temperatures are mild and sunshine is plentiful. Tourist season, from June to August, is the most expensive, crowded, and hottest time to visit, but the summer arts and music festivals are highlights in the city's cultural calendar. From late November until April a gray smog can hang over the city. However, Istanbul is still mild in

**Independence Day in Istanbul**

autumn and winter and, with very few tour groups around, you can enjoy the sights in peace. As well as arts and sports events, several public holidays and religious festivals punctuate the year. It is important to be aware of these when planning an itinerary, as some sights may be closed or else crammed with locals enjoying a day off. Some of these celebrations are also fascinating in their own right.

**Tulips growing in Emirgan Park, scene of the spring Tulip Festival**

## SPRING

As THE WINTER SMOG fades and sunshine increases, cafés and restaurants prepare for the first wave of alfresco dining. After a winter's diet of apples and oranges, a welcome crop of spring fruits, including fresh figs, strawberries, and tart green plums, arrives in stores. Toasted corn is sold from carts (see p200), and a spring catch of sea bream, sea bass, and turbot is on the menu. Tulips, hyacinths, daffodils, and pansies fill parks and gardens, and the distinctive pink buds of the Judas tree are seen along the Bosphorus. Monuments and museums are generally uncrowded in spring, and discounts are available at many hotels. In May the popular *son et lumière* shows outside the Blue Mosque (see pp78–9) begin and continue until September.

## EVENTS

**Easter** (*March or April*). Pilgrimage to the Monastery of St. George on Büyükada in the Princes' Islands (*see p159*).
**International Istanbul Film Festival** (*late March–mid-April*), selected theaters. Screening of Turkish and foreign films and related events.
**Tulip Festival** (*April*), Emirgan Park (*see p141*). Displays of springtime blooms.
**Independence Day** (*April 23*). Public holiday marking the inauguration of the Turkish Republic in 1923 (*see pp28–9*). Children take to the streets in folk costume.
**Commemoration of the Anzac Landings** (*April 25*), Gallipoli. Britons, Australians, and New Zealanders gather at the location of the Anzac landings at Gallipoli during World War I (*see pp170–71*).

**Spring Day and Worker's Day** (*May 1*). Unofficial public holiday when workers usually attend union-organized rallies.
**Kakava Festival** (*early May*), Edirne. A celebration of gypsy music and dance.
**Youth and Sports Day** (*May 19*). Public holiday in commemoration of the start of the War of Independence (*see p29*) in 1919, with sports events and other activities held throughout the city in stadiums and on the streets.
**International Istanbul Theater Festival** (*May–June*), various locations. European and Turkish productions.
**Conquest of Istanbul** (*May 29*), between Tophane and Karaköy and on the shores of the upper Bosphorus. Mehmet the Conqueror's taking of the city in 1453 (*see p24*) is re-enacted in street parades and mock battles.

**Colorful evening *son et lumière* show at the Blue Mosque**

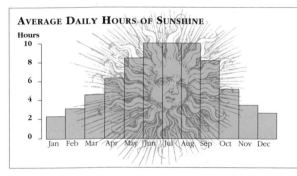

## AVERAGE DAILY HOURS OF SUNSHINE

Hours

Jan Feb Mar Apr May Jun Jul Aug Sep Oct Nov Dec

**Sunshine Chart**
*One of Istanbul's attractions is its summer sunshine – there are about 2,500 hours each year. From May to October, the city is bathed in light well into the evening, and a long Indian summer can sometimes linger into November. Winter, by contrast, is notoriously devoid of sun.*

## SUMMER

IN CONTRAST to an all-too-brief spring, the warm weather and clear skies of summer can linger on in Istanbul until November. In July and August, temperatures soar, and although luxury hotels have air conditioning, cheaper ones do not. Popular sights are packed with tourists throughout the summer. Picturesque locations outside Istanbul may, on the other hand, be overrun by locals. On weekends, city dwellers trek out to the Belgrade Forest and Black Sea beaches *(see p158)* or to health clubs along the Bosphorus. Those who can afford it flee to their coastal summer homes until autumn.

For those who stay behind, there is a strong summer culture. This includes a wild nightlife in hundreds of bars and night spots *(see p213)*, and enthusiastic support for many arts festivals, which attract world-famous performers. Also watch for events taking place in historical buildings. You may be able to listen to classical music in Hagia Eirene *(see p60)* or enjoy a pop concert in the Fortress of Europe on the Bosphorus *(see pp140–41)*. This is also the best time for outdoor activities such as water sports, hiking, horseback riding, golf, and parachuting.

In summer, the menu focuses more on meat than fish, but vegetables and fresh fruit – such as

**Silk Market in Bursa, which operates in June and July**

honeydew melons, cherries, mulberries, peaches, and apricots – are widely available. In July and August many stores have summer sales *(see p203)*.

### EVENTS

**Silk Market** *(June–July)*, Bursa. Special market for the sale of silk cocoons *(see p164)*.
**International Istanbul Music and Dance Festival** *(mid-June–July)*. Classical music, opera, and dance performed in historic locations. Mozart's *Abduction from the*

**Performance of Mozart's** *Abduction from the Seraglio* **in the Harem of Topkapı Palace**

*Seraglio* is staged annually in Topkapı Palace *(see pp54–9)*.
**Bursa Festival** *(June–July)*, Bursa Park. Music, folk dancing, plays, opera, and shadow puppetry.
**Navy Day** *(July 1)*. Parades of old and new boats along the Bosphorus.
**International Istanbul Jazz Festival** *(July)*, various locations. International event with a devoted following.
**International Sailing Races** *(July)*. Regatta held at the Marmara Islands *(see p169)*.
**Grease Wrestling** *(July)*, Kırkpınar, Edirne. Wrestlers smeared in olive oil grapple with each other *(see p154)*.
**Hunting Festival** *(3 days, late July)*, Edirne. Music, art, and fishing displays.
**Folklore and Music Festival** *(late July)*, Bursa. Ethnic dances and craft displays.
**Festival of Troy** *(August)*, Çanakkale. Reenactment of the tale of Troy *(see p171)*.
**Victory Day** *(August 30)*. Public holiday commemorating victory over Greece in 1922.

## AVERAGE MONTHLY RAINFALL

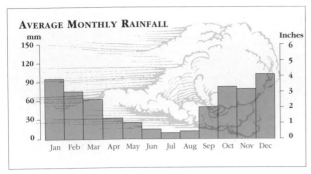

| mm | Inches |
|----|--------|
| 150 | 6 |
| 120 | 5 |
| 90 | 4 |
| 60 | 3 |
| 30 | 2 |
| 0 | 1 |
| Jan Feb Mar Apr May Jun Jul Aug Sep Oct Nov Dec | 0 |

**Rainfall Chart**
*Winter is the wettest season in Istanbul. Heavy showers of rain can sometimes continue into April and May, making spring seem shorter. Sudden snowstorms are not uncommon in winter, but these are short-lived and snowfalls will usually melt away as quickly as they come.*

## AUTUMN

RESIDENTS of Istanbul often consider their city to be at its best in autumn. As the summer heat loses its grip, chestnut sellers appear on the streets *(see p200)*, pumpkins are sold in the markets, and fresh figs are eaten in abundance. In the surrounding countryside, cotton, wheat, and sunflowers are harvested. Migratory grouper and bonito are among the tastiest types of fish that are caught at this time of year.

A popular spot for seeing the leaves change color is Lake Abant, 200 km (125 miles) east of Istanbul. Meanwhile, birdwatchers converge on the hills overlooking the Bosphorus to view great flocks of migratory birds heading to their warm wintering grounds in Africa *(see p141)*.

On the cultural side is a world-class arts biennial and an antique fair that blends

Turkish and Western aesthetics. Several public holidays reaffirm Turkey's commitment to secularism, including Republic Day in late October, during which flags are hung from balconies. The bridges over the Bosphorus *(see p138)* are hung with particularly huge flags.

**Street-side roasting of seasonal chestnuts**

## EVENTS

**Tüyap Arts Fair** *(September)*, opposite the Pera Palas Hotel *(see p104)*. A showcase of Istanbul's artistic talent.
**Yapı Kredi Festival** *(September)*, various locations. A celebration of music and dance promoting young performers.

**Republic Day** *(October 29)*. Public holiday commemorating Atatürk's proclamation of the Republic in 1923 *(see p29)*. The Turkish flag adorns buildings in the city.
**Akbank Jazz Festival** *(October)*, various locales. Jazz music *(see p213)*.
**International Istanbul Fine Arts Biennial** *(October–November every two years)*. International and local avant-garde artists exhibit work in historic locations such as Hagia Eirene and the Imperial Mint *(see p60)*, and the Basilica Cistern *(see p76)*.
**Anniversary of Atatürk's Death** *(November 10)*. A minute's silence is observed at 9:05am, the precise time of Atatürk's death in Dolmabahçe Palace *(see pp128–9)* in 1938.
**Tüyap Book Fair** *(first week of November)*, opposite the Pera Palas Hotel. Symposia featuring prominent publishers and writers. Manuscripts, prints, and books displayed.
**Efes Pilsen Blues Festival** *(early November)*, selected locales. Foreign and local blues bands play in popular music spots around the city.
**Interior Design Fair** *(first week of November)*, Çırağan Palace Hotel Kempinski *(see p123)*. Interior designers and antique dealers display upscale wares in this popular annual show.
**Elit's Küsav Antiques Fair** *(mid-November)*, Military Museum *(see p126)*. Sale of local and foreign paintings, furniture, carpets, maps, books, porcelain, textiles, silver, clocks, and bronze statuary.

**Crowds gathering to celebrate Republic Day on October 29**

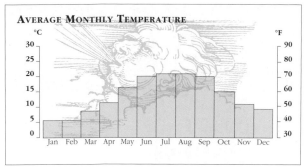

## AVERAGE MONTHLY TEMPERATURE

**Temperature Chart**
*The temperature of the city rarely drops below freezing in winter, and even very cold snaps seldom last longer than three days. The heat of the long, humid summer is intensified by the* lodos *wind, which blows in from the Sea of Marmara. However, the northerly* poyraz *occasionally provides a cooling breeze.*

## WINTER

THERE ARE distinct bonuses to visiting Istanbul in the winter, when sights are uncrowded, although the weather may be discouraging. Stores in the Akmerkez, Galleria, Capitol, and Carousel malls *(see p203)* hold sales, making the city a shopper's paradise for leather products, woolen goods, and fashion.

Outside Istanbul, when enough snow has fallen on the mountains, the ski season begins in Uludağ *(see p169)*, one of Turkey's most important winter sports resorts. Meanwhile, tea with baklava and cream cakes is consumed in the cozy cafés along the Bosphorus and in the old quarter of Beyoğlu *(see pp100–7)*.

**View of Bebek on the Bosphorus *(see pp136–49)* in winter**

founder of the famous Whirling Dervishes.

**Christmas** *(late December)*. Although Christmas Day is not a public holiday, major hotels organize seasonal festivities.

**New Year's Day** *(January 1)*. Public holiday incorporating Western Christmas traditions,

such as eating turkey and decorating trees. Strings of lights adorn the main roads.

**Karadam Ski Festival** *(second half of February)*, Uludağ Mountain. Competitions organized by local radio stations and the Uludağ Ski Instructors' Association.

**Multitude of lights to welcome in the New Year in Beyoğlu**

## EVENTS

**Mevlana Festival** *(December 17–24)*, Mevlevi Monastery *(see p104)*. Enthusiastic Istanbul devotees perform special dances in honor of the

## MUSLIM HOLIDAYS

The dates of Muslim holidays vary according to the phases of the moon and therefore change from year to year. In the holy month of **Ramazan**, Muslims refrain from eating and drinking between dawn and dusk. Some restaurants are closed during the day, and tourists should be discreet when eating in public. Right after this is the three-day **Şeker Bayramı** (Sugar Festival), when many sweets are prepared. Two months later, the four-day **Kurban Bayramı** (Feast of the Sacrifice) commemorates the Koranic version of Abraham's sacrifice. This is the main annual public holiday in Turkey, and hotels, trains, and roads are packed. Strict Muslims also observe the festivals of **Regaip Kandili**, **Miraç Kandili**, **Berat Kandili**, and **Mevlid-i-Nebi**.

**Festivities during Şeker Bayramı**

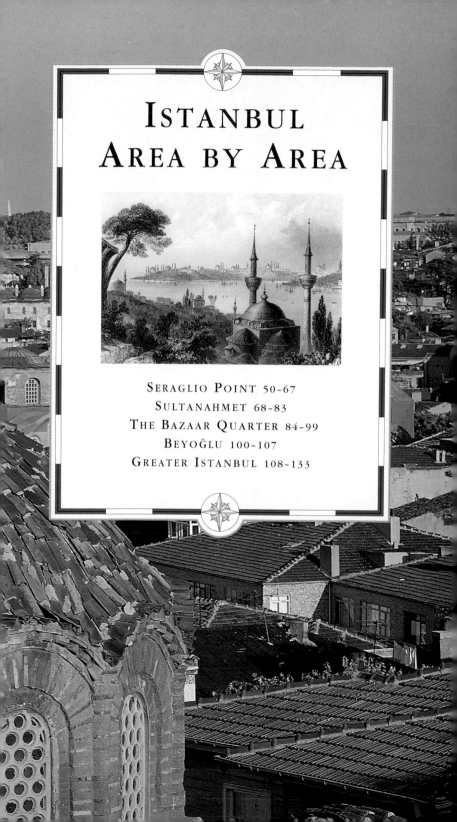

# ISTANBUL
# AREA BY AREA

# SERAGLIO POINT

THE HILLY, wooded promontory that marks the meeting point of the Bosphorus and the Sea of Marmara occupies a natural strategic position. In Byzantine times, monasteries and public buildings stood on this incomparable site. Today it is dominated by the grandiose complex of buildings forming Topkapı Palace, the residence of the Ottoman sultans and the women of the harem for 400 years.

Lion relief from the Ishtar Gate

The palace is now open to the public as a rambling museum, with lavish apartments and glittering collections of jewels and other treasures. Originally the palace covered almost the entire area with its extensive gardens and pavilions. Part of the grounds have now been turned into a public park. Adjacent to it is the Archaeological Museum, a renowned collection of finds from Turkey and the Near East.

## SIGHTS AT A GLANCE

**Museums and Palaces**
Archaeological Museum
  pp62–5 **2**
Topkapı Palace pp54–9 **1**

**Churches**
Hagia Eirene **4**

**Historic Buildings and Monuments**
Fountain of Ahmet III **5**
Imperial Mint **3**
Sirkeci Station **11**
Sublime Porte **9**

**Streets and Courtyards**
Cafer Ağa Courtyard **7**
Soğukçeşme Sokağı **6**

**Parks**
Gülhane Park **8**

**Turkish Baths**
Cağaloğlu Baths **10**

### GETTING AROUND
With little traffic, this small area is easily explored on foot. Trams from the Grand Bazaar and the ferry piers at Eminönü stop outside Gülhane Park.

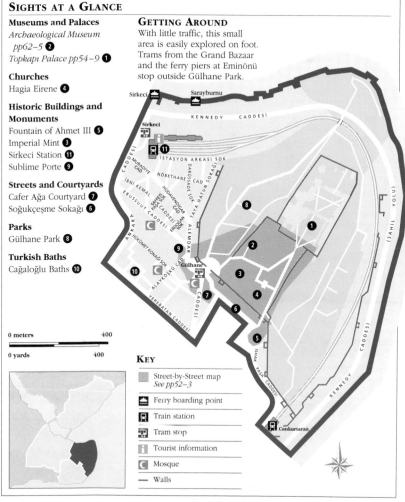

0 meters 400
0 yards 400

### KEY

| | Street-by-Street map See pp52–3 |
| --- | --- |
| | Ferry boarding point |
| | Train station |
| | Tram stop |
| | Tourist information |
| C | Mosque |
| — | Walls |

◁ **The Circumcision Pavilion in the third courtyard of Topkapı Palace**

# Street-by-Street: The First Courtyard of Topkapı

THE JUXTAPOSITION of Ottoman palace walls, intimately proportioned wooden houses, and a soaring Byzantine church lends plenty of drama to the First Courtyard, the outer part of Topkapı Palace. This was once a service area, housing the mint, a hospital, a college, and a bakery. It was also the mustering point of the Janissaries *(see p127)*. Nowadays, the Cafer Ağa Courtyard and the Fatih Büfe, just outside the courtyard wall, offer unusual settings for refreshments. Gülhane Park, meanwhile, is one of the few shady open spaces in a city of monuments.

**Gülhane Park**
*Once a rose garden in the outer grounds of Topkapı Palace, the wooded Gülhane Park provides welcome shade in which to escape from the heat of the city* **8**

**Soğukçeşme Sokağı**
*Traditional, painted wooden houses line this narrow street* **6**

**Sublime Porte**
*A Rococo gate stands in place of the old Sublime Porte, once the entrance to (and symbol of) the Ottoman government* **9**

**Museum of the Ancient Orient**

**Entrance to Gülhane Park**

**Gülhane tram stop**

**Alay Pavilion**

| 0 meters | 75 |
|---|---|
| 0 yards | 75 |

**KEY**

– – – Suggested route

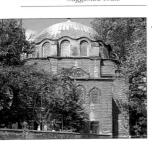

**Zeynep Sultan Mosque**
*Resembling a Byzantine church, this mosque was built in 1769 by the daughter of Ahmet III, Princess Zeynep.*

**Fatih Büfe**, a tiny, ornate kiosk, sells drinks and snacks.

**Otag Music Shop**
sells traditional Turkish instruments.

**Cafer Ağa Courtyard**
*The rooms of this former college, arranged around a tranquil courtyard café, are occupied by jewelers, calligraphers, and other artisans selling their wares* **7**

**STAR SIGHTS**

★ **Archaeological Museum**

★ **Topkapı Palace**

**★ Archaeological Museum**

*Classical statues, dazzling carved sarcophagi, Turkish ceramics, and other treasures from all over the former Ottoman Empire make this one of the world's great collections of antiquities* ❷

**Çinili Pavilion**
*(see p65)*

**LOCATOR MAP**
*See Street Finder maps 3 and 5*

**The Executioner's Fountain** is so named because the executioner washed his hands and sword here after a public beheading.

**★ Topkapı Palace**

*For 400 years the Ottoman sultans ruled their empire from this vast palace. Its fine art collections, opulent rooms, and leafy courtyards are among the highlights of a visit to Istanbul* ❶

**Entrance to Topkapı Palace**

**Topkapı Palace ticket office**

**Imperial Mint**
*This museum houses exhibitions on the historical background to Istanbul* ❸

**Hagia Eirene**
*The Byzantine church of Hagia Eirene dates from the 6th century. It is unusual, in that it has never been converted into a mosque* ❹

**Imperial Gate**

**Fountain of Ahmet III**
*Built in the early 18th century, the finest of Istanbul's Rococo fountains is inscribed with poetry likening it to the fountains of paradise* ❺

# Topkapı Palace ❶
## Topkapı Sarayı

**Süleyman I's tuğra over the main gate**

ETWEEN 1459 and 1465, shortly after his conquest of Constantinople *(see p24)*, Mehmet II built Topkapı Palace as his principal residence. Rather than a single building, it was conceived as a series of pavilions contained by four enormous courtyards, a stone version of the tented encampments from which the nomadic Ottomans had emerged. Initially, the palace served as the seat of government and contained a school in which civil servants and soldiers were trained. In the 16th century, however, the government was moved to the Sublime Porte *(see p61)*. Sultan Abdül Mecit I abandoned Topkapı in 1853 in favor of Dolmabahçe Palace *(see pp128–9)*. In 1924 it was opened to the public as a museum.

★ **Harem**
*The labyrinth of exquisite rooms, where the sultan's wives and concubines lived, can be visited on a guided tour (see pp58–9).*

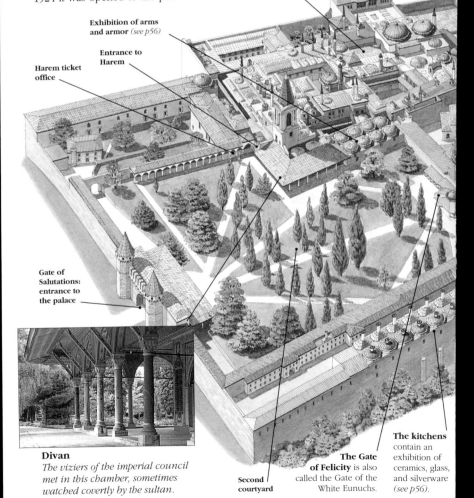

**Exhibition of arms and armor** *(see p56)*

**Entrance to Harem**

**Harem ticket office**

**Gate of Salutations: entrance to the palace**

**Divan**
*The viziers of the imperial council met in this chamber, sometimes watched covertly by the sultan.*

**Second courtyard**

**The Gate of Felicity** is also called the Gate of the White Eunuchs.

**The kitchens** contain an exhibition of ceramics, glass, and silverware *(see p56)*.

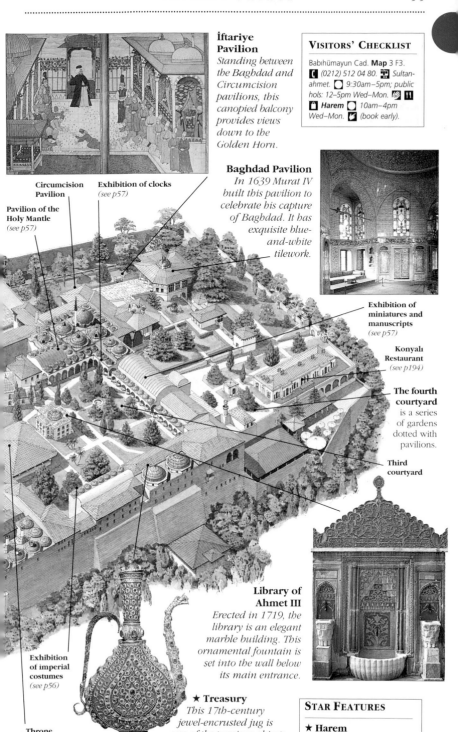

**İftariye Pavilion**
Standing between the Baghdad and Circumcision pavilions, this canopied balcony provides views down to the Golden Horn.

**VISITORS' CHECKLIST**

Babıhümayun Cad. **Map** 3 F3.
[C] (0212) 512 04 80. [T] Sultan-ahmet. [O] 9:30am–5pm; public hols: 12–5pm Wed–Mon. [icon] [icon]
[icon] **Harem** [O] 10am–4pm Wed–Mon. [icon] (book early).

**Circumcision Pavilion**

**Exhibition of clocks** (see p57)

**Pavilion of the Holy Mantle** (see p57)

**Baghdad Pavilion**
In 1639 Murat IV built this pavilion to celebrate his capture of Baghdad. It has exquisite blue-and-white tilework.

**Exhibition of miniatures and manuscripts** (see p57)

**Konyalı Restaurant** (see p194)

**The fourth courtyard** is a series of gardens dotted with pavilions.

**Third courtyard**

**Exhibition of imperial costumes** (see p56)

**Throne Room**

**Library of Ahmet III**
Erected in 1719, the library is an elegant marble building. This ornamental fountain is set into the wall below its main entrance.

**★ Treasury**
This 17th-century jewel-encrusted jug is one of the precious objects exhibited in the former treasury (see p57).

**STAR FEATURES**

★ Harem

★ Treasury

# Exploring the Palace's Collections

DURING THEIR 470-YEAR REIGN, the Ottoman sultans amassed a glittering collection of treasures. After the foundation of the Turkish Republic in 1923 (see p29), this was nationalized and the bulk of it put on display in Topkapı Palace. As well as diplomatic gifts and articles commissioned from the craftsmen of the palace workshops, a large number of items in the collection were brought back as booty from successful military campaigns. Many such trophies date from the massive expansion of the Ottoman Empire during the reign of Selim the Grim (1512–20), when Syria, Arabia, and Egypt were conquered.

**Royal crib displayed in the Treasury**

## CERAMICS, GLASS, AND SILVERWARE

THE KITCHENS contain the palace's collection of ceramics, glass, and silverware. Turkish and European pieces are massively overshadowed here by the vast display of Chinese and, to a lesser extent, Japanese porcelain. This was brought to Turkey along the Silk Route, the overland trading link between the Far East and Europe. Topkapı's collection of Chinese porcelain is the world's second best after China itself.

The Chinese porcelain on display spans four dynasties: the Sung (10–13th centuries), followed by the Yüan (13–14th centuries), the Ming (14–17th centuries), and the Ching (17–20th centuries). Celadon, the earliest form of Chinese porcelain collected by the sultans, was made to look like jade, a stone believed by the Chinese to be lucky. The Ottomans prized it because it was said to neutralize poison in food. More delicate than these are a number of exquisite blue-and-white pieces, mostly of the Ming era.

Chinese aesthetics were an important influence on Ottoman craftsmen, particularly in

**Japanese porcelain plate**

the creation of designs for their fledgling ceramics industry at İznik (see p161). Although there are no İznik pieces in the Topkapı collection, many of the tiles on the palace walls originated there. These clearly show the influence of designs used for Chinese blue-and-white porcelain, such as stylized flowers and cloud scrolls. Much of the later porcelain, particularly the Japanese Imari ware, was made specifically for the export market. The most obvious examples of this are some plates decorated with quotations from the Koran. A part of the kitchens, the old confectioners' pantry, has been preserved as it would have been when in use. On display are huge cauldrons and other utensils wielded by the palace's chefs as they prepared to feed its 12,000 residents and guests.

## ARMS AND ARMOR

TAXES AND TRIBUTES from all over the empire were once stored in this chamber, which was known as the Inner Treasury. Straight ahead as you enter is a series of horsetail standards. Carried in processions or displayed outside tents, these proclaimed the rank of their owners. Viziers

(see p27), for example, merited three, and the grand vizier five, while the sultan's banner would flaunt nine.

The weaponry includes ornately embellished swords and several bows made by sultans themselves (Beyazıt II was a particularly fine craftsman). Seen next to these exquisite items, the huge iron swords used by European crusaders look crude by comparison. Also on view are pieces of 15th-century Ottoman chain-mail and colorful shields. The shields have metal centers surrounded by closely woven straw, painted with flowers.

## IMPERIAL COSTUMES

A COLLECTION of imperial costumes is displayed in the Hall of the Campaign Pages, whose task was to look after the royal wardrobe. It was a palace tradition that on the death of a sultan, his clothes were carefully folded and placed in sealed bags. As a result, it is possible to see a perfectly preserved kaftan once worn by Mehmet the Conqueror (see p24). The reforms of Sultan Mahmut II included a revolution in the dress code (see p28). The end of an era came as plain gray serge replaced the earlier luxurious silken textiles.

**Sumptuous silk kaftan once worn by Mehmet the Conqueror**

## TREASURY

OF ALL THE exhibitions in the palace, the Treasury's collection is the easiest to appreciate, glittering brilliantly with thousands of precious and semiprecious stones. The only surprise is that there are so few women's jewels here. Whereas the treasures of the sultans and viziers were owned by the state and reverted to the palace on their deaths, those belonging to the women of the court did not.

In the first hall stands a full, diamond-encrusted suit of chainmail, designed for Mustafa III (1757–74) for ceremonial use. Diplomatic gifts include a fine pearl statuette of a prince seated beneath a canopy, which was sent to Sultan Abdül Aziz (1861–76) from India.

**The Topkapı dagger**

The greatest pieces are in the second hall. Foremost among these is the Topkapı dagger (1741). This splendid object was commissioned by the sultan from his own jewelers. It was intended as a present for the Shah of Persia, but he died before it reached him. Among other exhibits here are a selection of the bejeweled aigrettes (plumes) that added splendor to imperial turbans.

In the third hall, the 86-carat Spoonmaker's diamond is said to have been discovered in a trash pile in Istanbul in the 17th century and bought from a scrap merchant for three spoons. The gold-plated Bayram throne was given to Murat III *(see p30)* by the Governor of Egypt in 1574 and used for state ceremonies until early this century.

It was the throne in the fourth hall, given by the Shah of Persia, that was to have been acknowledged by the equally magnificent gift of the Topkapı dagger. In a cabinet near the throne is an unusual relic: a case containing bones said to be from the hand of St. John the Baptist.

## MINIATURES AND MANUSCRIPTS

IT IS POSSIBLE to display only a tiny fraction of Topkapı's total collection of over 13,000 miniatures and manuscripts at any one time. Highlights of it include a series of depictions of warriors and fearsome creatures, known as *Demons and Monsters in the Life of Nomads*, which was painted by Mohammed Siyah Qalem, possibly as early as the 12th century. It is from this Eastern tradition of miniature painting, which was also prevalent in Mogul India and Persia, that the ebullient Ottoman style of miniatures developed.

Also on show are some fine examples of calligraphy *(see p95)*, including copies of the Koran, manuscripts of poetry, and several firmans, the imperial decrees by which the sultan ruled his empire.

**Cover of a Koran, decorated in gold filigree work**

## CLOCKS

EUROPEAN CLOCKS given to, or bought by, various sultans form the majority of this collection, despite the fact that there had been makers of clocks and watches in Istanbul since the 17th century.

**A 17th-century watch made of gold, enamel, and precious stones**

The clocks range from simple, weight-driven 16th-century examples to an exquisite 18th-century English mechanism encased in mother-of-pearl and featuring a German organ that played tunes on the hour, to the delight of the harem.

Interestingly, the only male European eyewitness accounts of life in the harem were written by the mechanics sent to service these instruments.

## PAVILION OF THE HOLY MANTLE

SOME OF THE HOLIEST relics of Islam are displayed in these five domed rooms, which are a place of pilgrimage for Muslims. Most of the relics found their way to Istanbul as a result of the conquest by Selim the Grim *(see p24)* of Egypt and Arabia, and his assumption of the caliphate (the leadership of Islam) in 1517.

The most sacred treasure is the mantle once worn by the Prophet Mohammed. Visitors cannot actually enter the room in which it is stored; instead they look into it from an antechamber through an open doorway. Night and day, holy men continuously chant passages from the Koran over the gold chest in which the mantle is stored. A stand in front of the chest holds two of Mohammed's swords.

A glass cabinet in the anteroom contains hairs from the beard of the Prophet, a letter written by him, and an impression of his footprint.

In the other rooms you can see some of the ornate locks and keys for the Kaaba *(see p37)* that were sent to Mecca by successive sultans.

# Topkapı Palace: The Harem

THE WORD *harem* comes from the Arabic for "forbidden." It was the residence of the sultan's wives, concubines, and children, who were guarded by black slave eunuchs. The sultan and his sons were the only other men allowed access to the

**Stained-glass window in the Paired Pavilions**

Harem, which also included the Cage, a set of rooms where the sultan's brothers were confined to avoid succession contests. Topkapı's Harem was laid out by Murat III in the late 16th century and is a labyrinth of brilliantly tiled corridors and chambers. Visitors must take a guided tour, which lasts a little over half an hour and often gets booked early in the day.

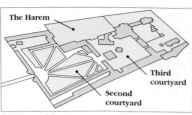

**LOCATOR MAP**
*See main illustration of the palace on pp54–5*

Apartments and courtyard of the favorites

Sultan's bathing chamber

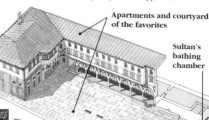

★ **Paired Pavilions**
*These twin apartments, built in the 17th century for the crown prince, boast superb İznik tiles (see p161) and a dome lined with gilded canvas.*

**The Library of Ahmet I** is pleasantly airy and bright, with ivory-faced shutters.

**The Salon of Murat III**, built by Sinan *(see p91)*, has fine tiled walls, a handsome fountain, and a large hearth.

★ **Dining Room of Ahmet III**
*A sumptuous array of fruit and flowers is painted on to the walls of this 18th-century chamber, which is also known as the Fruit Room.*

**Imperial Hall**
*The largest room in the Harem, this hall was used for entertainment. Against one wall stands a large throne, from which the sultan would view the proceedings.*

## LIFE IN THE HAREM

The women of the Harem were slaves, gathered from the farthest corners of the Ottoman Empire and beyond. Their dream was to become a favorite of the sultan *(see p26)* and bear him a son, which on some occasions led to marriage. Competition was stiff, however, for at its height the Harem contained over 1,000 concubines, many of whom never rose beyond the service of their fellow captives. The last women eventually left in 1909.

**A Western view of Harem life in a 19th-century engraving**

### Salon of the Valide Sultan
*The sultan's mother, the valide sultan (see p27), was the most powerful woman in the Harem and had some of the best rooms.*

**The Tower of Justice** can be climbed after a tour of the Harem, for a superb view of Topkapı's rooftops and beyond.

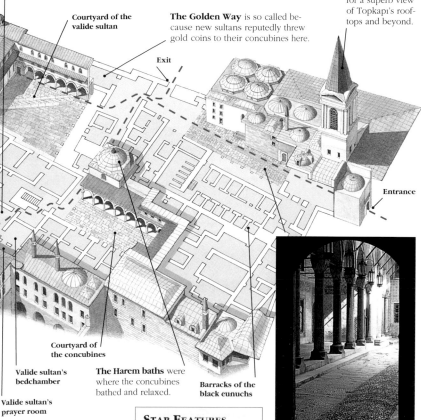

**Courtyard of the valide sultan**

**The Golden Way** is so called because new sultans reputedly threw gold coins to their concubines here.

**Exit**

**Entrance**

**Courtyard of the concubines**

**The Harem baths** were where the concubines bathed and relaxed.

**Barracks of the black eunuchs**

**Valide sultan's bedchamber**

**Valide sultan's prayer room**

### KEY

— — —  Route of guided tour

☐  Rooms on guided tour

☐  Areas closed to the public

### STAR FEATURES

★ **Paired Pavilions**

★ **Dining Room of Ahmet III**

### Courtyard of the Black Eunuchs
*Marble columns line this courtyard, which still has some old-fashioned, wrought-iron lamps.*

# Archaeological Museum ❷

*See pp62–5.*

# Imperial Mint ❸
Darphane-i Amire

First courtyard of Topkapı Palace.
**Map** 3 E4 (5 F3). **[** *(0212) 513 20 35.* **☷** *Gülhane or Sultanahmet.*
**☐** *10am–7pm Wed–Sun.*

THE OTTOMAN MINT opened here in 1727, but most of what can be seen today dates from the reign of Mahmut II (1808–39), when the complex was extended. In 1967, the mint moved to a new location. The buildings are now used for exhibitions on the history of Istanbul. There is a plan to convert them into a museum of social history.

# Hagia Eirene ❹
Aya İrini Kilisesi

First courtyard of Topkapı Palace.
**Map** 3 E4 (5 F3). **[** *(0212) 522 17 50.* **☷** *Gülhane or Sultanahmet.*
**☐** *for concerts.*

ALTHOUGH THE present church dates only from the 6th century, it is at least the third building to be erected on what is thought to be the oldest site of Christian worship in Istanbul. Within a decade of the Muslim conquest of the city in 1453 *(see p24)*, it had

One of the four elaborately decorated sides of the Fountain of Ahmet III

been included within the Topkapı Palace complex and pressed into use as an arsenal. Today the building, which has good acoustics, is the setting for concerts during the Istanbul Music Festival *(see p45)*.

Inside are three fascinating features that have not survived in any other Byzantine church in the city. The *synthronon*, the five rows of built-in seats hugging the apse, were occupied by clergymen officiating during services. Above this looms a simple black mosaic cross on a gold background, which dates from the iconoclastic period *(see p18)* when figurative images were forbidden. At the back of the church is a cloisterlike courtyard where deceased Byzantine emperors once lay in their porphyry sarcophagi. Most have been moved to the Archaeological Museum.

# Fountain of Ahmet III ❺
Ahmet III Çeşmesi

Junction of İshak Paşa Cad & Babıhümayun Cad. **Map** 3 E4 (5 F4).
**☷** *Gülhane or Sultanahmet.*

BUILT IN 1728, the most beautiful of Istanbul's countless fountains survived the violent deposition of Sultan Ahmet III two years later. Many of the other monuments constructed by the sultan during his reign, which has become known as the Tulip Period *(see p25)*, were destroyed. The fountain is in the delicate Turkish Rococo style, with five small domes, mihrab-shaped niches, and dizzying floral reliefs.

Ottoman fountains do not spout jets of water, but are more like ornate public faucets. They sometimes incorporated a counter, or *sebil*, from which refreshments would be served.

In this case, each of the fountain's four walls is equipped with a tap, or *çeşme*, above a carved marble basin. Over each faucet is an elaborate calligraphic inscription by the 18th-century poet Seyit Vehbi Efendi. The inscription, in gold on a blue-green background, is in honor of the fountain and its founder. At each of the four corners there is a *sebil* backed by three windows covered by ornate marble grilles. Instead of the customary ice water, passersby at this fountain would have been offered sherbets and flavored waters in silver goblets.

The apse of Hagia Eirene, with its imposing black-on-gold cross

# Soğukçeşme Sokağı ❻

**Map** 3 E4 (5 F3). 🚇 Gülhane.

CHARMING OLD wooden houses line this narrow, sloping cobblestone lane ("the street of the cold fountain"), which squeezes between the outer walls of Topkapı Palace and the towering minarets of Hagia Sophia. Traditional houses like these were built in the city from the late 18th century onward.

The buildings in the lane were renovated by the Turkish Touring and Automobile Club (TTOK, *see p175*) in the 1980s. Some of them now form the Ayasofya Pansiyonları *(see p180)*, a series of attractive, pastel-painted guesthouses popular with tourists. Another building has been converted by the TTOK into a library and archive of historical writings, engravings, and photographs of the city. A Roman cistern toward the bottom of the lane has been converted into the Sarnıç restaurant *(see p194)*.

**Traditional calligraphy on sale in Cafer Ağa Courtyard**

# Cafer Ağa Courtyard ❼
Cafer Ağa Medresesi

Caferiye Sok. **Map** 5 E3. 📞 (0212) 245 11 60. 🚇 Gülhane. ○ 8:30am–8pm daily.

THIS PEACEFUL courtyard at the end of an alley was built in 1559 by Sinan *(see p91)* for the chief black eunuch *(see p27)* as a *medrese* (theological college, *see p36*). Sinan's bust presides over the café tables in the courtyard. The former students' lodgings are now used to display a variety of craft goods typically including jewelry, silk prints, ceramics, and calligraphy.

**Restored Ottoman house on Soğukçeşme Sokağı**

# Gülhane Park ❽
Gülhane Parkı

Alemdar Cad. **Map** 3 E3 (5 F2). 🚇 Gülhane. ○ daily.

GÜLHANE PARK occupies what was the lower grounds of Topkapı Palace. Today it has a neglected air, but it is still a shady place to stroll, and it includes a couple of interesting landmarks.

Ignore the run-down zoo on the left of the road through the park, look for the aquarium by the abandoned cascade on the right. It is in the cavernous vaults of a Roman water cistern. At the far end of the park is the Goths' Column, a 3rd-century victory monument, surrounded by a cluster of clapboard teahouses. Its name comes from the Latin inscription that reads: "Fortune is restored to us now that the Goths are conquered."

Across Kennedy Caddesi, the main road running along the northeast side of the park, there is a view of the busy waters where the Golden Horn meets the Bosphorus.

## OTTOMAN HOUSES

The typical, fashionable town-house of 19th-century Istanbul had a stone ground floor above which were one or two wooden stories. The building invariably sported a *çıkma*, a section projecting out over the street. This developed from the enclosed Turkish balcony, traditionally used in the northern part of the country because of the colder climate. Wooden lattice covers, or *kafesler*, over the windows on the upper stories ensured that the women of the house were able to watch life on the street below without being seen themselves. Few wooden houses have survived. Those that remain usually owe their existence to tourism, and many have been restored as hotels. Even though the law forbids their demolition, it is extremely hard to obtain insurance for them in a city that has experienced many devastating fires.

# Sublime Porte ❾
Bab-ı Ali

Alemdar Cad. **Map** 3 E3 (5 E2). 🚇 Gülhane.

FOREIGN AMBASSADORS to Ottoman Turkey were known as Ambassadors to the Sublime Porte, after this monumental gateway that once led into the offices and palace of the grand vizier. The institution of the Sublime Porte filled an important role in Ottoman society because it could often provide an effective counterbalance to the whims of sultans.

The Rococo gateway you see today was built in the 1840s. Its guarded entrance now shields the offices of Istanbul's provincial government.

**Rococo decoration on the roof of the Sublime Porte**

# Archaeological Museum ❷

## Arkeoloji Müzesi

**Roman statue of Apollo**

ALTHOUGH THIS collection of antiquities was begun only in the mid-19th century, provincial governors were soon sending in objects from the length and breadth of the Ottoman Empire. Today the museum has one of the world's richest collections of classical artifacts and also includes treasures from the preclassical world. The main building was erected under the directorship of Osman Hamdi Bey (1881–1910) to house his finds. This archaeologist, painter, and scholar discovered the exquisite sarcophagi in the royal necropolis at Sidon in present-day Lebanon. A new four-story wing of the museum opened in 1991.

★ **Alexander Sarcophagus**

*This fabulously carved marble tomb from the late 4th century BC is thought to have been built for King Abdalonymos of Sidon. It is called the Alexander Sarcophagus because Alexander the Great is depicted on it winning a victory over the Persians.*

### KEY

- ☐ Classical Archaeology
- ☐ Children's Museum
- ☐ Thracian, Bithynian, and Byzantine Collections
- ☐ Istanbul Through the Ages
- ☐ Anatolia and Troy
- ☐ Anatolia's Neighboring Cultures
- ☐ Turkish Tiles and Ceramics
- ☐ Museum of the Ancient Orient
- ☐ Nonexhibition space

### GALLERY GUIDE

*The 20 galleries of the main building house the museum's important collection of classical antiquities. The new wing has displays on the archaeology of Istanbul and nearby regions, and includes the Children's Museum. There are two other buildings within the grounds: the Çinili Pavilion, which contains Turkish tiles and ceramics, and the Museum of the Ancient Orient.*

**Sarcophagus of the Mourning Women**

**The porticoes** of the museum take their design from the 4th-century BC Sarcophagus of the Mourning Women.

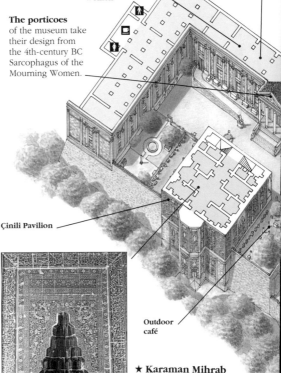

**Çinili Pavilion**

**Outdoor café**

### STAR EXHIBITS

- ★ **Alexander Sarcophagus**
- ★ **Karaman Mihrab**
- ★ **Treaty of Kadesh**

★ **Karaman Mihrab**

*This blue, richly tiled mihrab (see p36) comes from the city of Karaman in southeast Turkey, which was the capital of the Karamanid state from 1256–1483. It is the most important artistic relic of that culture.*

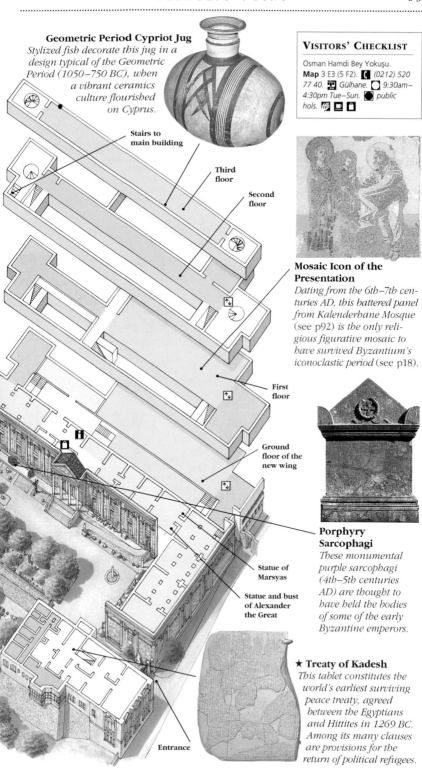

**Geometric Period Cypriot Jug**
*Stylized fish decorate this jug in a design typical of the Geometric Period (1050–750 BC), when a vibrant ceramics culture flourished on Cyprus.*

Stairs to main building

Third floor

Second floor

First floor

Ground floor of the new wing

Statue of Marsyas

Statue and bust of Alexander the Great

Entrance

**VISITORS' CHECKLIST**

Osman Hamdi Bey Yokuşu.
**Map** 3 E3 (5 F2). ( (0212) 520 77 40. 🚋 *Gülhane.* ◯ *9:30am–4:30pm Tue–Sun.* ● *public hols.* 🚫 🛒 🛆

**Mosaic Icon of the Presentation**
*Dating from the 6th–7th centuries AD, this battered panel from Kalenderhane Mosque (see p92) is the only religious figurative mosaic to have survived Byzantium's iconoclastic period (see p18).*

**Porphyry Sarcophagi**
*These monumental purple sarcophagi (4th–5th centuries AD) are thought to have held the bodies of some of the early Byzantine emperors.*

**★ Treaty of Kadesh**
*This tablet constitutes the world's earliest surviving peace treaty, agreed between the Egyptians and Hittites in 1269 BC. Among its many clauses are provisions for the return of political refugees.*

# Exploring the Archaeological Museum

THIS ENORMOUS COLLECTION spans over 5,000 years, from figurines of the Mother Goddess modeled in the 3rd millennium BC to Turkish pottery thrown in the 19th century. To cover everything in one visit is impossible. Visitors with little time should not miss the breathtaking sarcophagi from the royal necropolis at Sidon. To learn more about the history of Istanbul itself you should head for the gallery exploring this theme, on the first floor of the new wing. Youngsters may enjoy the displays in the Children's Museum.

## CLASSICAL ARCHAEOLOGY

MONUMENTAL BES, the ancient Egyptian god, greets visitors at the door to the main building. Very popular in the 1st–3rd centuries, Bes's comically grotesque appearance was an effective deterrent for evil spirits. Rooms 9 and 8 contain the highlights of the museum's entire collection: a group of sarcophagi unearthed in 1887 at Sidon (in present-day Lebanon). These are thought to have been made for a line of Phoenician kings who ruled in the 6th–4th centuries BC. Their decoration vividly shows the transition from Egyptian to Greek influence in the art of the Near East at that time.

**Marble bust of Emperor Augustus**

The latest and finest of them is the so-called Alexander Sarcophagus (late 4th century BC). Alexander the Great is featured in two decorative, high-relief friezes on the longest sides. These show a battle scene and a hunting

scene. The friezes survive in almost perfect condition, showing traces of their original coloring, but the metal weapons of the soldiers and hunters have been lost.

The Sarcophagus of the Mourning Women is thought to have been made for King Straton (374–358 BC), who was known for his fondness for women. The grief-stricken females may have been members of his harem.

Rooms 14–20 contain some remarkable statues. Among them is a Roman copy of a 3rd century BC statue of Marsyas, depicting the satyr about to be flayed after daring to challenge Apollo's musical ability. A statue and bust of Alexander the Great (3rd–2nd centuries BC) show the conqueror as the perfect hero, with a meditative expression on his face. Room 18 contains realistic busts of Roman emperors.

## CHILDREN'S MUSEUM

SPECIAL LOW CABINETS are used in this part of the museum, which is designed for visiting schoolchildren. Paper and colored crayons are on hand in a bid to stimulate future archaeologists.

## THRACIAN, BITHYNIAN, AND BYZANTINE COLLECTIONS

THIS GALLERY on the ground floor of the new wing displays religious and other artifacts from the ancient civilizations of Thrace and Bithynia and from Byzantium (see pp18–23) – including a statue of Byzantine Emperor Valens. This section of the musuem also covers the architecture of the ancient world.

**Bronze head of a snake from the Serpentine Column**

## ISTANBUL THROUGH THE AGES

WITH A FEW well-chosen pieces and explanatory texts in Turkish and English, this gallery brilliantly chronicles Istanbul's archaeological past.

The rare Mosaic Icon of the Presentation (c.AD 600) originally adorned the Kalenderhane Mosque (see p92). One of the three snakes' heads from the Serpentine Column, which has stood headless in the Hippodrome (see p80) since the 18th century, is also displayed here. Also look for a section of the iron chains that the Byzantines hung across both the Bosphorus and the Golden Horn to stop hostile ships (see p21).

**Frieze showing the battle of Issus (333 BC), on the side panel of the Alexander Sarcophagus**

Reconstruction of a mausoleum discovered at Palmyra in Syria

## ANATOLIA AND TROY

ONE SIDE OF this narrow, long hall chronicles the history of Anatolia (the Asiatic part of modern Turkey) from the Paleolithic era to the Iron Age. It culminates with a room devoted to the Phrygian culture, which centered on the city of Gordion. The highlight is a recreation of an 8th-century BC royal tomb, which was housed beneath a tumulus in a juniper-wood chamber. As well as cooking utensils, the king was buried with furniture made of oak, boxwood, yew, and juniper.

The other side of the gallery traces the excavations of nine different civilizations at Troy *(see p171),* from 3000 BC to the time of Christ. On display are a few pieces of the gold hoard known as the Schliemann treasure, after the archaeologist who first discovered it in the late 19th century. Most of the pieces were smuggled out of Turkey, however, and are now in museums around the world.

## ANATOLIA'S NEIGHBORING CULTURES

THIS LONG GALLERY is also divided in two, with one side devoted to Cyprus and the other to Syria-Palestine. The Cypriot collection was assembled by the joint American and Russian consul to Cyprus, Luigi Palma di Cesnola, who systematically looted its tombs from 1865–73. Apart from some beautiful pots, the most interesting objects are the figures of plump, naked temple boys (3rd century BC). They are thought to represent boy prostitutes at temples to Aphrodite, the Greek goddess of love.

Among the Syrian exhibits are funerary reliefs, the Gezer Calendar (925 BC) – a limestone tablet bearing the oldest known Hebrew inscription – and a reconstruction of a 1st- to 3rd-century mausoleum from Palmyra.

16th-century İznik tiled lunette in the Çinili Pavilion

## TURKISH TILES AND CERAMICS

APART FROM CARPETS, the most distinctive Turkish art form is ceramics. This is particularly seen in the sheets of tiles used to decorate the walls of mosques and pavilions such as the Çinili Pavilion, where the entrance archway is plastered with geometric and calligraphic tiles.

In the main room there is an exquisite early 15th-century tiled mihrab from central Anatolia. Rooms 3 and 4 contain tiles and mosque lamps from the famed İznik potteries, the hub of Turkish ceramics production *(see p161).* With the decline in quality of İznik ceramics in the late 16th century, other centers took over. One of these, Kütahya, also produced pieces of beauty and high quality (rooms 5 and 6).

## MUSEUM OF THE ANCIENT ORIENT

ALTHOUGH THIS collection contains antiquities of great rarity and beauty from the Egyptian and Hittite cultures, the best display shows artifacts from the early civilizations of Mesopotamia (present-day Iraq).

The monumental glazed brick friezes from Babylon's main entrance, the Ishtar Gate, (rooms 3 and 9) date from the reign of Nebuchadnezzar II (605–562 BC), when the capital of Babylon experienced its final flowering. The elegant, 30-kg (65-lb) duck-shaped weight in Room 4 comes from a much earlier Babylonian temple (c.2000 BC).

Room 5 contains some of the earliest known examples of writing, in the form of cuneiform inscriptions on clay tablets, dating from 2700 BC. The famous Treaty of Kadesh (room 7), concluded around 1269 BC between the Egyptian and Hittite empires, was originally written on a sheet of silver. The one in this collection is a Hittite copy. The treaty includes many sophisticated clauses, including one providing for the return of a political refugee, who was "not to be charged with his crime, nor his house and wives and his children be harmed."

Glazed frieze of a bull from Ishtar Gate, Babylon

## Cağaloğlu Baths ⑩
Cağaloğlu Hamamı

Prof Kazım İsmail Gürkan Cad 34,
Cağaloğlu. **Map** 3 E4 (5 D3).
█ (0212) 522 24 24.
🚇 Sultanahmet. ◯ daily 8am–9pm
(women); 8am–10pm (men).

AMONG THE city's more sumptuous Turkish baths, the
ones in Cağaloğlu were built
by Sultan Mahmut I in 1741.
The income from them was
designated for the maintenance
of Mahmut's library in Hagia
Sophia (see pp72–5).

The city's smaller baths have
different times at which men
and women can use the same
facilities. But in larger baths,

**Corridor leading into the Cağaloğlu
Baths, built by Mahmut I**

such as this one, there are
entirely separate sections. In
the Cağaloğlu Baths the men's
and women's sections are at
right angles to one another and
entered from different streets.
Each consists of three parts: a
camekan, a soğukluk, and the
main bath chamber, or hararet,
which centers on a massive
octagonal massage slab.

The Cağaloğlu Baths are
popular with tourists; the staff
are friendly and willing to
explain the procedure. Even
if you do not want to sweat it
out, you can still take a look
inside the entrance corridor
and camekan of the men's
section. Here there is a small
display of Ottoman bathing
regalia, including precarious
wooden clogs once worn by
women on what would fre-
quently be their only outing
from the confines of the
home. You can also sit and
have a drink by the fountain
in the peaceful camekan.

## Sirkeci Station ⑪
Sirkeci Garı

Sirkeci İstasyon Cad, Sirkeci. **Map** 3E3
(5 E1). █ (0212) 527 00 50.
🚇 Sirkeci. ◯ daily.

THIS MAGNIFICENT train
station was built to receive
the long-anticipated Orient
Express from Europe. It was
officially opened in 1890, even

**Sirkeci Station, final destination
of the historic Orient Express**

though the luxurious train had
been running into Istanbul for
a year by then. The design, by
the German architect Jasmund,
successfully incorporates features from the many different
architectural traditions of
Istanbul. Byzantine alternating
stone and brick courses are
combined with a Seljuk-style
monumental recessed portal
and Muslim horseshoe arches
around the windows.

The station café is a good
place to relax and escape the
bustle of the city for a while.
Sirkeci serves Greece and
other destinations in Europe
as well as the European part
of Turkey. Istanbul's other
mainline train station is
Haydarpaşa (see p133), on
the Asian side of the city.

## THE WORLD-FAMOUS ORIENT EXPRESS

The Orient Express made its first run from Paris to
Istanbul in 1889, covering the 2,900-km (1,800-mile)
trip in three days. Both Sirkeci Station and the Pera
Palas Hotel (see p104) in Istanbul were built
especially to receive its passengers. The wealthy and
often distinguished passengers of "The Train of
Kings, the King of Trains" did indeed include kings
among the many presidents, politicians, aristocrats,
and actresses. King Boris III of Bulgaria even made a
habit of taking over from the driver of the train when
he traveled on it through his own country.

A byword for exoticism and romance, the train was
associated with the orientalist view of Istanbul as a
treacherous melting pot of diplomats and arms dealers.
It inspired no fewer than 19 books – Murder on the
Orient Express by Agatha Christie and Stamboul Train
by Graham Greene foremost among them – six films,
and one piece of music. During the Cold War
standards of luxury crashed, although a service of
sorts, without even a restaurant car, continued twice
weekly to Istanbul until 1977.

**A 1920s poster for the Orient Express,
showing a romantic view of Istanbul**

# Turkish Baths

No TRIP TO ISTANBUL is complete without an hour or two spent in a Turkish bath *(hamam)*, which will leave your whole body feeling rejuvenated. Turkish baths differ little from the baths of ancient Rome, from which they derive, except there is no pool of cold water to plunge into at the end.

A full service will entail a period of relaxation in the steam-filled hot room, punctuated by bouts

**Ornate wash basin**

of vigorous soaping and massaging. There is no time limit, but allow at least an hour and a half for a leisurely bath. Towels and soap will be provided, but you can take special toiletries with you. Two historic baths located in the old city, Çemberlitaş *(see p81)* and Cağaloğlu (illustrated below), are used to catering to foreign tourists. Some luxury hotels have their own baths *(see pp174–85).*

**Choosing a Service**
*Services, detailed in a price list at the entrance, range from a self-service option to a luxury body scrub, shampoo, and massage.*

**The çamekan (entrance hall)** is a peaceful internal courtyard near the entrance of the building. Bathers change clothes in cubicles surrounding it. The *çamekan* is also the place to relax with a cup of tea after bathing.

**Changing Clothes**
*Before changing you will be given a cloth* (peştemal) *to wrap around you and a pair of slippers for walking on the hot, wet floor.*

**Corridor from street**

**Basin and tap for washing**

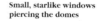

**Small, starlike windows piercing the domes**

## CAĞALOĞLU BATHS
The opulent, 18th-century Turkish baths at Cağaloğlu have separate, identical sections for men and women. The men's section is shown here.

**The soğukluk (intermediate room)** is a temperate passage between the changing room and the *hararet*. You will be given dry towels here on your way back to the *çamekan*.

**In the hararet (hot room)**, the main room of the Turkish bath, you may sit and sweat in the steam for as long as you like.

**The Exfoliating Body Scrub**
*In between steaming, you (or the staff at the baths) scrub your body briskly with a coarse, soapy mitt (kese).*

**The Body Massage**
*A marble plinth (göbek taşı) occupies the center of the hot room. This is where you will have your pummeling full-body massage.*

# SULTANAHMET

I STANBUL'S two principal monuments face each other across an area of gardens known informally as Sultanahmet Square. This part of the city gets its name from Sultan Ahmet I, who built the Blue Mosque. Opposite is Hagia Sophia, an outstanding example of early Byzantine architecture, and still one of the world's most remarkable churches. A neat, oblong square

**Mosaic of Empress Irene in Hagia Sophia**

next to the Blue Mosque marks the site of the Hippodrome, a chariot-racing stadium built by the Romans in around AD 200. On the other side of the Blue Mosque, Sultanahmet slopes down to the Sea of Marmara in a jumble of alleyways. Here, traditional-style Ottoman wooden houses have been built over the remains of the Great Palace of the Byzantine emperors.

## SIGHTS AT A GLANCE

### Mosques and Churches
Blue Mosque pp78–9 **7**
Church of SS. Sergius and Bacchus **14**
Hagia Sophia pp72–5 **1**
Sokollu Mehmet Paşa Mosque **13**

### Museums
Mosaics Museum **6**
Museum of Turkish and Islamic Arts **8**
Vakıflar Carpet Museum **5**

### Squares and Courtyards
Hippodrome **9**
Istanbul Crafts Center **3**

### Historic Buildings and Monuments
Basilica Cistern **2**
Baths of Roxelana **4**
Bucoleon Palace **15**
Cistern of 1,001 Columns **10**
Constantine's Column **12**
Tomb of Sultan Mahmut II **11**

### KEY

|   |   |
|---|---|
| ▦ | Street-by-Street map *See pp70–71* |
| 🚋 | Tram stop |
| 🛈 | Tourist information |
| C | Mosque |
| — | Walls |

### GETTING AROUND
Trams from Eminönü and Beyazıt stop in Sultanahmet by the Firuz Ağa Mosque on Divanyolu Caddesi. From there, most of the sights are easily reached on foot.

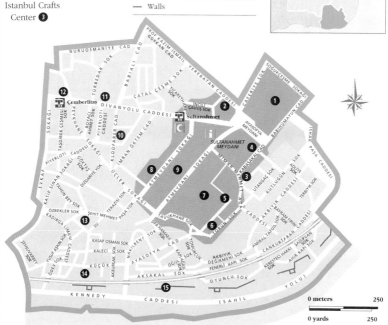

◁ **The elegant domes of the Blue Mosque, catching the evening sun**

# Street-by-Street: Sultanahmet Square

Two OF ISTANBUL's most venerable monuments, the Blue Mosque and Hagia Sophia, face each other across a leafy square, informally known as Sultanahmet Square (Sultanahmet Meydanı), next to the Hippodrome of Byzantium. Also in this fascinating historic quarter are a handful of museums, including the Mosaics Museum, built over part of the old Byzantine Great Palace *(see pp82–3)*, and the Museum of Turkish and Islamic Arts. No less diverting than the cultural sights are the cries of the *simit* (bagel) hawkers and carpet sellers, and the chatter of children selling postcards.

**Tomb of Sultan Ahmet I**
*Stunning, 17th-century İznik tiles (see p161) adorn the inside of this tomb, which is part of the outer complex of the Blue Mosque.*

**★ Blue Mosque**
*Towering above Sultanahmet Square are the six beautiful minarets of this world-famous mosque. It was built in the early 17th century for Ahmet I* **7**

Sultanahmet tram stop

**Firuz Ağa Mosque**

**Fountain of Kaiser Wilhelm II**

**Museum of Turkish and Islamic Arts**
*Yurts, used by Turkey's nomadic peoples, and rugs are included in this impressive collection* **8**

Egyptian Obelisk

**KEY**

– – – Suggested route

Serpentine Column

Brazen Column

**Hippodrome**
*This stadium was the city's focus for more than 1,000 years before it fell into ruin. Only a few sections, such as the central line of monuments, remain* **9**

**Vakıflar Carpet Museum**
*Part of the Blue Mosque complex, this museum displays fine antique carpets* **5**

**Mosaics Museum**
*Hunting scenes are one of the common subjects that can be seen in some of the mosaics from the Great Palace* **6**

0 meters          75

0 yards          75

### ★ Basilica Cistern
*This marble Medusa head is one of two classical column bases found in the Basilica Cistern. The cavernous cistern dates from the reign of Justinian (see p18) in the 6th century* ❷

**A stone pilaster** next to the remains of an Ottoman water tower is all that survives of the Milion *(see p83)*, a triumphal gateway.

**LOCATOR MAP**
*See Street Finder, maps 3 and 5*

### ★ Hagia Sophia
*The supreme church of Byzantium is over 1,400 years old but has survived in a remarkably good state. Inside it are several glorious figurative mosaics* ❶

**Baths of Roxelana**
*Sinan (see p91) designed these beautiful baths in the mid-16th century. They no longer serve their original function, however, having been converted into a state-run carpet store* ❹

**Yeşil Ev Hotel**
*(see p182)*

**Istanbul Crafts Center**
*Visitors have a rare opportunity here to observe Turkish craftsmen practicing a range of skills* ❸

**Cavalry Bazaar**
*Eager salesmen will call you over to peruse their wares – mainly carpets and crafts – in this bazaar. With two long rows of stores on either side of a lane, the bazaar was once a stable yard.*

**STAR SIGHTS**

★ Blue Mosque

★ Basilica Cistern

★ Hagia Sophia

# Hagia Sophia ❶
## Aya Sofya

THE "CHURCH OF HOLY WISDOM," Hagia Sophia is among the world's greatest architectural achievements. More than 1,400 years old, it stands as a testament to the sophistication of the 6th-century Byzantine capital and was of paramount influence on architecture in the following centuries. The vast edifice was built over two earlier churches and inaugurated by Emperor Justinian in 537. In the 15th century the Ottomans converted it into a mosque: the minarets, tombs, and fountains date from this period. To help support the structure's great weight, the exterior has been buttressed on numerous occasions, which has partly obscured its original shape.

**Print of Hagia Sophia from the mid-19th century**

**Seraphims** adorn the pendentives at the base of the dome.

**Calligraphic roundel**

**Kürsü**
*(see p37)*

**Byzantine Frieze**
*Among the ruins of the monumental entrance to the earlier Hagia Sophia (dedicated in AD 415) is this frieze of sheep.*

**Buttresses**

**Imperial Gate**

**Entrance**

**Outer Narthex**

**Inner Narthex**

**The galleries** were originally used by women during services.

## HISTORICAL PLAN OF HAGIA SOPHIA

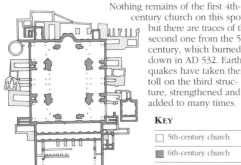

Nothing remains of the first 4th-century church on this spot, but there are traces of the second one from the 5th century, which burned down in AD 532. Earthquakes have taken their toll on the third structure, strengthened and added to many times.

**KEY**

☐ 5th-century church
■ 6th-century church
☐ Ottoman additions

### STAR FEATURES

★ **Nave**

★ **The Mosaics**

★ **Ablutions Fountain**

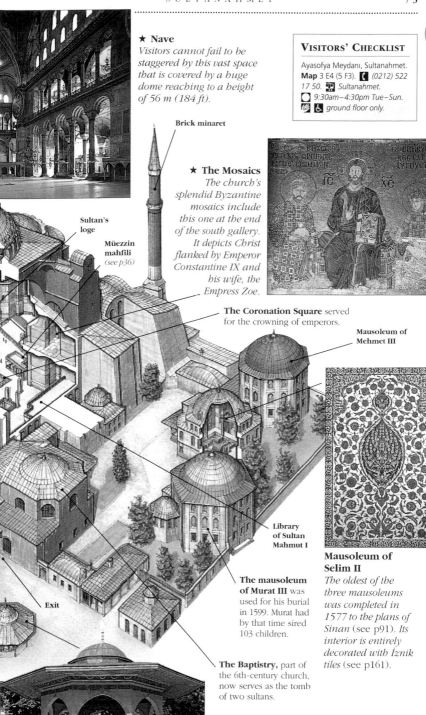

★ **Nave**
*Visitors cannot fail to be staggered by this vast space that is covered by a huge dome reaching to a height of 56 m (184 ft).*

Brick minaret

★ **The Mosaics**
*The church's splendid Byzantine mosaics include this one at the end of the south gallery. It depicts Christ flanked by Emperor Constantine IX and his wife, the Empress Zoe.*

Sultan's loge

Müezzin mahfili *(see p36)*

**The Coronation Square** served for the crowning of emperors.

Mausoleum of Mehmet III

**Mausoleum of Selim II**
*The oldest of the three mausoleums was completed in 1577 to the plans of Sinan (see p91). Its interior is entirely decorated with İznik tiles (see p161).*

Library of Sultan Mahmut I

**The mausoleum of Murat III** was used for his burial in 1599. Murat had by that time sired 103 children.

Exit

**The Baptistry,** part of the 6th-century church, now serves as the tomb of two sultans.

★ **Ablutions Fountain**
*Built around 1740, this fountain is an exquisite example of Turkish Rococo style. Its projecting roof is painted with floral reliefs.*

# Exploring Hagia Sophia

Calligraphic roundel

**D**ESIGNED AS AN EARTHLY mirror of the heavens, the interior of Hagia Sophia succeeds in imparting a truly celestial feel. The artistic highlights are a number of glistening figurative mosaics – remains of the decoration that once covered the upper walls but that has otherwise mostly disappeared. These remarkable works of Byzantine art date from the 9th century or later, after the iconoclastic era *(see p18)*. Some of the patterned mosaic ceilings, however, particularly those adorning the narthex and the neighboring Vestibule of the Warriors, are part of the cathedral's original 6th-century decoration.

Interior as it looked after restoration in the 19th century

## GROUND FLOOR

**T**HE FIRST of the surviving Byzantine mosaics can be seen over the Imperial Gate. This is now the public entrance into the church, although previously only the emperor and his entourage were allowed to pass through it. The mosaic shows **Christ on a throne with an emperor kneeling beside him** ① and has been dated to between 886 and 912. The emperor is thought to be Leo VI, the Wise *(see p19)*.

The most conspicuous features at ground level in the nave are those added by the Ottoman sultans after the conquest of Istanbul in 1453, when the church was converted into a mosque.

The **mihrab** ②, the niche indicating the direction of Mecca, was installed in the apse of the church directly opposite the entrance. The **sultan's loge** ③, on the left of the mihrab as you face it, was built by the Fossati brothers. These Italian-Swiss architects undertook a major restoration of Hagia Sophia for Sultan Abdül Mecit in 1847–9.

To the right of the mihrab is the **minbar** ④, or pulpit, which was installed by Murat III (1574–95). He also erected the four **müezzin mahfilis** ⑤, marble platforms for readers of the Koran *(see p37)*. The largest of these is adjacent to the *minbar*. The patterned marble **coronation square** ⑥ next to it marks the supposed site of the Byzantine emperor's throne, or omphalos (center of the world). Nearby, in the south aisle, is the **library of Mahmut I** ⑦, which was built in 1739 and is entered by a decorative bronze door.

Across the nave, between two columns is the 17th-century, marble **preacher's throne** ⑧, the contribution of Murat IV (1623–40). Behind it is one of several **maqsuras** ⑨. These low, fenced platforms were placed beside walls and pillars to provide places for elders to sit, listen, and read the Koran.

In the northwestern and western corners of the church are two **marble urns** ⑩, thought to date from the Hellenistic or early Byzantine period. A rectangular pillar behind one of the urns, the **pillar of St. Gregory the Miracle Worker** ⑪, is believed to have healing powers. As you leave the church you pass through the **Vestibule of the Warriors**, so called because the emperor's bodyguards would wait here for him when he came to worship. Look behind you as you enter it at the wonderful mosaic of the **Virgin with Constantine and Justinian** ⑫ above the door. It shows Mary seated

## FLOOR PLAN OF HAGIA SOPHIA

☐ Upper walls and domes
☐ Galleries
☐ Ground floor

Apse

Upper walls and domes

North gallery

West gallery

Ramp to gallery

South gallery

Apse

Nave

Entrance

Outer narthex       Narthex       Vestibule of the Warriors

on a throne holding the infant Jesus and flanked by two of the greatest emperors of the city. Constantine, on her right, presents her with the city of Constantinople, while Justinian offers her Hagia Sophia. This was made long after either of these two emperors lived, probably in the 10th century, during the reign of Basil II *(see p19)*. Visitors exit the church by the door that was once reserved for the emperor due to its proximity to the Great Palace *(see pp82–3)*.

Figure of Christ, detail from the Deesis Mosaic in the south gallery

## GALLERIES

A RAMP LEADS from the ground floor to the north gallery. Here, on the eastern side of the great northwest pier, you will find the 10th-century mosaic of **Emperor Alexander holding a skull** ⑬. On the west face of the same pier is a medieval drawing of a galleon in full sail. The only point of interest in the western

gallery is a green marble disk marking the location of the Byzantine **Empress's throne** ⑭.

There is much more to see in the south gallery. You begin by passing through the so-called **Gates of Heaven and Hell** ⑮, a marble doorway of which little is known except that it predates the Ottoman conquest *(see p24)*.

Around the corner to the right after passing through this doorway is the **Deesis Mosaic** ⑯ showing the Virgin Mary and John the Baptist with Christ Pantocrator (the All-Powerful). Set into the floor opposite it is the tomb of Enrico Dandalo, the Doge of Venice responsible for the sacking of Constantinople in 1204 *(see p22)*.

In the last bay of the southern gallery there are two more mosaics. The right-hand one of these is of the **Virgin holding Christ, flanked by Emperor John II Comnenus and Empress Irene** ⑰. The other shows **Christ with Emperor Constantine IX Monomachus and Empress Zoe** ⑱. The faces of the emperor and empress have been altered.

Eight great **wooden plaques** ⑲ bearing calligraphic inscriptions hang over the nave at the level of the gallery. An addition of the Fossati brothers, they bear the names of Allah, the Prophet Mohammed, the first four caliphs, and Hasan and Hussein, two of the Prophet's grandsons who are revered as martyrs.

Mosaic depicting the archangel Gabriel, adorning the lower wall of the apse

## UPPER WALLS AND DOMES

T HE APSE is dominated by a large and striking mosaic showing the **Virgin with the infant Jesus on her lap** ⑳. Two other mosaics in the apse show the archangels **Gabriel** ㉑ and, opposite him, Michael, but only fragments of the latter now remain. The unveiling of these mosaics on Easter Sunday 867 was a triumphal event celebrating victory over the iconoclasts *(see p19)*.

Three mosaic portraits of **saints** ㉒ adorn niches in the north tympanum and are visible from the south gallery and the nave. From left to right, they depict St. Ignatius the Younger, St. John Chrysostom, and St. Ignatius Theophorus.

In the four pendentives (the triangular, concave areas at the base of the dome) are mosaics of six-winged **seraphim** ㉓. The ones in the eastern pendentives date from 1346–55, but may be copies of much older ones. Those on the western side are 19th-century imitations that were added by the Fossati brothers.

The great **dome** ㉔ itself is decorated with Koranic inscriptions. It was once covered in golden mosaic, and the tinkling sound of pieces dropping to the ground was familiar to visitors until the building's 19th-century restoration.

Mosaic of the Virgin with Emperor John II Comnenus and Empress Irene

The cavernous interior of the Byzantine Basilica Cistern

## Basilica Cistern ❷
### Yerebatan Sarayı

13 Yerebatan Cad, Sultanahmet.
**Map** 3 E4 (5 E4). *(0212) 522 12 59.* ⛟ *Sultanahmet.* ○ *9am–5:30pm daily.*

THIS VAST underground water cistern, a beautiful piece of Byzantine engineering, is the most unusual tourist attraction in the city. Although there may have been an earlier, smaller cistern here, this cavernous vault was laid out under Justinian in 532, mainly to satisfy the growing demands of the Great Palace (*see pp82–3*) on the other side of the Hippodrome (*see p80*). For a century after the conquest (*see p24*), the Ottomans did not know of the cistern's existence. It was rediscovered after people were found to be collecting water, and even fish, by lowering buckets through holes in their basements.

Visitors tread walkways to the mixed sounds of classical music and dripping water. The cistern's roof is held up by 336 columns, each over 8 m (26 ft) high. Only about two-thirds of the original

structure is visible today, the rest having been bricked up in the 19th century.

In the far left-hand corner two columns rest on Medusa head bases. These bases show evidence of plundering by the Byzantines from earlier monuments. They are thought to mark a *nymphaeum*, a shrine to the water nymphs.

## Istanbul Crafts Center ❸
### Mehmet Efendi Medresesi

Kabasakal Cad, Sultanahmet.
**Map** 3 E4 (5 E4). *(0212) 517 67 82.* ⛟ *Sultanahmet.* ○ *9:30am–6:30pm daily.*

IF YOU ARE INTERESTED in Turkish crafts, this former Koranic college is worth a visit. You can watch skilled artisans at work: they may be binding a book, executing an elegant piece of calligraphy, or painting glaze onto ceramics. Items produced here are all for sale. Others include exquisite dolls, meerschaum pipes, and jewelry based on Ottoman designs.

Next door is the Yeşil Ev Hotel (*see p182*), a restored Ottoman building with a pleasant café in its courtyard.

## Baths of Roxelana ❹
### Haseki Hürrem Hamamı

Ayasofya Meydanı, Sultanahmet.
**Map** 3 E4 (5 E4). *(0212) 638 00 35.* ⛟ *Sultanahmet.* ○ *9am–5pm Wed–Mon.*

THESE BATHS were built for Süleyman the Magnificent (*see p24*) by Sinan (*see p91*), and are named after Roxelana, the sultan's scheming wife. They were designated for the

### ROXELANA

Süleyman the Magnificent's power-hungry wife Roxelana (1500–58, Haseki Hürrem in Turkish), rose from being a concubine in the imperial harem to become his chief wife, or first *kadın* (*see p26*). Thought to be of Russian origin, she was also the first consort permitted to reside within the walls of Topkapı Palace (*see pp54–9*).

Roxelana would stop at nothing to get her own way. When Süleyman's grand vizier and friend from youth, İbrahim Paşa, became a threat to her position, she persuaded the sultan to have him strangled. Much later, Roxelana performed her *coup de grâce*. In 1553 she persuaded Süleyman to have his handsome and popular heir, Mustafa, murdered by deaf mutes to clear the way for her own son, Selim (*see p24*), to inherit the throne.

**The 16th-century Baths of Roxelana, now housing an exclusive carpet shop**

use of the congregation of Hagia Sophia (see pp72–5) when it was used as a mosque. With the women's entrance at one end of the building and the men's at the other, their absolute symmetry makes them perhaps the most handsome baths in the city.

The building is now a government-run carpet shop, but the baths' original features are still clearly visible. A look around it is a must for those who have no intention of baring themselves in a public bath but are curious about what the interiors of Turkish baths (see p67) are like.

Each end starts with a *camekan*, a massive domed hall that would originally have been centered on a fountain. Next is a small *soğukluk*, or intermediate room, which opens into a *hararet*, or steam room. The hexagonal massage slab in each *hararet*, the *göbek taşı*, is inlaid with colored marbles, indicating that the baths are of imperial origin.

## Vakıflar Carpet Museum ❺
Vakıflar Halı Müzesi

Imperial Pavilion, Blue Mosque, Sultanahmet. **Map** 3 E5 (5 E4). ☎ *(0212) 518 13 30.* 🚋 *Sultanahmet.* ⭕ *9am–4pm Tue–Wed.*

A RAMP TO THE LEFT of the main doorway into the Blue Mosque (see pp78–9) leads up to the Vakıflar Carpet Museum. It has been installed

in what was formerly the mosque's imperial pavilion. This pavilion was built by Ahmet I and used on most Fridays by him and his successors when they attended prayers.

The carpets (see pp210–11) in this fine collection are hidden from potentially destructive sunlight by stained-glass windows. They date from the 16th to the 19th centuries and are mostly from the principal western Anatolian regions of Uşak, Bergama, and Konya. For many years mosques have played a vital role in the preservation of early rugs: all the carpets in this museum lay inside mosques until recently.

**Detail of a 5th-century mosaic in the Mosaics Museum**

## Mosaics Museum ❻
Mozaik Müzesi

Arasta Çarşısı, Sultanahmet. **Map** 3 E5 (5 E5). ☎ *(0212) 518 12 05.* 🚋 *Sultanahmet.* ⭕ *9:30am–4:30pm Wed–Mon.*

T HIS MUSEUM was created simply by roofing over a part of the Great Palace of the Byzantine Emperors (see pp82–3), which was discovered in the 1930s. In its heyday the palace boasted hundreds of rooms, many of them glittering with gold mosaics.

The surviving mosaic floor shows a lively variety of wild and domestic beasts, and includes some hunting and fighting scenes. It is thought to have adorned the colonnade leading from the royal apartments to the imperial enclosure beside the Hippodrome, and dates from the late 5th century AD.

## Blue Mosque ❼
See pp78–9.

## Museum of Turkish and Islamic Arts ❽
Türk ve İslam Eserleri Müzesi

Atmeydanı Sok, Sultanahmet. **Map** 3 D4 (5 D4). ☎ *(0212) 518 18 05.* 🚋 *Sultanahmet.* ⭕ *9:30am–5pm Tue–Sun.*

O VER 40,000 items are on display in the former palace of İbrahim Paşa (c.1493–1536), the most gifted of Süleyman's many grand viziers. The collection was begun in the 19th century and ranges from the earliest period of Islam, under the Omayyad caliphate (661–750), through to modern times.

Each room concentrates on a different chronological period or geographical area of the Islamic world, with detailed explanations in both Turkish and English. The museum is particularly renowned for its collection of rugs. These range from 13th-century Seljuk fragments to the palatial Persian silks that cover the walls from floor to ceiling in the palace's great hall.

On the ground floor, an ethnographic section focuses on the lifestyles of different Turkish peoples, particularly the nomads of central and eastern Anatolia. The exhibits include recreations of a round felt yurt (Turkic nomadic tent) and a traditional brown tent.

**Recreated yurt interior, Museum of Turkish and Islamic Arts**

# Blue Mosque ❼
## Sultan Ahmet Camii

THE BLUE MOSQUE, which takes its name from the mainly blue İznik tilework *(see p161)* decorating its interior, is one of the most famous religious buildings in the world. Serene at any time, it is at its most magical when floodlit at night, its minarets circled by keening seagulls. Sultan Ahmet I *(see p31)* commissioned the mosque during a period of declining Ottoman fortunes, and it was built between 1609–16 by Mehmet Ağa, the imperial architect. The splendor of the plans provoked great hostility at the time, especially because a mosque with six minarets was considered a sacrilegious attempt to rival the architecture of Mecca itself.

**A 19th-century engraving showing the Blue Mosque viewed from the Hippodrome *(see p80)***

**Thick piers** support the weight of the dome.

**Mihrab**

**The loge** *(see p37)* accommodated the sultan and his entourage during mosque services.

**The Imperial Pavilion** now houses the Vakıflar Carpet Museum *(see p77).*

**Minbar**
*The 17th-century minbar is intricately carved in white marble. It is used by the imam during prayers on Friday* (see pp36–7).

**Prayer hall**

**Exit for tourists**

**Müezzin mahfili** *(see p36)*

**Entrance to courtyard**

**★ İznik Tiles**
*No cost was spared in the decoration of the mosque. The tiles were made at the peak of tile production in İznik (see p161).*

### STAR FEATURES
★ İznik Tiles
★ Inside of the Dome
★ View of the Domes

★ **Inside of the Dome**
*Mesmerizing designs, employing flowing arabesques, are painted onto the interior of the mosque's domes and semidomes. The windows piercing the domes no longer have their original 17th-century stained glass.*

★ **View of the Domes**
*The graceful cascade of domes and semidomes makes a striking sight when viewed from the courtyard below.*

**Over 250 windows** allow light to flood into the mosque.

**Entrance**

**Ablutions Fountain**
*The hexagonal şadırvan is now purely ornamental, since ritual ablutions are no longer carried out at this fountain.*

**Each minaret** has two or three balconies.

**Exit to Hippodrome**

**Washing the Feet**
*The Muslim's ritual ablutions conclude with the washing of the feet (see p37). Taps outside the mosque are used by the faithful for this purpose.*

**The courtyard** covers the same area as the prayer hall, balancing the whole building.

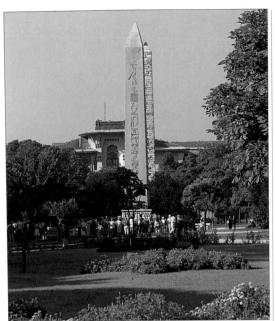

**Egyptian Obelisk and the Serpentine Column in the Hippodrome**

## Hippodrome ❾

At Meydanı

Sultanahmet. **Map** 3 E4 (5 D4).
🚋 *Sultanahmet*.

LITTLE IS LEFT of the gigantic stadium that once stood at the heart of the Byzantine city of Constantinople *(see pp20–21)*. It was originally laid out by Emperor Septimus Severus during his rebuilding of the city in the 3rd century AD *(see p17)*. Emperor Constantine *(see p18)* enlarged the Hippodrome and connected its *kathisma*, or royal box, to the nearby Great Palace *(see pp82–3)*. It is thought that the stadium held up to 100,000 people. The site is now an elongated public garden, At Meydanı, the Square of the Horses. There are, however, enough remains of the Hippodrome to get a sense of its scale and importance.

The road running around the square almost directly follows the line of the chariot racing track. You can also make out

**Relief carved on the base of the Egyptian Obelisk**

some of the arches of the *sphendone* (the curved end of the Hippodrome) by walking a few steps down İbret Sokağı. Constantine adorned the *spina*, the central line of the stadium, with obelisks and columns from Ancient Egypt and Greece, importing a sense of history to his new capital. Conspicuous by its absence is the column that once stood on the spot where the tourist information office is now located. This was topped by four bronze horses, which were pillaged during the Fourth Crusade *(see p22)* and taken to St. Mark's in Venice. Three ancient monuments remain, however. The **Egyptian Obelisk**, which was built in 1500 BC, stood outside Luxor until Constantine had it brought to his city. This beautifully carved monument is broken and probably only one-third of its original height. It stands on a base, made in the 4th century AD, showing Theodosius I *(see p18)* and his family in the *kathisma*

watching various events. The four sides depict a chariot race; Theodosius preparing to crown the winner with a wreath of laurel; prisoners paying homage to the emperor; and the erection of the obelisk itself.

Next to it is the **Serpentine Column**, which was shipped here from Delphi and is believed to date from 479 BC. The heads of the serpents were knocked off in the 18th century by a drunken Polish nobleman. One of them can be seen in the Archaeological Museum *(see pp62–5)*.

Another obelisk still standing, but of unknown date, is usually referred to as the **Column of Constantine Porphyrogenitus**, after the emperor who restored it in the 10th century AD. It is also sometimes called the Brazen Column, because it is thought to have once been sheathed in a case of bronze. Its dilapidated state owes much to the fact that young Janissaries *(see p127)* would routinely scale it as a test of their bravery.

The only other structure in the Hippodrome is a domed fountain that commemorates the visit of Kaiser Wilhelm II to Istanbul in 1898 *(see p43)*. The Hippodrome was the scene of one of the bloodiest events in Istanbul's history. In 532 a brawl between rival chariot-racing teams developed into the Nika Revolt, during which much of the city was destroyed. The end of the revolt came when an army of mercenaries, under the command of Justinian's general Belisarius, massacred an estimated 30,000 people trapped in the Hippodrome.

## Cistern of 1001 Columns ❿

Binbirdirek Sarnıcı

Klodfarer Cad, Sultanahmet.
**Map** 3 D4 (5 D4). 📞 *(0212) 638 22 38*. 🚋 *Çemberlitaş*. 🕐 *8am–midnight daily*. ♿

THIS CISTERN, dating back to the 4th century AD, is the second largest underground Byzantine cistern in Istanbul after the Basilica Cistern *(see p76)*. Covering an area of

## CEREMONIES IN THE HIPPODROME

**Sultan Murat III**

**Palace of İbrahim Paşa (Museum of Turkish and Islamic Arts,** *see p77*)

**Column of Constantine Porphyrogenitus**

**Serpentine Column**

**Egyptian Obelisk**

Beginning with the inauguration of Constantinople on May 11, 330 *(see p18)*, the Hippodrome formed the stage for the city's greatest public events for the next 1,300 years. The Byzantines' most popular pastime was watching chariot racing in the stadium. Even after the Hippodrome fell into ruins following the Ottoman conquest of Istanbul *(see p24)*, it continued to be used for great public occasions. This 16th-century illustration depicts Murat III watching the 52-day-long festivities staged for the circumcision of his son Mehmet. All the guilds of Istanbul paraded before the Sultan, displaying their crafts.

64 m (210 ft) by 56 m (185 ft), the herringbone brick roof vaults are held up by 264 marble columns – the 1,001 columns of its name is poetic exaggeration. Until not long ago, the cistern was filled with rubble and explored only by adventurous visitors. It has recently been transformed into an atmospheric shopping complex specializing in jewelry, carpets, tiles, and other merchandise inspired by Ottoman culture.

## Tomb of Sultan Mahmut II **⓫**

Mahmut II Türbesi

Divanyolu Cad, Çemberlitaş.
**Map** 3 D4 (4 C3). 🚋 Çemberlitaş.
🕐 9:30am–4:30pm daily.

THIS LARGE octagonal mausoleum is in the Empire style (modeled on Roman architecture), made popular by Napoleon. It was built in 1838, the year before Sultan Mahmut II's death, and is shared by sultans Mahmut II, Abdül Aziz, and Abdül Hamit II *(see pp30–31)*. Inside, Corinthian pilasters divide up walls that groan with symbols of prosperity and victory. The huge tomb dominates a cemetery that has beautiful headstones, a fountain, and, at the far end, a good café.

## Constantine's Column **⓬**

Çemberlitaş

Yeniçeriler Cad, Çemberlitaş.
**Map** 3 D4 (4 C3). 🚋 Çemberlitaş.
**Çemberlitaş Baths** Vezirhanı Cad 8.
📞 (0212) 511 25 35. 🕐 7am–
11pm daily (8am–11pm for women).

A SURVIVOR OF both storm and fire, this 35-m (115-ft) high column was constructed in AD 330 as part of the celebrations to inaugurate the new Byzantine capital *(see p18)*. It once dominated the magnificent Forum of Constantine *(see p21)*.

Made of porphyry brought from Heliopolis in Egypt, it was originally surmounted by a Corinthian capital bearing a statue of Emperor Constantine dressed as Apollo. This was brought down in a storm in 1106. Although what is left is relatively unimpressive, it has been carefully preserved. In the year 416 the 10 stone drums making up the column were reinforced with metal rings. These were renewed in 1701 by Sultan Mustafa III, and consequently the column is

**Constantine's Column**

known as Çemberlitaş (the Hooped Column) in Turkish. In English it is sometimes referred to as the Burned Column because it was damaged by several fires, especially one in 1779, which decimated the Grand Bazaar *(see pp98–9)*.

A variety of fantastic holy relics were supposedly entombed in the base of the column, which has since been encased in stone to strengthen it. These included the ax that Noah used to build the ark, Mary Magdalen's flask of anointing oil, and remains of the loaves of bread with which Christ fed the multitude.

Next to Constantine's Column, on the corner of Divanyolu Caddesi, stand the Çemberlitaş Baths. This splendid *hamam* complex *(see p67)* was commissioned by Nur Banu, wife of Sultan Selim II, and built in 1584 to a plan by the great Sinan *(see p91)*. Although the original women's section no longer survives, the baths still have separate facilities for men and women. The staff is used to foreign visitors, so this is a good place for your first experience in a Turkish bath.

# Sokollu Mehmet Paşa Mosque ⑬

Sokollu Mehmet
Paşa Camii

Şehit Çeşmesi Sok, Sultanahmet.
**Map** 3 D5 (4 C5). 🚋 Çemberlitaş or
Sultanahmet. ☐ daily.

**B**UILT BY THE ARCHITECT Sinan
*(see p91)* in 1571–2, this
mosque was commissioned by
Sokollu Mehmet Paşa, grand
vizier to Selim II *(see p30)*. The
simplicity of Sinan's design solution for the mosque's sloping
site has been widely admired.
A steep entrance stairway
leads up to the mosque courtyard from the street, passing
beneath the teaching hall of
its *medrese (see p36)*, which
still functions as a college.
Only the tiled lunettes above
the windows in the portico
give a hint of the jeweled
mosque interior to come.

Inside, the far wall around
the carved mihrab is entirely
covered in İznik tiles *(see
p161)* of a sumptuous green-
blue hue. This tile panel,
designed specifically for the
space, is complemented by
six stained-glass windows.
The "hat" of the *minbar* is
covered with the same tiles.
Most of the mosque's other
walls are of plain stone, but
they are enlivened by a few
more tile panels. Set into the
wall over the entrance there
is a small piece of greenish
stone that is supposedly from
the Kaaba, the holy building
at the center of Mecca.

The Byzantine Church of SS. Sergius and Bacchus, now a mosque

# SS. Sergius and Bacchus' Church ⑭

Küçük Ayasofya Camii

Küçük Ayasofya Cad. **Map** 3 D5 (4 C5).
🚋 Çemberlitaş or Sultanahmet.
☐ daily. ♿

**C**OMMONLY REFERRED TO as
"Little Hagia Sophia," this
church was built in 527, a few
years before its namesake *(see
pp72–5)*. It too was founded

by Emperor Justinian *(see p18)*,
together with his empress,
Theodora, at the beginning of
his long reign. Ingenious and
highly decorative, the church
gives a somewhat hodge-
podge impression both inside
and out and is one of the
most charming of the city's
architectural treasures.

Inside, an irregular octagon
of columns on two floors supports a broad central dome
composed of 16 vaults. The

Interior of the 16th-century
Sokollu Mehmet Paşa Mosque

## RECONSTRUCTION OF THE GREAT PALACE

In Byzantine times, present-day
Sultanahmet was the site of the Great
Palace, which, in its heyday, had no
equal in Europe and dazzled medieval
visitors with its opulence. This great
complex of buildings – including royal
apartments, state rooms, churches,
courtyards, and gardens – extended
over a sloping, terraced site from the
Hippodrome to the imperial harbor
on the shore of the Sea of Marmara.
The palace was built in stages, beginning under Constantine in the 4th
century. It was enlarged by Justinian
following the fire caused by the Nika
Revolt in 532 *(see p80)*. Later emperors,
especially the 9th-century Basil I *(see
p19)*, extended it further. After
several hundred years of occupation, it was finally abandoned in the second half
of the 13th century in
favor of Blachernae
Palace *(see p117)*.

**The Mese** was a colon-
naded street lined with
shops and statuary.

**Hippodrome**
*(see p80)*

**Hormisdas
Palace**

**Church of SS.
Peter and Paul**

**Church of SS. Sergius
and Bacchus**

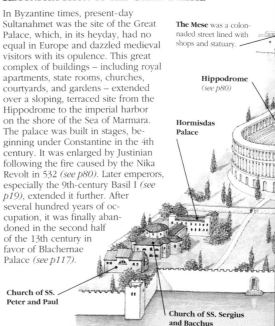

mosaic decoration that once adorned some of the walls has long since crumbled away. However, the green and red marble columns, the delicate tracery of the capitals, and the carved frieze running above the columns are original features of the church.

The inscription on this frieze, in boldly carved Greek script, mentions the founders of the church and St. Sergius, but not St. Bacchus. The two saints were Roman centurions who converted to Christianity and were martyred. Justinian credited them with saving his life when, as a young man, he was implicated in a plot to kill his uncle, Justin I. The saints supposedly appeared to Justin in a dream and told him to release his nephew. The Church of SS. Sergius and Bacchus was built between two important edifices to which it was connected, the Palace of Hormisdas and the Church of SS. Peter and Paul, but has outlived them both. After the conquest of Istanbul in 1453 *(see p24)* it was converted into a mosque.

## Bucoleon Palace ⓕ

### Bukoleon Sarayı

Kennedy Cad, Sultanahmet. **Map** 3 E5. 🚇 *Sultanahmet.*

**F**INDING THE SITE of what remains of the Great Palace of the Byzantine emperors requires precision. It is not advisable to visit the ruins alone as they are usually inhabited by tramps.

Take the path under the railroad from the Church of SS. Sergius and Bacchus, turn left, and walk beside Kennedy Caddesi, the main road along the shore of the Sea of Marmara for about 400 m (450 yards). This will bring you to a stretch of the ancient seawalls, constructed to protect the city from a naval assault. Within these walls you will find a vine-clad section of stonework pierced by three vast windows framed in

marble. This is all that now survives of the Bucoleon Palace, a maritime residence that formed part of the sprawling Great Palace. The waters of a small private harbor lapped right up to the palace and a private flight of steps led down in to the water, allowing the emperor to board imperial caïques. The ruined tower just east of the palace was a lighthouse, called the Pharos, in Byzantine times.

**Wall of Bucoleon Palace, the only part of the Byzantine Great Palace still standing**

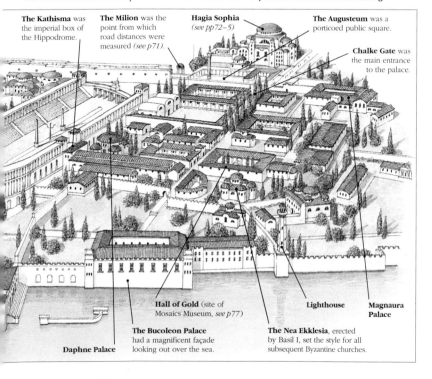

**The Kathisma** was the imperial box of the Hippodrome.

**The Milion** was the point from which road distances were measured *(see p71).*

**Hagia Sophia** *(see pp72–5)*

**The Augusteum** was a porticoed public square.

**Chalke Gate** was the main entrance to the palace.

**Hall of Gold** (site of Mosaics Museum, *see p77*)

**Lighthouse**

**Magnaura Palace**

**The Bucoleon Palace** had a magnificent façade looking out over the sea.

**The Nea Ekklesia**, erected by Basil I, set the style for all subsequent Byzantine churches.

**Daphne Palace**

# THE BAZAAR QUARTER

RADE HAS always been important in a city straddling the continents of Asia and Europe. Nowhere is this more evident than in the warren of streets lying between the Grand Bazaar and Galata Bridge. Everywhere, goods tumble out of stores onto the sidewalk. Look through any of the archways between stores and you will discover hidden courtyards, or hans *(see p96)*, with industrious

**Window from Nuruosmaniye Mosque**

workshops. With its seemingly limitless range of goods, the labyrinthine Grand Bazaar is at the center of all this commercial activity. The Spice Bazaar is equally colorful but smaller and more manageable.

Up on the hill, next to the university, is Süleymaniye Mosque, a glorious expression of 16th-century Ottoman culture. It is just one of numerous beautiful mosques in this area.

## SIGHTS AT A GLANCE

### Mosques and Churches
Atik Ali Paşa Mosque **20**
Bodrum Mosque **12**
Church of St. Theodore **6**
Kalenderhane Mosque **10**
Mahmut Paşa Mosque **22**
New Mosque **1**
Nuruosmaniye Mosque **21**
Prince's Mosque **9**
Rüstem Paşa Mosque **3**
*Sülemaniye Mosque pp90–91* **5**
Tulip Mosque **11**

### Bazaars, Hans, and Stores
Book Bazaar **16**
*Grand Bazaar pp98–9* **18**
Spice Bazaar **2**
Valide Hanı **17**
Vefa Bozacısı **8**

### Museums and Monuments
Forum of Theodosius **13**
Museum of Calligraphy **14**
Valens Aqueduct **7**

### Squares and Courtyards
Beyazıt Square **15**
Çorlulu Ali Paşa Courtyard **19**

### Waterways
Golden Horn **4**

### KEY

|   |   |
|---|---|
| | Street-by-Street map See pp86–7 |
| | Ferry boarding point |
| | Tram stop |
| | Main bus stop |
| C | Mosque |

Haliç Hattı
ÇARDAK CAD
Eminönü
Eminönü

## GETTING AROUND
Trams from Sultanahmet run down Yeniçeriler Caddesi and stop outside the Grand Bazaar. Ferries from various destinations dock at Eminönü, opposite the Spice Bazaar.

| 0 meters | 500 |
| 0 yards | 500 |

◁ **The inside of the Grand Bazaar, always thronging with bargain hunters**

# Street-by-Street: Around the Spice Bazaar

THE NARROW STREETS around the Spice Bazaar encapsulate the spirit of old Istanbul. From here buses, taxis, and trams head off across the Galata Bridge and into the interior of the city. The blast of ships' horns signals the departure of ferries from Eminönü to Asian Istanbul. It is the quarter's shops and markets, though, that are the focus of attention for the eager shoppers who crowd the Spice Bazaar and the streets around it, sometimes breaking for a leisurely tea beneath the trees in its courtyard. Across the way, and entirely aloof from the bustle, rise the domes of the New Mosque. On one of the commercial alleyways which radiate out from the mosque, an inconspicuous doorway leads up stairs to the terrace of the serene, tile-covered Rüstem Paşa Mosque.

**Nargile on sale near the Spice Bazaar**

★ **Rüstem Pasa Mosque**
*The interior of this secluded mosque is a brilliant pattern-book made of İznik tiles (see p161) of the finest quality* ❸

**The *pastırma* shop** at 11 Hasırcılar Caddesi sells thin slices of dried beef, spiced with fenugreek – a Turkish delicacy.

**Tahtakale Hamamı Çarşısı,** now a bazaar, was formerly a Turkish bath.

**Dolmuş and bus station**

**Kurukahveci Mehmet Efendi** is one of Istanbul's oldest and most popular coffee shops. You can drink coffee on the premises or buy a packet to take away with you *(see p205).*

0 meters          75
0 yards           75

## STAR SIGHTS

★ **Rüstem Pasa Mosque**

★ **New Mosque**

★ **Spice Bazaar**

**Street sellers,** such as this man selling garlic cloves, ply their wares in Sabuncuhanı Sokağı and the other narrow streets around the Spice Bazaar.

Eminönü is the port where ferries depart to many destinations *(see p236)* and for trips along the Bosphorus *(see pp144–9)*. It bustles with activity as merchants compete to sell drinks and snacks.

**LOCATOR MAP**
*See Street Finder map 2*

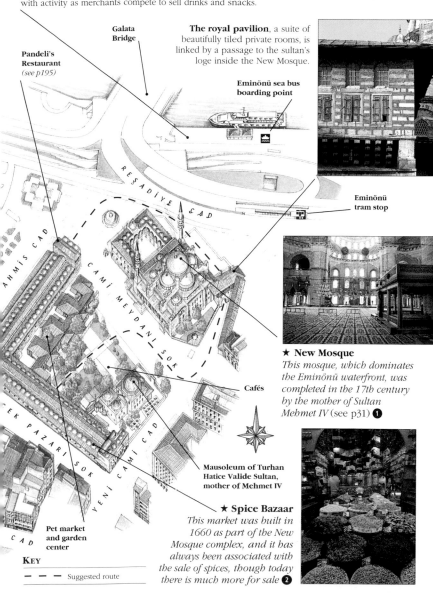

**Galata Bridge**

**Pandeli's Restaurant**
*(see p195)*

**The royal pavilion**, a suite of beautifully tiled private rooms, is linked by a passage to the sultan's loge inside the New Mosque.

**Eminönü sea bus boarding point**

**Eminönü tram stop**

RESADIYE CAD

AHMIS CAD

CAMI MEYDANI SOK

YENI CAMI CAD

EK PAZARI SOK

CAD

**Cafés**

★ **New Mosque**
*This mosque, which dominates the Eminönü waterfront, was completed in the 17th century by the mother of Sultan Mehmet IV (see p31)* ❶

**Mausoleum of Turhan Hatice Valide Sultan, mother of Mehmet IV**

**Pet market and garden center**

★ **Spice Bazaar**
*This market was built in 1660 as part of the New Mosque complex, and it has always been associated with the sale of spices, though today there is much more for sale* ❷

**KEY**

– – – Suggested route

# New Mosque ❶
Yeni Cami

Yeni Cami Meydanı, Eminönü.
**Map** 3 D2. 🚊 *Eminönü.* ⬤ *daily.*

Sの ITUATED AT the southern end of Galata Bridge, the New Mosque is one of the most prominent mosques in the city. It dates from the time when a few women from the harem became powerful enough to dictate the policies of the Ottoman sultans *(see p25)*. The mosque was started in 1597 by Safiye, mother of Mehmet III. Building was suspended when the sultan died, since his mother had lost her position. It was not completed until 1663, after Turhan Hadice, mother of Mehmet IV, had taken up the project.

Although the mosque was built after the classical period of Ottoman architecture, it shares many traits with earlier imperial foundations, including a monumental courtyard. The mosque once had a hospital, school, and public baths.

The turquoise, blue, and white floral tiles decorating the interior are from İznik *(see p161)* and date from the mid-17th century, although by this time the quality of the tiles produced there was already in decline. More striking are the tiled lunettes and bold Koranic frieze decorating the porch between the courtyard and the prayer hall.

At the far left-hand corner of the upper gallery is the sultan's loge *(see p37)*, which is linked to his personal suite of rooms *(see p87)*.

**A selection of nuts and seeds for sale in the Spice Bazaar**

# Spice Bazaar ❷
Mısır Çarşısı

Cami Meydanı Sok. **Map** 3 D2 (4 C1). 🚊 *Eminönü.* ⬤ *8am–7pm Mon–Sat.*

THIS CAVERNOUS, L-shaped market was built in the early 17th century as an extension of the New Mosque complex. Its revenues once helped maintain the mosque's philanthropic institutions.

In Turkish the market is named the Mısır Çarşısı – the Egyptian Bazaar – because it was built with money paid as duty on Egyptian imports. In English it is usually known as the Spice Bazaar. From medieval times spices were a vital and expensive part of cooking, and they became the market's main produce. The bazaar came to specialize in spices from the Orient, taking advantage of Istanbul's site on the trade route between the East (where most spices were grown) and Europe.

Stalls in the bazaar stock spices, herbs, and other foods such as honey, nuts, sweetmeats, and *pastırma* (dried beef). Today's expensive Eastern commodity, caviar, is also available, the best variety being Iranian.

Today an eclectic range of other items can be found in the Spice Bazaar, including everything from household goods, toys, and clothes, to exotic aphrodisiacs. The square between the two arms of the bazaar is full of commercial activity, with cafés, and stalls selling plants and pets.

**Floral İznik tiles adorning the interior of Rüstem Paşa Mosque**

# Rüstem Paşa Mosque ❸
Rüstem Paşa Camii

Hasırcılar Cad, Eminönü.
**Map** 3 D2. 🚊 *Eminönü.* ⬤ *daily.*

RAISED ABOVE the busy shops and warehouses around the Spice Bazaar, this mosque was built in 1561 by the great architect Sinan *(see p91)* for Rüstem Paşa, son-in-law of and grand vizier to Süleyman I *(see p24)*. Rents from the businesses in the bazaar were intended to pay for the upkeep of the mosque.

The staggering wealth of its decoration says something about the amount of money that the corrupt Rüstem managed to salt away during his career. Most of the interior is covered in İznik tiles of the very highest quality.

**The New Mosque, a prominent feature on the Eminönü waterfront**

The four piers are adorned with tiles of one design, but the rest of the prayer hall is a riot of different patterns, from abstract to floral. Some of the finest tiles can be found on the galleries. All in all, there is no other mosque in the city adorned with such a magnificent blanket of tiles.

The mosque is also notable for its numerous windows: it was built with as many as the structure would allow.

## Golden Horn ❹
Haliç

**Map** 3 D2. 🚇 *Eminönü.*
🚌 *55T, 99A.*

OFTEN DESCRIBED as the world's greatest natural harbor, the Golden Horn is a flooded river valley that flows southwest into the Bosphorus. The estuary attracted settlers to its shores in the 7th century BC and later enabled Constantinople to become a rich and powerful port. According to legend, the Byzantines threw so many valuables into it during the Ottoman conquest *(see p24)* that the waters glistened with gold. Today, however, belying its name, the Golden Horn has become polluted by the numerous nearby factories.

For hundreds of years the city's trade was conducted by ships that off-loaded their goods into warehouses lining the Golden Horn. Today, the great container ships coming to Istanbul use ports on the Sea of Marmara. Spanning the mouth of the Horn is the Galata Bridge, which joins Eminönü to Galata. The bridge, built in 1992, opens in the middle to allow access for tall ships. It is a good place from which to appreciate the complex geography of the city and admire the minaret-filled skyline. Fishermen's boats selling mackerel sandwiches are usually moored at each end.

The functional Galata Bridge replaced the raffish charm of a pontoon bridge with a busy lower level of restaurants. The old bridge has been reconstructed just south of the Rahmi Koç Museum *(see p127)*. There is another bridge, Atatürk, between these, and a fourth, Fatih, farther up the Horn near the end of the city walls.

## Süleymaniye Mosque ❺

*See pp90–91.*

## Church of St. Theodore ❻
Kilise Camii

Vefa Cad, Cami Sok, Vefa.
**Map** 2 B2. 🚌 *28, 61B, 87.*

APART FROM ITS delightfully disheveled ancient exterior, very little else remains of the former Byzantine Church of St. Theodore. The elaborate church was built in the 12th–14th centuries, the last great era of Byzantine construction. It was converted into a mosque following the Ottoman conquest of the city in 1453 *(see p24).*

One feature that is still evident in the south dome in its outer porch is a 14th-century mosaic of the Virgin Mary surrounded by the Prophets. The fluted minaret makes a sympathetic addition.

**The 4th-century Valens Aqueduct crossing Atatürk Bulvarı**

## Valens Aqueduct ❼
Bozdoğan Kemeri

Atatürk Bulvarı, Saraçhane.
**Map** 2 A3. 🚇 *Laleli.* 🚌 *28, 61B, 87.*

EMPEROR VALENS built this mighty aqueduct, supported by two imposing rows of arches, in the late 4th century AD. Part of the elaborate water system feeding the palaces and fountains of the Byzantine capital, it brought water from the Belgrade Forest *(see p158)* and mountains more than 200 km (125 miles) away to a vast cistern that stood in the vicinity of what is now Beyazıt Square *(see p94).*

The aqueduct supplied the city's water until the late 19th century, when it was made obsolete by a modern water-distribution network. However, by this time, the original open channels had already been replaced, first by clay pipes and then by iron ones.

The structure was repaired many times, most recently by sultans Mustafa II (1695–1703) and Ahmet III *(see p25).* It was originally 1,000 m (3,300 ft) long, of which only 625 m (2,050 ft) remain.

**Fisherman on the modern Galata Bridge spanning the Golden Horn**

# Süleymaniye Mosque ❺
## Süleymaniye Camii

ISTANBUL'S MOST IMPORTANT MOSQUE is both a tribute to its architect, the great Sinan, and a fitting memorial to its founder, Süleyman the Magnificent *(see p24)*. It was built above the Golden Horn in the grounds of the old palace, Eski Saray *(see p94)*, between 1550–57. Like the city's other imperial mosques, the Süleymaniye Mosque was not only a place of worship but also a charitable foundation, or *külliye (see p36)*. The mosque is surrounded by its former hospital, soup kitchen, schools, caravanserai, and bath house. This complex provided a welfare system which fed over 1,000 of the city's poor – Muslims, Christians, and Jews alike – every day.

**Courtyard**
*The ancient columns that surround the courtyard are said to have come originally from the* kathisma, *the Byzantine royal box in the Hippodrome (see p80).*

**Muvakkithane Gateway**
*The main courtyard entrance (now closed) contained the rooms of the mosque astronomer, who determined prayer times.*

**Minaret**

**Tomb of Sinan**

**The caravanserai** provided lodging and food for travelers and their animals.

**İmaret Gate**

**Café in a sunken garden**

**İmaret**
*The kitchen – now a restaurant (see p195) – fed the city's poor as well as the mosque staff and their families. The size of the millstone in its courtyard gives some idea of the amount of grain needed to feed everyone.*

★ **Mosque Interior**
*Both soaring space and calm strike you as you enter the mosque. The effect is enhanced by the fact that the height of the dome from the floor is exactly double its diameter.*

**VISITORS' CHECKLIST**

Prof Sıddık Sami Onar Caddesi, Vefa. **Map** 2 C3 (4 A1).
(0212) 514 01 39. *Beyazıt or Eminönü, then 10 mins walk.* daily.

**The Tomb of Roxelana** contains Süleyman's beloved wife *(see p76)*.

**Entrance**

**Graveyard**

★ **Tomb of Süleyman**
*Ceramic stars said to be set with emeralds sparkle above the coffins of Süleyman, his daughter Mihrimah, and two of his successors, Süleyman II and Ahmet II.*

**These marble benches** were used to support coffins before burial.

**"Addicts Alley"** is so called because the cafés here once sold opium and hashish, as well as coffee and tea.

**The *medreses*** *(see p36)* to the south of the mosque house a library containing 110,000 manuscripts.

**Former hospital and asylum**

### SINAN, THE IMPERIAL ARCHITECT

Like many of his eminent contemporaries, Koca Mimar Sinan (c.1491–1588) was brought from Anatolia to Istanbul in the *devşirme*, the annual roundup of talented Christian youths, and educated at one of the elite palace schools. He became a military engineer but won the eye of Süleyman I, who made him chief imperial architect in 1538. With the far-sighted patronage of the sultan, Sinan – Turkey's equivalent of a Renaissance architect – created masterpieces that demonstrated his master's status as the most magnificent of **Bust of the great** monarchs. Sinan died aged 97, having built **architect Sinan** 131 mosques and 200 other buildings.

**STAR FEATURES**

★ **Mosque Interior**

★ **Tomb of Süleyman**

## Vefa Bozacısı 8

Katip Çelebi Cad 102, Vefa.
**Map** 2 B2. ☎ *(0212) 519 49 22.*
🚌 *61B, 90.* ⬤ *8am–11pm daily.*

WITH ITS wood-and-tile interior and glittering glass-mosaic columns, this unusual shop and bar has changed little since the 1930s. It was founded in 1876 to sell *boza,* a popular winter drink made from bulgur (cracked wheat, *see p191*). In summer a slightly fermented grape juice known as *şıra* is sold. The shop's main trade throughout the whole year, however, is in wine vinegar.

Inside the shop you will see a glass from which Kemal Atatürk *(see p29)* drank *boza* in 1937, enshrined in a display beneath a glass dome.

**Dome of the Prince's Mosque, Sinan's first imperial mosque**

**Bottles of *boza*, a wheat-based drink, lining the interior of Vefa Bozacısı**

## Prince's Mosque 9
Şehzade Camii

Şehzade Başı Cad 70, Saraçhane.
**Map** 2 B3. 🚇 *Laleli.* ⬤ *daily.*
**Tombs** ⬤ *9am–5pm Tue–Sun.*

THIS MOSQUE complex was erected by Süleyman the Magnificent *(see p24)* in memory of his oldest son by Roxelana *(see p76)*, Şehzade (Prince) Mehmet, who died of smallpox at the age of 21. The building was Sinan's *(see p91)* first major imperial commission and was completed in 1548. The architect used a delightful decorative style in designing this mosque before abandoning it in favor of the classical austerity of his later work. The mosque is approached

through an elegant, porticoed inner courtyard, while the other institutions making up the mosque complex, including a *medrese (see p36)*, are enclosed within an outer courtyard.

The interior of the mosque is unusual and was something of an experiment in that it is symmetrical, having a semidome on each of its four sides.

The three tombs located to the rear of the mosque, belonging to Şehzade Mehmet himself and grand viziers İbrahim Paşa and Rüstem Paşa *(see p88)*, are the finest in the city. Each has beautiful İznik tiles *(see p161)* and lustrous original stained glass. That of Şehzade Mehmet also boasts the finest painted dome in Istanbul.

On Fridays you will notice a crowd of women flocking to another tomb within the

complex, that of Helvacı Baba, as they have done for over 400 years. Helvacı Baba is said to miraculously cure crippled children, solve fertility problems, and find husbands or accommodations for those who beseech him.

## Kalenderhane Mosque 10
Kalenderhane Camii

16 Mart Şehitleri Cad, Saraçhane.
**Map** 2 B3. 🚇 *Üniversite.*
⬤ *prayer times only.*

SHELTERING UNDER the Valens Aqueduct *(see p89)*, on the site where a Roman bath once stood, is this Byzantine church with a checkered history. It was built and rebuilt several times between the 6th and 12th centuries, before finally being converted into a mosque shortly after the conquest in 1453 *(see p24)*. The mosque is named after the Kalender brotherhood of dervishes, which used the church as its headquarters for some years after the conquest.

The building has the cruciform layout characteristic of Byzantine churches of the period. Some of the decoration remaining from its last incarnation, as the Church of Theotokos Kyriotissa (her Ladyship Mary, Mother of God), also survives in the prayer hall with its marble paneling and in the fragments of fresco in the narthex (entrance hall). A series of frescoes depicting the life of St. Francis of Assisi were removed in the 1970s and are no longer on public view.

**A shaft of light illuminating the interior of Kalenderhane Mosque**

The Baroque Tulip Mosque, housing a marketplace in its basement

## Tulip Mosque ⓫
### Laleli Camii

Ordu Cad, Laleli. **Map** 2 B4.
🚇 *Laleli.* ⭕ *prayer times only.*

**B**UILT IN 1759–63, this mosque complex is the best example in the city of the Baroque style, of which its architect, Mehmet Tahir Ağa, was the greatest exponent. Inside the mosque, a variety of gaudy, colored marble covers all of its surfaces.

More fascinating is the area underneath the main body of the mosque. This is a great hall supported on eight piers, with a fountain in the middle. The hall is now used as a subterranean marketplace, packed with Eastern Europeans and Central Asians haggling over items of clothing.

The nearby Büyük Taş Hanı *(see p96)*, or Big Stone Han, is likely to have been part of the mosque's original complex but now houses leather shops and a restaurant. To get to it, turn left outside the mosque into Fethi Bey Caddesi and then take the second left into

Çukur Çeşme Sokağı. The main courtyard of the han is at the end of a long passage situated off this lane.

## Bodrum Mosque ⓬
### Bodrum Camii

Sait Efendi Sok, Laleli. **Map** 2 A4.
🚇 *Laleli.* ⭕ *prayer times only.*

**N**ARROW COURSES of brick forming the outside walls, and a window-pierced dome, betray the early origins of this mosque as a Byzantine church. It was built in the early 10th century by co-Emperor Romanus I Lacapenus (919–44) as part of the Monastery of Myrelaion and adjoined a small palace. The palace was later converted into a nunnery where the emperor's widow, Theophano, lived out her final years. She was eventually buried in a sanctuary chapel beneath the church, which is closed to the public.

In the late 15th century the church was converted into a mosque by Mesih Paşa, a descendant of the Palaeologus family, the last dynasty to rule

Byzantium. The building was gutted by fire several times and nothing remains of its internal decoration. Today it is still a working mosque and is accessed via a stairway that leads up to a raised piazza filled with coat stalls.

## Forum of Theodosius ⓭

Ordu Cad, Beyazıt. **Map** 2 C4 (4 A3).
🚇 *Üniversite or Beyazıt.*

**C**ONSTANTINOPLE *(see p18)* was built around several large public squares or forums. The largest of them stood on the site of present-day Beyazıt Square. It was originally known as the Forum Tauri (the Forum of the Bull) because of the huge bronze bull in the middle of it in which sacrificial animals, and sometimes even criminals, were roasted.

After Theodosius the Great enlarged it in the late 4th century, the forum took his name. Relics of the triumphal arch and other structures can be found lying and stacked on either side of the tram tracks along Ordu Caddesi. The huge columns, decorated with a motif reminiscent of a peacock's tail, are particularly striking. Once the forum had become derelict, these columns were reused all over the city. Some can be seen in the Basilica Cistern *(see p76)*. Other fragments from the forum were built into Beyazıt Hamamı, a Turkish bath *(see p67)* farther west down Ordu Caddesi, now a bazaar.

Peacock feather design on a column from the Forum of Theodosius

# Museum of Calligraphy ⑭

Türk Vakıf Hat Sanatları Müzesi

Beyazıt Meydanı, Beyazıt. **Map** 2 C4 (4 A3). ☎ (0212) 527 58 51. ⊟ Üniversite. ◯ 9am–4pm Tue & Wed. 🅮 🅿 &.

THE DELIGHTFUL courtyard in which this museum has been installed was once a *medrese (see p36)* of Beyazıt Mosque, situated on the other side of the square.

Its changing displays are taken from the massive archive belonging to the Turkish Calligraphy Foundation. There are some beautiful manuscripts as well as examples of calligraphy on stone and glass. There is also an exhibition of tools used in calligraphy. One of the cells in the *medrese* now contains a waxwork tableau of a master calligrapher with his pupils.

**Beyazıt Tower, within the wooded grounds of Istanbul University**

# Beyazıt Square ⑮

Beyazıt Meydanı

Ordu Cad, Beyazıt. **Map** 2 C4 (4 A3). ⊟ Beyazıt.

ALWAYS FILLED with crowds of people and huge flocks of pigeons, Beyazıt Square is the most vibrant space in the old part of the city. Throughout the week the square is the site of a flea market, where everything from carpets *(see pp210–11)* and Central Asian silks to general bric-a-brac can be purchased. When you

**The fortress-like entrance to Istanbul University, Beyazıt Square**

are tired of rummaging, you can choose among a number of cafés located beneath shady plane trees.

On the northern side of the square is the Moorish-style gateway leading into Istanbul University. The university's main building dates from the 19th century and once served as the Ministry of War. Within the wooded grounds rises Beyazıt Tower. This marble fire-watching station was built in 1828 on the site of Eski Saray, the palace first inhabited by Mehmet the Conqueror *(see p24)* after Byzantium fell to the Ottomans. A climb of 180 steps inside the tower leads to the top for a panoramic view of Istanbul.

On the square's eastern side is Beyazıt Mosque, which was commissioned by Beyazıt II and completed in 1506. It is the oldest surviving imperial mosque in the city. Behind the impressive outer portal is a harmonious courtyard with an elegant domed fountain at its center. Around the courtyard are columns made of granite and green and red Egyptian porphyry, and a pavement of multi-colored marble. The layout of the mosque's interior, with its central dome and surrounding semi-domes, is heavily inspired by the design of Hagia Sophia *(see pp72–5)*.

# Book Bazaar ⑯

Sahaflar Çarşısı

Sahaflar Çarşısı Sok, Beyazıt. **Map** 2 C4 (4 A3). ⊟ Üniversite. ◯ 8am–8pm daily. &.

THIS CHARMING booksellers' courtyard, on the site of the Byzantine book and paper market, can be entered either from Beyazıt Square or from inside the Grand Bazaar *(see pp98–9)*. Racks are laden with all sorts of books, from tourist guides to academic tomes.

During the early Ottoman period *(see pp23–5)*, printed books were seen as a corrupting European influence and were banned in Turkey. As a result, the bazaar sold only manuscripts. Then on January 31, 1729, İbrahim Müteferrika (1674–1745) produced the first printed book in the Turkish language, an Arabic dictionary. His bust stands in the center of the market today. Note that book prices are fixed and cannot be haggled over.

**Customers browsing in the Book Bazaar**

# The Art of Ottoman Calligraphy

CALLIGRAPHY IS one of the noblest of Islamic arts. Its skills were handed down from master to apprentice, with the goal of the pupil being to replicate perfectly the hand of his master. In Ottoman Turkey, calligraphy was used to adorn firmans (imperial decrees) as well as poetry and copies of the Koran. However, many examples are also to be found on buildings, carved in wood and applied to architectural ceramics. The art of the calligrapher in all cases was to go as far as possible in beautifying the writing without altering the sense of the text. It was particularly important that the text of the Koran be accurately transcribed. With the text of a firman, made to impress as much as to be read, the calligrapher could afford to add more flourishes.

*The great calligraphers* of the Ottoman period were Şeyh Hamdullah (1436–1520), whose work is seen in this Koran, Hafiz Osman (1642–98), and Ahmet Karahisari (d.1556). Their pupils also achieved great renown.

**Floral decorations**

**Ornamental loops**

*The sultan's* **tuğra** *was his personal monogram, used in place of his signature. It would either be drawn by a calligrapher or engraved on a wooden block and then stamped on documents. The* tuğra *incorporated the sultan's name and title, his patronymic, and wishes for his success or victory – all highly stylized. This is the* tuğra *of Selim II (1566–74).*

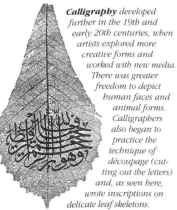

*Calligraphy* developed further in the 19th and early 20th centuries, when artists explored more creative forms and worked with new media. There was greater freedom to depict human faces and animal forms. Calligraphers also began to practice the technique of découpage (cutting out the letters) and, as seen here, wrote inscriptions on delicate leaf skeletons.

*The later sultans* were taught calligraphy as part of their education and became skilled artists. This panel, from the 19th century, is by Mahmut II (1808–39).

*Breathing techniques* were probably practiced by some calligraphers in order to achieve the steadiness of hand required for their craft.

**Burnisher**

**Knife for cutting pen nib**

*The calligrapher's tools* and materials included a burnisher, usually made of agate, that was used to prepare the paper. A knife was used to slit the reed nib of the pen before writing.

## Valide Han ⓱
Valide Hanı

Junction of Çakmakçılar Yokuşu & Tarakçılar Cad, Beyazıt. **Map** 2 C3 (4 B2). 🚇 Beyazıt, then 10 mins walk. ◯ 9:30am–5pm Mon–Sat.

Carpet shops in Çorlulu Ali Paşa Courtyard

IF THE GRAND BAZAAR (see pp98–9) seems large, it is sobering to realize that it is nothing more that the covered part of an huge area of seething commercial activity reaching all the way to the Golden Horn (see p89). As in the Grand Bazaar, most manufacturing and trade takes place in hans, courtyards hidden away from the street behind shaded gateways.

The largest han in Istanbul is Valide Han. It was built in 1651 by Kösem, the mother of Sultan Mehmet IV. You enter it from Çakmakçılar Yokuşu through a massive portal. After passing through an irregularly shaped area, you come out into a large courtyard centering on a Shiite mosque. This was built when the han became the center of Persian trade in the city. Today, the han throbs to the rhythm of hundreds of weaving looms.

A short walk farther down Çakmakçılar Yokuşu is Büyük Yeni Han, hidden behind another impressive doorway. This Baroque han, built in

1764, has three arcaded levels. The entrance is on the top level, where distinctive birdcages are among the wares.

In the labyrinth of narrow streets around these hans, artisans are grouped according to their wares: on Bakırcılar Caddesi, for instance, you will find metal workers, while the craftsmen of Uzunçarşı Caddesi make wooden items.

## Grand Bazaar ⓲

See pp98–9.

Café in Büyük Taş Han, near the Tulip Mosque (see p93)

### HANS OF ISTANBUL

The innumerable hans that dot the center of Istanbul originally provided temporary accommodations for travelers, their pack animals, and their wares. The typical han was built as part of a mosque complex (see pp36–7). It consists of two- or three-story buildings around a courtyard. This is entered through a large gateway that can be closed off by a heavy wooden door at night. When vans and trucks replaced horses and mules, the city's hans lost their original function, and most of them were converted into warrens of small factories and workshops. These working hans are frequently in bad repair, but in them you can still sense the entrepreneurial, oriental atmosphere of bygone Istanbul.

## Çorlulu Ali Paşa Courtyard ⓳
Çorlulu Ali Paşa Külliyesi

Yeniçeriler Cad, Beyazıt. **Map** 4 B3. 🚇 Beyazıt. ◯ daily.

LIKE MANY OTHERS in the city, the medrese (see p36) of this mosque complex outside the Grand Bazaar has become the setting for a tranquil outdoor café. It was built for Çorlulu Ali Paşa, son-in-law of Mustafa II, who served as grand vizier under Ahmet III (see p25). Ahmet later exiled him to the island of Lésvos and had him executed there in 1711. Some years later his family smuggled his head back to Istanbul and interred it in the tomb built for him.

The complex is entered from Yeniçeriler Caddesi by two alleyways. Several carpet shops now inhabit the medrese, and rugs are hung and spread all around, waiting for prospective buyers. The carpet shops share the medrese with a kahve, a traditional café (see p200), which is popular with locals and students from the nearby university. It advertises itself irresistibly as the "Traditional Mystic Water Pipe and Erenler Tea Garden." Here you can sit and drink tea, and perhaps smoke a nargile (bubble pipe), while deciding which carpet to buy (see pp210–11).

Situated across Bıleycıler Sokak, an alleyway off Çorlulu Ali Paşa Courtyard, is the Koça Sinan Paşa tomb complex, the courtyard of which is another tea garden. The charming *medrese*, mausoleum, and *sebil* (a fountain where water was handed out to passersby) were built in 1593 by Davut Ağa, who succeeded Sinan *(see p91)* as chief architect of the empire. The tomb of Koça Sinan Paşa, grand vizier under Murat III and Mehmet III, is a striking 16-sided structure.

Just off the other side of Yeniçeriler Caddesi is Gedik Paşa Hamamı, thought to be the oldest working Turkish baths *(see p67)* in the city. It was built around 1475 for Gedik Ahmet Paşa, grand vizier under Mehmet the Conqueror *(see p24)*.

**The dome and minaret of the mosque of Atik Ali Paşa, dating from 1496**

## Atik Ali Paşa Mosque ⓴
Atik Ali Paşa Camii

Yeniçeriler Cad, Beyazıt. **Map** 3 D4 (4 C3). 🚇 Çemberlitaş. ⭕ 8:30am–11pm daily. 🚫

SECRETED BEHIND walls in the area north of the Grand Bazaar, this is one of the oldest mosques in the city. It was built in 1496 during the reign of Beyazıt II, the successor of Mehmet the Conqueror, by his eunuch grand vizier, Atik Ali Paşa. The mosque stands in a small garden. It is a simple rectangular structure entered through a deep stone porch. In an unusual touch, its mihrab

is contained in a kind of apse. The other buildings that formed part of the mosque complex – its kitchen *(imaret)*, *medrese* and Sufi monastery *(tekke)* – have all but disappeared during the widening of the busy Yeniçeriler Caddesi.

## Nuruosmaniye Mosque ㉑
Nuruosmaniye Camii

Vezirhanı Cad, Beyazıt. **Map** 3 D4 (4 C3). 🚇 Çemberlitaş. ⭕ 8:30am–11pm daily. 🚫

NURUOSMANIYE CADDESİ, a street lined with top-of-the-market carpet and antique shops, leads to the gateway of the mosque from which it gets its name. Mahmut I began the mosque in 1748, and it was finished by his brother, Osman III. It was the first in the city to exhibit the exaggerated traits of the Baroque, as seen in its massive cornices. Its most striking features, however, are the enormous unconcealed arches supporting the dome, each pierced by a mass of windows.

Light floods into the plain square prayer hall, allowing you to see the finely carved wooden calligraphic frieze that runs around the walls above the gallery.

On the other side of the mosque complex is the Nuruosmaniye Gate. This leads into Kalpakçılar Caddesi, the Grand Bazaar's street of jewelry shops *(see p204)*.

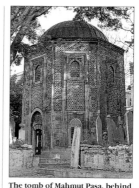

**The tomb of Mahmut Paşa, behind the mosque named after him**

## Mahmut Paşa Mosque ㉒
Mahmut Paşa Camii

Vezirhanı Cad, Beyazıt. **Map** 3 D3 (4 C3). 🚇 Çemberlitaş. ⭕ daily 8:30am–11pm. 🚫

BUILT IN 1462, just nine years after Istanbul's conquest by the Ottomans, this was the first large mosque to be erected within the city walls. Unfortunately, it has been over-restored and much of its original charm lost.

The mosque was funded by Mahmut Paşa, a Byzantine aristocrat who converted to Islam and became grand vizier under Mehmet the Conqueror. In 1474 his disastrous military leadership incurred the sultan's fury, and he was executed. His tomb, behind the mosque, is unique in Istanbul for its Moorish style of decoration, with small tiles in blue, black, turquoise, and green set in swirling geometric patterns.

**Rows of windows illuminating the prayer hall of Nuruosmaniye Mosque**

# The Grand Bazaar ⑱

## Kapalı Çarşı

NOTHING CAN PREPARE YOU for the Grand Bazaar. This labyrinth of streets covered by painted vaults is lined with thousands of boothlike shops, whose wares spill out to tempt you and whose shopkeepers are relentless in their quest for a sale. The bazaar was established by Mehmet II shortly after his conquest of the city in 1453 *(see p24)*. It can be entered by several gateways, two of the most useful being Çarşıkapı Gate (from Beyazıt tram stop) and Nuruosmaniye Gate (from Nuruosmaniye Mosque). It is easy to get lost in the bazaar in spite of the signs. Many of the bazaar's goods are made behind the scenes in secluded hans *(see p96)*.

**Muhlis Günbattı** is a well-known textile and carpet store *(see p204)*.

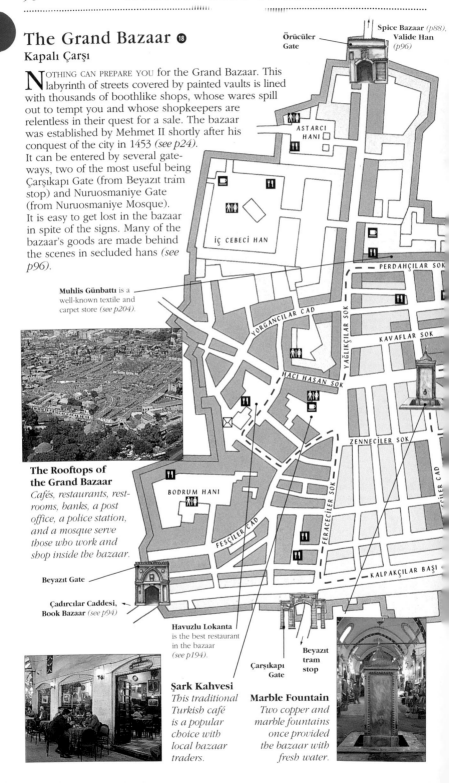

Spice Bazaar *(p88)*, Valide Han *(p96)*

Örücüler Gate

ASTARCI HANI

İÇ CEBECİ HAN

PERDAHÇILAR SOK

YORGANCILAR CAD

YAĞLIKÇILAR SOK

KAVAFLAR SOK

HACI HASAN SOK

ZENNECİLER SOK

...ÇİLER CAD

FERACECİLER SOK

BODRUM HANI

FESÇİLER CAD

KALPAKÇILAR BAŞI

### The Rooftops of the Grand Bazaar

*Cafés, restaurants, restrooms, banks, a post office, a police station, and a mosque serve those who work and shop inside the bazaar.*

**Beyazıt Gate**

**Çadırcılar Caddesi, Book Bazaar** *(see p94)*

**Havuzlu Lokanta** is the best restaurant in the bazaar *(see p194).*

Beyazıt tram stop

Çarşıkapı Gate

### Şark Kahvesi

*This traditional Turkish café is a popular choice with local bazaar traders.*

### Marble Fountain

*Two copper and marble fountains once provided the bazaar with fresh water.*

**Zincirli Han**
*This is one of the prettiest hans in the bazaar. Here a piece of jewelry can be made to your own choice of design.*

**VISITORS' CHECKLIST**

Çarşıkapı Cad, Beyazıt. **Map** 2 C4 (4 B3). 🚇 *Beyazıt (for Çarşıkapı Gate), Çemberlitaş (for Nuruosmaniye Gate).* 🚌 *61B.* ⏰ *9am–7pm Mon–Sat.*

**The İç Bedesten** is the oldest part of the bazaar. Once a locked warehouse, it also served as a place where jewelers could make and sell their wares.

**The Oriental Kiosk** was built as a coffeehouse in the 17th century and is now a jewelry shop.

**Rugs on Display**
*Carpets and kilims* (see pp210–11) *from all over Turkey and Central Asia are on sale in the bazaar.*

ZİNCİRLİ HAN

**Mahmut Paşa Gate**

AYNACILAR SOK

**Money trading** is conducted on cellular phones.

HALICILAR ÇARŞISI CAD

AĞA SOK

İÇ BEDESTEN

**Gateway to the İç Bedesten**
*Though the eagle was a symbol of the Byzantine emperors* (see p23), *this eagle, like the bazaar itself, postdates the Byzantine era.*

MUHAFAZACILAR SOK

KESECİLER CAD

SANDAL BEDESTENİ

TERZİ BAŞI SOK

SANDAL BEDESTENİ SOK

**The Sandal Bedesteni** dates from the 16th century and is covered by 20 brick domes supported on piers.

**Nuruosmaniye Mosque** (see p97), **Çemberlitaş tram stop**

**Nuruosmaniye Gate**

**KEY**

| | |
|---|---|
| ━ ━ | Suggested route |
| ▨ | Antiques and carpets |
| ▨ | Leather and denim |
| ☐ | Gold and silver |
| ▨ | Fabrics |
| ▨ | Souvenirs |
| ▨ | Household goods and workshops |
| ▨ | Boundary of the bazaar |

**Souvenirs**
*Traditionally crafted items, such as this brass coffee pot, are for sale in the bazaar.*

**Kalpakçılar Başı Caddesi,** the widest of the streets in the bazaar, is lined with the glittering windows of countless jewelry shops.

0 meters 40

0 yards 40

# BEYOĞLU

FOR CENTURIES Beyoğlu, a steep hill north of the Golden Horn, was home to the city's foreign residents. First to arrive here were the Genoese. As a reward for their help in the reconquest of the city from the Latins in 1261 *(see p22)*, they were given the Galata area, which is now dominated by the Galata Tower. During the Ottoman period, Jews from Spain, Arabs, Greeks, and Armenians settled in communities here. From the 16th century on the great European powers established embassies in the area to further their own interests within the lucrative territories of the Ottoman Empire. The district has not changed much in character over the centuries and is still a thriving commercial quarter today.

**Monument of Independence, Taksim Square**

## SIGHTS AT A GLANCE

**Historic Buildings and Monuments**
Galata Tower **3**
Mevlevi Monastery **2**
Pera Palas Hotel **1**
Tophane Fountain **9**

**Mosques and Churches**
Arab Mosque **5**
Azap Kapı Mosque **6**
Church of SS. Peter and Paul **4**
Kılıç Ali Paşa Mosque **8**

Nusretiye Mosque **10**
Yeraltı Mosque **7**

**Quarters**
Çukurcuma **11**
Taksim **12**

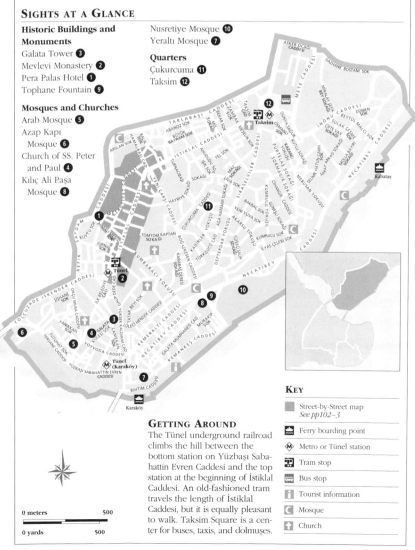

### KEY

| | |
|---|---|
| ▨ | Street-by-Street map *See pp102–3* |
| ⚓ | Ferry boarding point |
| Ⓜ | Metro or Tünel station |
| 🚊 | Tram stop |
| 🚌 | Bus stop |
| ℹ | Tourist information |
| C | Mosque |
| ✚ | Church |

## GETTING AROUND

The Tünel underground railroad climbs the hill between the bottom station on Yüzbaşı Sabahattin Evren Caddesi and the top station at the beginning of İstiklal Caddesi. An old-fashioned tram travels the length of İstiklal Caddesi, but it is equally pleasant to walk. Taksim Square is a center for buses, taxis, and dolmuşes.

0 meters       500
0 yards        500

◁ **The Galata Tower and backstreets of Beyoğlu, seen from the mouth of the Golden Horn**

# Street-by-Street: İstiklal Caddesi

Crest on top of the Russian Consulate gate

THE PEDESTRIANIZED İstiklal Caddesi is Beyoğlu's main street. Once known as the Grande Rue de Pera, it is lined by late 19th-century apartment houses and European embassy buildings, whose grandiose gates and façades belie their use as mere consulates since Ankara became the Turkish capital in 1923 *(see p29)*. Hidden from view stand the churches, which used to serve the foreign communities of Pera (as this area was formerly called), some still buzzing with worshipers, others just quiet echoes of a bygone era. Today, the once seedy backstreets of Beyoğlu, off İstiklal Caddesi, are taking on a new lease of life, with trendy jazz bars opening and shops selling handcrafted jewelry, furniture, and the like. Crowds are also drawn by the area's movie theaters and numerous stylish restaurants.

★ **Pera Palas Hotel**
*This hotel is an atmospheric period piece. Many famous guests, including Agatha Christie, have stayed here since it opened in 1892. Non-residents can enjoy a drink in the bar* ❶

**St. Mary Draperis**
is a Franciscan church dating from 1789. This small statue of the Virgin stands above the entrance from the street. The vaulted interior of the church is colorfully decorated. An icon of the Virgin, said to perform miracles, hangs over the altar.

★ **Mevlevi Monastery**
*A peaceful garden surrounds this small museum of the Mevlevi Sufi sect (see p104). On the last Sunday of every month visitors can see dervishes perform their famous swirling dance* ❷

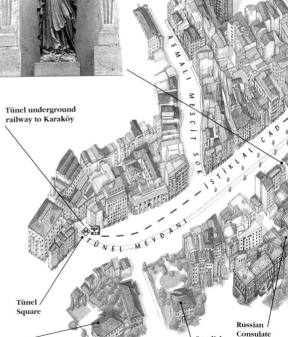

**Tünel underground railway to Karaköy**

**Tünel Square**

**Swedish Consulate**

**Russian Consulate**

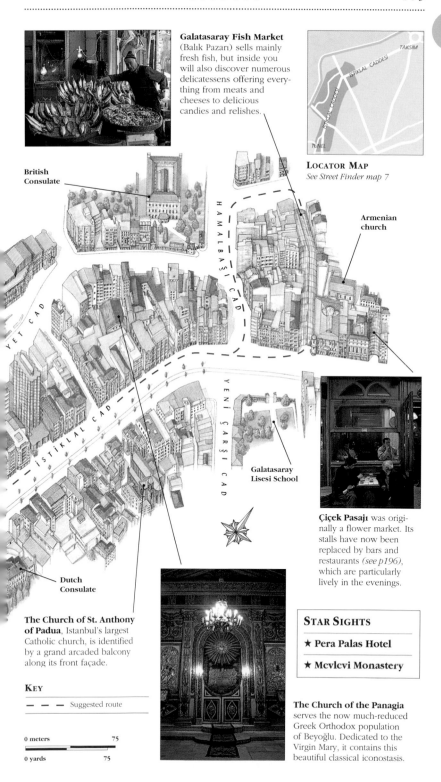

**Galatasaray Fish Market** (Balık Pazarı) sells mainly fresh fish, but inside you will also discover numerous delicatessens offering everything from meats and cheeses to delicious candies and relishes.

**LOCATOR MAP**
*See Street Finder map 7*

**British Consulate**

**Armenian church**

**Çiçek Pasajı** was originally a flower market. Its stalls have now been replaced by bars and restaurants *(see p196)*, which are particularly lively in the evenings.

**Galatasaray Lisesi School**

**Dutch Consulate**

**The Church of St. Anthony of Padua**, Istanbul's largest Catholic church, is identified by a grand arcaded balcony along its front façade.

**KEY**

– – – Suggested route

0 meters 75

0 yards 75

**STAR SIGHTS**

★ **Pera Palas Hotel**

★ **Mevlevi Monastery**

**The Church of the Panagia** serves the now much-reduced Greek Orthodox population of Beyoğlu. Dedicated to the Virgin Mary, it contains this beautiful classical iconostasis.

**The elegant Grand Orient bar in the Pera Palas Hotel**

# Pera Palas Hotel ❶
Pera Palas Oteli

Meşrutiyet Cad 98–100, Tepebaşı.
**Map** 7 D5. ☎ *(0212) 251 45 60.*
🚇 *Tünel.* ♿ *by arrangement.* ▣

THROUGHOUT the world there are hotels that have attained an almost legendary status. One such is the Pera Palas *(see p183)*. Relying on the hazy mystique of yester-year, it has changed little since it opened in 1892, principally to cater to travelers on the Orient Express *(see p66)*. It still evokes images of uniformed porters and such exotic onward destinations as Baghdad and Isfahan. The Grand Orient bar serves cocktails beneath its original chandeliers, while the patisserie still offers irresistible cakes and genteel ambience.

Former guests who have contributed to the hotel's reputation include Mata Hari, Greta Garbo, Jackie Onassis, Sarah Bernhardt, Josephine Baker, and Atatürk *(see p29)*. A room used by the thriller writer Agatha Christie *(see p42)* can be visited on request.

# Mevlevi Monastery ❷
Mevlevi Tekkesi

Galip Dede Cad 15, Beyoğlu. **Map** 7 D5. ☎ *(0212) 243 50 45.* 🚇 *Tünel.* ⏱ *9:30am–4:30pm Tue–Sun.*

ALTHOUGH SUFISM was banned by Atatürk in 1924, this monastery has survived as the Divan Edebiyatı Müzesi, a museum of *divan* literature (classical Ottoman poetry). The monastery belonged to the most famous sect of Sufis, who were known as the Whirling Dervishes. The original dervishes were disciples of the mystical poet and great Sufi master "Mevlana" (Our Leader) Jelaleddin Rumi, who died in Konya, in south central Anatolia, in 1273.

Tucked away off a street named after one of the great poets of the sect, Galip Dede, the museum centers on an 18th-century lodge, within which is a beautiful octagonal wooden dance floor. Here, for the benefit of visitors, the *sema* (ritual dance) is performed by a group of latter-day Sufi devotees on the last Sunday of every month. Between 5pm and 7pm, a dozen or so dancers unfurl their great circular skirts to whirl around the room in an extraordinary state of ecstatic meditation, accompanied by haunting music.

Around the dance floor are glass cases containing a small exhibition of artifacts belonging to the sect, including hats, clothing, manuscripts, photographs, and musical instruments. Outside, in the calm,

## SUFISM AND THE WHIRLING DERVISHES

Sufism is the mystical branch of Islam *(see pp36–7)*. The name comes from *suf*, the Arabic for wool, for Sufis were originally associated with poverty and self-denial, and often wore rough woollen clothes next to the skin. Sufis aspire to a personal experience of the divine. This takes the form of meditative rituals, involving recitation, dance, and music, to bring the practitioner into direct, ecstatic communion with Allah. There are several sects of Sufis, the most famous of which are the Mevlevi, better known as the Whirling Dervishes because of their ritual spinning dance.

**Painting of the Whirling Dervishes (1837) at the Mevlevi Monastery**

**The peaceful courtyard of the Mevlevi Monastery**

terraced garden, stand the ornate tombstones of ordinary members and prominent sheikhs (leaders) of the sect. Surrounding the elegantly carved tombs is a profusion of delicately scented roses.

## Galata Tower ❸
### Galata Kulesi

Büyük Hendek Sok, Beyoğlu.
**Map** 3 D1. ☎ (0212) 245 11 60.
Ⓜ Tünel. ⏲ 9am–9pm daily. 📷
**Restaurant & Nightclub** ⏲
8pm–midnight daily.

THE MOST distinctive silhouette on the Galata skyline is a 62-m (205-ft) high round tower topped by a conical roof. It was built in 1348 by the Genoese (see p23) as part of their fortifications. Throughout the Ottoman period the building was used as a watchtower, but it has since been converted to cater to tourism. The top two floors, the 8th and 9th, are occupied by a restaurant and nightclub (see p213). Sadly, the interior decor no longer reflects the building's medieval origins.

You can reach the top of the tower by elevator or by way of a narrow spiral staircase. It is worth the climb simply to admire the fabulous panoramic view from the balcony, which encompasses the main monuments of Istanbul and, beyond, the Princes' Islands.

**Doorway to the main courtyard of the Church of SS. Peter and Paul**

## Church of SS. Peter and Paul ❹
### Sen Piyer Kilisesi

Galata Kulesi Sok 44, Karaköy.
**Map** 3 D1. ☎ (0212) 249 23 85.
Ⓜ Tünel. ⏲ 9–11am & 4–6pm daily.

WHEN THEIR original church was requisitioned as a mosque (to become the nearby Arab Mosque) in the early 16th century, the Dominican brothers of Galata moved to this site, just below the Galata Tower. The present building, dating from 1841, was built by the Fossati brothers, architects of Italian-Swiss origin who

also worked on the restoration of Hagia Sophia (see pp72–5). The church's rear wall is built into a section of Galata's old Genoese ramparts.

According to Ottoman regulations, the main façade of the building could not be directly on a road, so the church is reached through a courtyard, the entrance to which is by a tiny door on the street. Ring the bell to gain admittance.

The church is built in the style of a basilica, with four side altars. The cupola over the choir is sky blue, studded with gold stars. Mass is said here in Italian every morning.

Set inside a large silver case is the revered icon of the Virgin Hodegetria ("the Guide"), which is said to have been one of the protective icons of Byzantine Constantinople and is attributed to St. Luke. In support of this reputation, the icon miraculously survived a fire in 1731 that destroyed the earlier church that stood on this site.

## Arab Mosque ❺
### Arap Camii

Kalyon Sok 1, Galata. **Map** 3 D1.
Ⓜ Tünel. ⏲ prayer times only.

THE ARABS after whom this mosque was named were Moorish refugees from Spain. Many settled in Galata after their expulsion from Andalusia following the fall of Granada in 1492. The church of SS. Paul and Dominic, built in the first half of the 14th century by Dominican monks, was given to the settlers for use as a mosque. It is an unusual building for Istanbul: a vast, strikingly rectangular Gothic church with a tall square belfry that now acts as a minaret. The building has been restored several times, but of all the converted churches in the city it makes the least convincing mosque.

**The distinctive Galata Tower, as seen from across the Golden Horn**

**Azap Kapı Mosque, built by the great architect Sinan**

## Azap Kapı Mosque **6**
Azap Kapı Camii

Tersane Cad, Azapkapı. **Map** 2 C1.
Ⓜ *Tünel.* 🚌 *46H, 61B.* 🕐 *prayer times only.*

CHARMING though they are, this little mosque complex and fountain are somewhat overshadowed by the stream of traffic thundering over the adjacent Atatürk Bridge. The trees surrounding the mosque, however, help to screen it from the noise. It was built in 1577–8 by Sinan (*see p91*) for Grand Vizier Sokollu Mehmet Paşa and is considered to be one of Sinan's more attractive mosques. Unusual for a mosque, the entrance is up a flight of internal steps leading to the porch and prayer hall. The building was rescued from ruin when the bridge was built in 1942, and its vanished İznik tiles were replaced with Kütahya tiles (*see p204*).

The lavishly decorated Baroque fountain to the north of the mosque dates from 1732. It has been restored, too, although vagrants sometimes sleep in its water troughs.

## Yeraltı Mosque **7**
Yeraltı Camii

Karantina Sok, Karaköy. **Map** 3 E1.
Ⓜ *Tünel.* 🕐 *daily.*

THIS STRANGE, secluded sight, literally "the underground mosque," contains the shrines of two Muslim saints, Abu Sufyan and Amiri Wahibi, who died during the first Arab siege of the city in the 7th century (*see p19*). It was the discovery of their bodies in the cellar of an ancient Byzantine fortification in 1640 that led to the creation of first a shrine on the site and later, in 1757, a mosque. The building may even have been part of the Galata Castle, from which one end of the chain protecting the Byzantine harbor on the Golden Horn was suspended (*see p21*).

The tombs of the saints are behind grates at the end of a low, dark prayer hall, the roof of which is supported by a forest of pillars. Adorning the entrance and mihrab are beautiful İznik tiles (*see p161*).

## Kılıç Ali Paşa Mosque **8**
Kılıç Ali Paşa Camii

Necatibey Cad, Tophane. **Map** 7 E5.
🚌 *25E, 56.* 🕐 *daily.*

THIS MOSQUE WAS built in 1580 by Sinan, who was by then in his 90s. The church of Hagia Sophia (*see pp72–5*) provided the architect with his inspiration. Although the mosque's smaller proportions stop it from soaring heavenward like Hagia Sophia, it is still a pleasing building, with İznik tiles around the mihrab and a beautiful deep porch before the main

door. Above the entrance portal is an inscription giving the date when the mosque was established.

Kılıç Ali Paşa, who commissioned the mosque, had a colorful life. Born in Italy, he was captured by Muslim pirates and later converted to Islam in the service of Süleyman the Magnificent (1520–66). He served as a naval commander under three sultans, and after retiring asked Murat III (*see p25*) where to build his mosque. The sultan is said to have replied "in the admiral's domain, the sea." Taking him at his word, Kılıç Ali Paşa reclaimed part of the Bosphorus for his complex. He died in 1587 at the age of 90, allegedly in the arms of a concubine, and was buried in the *türbe* (tomb) behind the mosque.

**Detail of a carved panel on Tophane Fountain**

## Tophane Fountain **9**
Tophane Çeşmesi

Tophane İskele Cad, Tophane.
**Map** 7 E5. 🚌 *25E, 56.*

ACROSS the small road beside Kılıç Ali Paşa Mosque stands a beautiful but abandoned Baroque fountain, built in 1732 by Mahmut I. With its elegant roof and dome, it resembles the fountain of Ahmet III (*see p60*). Each of the four walls is entirely covered in bas-relief floral carving, which would once have been brightly painted. The name,

**Koranic inscription in İznik tiles at the Kılıç Ali Paşa Mosque**

meaning "cannon foundry fountain," comes from the brick and stone foundry building on the hill nearby. Established in 1453 by Mehmet the Conqueror *(see p24)* and rebuilt several times, the foundry no longer produces weapons but is still owned by the military.

## Nusretiye Mosque ❿
Nusretiye Camii

Necatibey Cad, Tophane. **Map** 7 E5. ▥ *25E, 56.* ⬭ *daily.*

THE BAROQUE "Mosque of Victory" was built in the 1820s by Kirkor Balyan *(see p128)*, who went on to found a dynasty of architects. This ornate building seems more like a large palace pavilion than a mosque, with its decorative outbuildings and marble terrace.

Commissioned by Mahmut II to commemorate his abolition of the Janissary corps in 1826 *(see p28)*, it faces the Selimiye Barracks *(see p132)*, across the Bosphorus, which housed the New Army that replaced the Janissaries. In the high-domed interior, the Empire-style swags and embellishments celebrate the sultan's victory. The marble panel of calligraphy around the interior of the mosque is particularly ornate, as is the pair of *sebils* (kiosks for serving drinks) outside.

**The window-filled dome and arches of Nusretiye Mosque**

**Fountain in the park at the center of Taksim Square**

## Çukurcuma ⓫

**Map** 7 E4. ⬙ *Tünel.*

THIS CHARMING OLD quarter of Beyoğlu, radiating from a neighborhood mosque on Çukurcuma Caddesi, has become an important center for Istanbul's furnishings and antique trades. The old warehouses and houses have been converted into stores and showrooms, where modern upholstery materials are piled on carved marble basins and antique cabinets. It is worth browsing here to discover anything from 19th-century Ottoman embroidery to 1950s cookie boxes.

**Suzani textiles *(see p204)* on sale in Çukurcuma**

## Taksim ⓬

**Map** 7 E3. ▤ *Taksim.* ⬙ *Taksim.* **Taksim Art Gallery** ▮ *(0212) 245 20 65.* ⬭ *11am–7pm daily.*

CENTERING ON THE vast, open Taksim Square (Taksim Meydanı), the Taksim area is the hub of activity in modern Beyoğlu. Taksim means "water distribution center," and from the early 18th century it was from this site that water from the Belgrade Forest *(see p158)* was distributed throughout the modern city. The original stone reservoir, built in 1732 by Mahmut I, still stands at the top of İstiklal Caddesi. In the southwest of the square is the Monument of Independence, sculpted by the Italian artist Canonica in 1928. It shows Atatürk *(see pp28–9)* and the other founding fathers of the modern Turkish Republic.

Farther up, on Cumhuriyet Caddesi, is the modern building of the **Taksim Art Gallery**. As well as temporary exhibitions, it has a permanent display of Istanbul landscapes by some of Turkey's most important 20th-century painters.

At the far end of Taksim Park, to the north of Taksim Square, breathtaking views of Istanbul and the Bosphorus can be enjoyed from the bars on the top floor of the Inter-Continental Hotel *(see p183)*.

# GREATER ISTANBUL

AWAY FROM the city center there are many sights that are worth the trip. Greater Istanbul has been divided into five areas shown on the map below; each also has its own map to help you get around. Closest to the center are the mosques and churches of Fatih, Fener, and Balat: most conspicuously the gigantic Fatih Mosque. Across the Golden Horn *(see p89)* from Balat are two sights worth seeing: Aynalı Kavak Palace and a fascinating industrial

Tiles depicting Mecca, Cezri Kasım Paşa Mosque, Eyüp

museum. The Theodosian Walls, stretching from the Golden Horn to the Sea of Marmara, are one of the city's most impressive monuments. Along these walls stand several ancient palaces and churches: particularly interesting is the Church of St. Savior in Chora, with its stunning Byzantine mosaics. Beyond the walls, up the Golden Horn, is Eyüp, a focus of pilgrimage to Muslims. There, you can visit several mausoleums and walk up the hill to the historic café associated with the French writer Pierre Loti *(see p42)*. Following the Bosphorus northward past Beyoğlu *(see pp100–7)* brings you to Dolmabahçe Palace, one of the best sights of Istanbul. This opulent fantasy created in the 19th century by Sultan Abdül Mecit I requires a lengthy visit. Beyond it is peaceful Yıldız Park, with still more beautiful palaces and pavilions. Not all visitors to Istanbul make it to the Asian side, but if you have half a day to spare, it is only a short ferry trip from Eminönü *(see pp234–5)*. Its attractions include some splendid mosques, a handsome train station, and a small museum dedicated to Florence Nightingale.

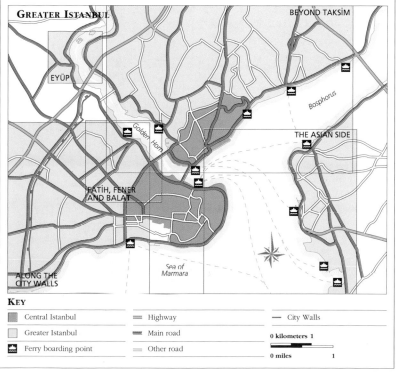

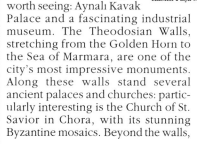

## KEY

| | | |
|---|---|---|
| ▦ Central Istanbul | ▬ Highway | — City Walls |
| ▢ Greater Istanbul | ▬ Main road | **0 kilometers 1** |
| ⚓ Ferry boarding point | ▭ Other road | **0 miles     1** |

◁ **Fountain in the grounds of the sumptuous Dolmabahçe Palace**

# Fatih, Fener, and Balat

A VISIT TO THESE NEIGHBORHOODS is a reminder that for centuries after the Muslim conquest *(see p24)*, Jews and Christians made up around 40 percent of Istanbul's population. Balat was home to Greek-speaking Jews from the Byzantine era onward; Sephardic Jews from Spain joined them in the 15th century. Fener became a Greek enclave in the early 16th century, and many wealthy residents rose to positions of prominence in the Ottoman Empire. Hilltop Fatih is linked to the city's radical Islamic tradition, and you will see far more devout Muslims here than anywhere else in Istanbul. All three areas are residential, their maze of streets the preserve of clothes lines and children playing.

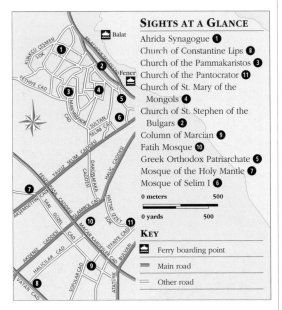

## SIGHTS AT A GLANCE

Ahrida Synagogue **1**
Church of Constantine Lips **8**
Church of the Pammakaristos **3**
Church of the Pantocrator **11**
Church of St. Mary of the Mongols **4**
Church of St. Stephen of the Bulgars **2**
Column of Marcian **9**
Fatih Mosque **10**
Greek Orthodox Patriarchate **5**
Mosque of the Holy Mantle **7**
Mosque of Selim I **6**

| 0 meters | 500 |
| 0 yards | 500 |

## KEY

⛴ Ferry boarding point

━ Main road

═ Other road

## Ahrida Synagogue **1**
### Ahrida Sinagogu

Gevgili Sok, Balat. **Map** 1 C1.
🚌 55T, 99A. ⭘ *by appointment.* 🚫

T HE NAME OF Istanbul's oldest and most beautiful synagogue is a corruption of Ohrid, a town in Macedonia from which its early congregation came. It was founded before the Muslim conquest of the city in 1453, and with a capacity for up to 500 worshipers, it has been in constant use ever since. However, tourists can visit only by prior arrangement with a guided tour company *(see p220)*. The

synagogue's painted walls and ceilings, dating from the late 17th century, have been restored to their Baroque glory. Pride of place, however, goes to the central Holy Ark, covered in rich tapestries, which contains rare holy scrolls.

During an explosion of fervor that swept the city's Jewish population in the 17th century, the religious leader Shabbetai Zevi (1629–76), a self-proclaimed messiah, started preaching at this synagogue. He was banished from the city and later converted to Islam. However, a significant number of Jews held that Zevi's conversion was a subterfuge, and his followers, the Sabbatians, exist to this day.

## Church of St. Stephen of the Bulgars **2**
### Bulgar Kilisesi

Mürsel Paşa Cad 85, Balat.
**Map** 1 C1. 🚌 55T, 99A. ⛴ *Balat.*
⭘ *9am–4pm daily.*

A STONISHINGLY, this entire church was cast in iron, even the internal columns and galleries. It was created in Vienna in 1871, shipped all the way to the Golden Horn *(see p89)*, and assembled on its shore. The church was needed for the Bulgarian community, who had broken away from the authority of the Greek Orthodox Patriarchate just up the hill. Today, it is still used by this community, who keep the marble tombs of the first Bulgarian patriarchs permanently decorated with flowers. The church stands in a charming little park that is dotted with trees and flowering shrubs and which runs down to the edge of the Golden Horn.

**The Church of St. Stephen of the Bulgars, wholly made of iron**

## Church of the Pammakaristos **3**
### Fethiye Camii

Fethiye Cad, Draman. **Map** 1 C2. 🚌 90, 90B. ⭘ *prayer times only.* 📷

T HIS BYZANTINE church is one of the hidden secrets of Istanbul. It is rarely visited despite the important role it has played in the history of the city and its breathtaking series of mosaics. For over 100 years after the Ottoman

**Byzantine façade of the Church of the Pammakaristos**

conquest, it housed the Greek Orthodox Patriarchate, but was converted into a mosque in the late 16th century by Murat III *(see p30)*. He named it the Mosque of Victory to commemorate his conquests of Georgia and Azerbaijan.

The exterior is obviously Byzantine, with its attractive, alternating stone and brick courses and finely carved marble details. The main body of the building is the working mosque, while the extraordinary mosaics are in a side chapel. This now operates as a museum and officially you need to get permission in advance from Hagia Sophia *(see pp72–5)* to see it. However there is a chance that if the caretaker is around he may go ahead and let you in.

Dating from the 14th century, the great Byzantine renaissance *(see p23)*, the mosaics show holy figures isolated in a sea of gold, a reflection of the heavens. From the center of the main dome, Christ Pantocrator ("the All-Powerful"), surrounded by the Old Testament prophets, stares solemnly down. In the apse, another figure of Christ, seated on a jewel-encrusted throne, gives his benediction. On either side are portraits of the Virgin Mary and John the Baptist beseeching Christ. They are overlooked by the four archangels, while the side apses are filled with other saintly figures.

## Church of St. Mary of the Mongols ❹
Kanlı Kilise

Tevkii Cafer Mektebi Sok, Fener.
**Map** 1 C2. (0212) 521 71 39.
55T, 99A. 9am–5pm daily.

CONSECRATED in the late 13th century, the Church of St. Mary of the Mongols is the only Greek Orthodox church in Istanbul to have remained continuously in the hands of the Greek community since the Byzantine era. Its immunity from conversion into a mosque was

**Detail on Church of St. Mary of the Mongols**

decreed in an order signed by Mehmet the Conqueror *(see p24)*. A copy of this is kept by the church to this day.

The church gets its name from the woman who founded it, Maria Palaeologina, an illegitimate Byzantine princess who was married off to a Mongol khan, Abagu, and lived piously with him in Persia for 15 years. On her husband's assassination, she returned to Constantinople, built this church, and lived out her days in it as a nun.

A beautiful Byzantine mosaic which depicts Theotokos Pammakaristos ("the All-Joyous Mother of God") is the church's greatest treasure.

## Greek Orthodox Patriarchate ❺
Ortodoks Patrikhanesi

Sadrazam Ali Paşa Cad 35, Fener.
(0212) 525 21 17. 55T, 99A.
9am–5pm daily.

THIS WALLED COMPLEX has been the seat of the patriarch of the Greek Orthodox Church since the early 17th century. Though nominally head of the whole church, the patriarch is now shepherd to a diminishing flock in and around Istanbul.

As you walk up the steps to enter the Patriarchate through a side door you will see that the main door has been welded shut. This was done in memory of Patriarch Gregory V, who was hanged here for treason in 1821 after encouraging the Greeks to overthrow Ottoman rule at the start of the Greek War of Independence (1821–32). Antagonism between the Turkish and Greek communities worsened with the Greek occupation of parts of Turkey in the 1920s *(see p29)*. There were anti-Greek riots in 1955, and in the mid-1960s many Greek residents were expelled. Today the clergy here is protected by a metal detector at the entrance.

The Patriarchate centers on the basilica-style Church of St. George, which dates back to 1720. Yet the church contains much older relics and furniture. The patriarch's throne, the high structure to the right of the nave, is thought to be Byzantine, while the pulpit on the left is adorned with fine Middle Eastern wooden inlay and Orthodox icons.

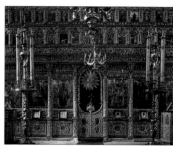

**The ornate, gilded interior of the Church of St. George in the Greek Orthodox Patriarchate**

**İznik tile panel capping a window in the Mosque of Selim I**

# Mosque of Selim I ❻
Selim I Camii

Yavuz Selim Cad, Fener. **Map** 1 C2. 🚌 55T, 90, 90B, 99A. ◯ daily.

THIS MUCH-ADMIRED mosque is also known locally as Yavuz Sultan Mosque: Yavuz, "the Grim" being the nickname the infamous Selim acquired *(see p24)*. It is idyllic in a rather offbeat way, which seems at odds with the barbaric reputation of the sultan.

The mosque, built in 1522, sits alone on a hill beside a vast sunken parking lot, once the Byzantine Cistern of Aspar. Sadly, it is rarely visited and has an air of neglect, yet the mosque's intimate courtyard gives an insight into concept of paradise in Islam. At the center of this lovely garden is an octagonal, domed fountain, surrounded by trees filled with chirping birds.

The windows set into the porticoes in the courtyard are capped by early İznik tiles *(see p161)*. These were made by the *cuerda seca* technique, where each color is separated during the firing process, giving the patterns greater depth and definition.

Similar tiles lend decorative effect to the simple prayer hall, with its fine mosque furniture *(see pp36–7)* and original painted woodwork.

# Mosque of the Holy Mantle ❼
Hırka-i Şerif Camii

Keçeciler Cad, Karagümrük. **Map** 1 B3. 🚌 28, 87, 90, 91. ◯ daily.

BUILT IN the Empire style in 1851, this mosque was designed to house a cloak *(hırka)* in the imperial collection that once belonged to and was worn by the Prophet Mohammed. This rests in a sanctuary directly behind the mihrab. The mosque's minarets are in the form of Classical columns and its balconies styled like Corinthian capitals. The interior of the octagonal prayer hall, meanwhile, has a plethora of decorative marble. Abdül Mecit I, the mosque's patron, was jointly responsible for the design of its calligraphic frieze.

**Knocker, Mosque of the Holy Mantle**

# Church of Constantine Lips ❽
Fenari İsa Camii

Vatan Cad, Fatih. **Map** 1 B4. 🚌 90B. ◯ daily.

THIS 10TH-CENTURY monastic church, dedicated to the Immaculate Mother of God, was founded by Constantine Lips Dungarios, a commander of the Byzantine fleet. Following the Byzantine reconquest

**Byzantine brickwork exterior of the Church of Constantine Lips**

of the city in 1261 *(see p22)*, Empress Theodora, wife of Michael VIII Palaeologus *(see pp22–3)*, added a second church. She also commissioned a funerary chapel, where she and her sons were buried.

This unusual history has given the structure its present rambling appearance. In an idiosyncratic touch, there are also four tiny chapels perched on the roof around the main dome. Another highlight is the building's eastern exterior wall. This is decorated with a *tour de force* of brick friezes, of the kind that are a hallmark of Byzantine churches of this period. When the church was converted into a mosque in 1496, it adopted the name Fenari İsa, or the Lamp of Jesus. This was in honor of İsa (Turkish for Jesus), the leader of a Sufi brotherhood *(see p104)* who worshiped here at that time. Inside the mosque, which is still in use today, there are some well-restored capitals and decorated cornices.

# Column of Marcian ❾
Kız Taşı

Kıztaşı Cad, Saraçhane. **Map** 1 C4 (2 A3). 🚌 28, 87, 90, 91.

STANDING IN a little square, this 5th-century Byzantine column was once surmounted by a statue of the Emperor Marcian (AD 450–57). On its base you can still see a pair of Greek winged goddesses of victory, holding an inscribed medallion.

Interestingly enough, the column's Turkish name translates as the Maiden's Column, suggesting that it was mistaken for the famous Column of Venus. According to legend, this column was said to sway at the passing of an impure maid. It originally stood nearby and is thought to have been used as one of the largest columns in the Süleymaniye Mosque *(see pp90–91)*.

Chandelier hanging in the light and airy interior of Fatih Mosque

# Fatih Mosque ⑩
## Fatih Camii

Macar Kardeşler Cad, Fatih. **Map** 1 C3.
🚌 28, 87, 90, 91. ☐ daily.

A SPACIOUS OUTER courtyard surrounds this vast Baroque mosque, which is the third major structure on this site. The first was the Church of the Holy Apostles (see p21), the burial place of most of the Byzantine emperors. When Mehmet the Conqueror (see p24) came to construct a mosque here, the church's crumbling remains provided a symbolic location. But the first Fatih Mosque collapsed in an earthquake in 1766, and most of what you see today was the work of Mehmet Tahir Ağa, the chief imperial architect under Mustafa III. Many of the buildings he constructed around the prayer hall, including eight Koranic colleges (medreses) and a hospice, still stand.

The only parts of Mehmet the Conqueror's mosque to have survived are the three porticoes of the courtyard, the ablutions fountain, the

main gate into the prayer hall, and, inside, the mihrab. Two exquisite forms of 15th-century decoration can be seen over the windows in the porticoes: İznik tiles made using the *cuerda seca* technique, and lunettes adorned with calligraphic marble inlay.

Inside the prayer hall, stenciled patterns decorate the domes, while the lower level of the walls is faced with yet more tiles – although these are inferior to those used in the porticoes.

The tomb of Mehmet the Conqueror stands behind the prayer hall, near that of his consort Gülbahar. His sarcophagus and turban are both appropriately large. It is a place of enormous gravity, always busy with supplicants.

If you pay a visit to the mosque on a Wednesday, you will also see the weekly market (see p206), which turns the streets around it into a circus of commerce. From tables piled high with fruit and vegetables to trucks loaded with unspun wool, this is a real spectacle, even if you don't buy anything.

# Church of the Pantocrator ⑪
## Zeyrek Camii

İbadethane Sok, Küçükpazar.
**Map** 2 B2. 🚌 28, 61B, 87.
☐ prayer times daily. ♿

E MPRESS IRENE, the wife of John II Comnenus (see p19), founded the Church of the Pantocrator ("Christ the Almighty") during the 12th century. This hulk of Byzantine masonry was once the centerpiece of one of the city's most important religious foundations, the Monastery of the Pantocrator. As well as a monastery and church, the complex included a hospice for the elderly, an asylum, and a hospital. In this respect it prefigured the social welfare system provided by the great imperial mosque complexes, which the Ottomans later built in the city (see p36).

The church, now a mosque, boasts a magnificent figurative marble floor. It is composed of three interlinked chapels. The one with the highest dome was built by Empress Irene. Emperor John II added another as a mortuary chapel when Irene died in 1124, and he later filled the area between with a third apsed chapel. The rest of the Comnenus dynasty and many of the Palaeologus imperial family were interred within these chapels.

Shortly after the Muslim conquest in 1453 (see p24), the building was converted into a mosque. A caretaker may let you in outside prayer times in the afternoons.

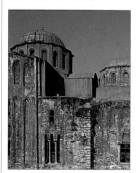

Church of the Pantocrator, built by Empress Irene in the 12th century

# Along the City Walls

ISTANBUL'S LAND WALLS are one of the most impressive remains of the city's Byzantine past. Pierced by monumental gates and strengthened by towers, they encompass the city center in a great arc, stretching all the way from Yedikule, on the Sea of Marmara, to Ayvansaray, on the Golden Horn (see p89). The suburbs that lie adjacent to the walls, particularly Edirnekapı and Topkapı, are mainly working-class, residential districts, interspersed with areas of wasteland that are unsafe to explore alone. Dotted around these suburbs, however, are important remnants of the city's past, particularly the Byzantine period. The outstanding sight here is the Church of St. Savior in Chora (see pp118–19), which has beautifully preserved mosaics and frescoes.

Silivrikapı, one of the gateways through the Theodosian Walls

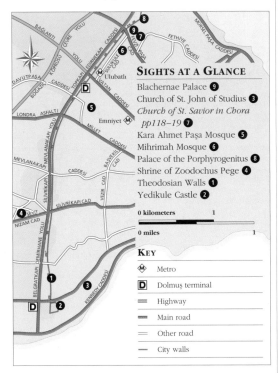

## SIGHTS AT A GLANCE

Blachernae Palace **9**
Church of St. John of Studius **3**
*Church of St. Savior in Chora pp118–19* **7**
Kara Ahmet Paşa Mosque **5**
Mihrimah Mosque **6**
Palace of the Porphyrogenitus **8**
Shrine of Zoodochus Pege **4**
Theodosian Walls **1**
Yedikule Castle **2**

```
0 kilometers        1
0 miles             1
```

## KEY

| | |
|---|---|
| Ⓜ | Metro |
| Ⓓ | Dolmuş terminal |
| ═ | Highway |
| ━ | Main road |
| ═ | Other road |
| — | City walls |

The walls were built between AD 412–22, during the reign of Theodosius II (408–50). In 447 an earthquake destroyed 54 of the towers, but these were immediately rebuilt, under threat of the advancing Attila the Hun. Subsequently the walls resisted sieges by Arabs, Bulgarians, Russians, and Turks. Even the determined armies of the Fourth Crusade (see p22) only managed to storm the ramparts along the Golden Horn, while the land walls stood firm.

Mehmet the Conqueror finally breached the walls in May 1453 (see p24). Successive Ottoman sultans then kept the walls in good repair until the end of the 17th century.

Recently, large stretches of the walls, particularly around Belgratkapı (Belgrade Gate) have been rebuilt. Byzantine scholars have criticized the restoration for insensitive use of modern building materials, but the new sections do give you an idea of how the walls used to look. Many (although not all) of the gateways are still in good repair. Mehmet the Conqueror directed his heaviest cannon at the St. Romanus and Charsius gates. Under the Ottomans, the former became known as Topkapı, the Gate

## Theodosian Walls **1**

Teodos II Surları

From Yedikule to Ayvansaray. **Map 1** A1. Ⓜ *Ulubatlı.* 🚐 *Topkapı.*

WITH ITS 11 fortified gates and 192 towers, this great chain of double walls sealed Constantinople's landward side against invasion for more than a thousand years. Extending for a distance of 6.5 km (4 miles) from the Sea

of Marmara to the Golden Horn, the walls are built in layers of red tile alternating with limestone blocks. Different sections can be reached by metro, tram, train, or bus; but to see their whole length you will need to take a taxi or dolmuş (see p230) along the main road that runs outside them.

Carving of the Byzantine eagle over Yedikule Gate

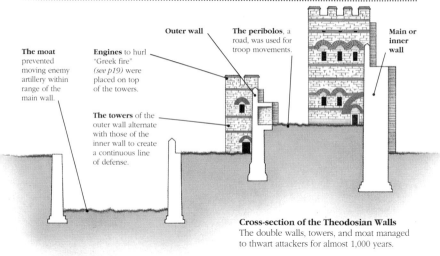

**The moat** prevented moving enemy artillery within range of the main wall.

**Engines** to hurl "Greek fire" *(see p19)* were placed on top of the towers.

**Outer wall**

**The towers** of the outer wall alternate with those of the inner wall to create a continuous line of defense.

**The peribolos**, a road, was used for troop movements.

**Main or inner wall**

**Cross-section of the Theodosian Walls**
The double walls, towers, and moat managed to thwart attackers for almost 1,000 years.

of the Cannon (not to be confused with Topkapı Palace, *see pp54–9*). Unfortunately, a section of walls close to this gate was demolished in the 1950s to make way for a road, Millet Caddesi. The Charsius Gate (now called Edirnekapı), Silivrikapı, Yeni Mevlanakapı, and other original gates still give access to the city. The Yedikule Gate (which stands beside the castle of the same name) has an imperial Byzantine eagle *(see p23)* carved above its main archway.

## Yedikule Castle ❷
Yedikule Müzesi

Yedikule Meydanı Sok, Yedikule.
🚌 80, 93T. ⬜ 9am–5pm Tue–Sun.

YEDİKULE, the "Castle of the Seven Towers," is built on to the southern section of the Theodosian Walls. Its seven towers are connected by thick walls to make a five-sided fortification. One of the sides, with four towers spaced along it, is formed by a stretch of the land walls themselves.

The fortress as it is today incorporates both Byzantine and Ottoman features. The two stout, square marble towers built into the land walls once flanked the Golden Gate (now blocked up), the triumphal entrance into medieval Byzantium *(see p20)* built by Theodosius II. Imperial processions would enter the city

through this gate to mark the investiture of a new emperor or in celebration of a successful military campaign. When it was first built, the gate was covered in gold plate and the façade decorated with sculptures, including a statue of a winged Victory, four bronze elephants, and an image of Emperor Theodosius himself.

In the 15th century, Mehmet the Conqueror added the three tall, round towers that are not part of the land walls, and the connecting curtain walls, to complete the fortress.

After viewing the castle from the outside, you can enter through a doorway in the northeastern wall. The tower immediately to your left as you enter is known as the *yazılı kule*, "the tower with inscriptions." This was used as a prison for foreign envoys

and others who fell afoul of the sultan. These hapless individuals carved their names, dates, and other details on the walls, and some of these inscriptions are still visible.

Executions were carried out in Yedikule Castle, in the northern of the two towers flanking the Golden Gate. Among those executed here was the 17-year-old Osman II *(see p31)*. In 1622 he was dragged to Yedikule by his own Janissaries *(see p127)*, after four years of misrule, which included, it is alleged, using his own pages as targets for archery practice.

The walkway around the ramparts is accessible via a steep flight of stone steps. It offers good views of the land walls and nearby suburbs, and also of the cemeteries that lie outside the walls.

**Aerial view of Yedikule Castle with the Sea of Marmara behind**

## Church of St. John of Studius ❸
İmrahor Camii

İmam Aşir Sok, Yedikule. 🚌 *80, 80B, 80T.* 🚉 *Yedikule.*

I STANBUL'S OLDEST surviving church, St. John of Studius, is now a mere shell consisting only of its outer walls. However, you can still get an idea of the original beauty of what was once part of an important Byzantine institution.

The church was completed in AD 463 by Studius, a Roman patrician who served as consul during the reign of Emperor Marcian (450–57). Originally connected to the most powerful monastery in the Byzantine Empire, in the late 8th century it was a spiritual and intellectual center under the rule of Abbot Theodore, who was buried in the church's garden. The abbot is venerated today in the Greek Orthodox Church as St. Theodore.

Until its removal by the soldiers of the Fourth Crusade *(see p22)*, the most sacred relic housed in the church was the head of St. John the Baptist. The emperor would visit the church each year for the Beheading of the Baptist feast on August 29.

In the 15th century, the church housed a university and was converted into a mosque. The building was abandoned in 1894 when it was severely damaged by an earthquake.

The church is a perfect basilica, with a single apse at the east end, preceded by a narthex and a courtyard. It has a magnificent entrance portal, with carved Corinthian capitals and a sculpted architrave and cornice. Except for six columns of verdigris, the church is empty inside.

**Ruins of the Church of St. John of Studius**

**The Shrine of Zoodochus Pege, founded on a sacred spring**

## Shrine of Zoodochus Pege ❹
Balıklı Kilise

Seyit Nizam Cad 3, Silivrikapı. 📞 *(0212) 582 30 81.* 🚉 *Seyitnizam.* 🚌 *93T.* ⏰ *8am–4pm daily.*

T HE FOUNTAIN OF Zoodochus Pege ("Life-Giving Spring") is built over Istanbul's most famous sacred spring, that is believed to have miraculous powers. The fish swimming in it are supposed to have arrived though a miracle that occurred shortly before the fall of Constantinople *(see p24).* They are said to have leaped into the spring from a monk's frying pan on hearing him declare that a Turkish invasion of Constantinople was as likely as fish coming back to life.

The spring was probably the site of an ancient sanctuary of Artemis. Later, with the arrival of Christianity, a church dedicated to the Virgin Mary was built around it. The spring was popular throughout the Byzantine era, especially on Ascension Day, when the emperor would visit it. The church was destroyed and rebuilt many times over the years by various Byzantine emperors, but the present one dates from 1833. The inner courtyard is filled with tombs of bishops and patriarchs of the Greek Orthodox Church.

## Kara Ahmet Paşa Mosque ❺
Kara Ahmet Paşa Camii

Undeğirmeni Sok, Fatma Sultan. ⏰ *Prayer times only.* ⊘ *Ulubatlı.* 🚉 *Topkapı.* 🚌 *93T.*

O NE OF THE most worthwhile detours along the city walls is the Kara Ahmet Paşa Mosque, also known as Gazi Ahmet Paşa. This lovely building, with its peaceful, leafy courtyard and graceful proportions, is one of Sinan's *(see p91)* lesser known achievements. He built it in 1554 for Kara Ahmet Paşa, a grand vizier of Süleyman the Magnificent *(see p24).*

The courtyard is surrounded by the cells of a *medrese* and a *dershane*, or main classroom. Attractive apple-green and yellow Iznik tiles *(see p161)* grace the porch, while blue-and-white ones are found on the east wall of the prayer hall. These tiles date from the mid-16th century. Of the three galleries, the wooden ceiling under the west one is elaborately painted in red, blue, gold, and black.

**Tilework over *medrese* doorway at Kara Ahmet Paşa Mosque**

Outside the city walls, nearby, is tiny Takkeci İbrahim Ağa Mosque, which dates from 1592. Wooden-domed, it has some particularly fine İznik tile panels.

## Mihrimah Mosque ❻
Mihrimah Camii

Sulukule Cad, Edirnekapı. **Map** 1 A2. 🚌 *28, 87, 91.* ⏰ *daily.*

A N IMPOSING monument located just inside the city walls, the Mihrimah Mosque complex was built by Sinan between 1562 and 1565. Mihrimah, the daughter of Süleyman the Magnificent (see p24), was then the recently widowed wife of Rüstem Paşa, a grand vizier who gave his name to the tiled mosque near the Spice Bazaar (see pp88–9).

This mosque rests on a platform occupying the highest point in the city. Its profile is visible from far away on the Bosphorus and also when approaching Istanbul from Edirne (see pp154–7).

The building is square in shape, with four strong turrets at its corners, and is surmounted by a 37-m (121-ft) high dome. The single minaret is tall and slender, so much so that it has twice been destroyed by earthquakes. On the second occasion, in 1894, the minaret crashed through the roof of the mosque. The 20th-century stenciling on the inside of the prayer hall was added following this accident.

**Stained-glass window in the Mihrimah Mosque**

The interior is illuminated by numerous windows, some of which have stained glass. The supporting arches of the sultan's loge (see p37) have been skillfully painted to resemble green-and-white marble. The carved marble *minbar* is also impressive.

## Church of St. Savior in Chora ❼

See pp118–19.

## Palace of the Porphyrogenitus ❽
Tekfur Sarayı

Şişehane Cad, Edirnekapı. **Map** 1 B1.
🚌 87, 90, 126.

ONLY GLIMPSES of the former grandeur of the Palace of the Porphyrogenitus (Sovereign) during its years as an imperial residence are discernible from the sketchy remains. Its one extant hall, now open to the elements, does, however, have an attractive three-story façade in typically Byzantine style. This is decorated in red brick and white marble, with arched doorways at ground level and two rows of windows looking down onto a courtyard.

The palace dates from the late Byzantine era. Its exact age is debatable, since the technique of alternating stone with three courses of brick is typical of the 10th century, whereas its geometrical designs were common in the 14th century. It was most likely constructed as an annex of nearby Blachernae Palace. These two palaces became the principal residences of the imperial sovereigns during the last two centuries before the fall of Byzantium in 1453 (see p24).

During the reign of Ahmet III (1703–30, see p25) the last remaining İznik potters (see p161) moved to the palace, and it became a center for tile production. However, by this time their skills were in decline, and the tiles made here never acquired the excellence of those created at the height of production in İznik. Still, some strong colors, including a rich red, were used. Cezri Kasım Paşa Mosque (see p121) in Eyüp has several examples of these tiles.

## Blachernae Palace ❾
Anemas Zindanları

İvaz Ağa Cad, Ayvansaray.
🚌 55T, 99A.

AS THE CITY WALLS approach the Golden Horn, you come to the scant remains of Blachernae Palace. These consist of a tower in the city wall, known as the Prison of Anemas, a terrace to the east (the present site of the İvaz Efendi Mosque), and another tower to the south of the terrace, known as the Tower of Isaac Angelus.

The origins of the palace date as far back as AD 500, when it was an occasional residence for imperial visitors to the shrine of Blachernae. It was the great Comnenus emperors (see p19) who rebuilt the structure in the 12th century, transforming it into a magnificent palace.

The remains of the marble decoration and wall frescoes in the Anemas tower indicate that this was probably an imperial residence. Although you can walk around the site, you will be unable to gain access into the towers unless the caretaker is there.

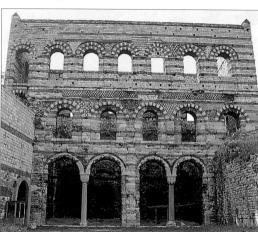

**Brick and marble façade in the Palace of the Porphyrogenitus**

# Church of St. Savior in Chora ⑦

Kariye Camii

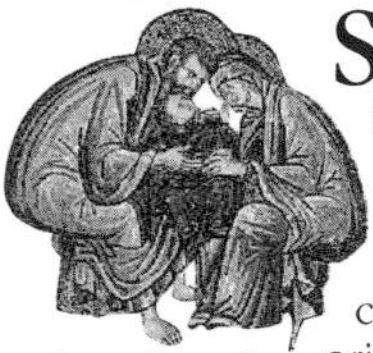

Scene from the Life of the Virgin

SOME OF THE VERY FINEST Byzantine mosaics and frescoes can be found in the Church of St. Savior in Chora. Little is known of the early history of the church, although its name "*in Chora*," which means "in the country," suggests that the church originally stood in a rural setting. The present church dates from the 11th century. Between 1315 and 1321 it was remodeled, and the mosaics and frescoes were added by Theodore Metochites, a theologian, philosopher, and one of the elite Byzantine officials of his day.

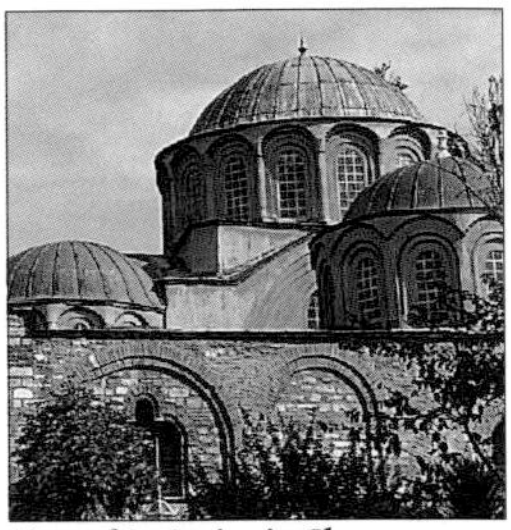

View of St. Savior in Chora

## The Genealogy of Christ

THEODORE METOCHITES, who restored St. Savior, wrote that his mission was to relate how "the Lord himself became a mortal on our behalf." He takes the *Genealogy of Christ* as his starting point: the mosaics in the two domes of the inner narthex portray 66 of Christ's forebears.

The crown of the southern dome is occupied by a figure of Christ. In the dome's flutes are two rows of his ancestors: Adam to Jacob arranged above the 12 sons of Jacob. In the northern dome, there is a central image of the Virgin and Child with the kings of the House of David in the upper row and lesser ancestors of Christ in the lower row.

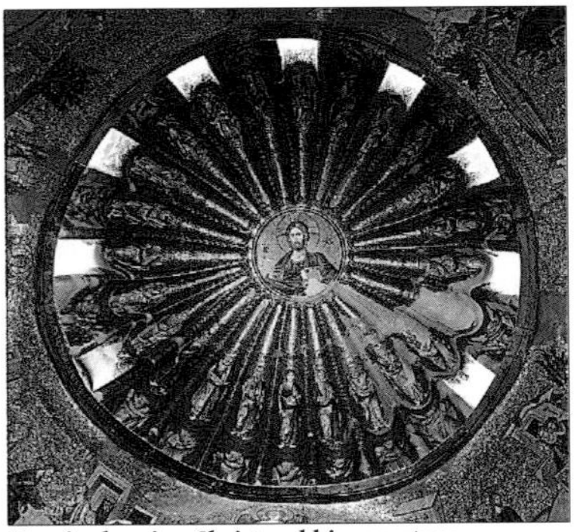

Mosaic showing Christ and his ancestors, in the southern dome of the inner narthex

## The Life of the Virgin

ALL BUT ONE of the 20 mosaics in the inner narthex depicting the *Life of the Virgin* are well preserved. This cycle is based mainly on the apocryphal Gospel of St. James, written in the 2nd century, which gives an account of the Virgin's life. This was popular in the Middle Ages and was a rich source of material for ecclesiastical artists.

Among the events shown are the first seven steps of the Virgin, the Virgin entrusted to Joseph, and the Virgin receiving bread from an angel.

## The Infancy of Christ

SCENES FROM the *Infancy of Christ*, based largely on the New Testament, occupy the semicircular panels of the outer narthex. They begin on

## Guide to the Mosaics and Frescoes

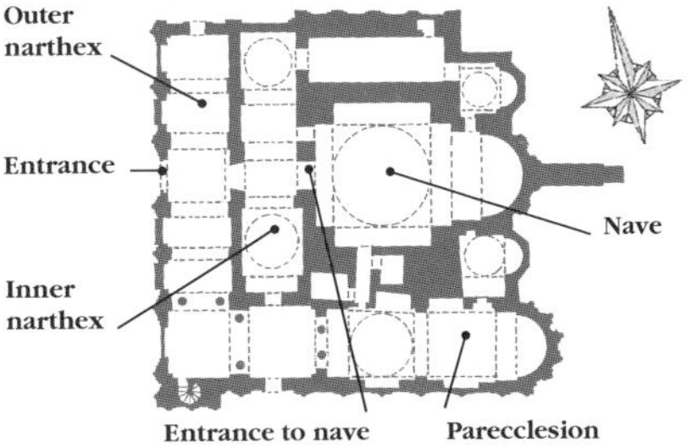


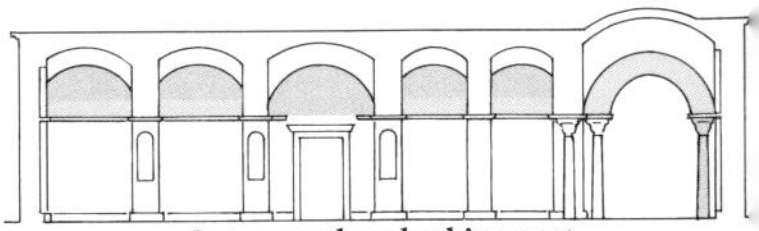

Outer narthex looking east

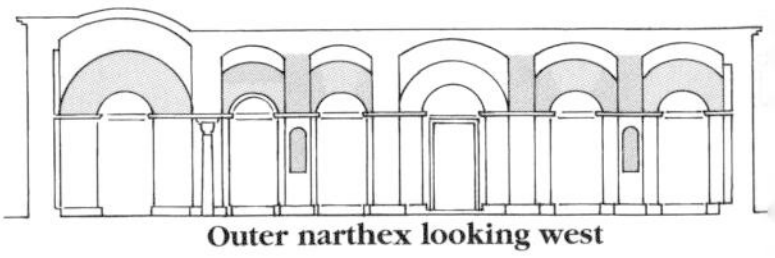

Outer narthex looking west

**Key**

- The Genealogy of Christ
- The Life of the Virgin
- The Infancy of Christ
- Christ's Ministry
- Other Mosaics
- The Frescoes

the north wall of the outer narthex with a scene of Joseph being visited by an angel in a dream. Subsequent panels include Mary and Joseph's *Journey to Bethlehem*, their *Enrollment for Taxation*, the *Nativity of Christ*, and finally, Herod ordering the *Massacre of the Innocents*.

**The *Enrollment for Taxation***

## CHRIST'S MINISTRY

WHILE MANY of the mosaics in this series are badly damaged, some beautiful panels remain. The cycle occupies the vaults of the seven bays of the outer narthex and some of the south bay of the inner narthex. The most striking mosaic is the portrayal of Christ's temptation in the wilderness, in the second bay of the outer narthex.

**Theodore Metochites presents St. Savior in Chora to Christ**

## OTHER MOSAICS

THERE ARE three panels in the nave of the church, one of which, above the main door from the inner narthex, illustrates the *Dormition of the Virgin*. This mosaic, protected by a marble frame, is the best

preserved in the church. The Virgin is depicted laid out on a bier, watched over by the Apostles, with Christ seated behind. Other devotional panels in the two narthexes include one of the *Deësis*, on the east wall of the south bay of the inner narthex, depicting Christ with the Virgin Mary, and unusually, without St. John. Another, in the inner narthex over the door into the nave, is of Theodore Metochites himself, shown wearing a large turban and presenting the restored church as an offering to Christ.

## THE FRESCOES

THE FRESCOES IN the parecclesion are thought to have been painted just after the mosaics were completed, probably in around 1320. The

most engaging of the frescoes – which reflect the purpose of the parecclesion as a place of burial – is the *Anastasis*, in the semidome above the apse. In it, the central figure of Christ, the vanquisher of death, is shown dragging Adam and Eve out of their tombs. Under Christ's feet are the gates of hell, while Satan lies before him. The fresco in the vault overhead depicts *The Last Judgment*, with the souls of the saved on the right and those of the damned to the left.

**Figure of Christ from the *Anastasis* fresco in the parecclesion**

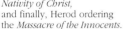

**Inner narthex looking east**

**Parecclesion and outer narthex looking south**

**Inner narthex looking west**

**Parecclesion and outer narthex looking north**

# Eyüp

As THE BURIAL PLACE of Eyüp Ensari, the standard
bearer of the Prophet Mohammed, the village of
Eyüp is a place of pilgrimage for Muslims from all over
the world. Its sacrosanct status has kept it a peaceful
place of contemplation, far removed from the squalid
effects of industrialization elsewhere on the Golden
Horn (see p89). The wealthy elite established mosques
and street fountains in the village, but above all, they
chose Eyüp as a place of burial. Their grand mausoleums line the streets surrounding Eyüp Mosque, while
the cypress groves in the hills above the village are
filled with the gravestones of ordinary people.

**Gateway to the Baroque Complex
of Valide Sultan Mihrişah**

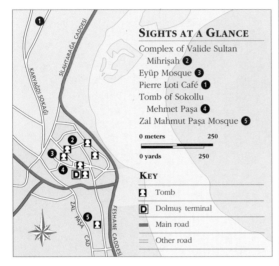

### SIGHTS AT A GLANCE

Complex of Valide Sultan
Mihrişah ❷
Eyüp Mosque ❸
Pierre Loti Café ❶
Tomb of Sokollu
Mehmet Paşa ❹
Zal Mahmut Paşa Mosque ❺

| 0 meters | | 250 |
|---|---|---|
| 0 yards | | 250 |

### KEY

🔲 Tomb

🔲 Dolmuş terminal

▬ Main road

═ Other road

## Pierre Loti Café ❶
Piyer Loti Kahvesi

Gümüşsuyu Balmumcu Sok 1.
📞 (0212) 581 26 96. 🚌 39, 55T,
99A. 🕒 8am–midnight daily.

THIS FAMOUS CAFÉ stands at
the top of the hill in Eyüp
Cemetery, about 20 minutes'
walk up Karyağdı Sokağı
from Eyüp Mosque, from
where it commands sweeping
views down over the Golden
Horn. It is named after
the French novelist
and Turkophile Pierre
Loti, who frequented a
café in Eyüp – claimed
to be this one – during
his stay here in 1876.
Loti (see p42), a
French naval officer,
fell in love with a
married Turkish
woman and wrote
an autobiographical

novel, Aziyade, about their
affair. The café is charmingly
decorated with 19th-century
furniture and, to add to the
atmosphere, the waiters wear
period clothing.
The path up to the café
passes by a picturesque array
of tombstones, most of which
date from the Ottoman era.
Just before the café on the
right, a few tall, uninscribed
tombstones mark the graves
of executioners.

**Period interior of the Pierre Loti Café**

## Complex of Valide
## Sultan Mihrişah ❷
Mihrişah Valide Sultan
Külliyesi

Seyit Reşat Cad. 🚌 39, 55T, 99A.
🕒 9:30am–4:30pm Tue–Sun.

MOST OF THE northern side
of the street leading from
Eyüp Mosque's northern gate
is occupied by the largest
Baroque külliye (see p36) in
Istanbul, although unusually
it is not centered on a mosque.
Built for Mihrişah, mother of
Selim III (see p31), the külliye
was completed in 1791.
The complex includes the
ornate marble tomb of Mihrişah
and a soup kitchen, which is
still in use today. There is also
a beautifully ornamented fountain (sebil), from which an
attendant once served water
and refreshing drinks of
sherbet to passersby.

## Eyüp Mosque ❸
Eyüp Camii

Cami-i Kebir Sok. 🚌 39, 55T, 99A.
🕒 daily.

MEHMET THE Conqueror
built the original mosque
on this site in 1458, five years
after his conquest of Istanbul
(see p24), in honor of Eyüp
Ensari. That building fell into
ruins, probably as a result of
an earthquake, and the present
mosque was completed in
1800 by Selim III (see p31).
The mosque's delightful
inner courtyard is a garden in
which two huge plane trees
grow on a platform. This platform was the setting for the
Girding of the Sword of

Osman, part of a sultan's inauguration from the days of
Mehmet the Conqueror.

The mosque itself is pre-
dominantly covered in gleam-
ing white marble, and inside
there is a magnificent green
carpet underfoot.

Opposite the mosque is the
tomb of Eyüp Ensari himself,
believed to have been killed
during the first Arab siege of
Constantinople in the 7th
century *(see p19)*. The tomb
dates from the same period
as the mosque and most of its
decoration is in the Ottoman
Baroque style. Both the outer
wall of the tomb facing the
mosque, and most of its
interior, have an impressive
covering of tiles, some of
them from İznik *(see p160)*.

Zal Mahmut Paşa Mosque, as viewed from its tomb garden

**Visitors at the tomb of Eyüp Ensari,
Mohammed's standard bearer**

# Tomb of Sokollu
# Mehmet Paşa ❹
Sokollu Mehmet Paşa
Türbesi

Cami-i Kebir Sok. 🚌 *39, 55T, 99A.*
🚪 *9:30am–4:30pm Tue–Sun.*

**G**RAND VIZIER *(see p27)*
Sokollu Mehmet Paşa
commissioned his tomb around
1574, five years before he was
assassinated by a madman in
Topkapı Palace *(see pp54–7)*.
Of Balkan royal blood, he
started his career as falconer
royal and steadily climbed the
social order until he became
grand vizier to Süleyman the
Magnificent *(see p24)* in 1565.
He held this position through
the reign of Selim II *(see p25)*
and into that of Murat III.
The architect Sinan *(see p91)*

built this elegantly proportioned octagonal tomb. It is
notable for its stained glass,
some of which is original.
A roofed colonnade connects
the tomb to what was formerly
a Koranic school.

# Zal Mahmut Paşa
# Mosque ❺
Zal Mahmut Paşa Camii

Zal Paşa Cad. 🚌 *39, 55T, 99A.*
🚪 *daily.*

**H**EADING SOUTH from the
center of Eyüp, it is a
short walk to Zal Mahmut
Paşa Mosque. The complex
was built by Sinan for the
man who assassinated Mustafa,

the first-born heir of Süleyman the Magnificent.

Probably erected some time
in the 1560s, the mosque is
notable for the lovely floral
tiles around its mihrab, and
for its carved marble *minbar*
and *müezzin mahfili (see
p36)*. Proceeding down some
stone steps to the north of the
mosque, you will come to a
garden. In it stands the large
tomb of Zal Mahmut Paşa and
his wife, said to have both
died on the same day.

On the same street, Cezri
Kasım Paşa Mosque (1515) is
a small mosque with a pretty
portal and a tiled mihrab. Most
of the tiles were produced at
the Palace of the Porphyrogenitus *(see p117)* in the first
half of the 18th century.

---

## OTTOMAN GRAVESTONES

The Ottoman graveyard was a garden
of the dead, where the living happily
strolled without morbid thoughts. The
gravestones within it were often lavishly
symbolic: from their decoration you can
tell the sex, occupation, rank, and
even the number of children of the deceased. As the turban was banned in
1828 *(see p28)*, only the fez appears on
men's gravestones erected after that date.

**Women's** *graves
have a flower
for each child.*

**A turban's** *size
reflected a gentle-
man's status.*

**This hat** *indicates
the grave of a mem-
ber of a Sufi order.*

**A fez** *was worn by
a paşa, or public
servant (see p27).*

# Beyond Taksim

The area to the north of Taksim Square *(see p107)* became fashionable in the 19th century, when sultans built palaces along the Bosphorus and in the wooded hills above it. The extravagant Dolmabahçe Palace, built by Abdül Mecit I *(see p28)*, started the trend. High-ranking court officials soon followed, and the area achieved a glamour that it retains to this day. Two other sights worth seeing are on the northern shore of the Golden Horn. Aynalı Kavak Palace is the last surviving trace of a grand palace built by Ahmet III *(see p25)*, while the Rahmi Koç Museum, in nearby Hasköy, is an interesting industrial museum. Hasköy became a royal park in the 15th century and later supported fruit orchards, before dockyards brought industrialization to the area in the 19th century.

Ortaköy's fashionable waterfront square and ferry landing

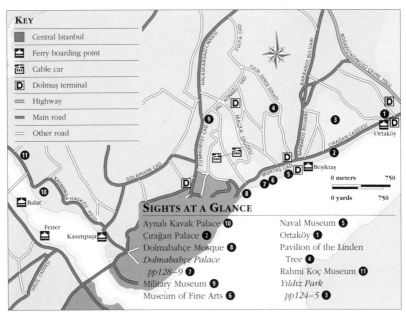

**Key**

- ▇ Central Istanbul
- ⛴ Ferry boarding point
- 🚡 Cable car
- Ⓓ Dolmuş terminal
- ▬ Highway
- ▬ Main road
- — Other road

**Sights at a Glance**

Aynalı Kavak Palace ❿
Çırağan Palace ❷
Dolmabahçe Mosque ❽
*Dolmabahçe Palace pp128–9* ❼
Military Museum ❾
Museum of Fine Arts ❻

Naval Museum ❺
Ortaköy ❶
Pavilion of the Linden Tree ❹
Rahmi Koç Museum ⓫
*Yıldız Park pp124–5* ❸

Cobbled Ortaköy side street lined with cafés and shops

## Ortaköy ❶

**Map** 9 F3. ⛴ *25E, 40.*

Crouched at the foot of Bosphorus Bridge *(see p138)*, the suburb of Ortaköy has retained a village feel. Life centers on İskele Meydanı, the dockside square, which was until recently busy with fishermen unloading the day's catch. Nowadays, though, Ortaköy is better known for its lively Sunday market *(see p207)*, which crowds out the square and surrounding streets, and for its stores selling the wares of local artisans. It is also the

location for a lively bar and café scene, which is the hub of Istanbul's nightlife *(see p213)*, especially in summer.

Mecidiye Mosque, Ortaköy's most impressive landmark, is located on the waterfront. It was built in 1855 by Nikoğos Balyan, who was responsible for Dolmabahçe Palace *(see pp128–9)*. A simple structure, it has grace and originality, with window-filled tympanum arches and corner turrets.

Ortaköy also has a Greek Orthodox church, Haghios Phocas, and a synagogue, Etz Ahayim. The origins of both date from the Byzantine era.

# Çırağan Palace ❷
## Çırağan Sarayı

Çırağan Cad 84, Beşiktaş. **Map** 9 D3.
📞 *(0212) 258 33 77.* 🚌 *25E, 40.*

SULTAN ABDÜL MECİT I started work on Çırağan Palace in the 1850s, but it was not completed until 1874, during the reign of Abdül Aziz *(see p28).* It replaced an earlier wooden palace where torchlit processions were held during the Tulip Period *(see p25).*

The palace was designed by Nikoğos Balyan. At the sultan's request, he added Arabic touches from sketches of Moorish buildings, such as the Alhambra at Granada in Spain. Externally this is evidenced in the honeycomb capitals over its windows. The sultan entered Çırağan Palace directly from the Bosphorus, through the ornate ceremonial gates along its shoreline.

Çırağan Palace had a sad, short history as an imperial residence. Abdül Aziz died here in 1876, supposedly committing suicide – although his friends believed he had been murdered. His successor, Murat V *(see p31),* was imprisoned in the palace for a year after a brief reign of only three months. He died in the Malta Pavilion *(see p125)* 27 years later, still a prisoner. In 1910 the palace was destroyed by fire. It remained a burned-out shell for many years, before

**Çırağan Palace, notable for the Moorish-style embellishments above its windows**

**Baroque-style staircase at the Pavilion of the Linden Tree**

being restored in 1990 as the Çırağan Palace Hotel Kempinski *(see p184),* one of Turkey's most luxurious hotels.

# Yıldız Park ❸

*See pp124–5.*

# Pavilion of the Linden Tree ❹
## Ihlamur Kasrı

Ihlamur Teşvikiye Yolu, Beşiktaş.
**Map** 8 B2. 📞 *(0212) 259 50 86.*
🚌 *26 (from Eminönü).* ⏰ *9:30am–5pm Tue–Wed & Fri–Sun.* 📷 ✔

THIS ONE-TIME residence of sultans, dating from the mid-19th century, stands in beautiful, leafy gardens planted with magnolias and camellias and decorated with ornamental fountains. The gardens are separated by walls from the neighboring modern suburb of Ihlamur, where they are left as a somewhat incongruous remnant of the city's Ottoman past.

As the pavilion's name suggests, the area was once a grove of lime (linden) trees, and the gardens are all that remain of what was previously a vast, wooded park. This park was a favorite retreat and hunting ground of the Ottoman

sultans. In the early 19th century, Abdül Mecit I *(see p28)* often came here and stayed in the original pavilion on this site. That building was so unassuming that the French poet Alphonse de Lamartine (1790–1869) expressed great surprise that a sultan had entertained him in such a humble cottage, with a gardener working in plain view through the windows.

In 1857 Abdül Mecit chose Nikoğos Balyan, who had by then finished the Dolmabahçe Palace with his father, to design another residence here. Two separate pavilions were built, the grander of which is the Ceremonial Pavilion, or Mabeyn Köşkü, used by the sultan and his guests. The Entourage Pavilion, or Maiyet Köşkü, a short distance away, was reserved for the sultan's retinue, including the women of the harem. Both buildings are open to visitors – the Entourage Pavilion is currently a café and bookstore.

The pavilions are constructed mainly of sandstone and marble. Their façades are in the Baroque style, with double stairways, many decorative embellishments, and hardly a single straight line to be seen. The ornate interiors of the buildings reflect 19th-century Ottoman taste, incorporating a mixture of European styles. With their mirrors, lavish furnishings, and gilded details, they are similar to, but less ostentatious than, those of Dolmabahçe Palace.

# Yıldız Park **4**

## Yıldız Parkı

Fountain, Yıldız
Palace Theater

YILDIZ PARK WAS ORIGINALLY laid out as the garden of the first Çırağan Palace *(see p123)*. It later formed the grounds of Yıldız Palace, an assortment of buildings from different eras, now enclosed behind a wall and entered separately from Ihlamur-Yıldız Caddesi. Other pavilions dot Yıldız Park, which, with its many ancient trees and exotic shrubs, is a favorite spot for family picnics. The whole park is situated on a steep hill, and, as it is a fairly long climb, you may prefer to take a taxi up to the Şale Pavilion and walk back down past the other sights.

**Bridge over the lake in the grounds of Yıldız Palace**

### Yıldız Palace

The palace is a collection of pavilions and villas built in the 19th and 20th centuries. Many of them are the work of the eccentric Sultan Abdül Hamit II (1876–1909, *see p31*), who made it his principal residence as he feared a sea-borne attack on Dolmabahçe Palace *(see pp128–9)*.

The main building in the entrance courtyard is the **State Apartments** (Büyük Mabeyn), dating from the reign of Sultan Selim III (1789–1807, *see p31*), but not presently open to the public. Around the corner, the **City Museum** (Şehir Müzesi) has a display of Yıldız porcelain. The Italianate building opposite it is the former armory, or Silahhane. Next door to the City Museum is the **Yıldız Palace Museum**, housed in what was once the Marangozhane, Abdül Hamit's carpentry workshop. This has a changing collection of art and objects from the palace.

A monumental arch leads from the first courtyard to the harem section of the palace.

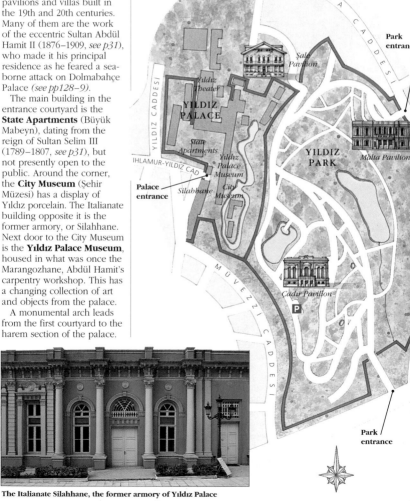

**The Italianate Silahhane, the former armory of Yıldız Palace**

On the left beside the arch is a pretty green-house, the Limonluk Serası (Lemon House).

Farther on, **Yıldız Palace Theatre** is now a museum. It was completed in 1889 by Abdül Hamit, who en-couraged all forms of Western art. The decor of the theater's restored interior is mainly blue and gold. The stars on the domed ceiling are a reference to the name of the palace: *yıldız* means "star" in Turkish.

Abdül Hamit sat alone in a box over the en-trance. Since no one was allowed to sit with his back to the sultan, the first row of orchestra seats were not used. Backstage, the former dressing rooms now have displays on the theater, including costumes.

The lake in the palace grounds is shaped like Abdül Hamit's *tuğra (see p95)*. A menagerie was kept on the islands in the lake where 30 keepers tended tigers, lions, giraffes, and zebras.

Salon in the lavish Şale Pavilion

**Park entrance**

PALANGA CADDESİ

*perial Porcelain Factory*

ÇIRAĞAN CADDESİ

0 meters                    250
0 yards                     250

**KEY**

| | |
|---|---|
| ▨ | Buildings of palace |
| — | Park wall/Palace wall |
| P | Parking |

**VISITORS' CHECKLIST**

Çırağan Cad, Beşiktaş. **Map** 9 D2.
🚌 25E, 40. ◯ daily.
**Yıldız Palace** 📞 (0212) 258 30 80. 🚌 56. ◯ 9:30am–4:30pm Wed–Sun. 🎫 **Şale Pavilion** 📞 (0212) 259 45 70. ◯ 9:30am–5pm (9am–4pm in winter) Fri–Sun, Tue & Wed. 🎫 **Malta & Çadır Pavilions** 📞 (0212) 258 94 53. ◯ 8am–8pm daily. (Malta Pavilion open until 10pm.) **Imperial Porcelain Factory** 📞 (0212) 260 23 70. ◯ 9am–5pm Mon–Fri. 🎫

**Şale Pavilion**

The single most impressive building in the park, the Şale Pavilion (Şale Köşkü) was among those erected by Abdül Hamit II. Although its façade appears as a whole, it was in fact built in three stages.

The first, left-hand section of the building was designed to resemble a Swiss chalet. It probably dates from the 1870s. Winston Churchill, Charles de Gaulle, and Nicolae Ceauşescu have all stayed in its rooms.

The second section was added in 1889, to accommo-date Kaiser Wilhelm II on the first-ever state visit of a foreign monarch to the Ottoman capital. The 14-room suite includes a dining room known as the Mother-of-Pearl Salon (Sedefli Salon) after the delicate inlay that covers almost all of its surfaces.

The third section was also built for a visit by Kaiser Wilhelm II, this time in 1898. Its reception chamber is the grandest room in the whole pavilion. The vast silk Hereke carpet *(see p210)* covering its floor was painstakingly hand-knotted by 60 weavers.

**Malta and Çadır Pavilions**

These two lovely pavilions were built in the reign of Abdül Aziz (1861–76, see p28). Both formerly served as pris-ons but are now open as cafés. Malta Pavilion, also a restaurant, has a superb view and on Sunday is a haunt for locals wanting to relax and read the newspapers.

Midhat Paşa, reformist and architect of the constitution, was among those imprisoned in Çadır Pavilion, for instigating the murder of Abdül Aziz. Meanwhile, Murat V and his mother were locked away in Malta Pavilion for 27 years after a brief incarceration in Çırağan Palace *(see p123)*.

**Façade of Çadır Pavilion, which has now been refurbished as a café**

**Imperial Porcelain Factory**

In 1895 this factory opened to feed the demand of the upper classes for European-style ceramics to decorate their homes. The unusual building was designed to look like a stylized European medieval castle, complete with turrets and portcullis windows.

The original sugar bowls, vases, and plates produced here depict idealized scenes of the Bosphorus and other local viewpoints; they can be seen in museums and palaces all over Istanbul. The mass-produced china made today is for sale in the store, and the factory is open to visitors.

## Naval Museum ❺
Deniz Müzesi

Hayrettin Paşa İskelesi Sok, Beşiktaş.
**Map** 8 B4. 📞 *(0212) 361 01 30.*
🚌 *25E, 28, 40, 56.* ⏱ *1:30–5pm
Fri–Tue.* 📷 ✔

T HIS MUSEUM is located in
two buildings next to the
ferry landing in Beşiktaş. One
of them is the Caïques Gallery,
which is devoted to huge imperial rowboats, or caïques
(some of them manned by
replica oarsmen), dating from
the 17th century. The largest
of these, at 40 m (130 ft), was
used by Mehmet IV and powered by 144 oarsmen. The
row boats used by Atatürk
*(see p28)* look

tiny in compar-
ison; it is re-
markable to
think that he
entertained
heads of state
in them.

**Rowboat
used by
Atatürk**

The exhibits in
the neighboring
main museum
include a 16th-
century map of
America by Turk-
ish cartographer Piri Reis, oil
paintings of various military
scenes, ship figureheads, naval
uniforms, and objects from
Atatürk's yacht, the *Savarona*.

## Museum of Fine Arts ❻
Resim ve Heykel Müzesi

Hayrettin Paşa İskelesi Sok, Beşiktaş.
**Map** 8 B4. 📞 *(0212) 261 42 98.*
🚌 *25E, 28, 40, 56.* ⏱ *10:30am–
4:30pm Wed–Sun.*

F ORMERLY THE Crown Prince
Pavilion, this building, adjacent to Dolmabahçe Palace
*(see pp128–9),* houses a fine
collection of 19th- and 20th-
century paintings and sculpture. In the 19th century, the
westernization of the Ottoman
Empire *(see pp28–9)* led
artists such as Osman Hamdi
Bey (1842–1910, *see p62*) to
experiment with Western-
style painting. While their
styles rely heavily on European art forms, the subject
matter of their work gives a
glimpse into the oriental

**Woman with Mimosas by Osman
Hamdi Bey, Museum of Fine Arts**

history of the city. Look for
*Woman with Mimosas,
Portrait of a Young Girl,* and
*Man with a Yellow Robe,* all
by Osman Hamdi Bey, *Sultan
Ahmet Mosque* by Ahmet Ziya
Akbulut (1869–1938) and
*Âşık,* a statue of a poet by
İsa Behzat (1867–1944).

## Dolmabahçe Palace ❼

*See pp128–9.*

## Dolmabahçe Mosque ❽
Dolmabahçe Camii

Meclis-i Mebusan Cad, Kabataş.
**Map** 8 A5. 🚌 *25E, 40.* ⏱ *daily.*

C OMPLETED AT THE same
time as Dolmabahçe
Palace, in 1853, the mosque
standing beside it was also
built by the wealthy Balyan
family. Its narrow minarets
were constructed in the form

of Corinthian columns, while
great arching windows lighten
the interior. Inside, the decoration includes fake marbling
and trompe l'oeil painting,
two highly fashionable effects
in the mid-19th century.

## Military Museum ❾
Askeri Müze

Vali Konağı Cad, Harbiye. **Map** 7 F1.
📞 *(0212) 233 71 15.* 🚌 *46H.*
⏱ *9am–5pm Wed–Sun.* **Mehter
Band performances** *3–4pm
Wed–Sun.* 📷 ✔

O NE OF ISTANBUL'S most
impressive museums, the
Military Museum traces the
history of the country's con-
flicts from the conquest of
Constantinople in 1453 *(see
p24)* through modern war-
fare. The building used to be
the military academy where
Atatürk studied from 1899 to
1905. His classroom has been
preserved as it was then.

The museum is also the
main location for performances
by the Mehter Band, which
was first formed in the 14th
century during the reign of
Osman I *(see p23)*. From then
until the 19th century, the
band's members were Janissaries, who would accompany
the sultan into battle and perform songs about Ottoman
hero-ancestors and battle
victories. The band had much
influence in Europe and is
thought to have provided
some inspiration for Mozart
and Beethoven.

Some of the most striking
weapons on display on the
ground floor are the curved

**Dolmabahçe Mosque, a landmark on the Bosphorus shoreline**

*Cembiyes* – Ottoman curved daggers – on display in the Military Museum

daggers (*cembiyes*) carried at the waist by foot soldiers in the 15th century. These are ornamented with plant, flower, and geometric motifs in relief and silver filigree. Other exhibits include 17th-century copper head armor for horses and Ottoman shields made from cane and willow, covered in silk thread.

A moving portrayal of trench warfare, commissioned in 1995, is included in the section concerned with the ANZAC landings of 1915 at Chunuk Bair on the Gallipoli peninsula *(see p28)*.

Upstairs, the most spectacular of all the exhibits are the tents used by sultans on their campaigns. They are made of silk and wool with embroidered decoration.

Not far from the museum, from the station on Taşkışla Caddesi, you can take the cable car across Maçka Park to Abdi İpekçi Caddesi in Teşvikiye. Also, some of the city's best designer clothes, jewelry, furniture, and art stores are to be found in this area *(see pp204–5)*.

## Aynalı Kavak Palace ❿
### Aynalı Kavak Kasrı

Kasımpaşa Cad, Hasköy. **Map** 6 A3.
📞 *(0212) 250 40 94.* 🚌 *47, 54.*
🕐 *9am–5pm Tue, Wed, Fri–Sun.* 📷

AYNALI KAVAK PALACE is the last vestige of a large Ottoman palace complex on the once-lovely Golden Horn *(see p89)*. Originally it stood in extensive gardens covering an area of 7,000 sq m (75,300 sq ft). Inscriptions dated 1791 can be found all over the palace, but it is thought to have been built earlier by Ahmet III during the Tulip Period *(see p25)* because of traces around the building of an older style of architecture.

The palace is built on a hill and, as a result, has two stories on the southwest side and a single story to the northeast. It retains some beautiful Ottoman features. These include the upper windows on the southwest façade, which are decorated with stained glass set in curvilinear

stucco tracery. Particularly striking is the composition room, which Sultan Selim III (1789–1807) is thought to have used for writing music.

The audience chamber is adorned with an inscription in gold on blue that describes the activities of Selim III while he stayed at the palace.

Restoration of Aynalı Kavak in 1984 has enabled it to be opened to the public. There is also a superb exhibition of archaic Turkish musical instruments permanently displayed in honor of Selim III, who contributed a great deal to Turkish classical music.

**Audience chamber of Aynalı Kavak Palace on the Golden Horn**

## Rahmi Koç Museum ⓫
### Rahmi Koç Müzesi

Hasköy Cad, Hasköy. 📞 *(0212) 256 71 53.* 🚌 *47.* 🕐 *10am–5pm Tue–Sun.* 📷

SITUATED IN Hasköy, this old 19th-century factory, which once produced anchors and chains, now houses an eclectic collection named after its industrialist founder, Rahmi Koç. The building itself, with its four small domes, vaulted passageways, and original wooden fixtures, is one of the museum's highlights.

The theme of the industrial age connects exhibitions on aviation, transport, steam engines, and scientific instruments. Exhibits range from mechanical toys and scale models of transportation and machinery to a re-created ship's bridge, an operational coin press, and an old tram.

## JANISSARIES

The Janissary (New Army) corps was formed in the 14th century to serve as the sultan's elite fighting force. Its ranks were filled by *devşirme*, the levy of Christian youths brought to Istanbul to serve the sultan. A highly professional and strong army, it was instrumental in the early expansion of the Ottoman Empire, and as well as a fighting force, it acted as the sultan's personal guard. However, discipline eventually began to weaken, and by 1800 the Janissaries had become a destabilizing element in society. They mutinied and overthrew many sultans until their final demise under Mahmut II in 1826 *(see p28)*.

**Janissaries depicted in a 16th-century miniature**

# Dolmabahçe Palace ❼
## Dolmabahçe Sarayı

S ULTAN ABDÜL MECİT *(see p31)* built Dolmabahçe Palace in 1856. As its designers he employed Karabet Balyan and his son Nikoğos, members of the great family of Armenian architects who lined the Bosphorus *(see pp137–49)* with many of their creations in the 19th century. The extravagant opulence of the Dolmabahçe belies the fact that it was built when the Ottoman Empire was in decline.

**Sèvres vase at the foot of the Crystal Staircase**

The sultan financed his great palace with loans from foreign banks. The palace can be visited only on a guided tour, of which there are two. The best tour takes you through the Selamlık (or Mabeyn-i Hümayun), the part of the palace that was reserved for men and contains the state rooms and the enormous Ceremonial Hall. The other tour goes through the Harem, the living quarters of the sultan and his entourage. If you want to go on only one tour, visit the Selamlık.

### ★ Crystal Staircase
*The apparent fragility of this glass staircase stunned observers when it was built. In the shape of a double horseshoe, it is made from Baccarat crystal and brass and has a polished mahogany rail.*

**Imperial Gate**
*Once used only by the sultan and his ministers, this gate is now the main entrance to the palace. The Mehter, or Janissary, Band (see pp126–7) performs in front of the gate every Tuesday afternoon throughout the summer.*

**The Süfera Salon**, where ambassadors waited for an audience with the sultan, is one of the most luxurious rooms in the palace.

**Entrance**

**Swan Fountain**
*This fountain stands in the Imperial Garden. The original 16th-century garden here was created from recovered land, hence the palace's name, Dolmabahçe, meaning "Filled-in Garden."*

**Selamlık**

**The Red Room** was used by the sultan to receive ambassadors.

### ★ Ceremonial Hall
*This magnificent domed hall was designed to hold 2,500 people. Its chandelier, reputedly the heaviest in the world, was bought in England.*

**Blue Salon**
*On religious feast days the sultan's mother would receive his wives and favorites in the Harem's principal room.*

**The Zülvecheyn, or Panorama Room**

**Harem**

**The Rose-colored salon** was the assembly room of the Harem.

**Reception room of the sultan's mother**

**Atatürk's Bedroom**
*Atatürk (see pp28–9) died in this room at 9:05am on November 10, 1938. All the clocks in the palace, such as this one near the crystal staircase, are stopped at this time.*

**Main shore gate**

**Sultan Abdül Aziz's bedroom** had to accommodate a huge bed built especially for the 150-kg (331-lb) amateur wrestler.

### ★ Main Bathroom
*The walls of this bathroom are lined in the finest Egyptian alabaster, and the faucets are solid silver. The brass-framed bathroom windows afford stunning views across the Bosphorus.*

**STAR FEATURES**

★ Crystal Staircase

★ Ceremonial Hall

★ Main Bathroom

# The Asian Side

THE ASIAN SIDE of Istanbul comprises the two major suburbs of Üsküdar and Kadıköy, which date from the 7th century BC *(see p17)*. Üsküdar (once known as Scutari after the 12th-century Scutarion Palace, which was located opposite Leander's Tower) was the starting point of Byzantine trade routes through Asia. It retained its importance in the Ottoman period and today is renowned for its many classical mosques.

A number of residential districts radiate from Üsküdar and Kadıköy. Moda is a pleasant, leafy suburb famous for its ice cream, while there is a lighthouse and an attractive park at Fenerbahçe. From there, it is a short walk up to Bağdat Caddesi, one of Istanbul's best-known shopping streets.

Leander's Tower, on its own small island

## SIGHTS AT A GLANCE

Atik Valide Mosque **5**
The Great Hill of Pines **10**
Haydarpaşa Station **9**
İskele Mosque **3**
Karaca Ahmet Cemetery **7**
Leander's Tower **1**
Selimiye Barracks **8**
Şemsi Paşa Mosque **2**
Tiled Mosque **6**
Yeni Valide Mosque **4**

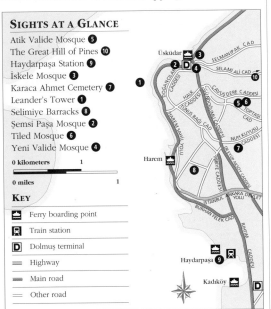

KEY

🚢 Ferry boarding point
🚉 Train station
Ⓓ Dolmuş terminal
═══ Highway
═══ Main road
── Other road

## Leander's Tower **1**

Kız Kulesi

Üsküdar. **Map** 10 A3. 🚢 *Üsküdar.*

LOCATED OFFSHORE from Üsküdar, the tiny, white Leander's Tower is a well-known Bosphorus landmark. The islet on which this 18th-century tower stands was the site of a 12th-century Byzantine fortress built by Manuel I Comnenus. In more recent years, the tower has served as a quarantine center during a cholera outbreak, a lighthouse, a customs control point, and a maritime tollgate. It is currently used by the Turkish navy to monitor shipping and is not open to the public.

The tower is known in Turkish as the "Maiden's Tower," after a legendary princess, said to have been confined here. A prophet foretold that she would die from a snakebite; the snake duly appeared from a basket of figs and struck the fatal blow. The English name of the tower derives from the Greek myth of Leander, who swam the Hellespont (the modern-day Dardanelles, *see p170*) to see his lover Hero.

## Şemsi Paşa Mosque **2**

Şemsi Paşa Camii

Sahil Yolu, Üsküdar. **Map** 10 A2.
🚢 *Üsküdar.* ⭕ *daily.*

THIS IS ONE OF the smallest mosques to be commissioned by a grand vizier *(see p27)*. Its miniature dimensions combined with its picturesque waterfront location make it one of the most attractive mosques in the city.

Şemsi Ahmet Paşa succeeded Sokollu Mehmet Paşa *(see p82)* as grand vizier and may have been involved in his murder. Sinan *(see p91)* built this mosque for him in 1580.

The garden, which overlooks the Bosphorus, is surrounded on two sides by the *medrese (see p36)*, with the mosque on the third side and the sea wall on the fourth. The mosque itself is unusual in that the tomb of Şemsi Ahmet is joined to the main building, divided from the interior by a grille.

Şemsi Paşa Mosque, built by Sinan for Grand Vizier Şemsi Ahmet Paşa

# İskele Mosque ❸
İskele Camii

Hakimiyeti Milliye Cad, Üsküdar.
**Map** 10 B2. 🚢 *Üsküdar.* ⬤ *daily.*

ONE OF ÜSKÜDAR'S most prominent landmarks, the İskele Mosque (also known as Mihrimah Sultan Mosque), takes its name from the ferry landing where it stands. A massive structure on a raised platform, it was built by Sinan between 1547 and 1548 for Mihrimah Sultan, favorite daughter of Süleyman the Magnificent and wife of Grand Vizier Rüstem Paşa *(see p88)*.

Without space to build a courtyard, Sinan constructed a large protruding roof that extends to cover the *şadırvan* (ablutions fountain) in front of the mosque. The porch and interior are rather dark as a result. This raised portico is an excellent place from which to look down on the main square below, in which stands the Baroque Fountain of Ahmet III, built in 1726.

The *mektep* (Koranic school) over the gate of Yeni Valide Mosque

**Fountain set into the platform below the İskele Mosque**

# Yeni Valide Mosque ❹
Yeni Valide Camii

Hakimiyeti Milliye Cad, Üsküdar.
**Map** 10 B2. 🚢 *Üsküdar.* ⬤ *daily.*

ACROSS THE main square from İskele Mosque, the Yeni Valide Mosque, or New Mosque of the Sultan's Mother, was built by Ahmet III between 1708 and 1710 to honor his mother, Gülnuş Emetullah. The complex is entered through a large gateway, with the *mektep* (Koranic school) built above it. This leads into a spacious courtyard. The buildings in the complex date from an important turning point in Ottoman architecture. The mosque is in the classical style, yet there are Baroque embellishments on the tomb of the Valide Sultan, the neighboring *sebil* (kiosk from which drinks were served), and the *şadırvan*.

# Atik Valide Mosque ❺
Atik Valide Camii

Çinili Camii Sok, Üsküdar. **Map** 10 C3.
🚌 *12C (from Üsküdar).* ⬤ *prayer times only.*

THE ATİK VALİDE MOSQUE, set on the hill above Üsküdar, was one of the most extensive mosque complexes in Istanbul. The name translates as the Old Mosque of the Sultan's Mother, as the mosque was built for Nur Banu, the Venetian-born wife of Selim II ("the Sot") and mother of Murat III. She was the first of the sultans' mothers to rule the Ottoman Empire from the harem *(see p25)*.

**Dome in the entrance to Atik Valide Mosque**

Sinan completed the mosque, which was his last major work, in 1583. It has a wide, shallow dome that rests on five semidomes, with a flat arch over the entrance portal.

The interior is surrounded on three sides by galleries, the undersides of which retain the rich black, red, and gold stenciling typical of the period. The mihrab apse is almost completely covered with panels of fine İznik tiles *(see p161)*, while the mihrab itself and the *minbar* are both made of beautifully carved marble. Side aisles were added to the north and south in the 17th century, and the grilles and architectural trompe l'oeil paintings on the royal loge in the western gallery date from the 18th century.

Outside, a door in the north wall of the courtyard leads down a flight of stairs to the *medrese*, where the *dershane* (classroom) projects out over the narrow street below, supported by an arch. Of the other buildings in the complex, the *şifahane* (hospital) is the only one that has been restored and is open to the public. Located just to the east of the mosque, it consists of 40 cells around a courtyard and was in use well into the 20th century.

**Women attending an Islamic class in the Tiled Mosque**

## Tiled Mosque ❻
Çinili Camii

Çinili Camii Sok, Üsküdar. **Map** 10 C3.
Üsküdar, then 20 mins walk.
prayer times only.

THIS ATTRACTIVE mosque is best known for the fine tiles from which it takes its name. It dates from 1640 and is noticeably smaller than other royal foundations of the 17th century. This is partly because by the middle of the century, much of Istanbul's prime land had already been built on, and the size of the plot did not allow for a larger building. There was also a trend away from endowing yet more enormous mosque complexes in the city.

The mosque was founded by Mahpeyker Kösem Sultan. As the wife of Sultan Ahmet I (see p31) and mother of sultans Murat IV and İbrahim the Mad, she wielded great influence. Indeed, she was one of the last of the powerful harem women (see p25).

In the courtyard is a massive, roofed ablutions fountain. The adjacent medrese (see p36), however, is tiny. The facade and interior of the mosque are covered with İznik tiles (see p161) in turquoise, white, gray, and a range of blues. There are none of the red and green pigments associated with the heyday of İznik tile production, but the designs are still exquisite. Even the conical cap of the marble minbar is tiled, and the carving on the minbar itself is picked out in green, red, and gold paint.

The mosque's Turkish bath is on Çinili Hamam Sokağı. It has been renovated and is used by local residents.

## Karaca Ahmet Cemetery ❼
Karaca Ahmet Mezarlığı

Nuh Kuyusu Cad, Selimiye. **Map** 10 C4. 12. 8:30am–5:30pm daily. **Tomb** 9:30am–4:30pm daily.

SPRAWLING OVER a large area, this cemetery is a pleasant place in which to stroll among old cypress trees and look at ancient tombstones. The earliest dated stone is from 1521, although the cemetery itself, one of the largest in Turkey, is thought to date from 1338.

The carvings on each tombstone tell a story (see p121). A man's tomb is indicated by a fez or a turban. The style of the turban denotes the status of the deceased. Women's stones are adorned with carved flowers, hats, and shawls.

**Crimean War memorial in the British War Cemetery**

Standing on the corner of Gündoğumu Caddesi and Nuh Kuyusu Caddesi is the tomb of Karaca Ahmet himself. This warrior died fighting in the Turkish conquest of the Byzantine towns of Chrysopolis and Chalcedon (Üsküdar and Kadıköy) in the mid-14th century. The tomb and monument to his favorite horse date from the 19th century.

## Selimiye Barracks ❽
Selimiye Kışlası

Çeşme-i Kebir Cad, Selimiye.
**Map** 10 B5. (0216) 343 73 10.
Harem. 12. by appointment only.

THE SELİMİYE BARRACKS were originally built by Selim III in 1799 to house his New Army, with which he hoped to replace the Janissaries (see p127). He failed in his attempt and was deposed and killed in a Janissary insurrection in 1807–8 (see p28). The barracks burned down shortly afterward. The present building, which dominates the skyline of the Asian shore, was started by Mahmut II in 1828, after he had finally disbanded the Janissary corps. Abdül Mecit I added three more wings between 1842 and 1853.

The barracks were used as a military hospital during the Crimean War (1853–6). They became associated with Florence Nightingale (see p43), who lived and worked in the northeast tower from 1854. The rooms she occupied are now a museum, and are the only part of the barracks open to the public. They contain their original furniture, copies of some of the pamphlets she wrote on military nursing, and the lamp from which she gained the epitaph "Lady of the Lamp."

**Visitor praying at the tomb of the warrior Karaca Ahmet**

**Haydarpaşa Station, terminus for trains arriving from Anatolia**

Two other sites near the barracks – the Selimiye Mosque and the British War Cemetery – are both worth seeing. Built in 1804, the mosque is in a lovely garden courtyard. The interior is filled with light from tiers of windows set in high arches. It is simply decorated with a classically painted dome and gray marble *minbar*. The royal pavilion in the northwest corner of the mosque compound is flanked by graceful arches.

The British War Cemetery is a short walk south, on Burhan Felek Caddesi. It contains the graves of men who died in the Crimean War, in World War I at Gallipoli *(see p170)*, and in World War II in the Middle East. There is no sign outside and opening hours vary, but the caretaker will usually be there to let you in.

## Haydarpaşa Station **9**
### Haydarpaşa Garı

Haydarpaşa İstasyon Cad, Haydarpaşa. **(0216) 336 04 75.** Haydarpaşa or Kadıköy. ☐ daily.

THE WATERFRONT location and grandeur of Haydarpaşa Station, together with the neighboring tiled jetty, make it the most impressive point of arrival or departure in Istanbul. The first Anatolian railroad line, which was built in 1873, ran from here to İznik *(see p160)*. The extension of this railroad was a major part of Abdül Hamit II's drive to modernize

the Ottoman Empire. Lacking sufficient funds to continue the project, he applied for help to his German ally, Kaiser Wilhelm II *(see p43)*. The Deutsche Bank agreed to invest in the construction and operation of the railroad. In 1898 German engineers were contracted to build the new railroad lines running across Anatolia and beyond into the far reaches of the Ottoman Empire. At the same time a number of stations were built. Haydarpaşa, the grandest of these, was completed in 1908. Trains run from Haydarpaşa into the rest of Asia.

## The Great Hill of Pines **10**
### Büyük Çamlıca

Çamlıca. 🚌 11F, KÇ1, then 30 mins walk. **Park** ☐ 9am–midnight daily.

ON A CLEAR DAY the view from the top of this hill takes in the Princes' Islands, the Sea of Marmara, the Golden Horn and Beyoğlu, and the Bosphorus as far as the Black Sea. It is even possible to see snow-capped Mount Uludağ near Bursa *(see p169)* to the south. The Great Hill of Pines, 4 km (2.5 miles) east of Üsküdar, is the highest point in Istanbul, at 261 m (856 ft) above sea level. Even the forest of radio and TV antennas farther down the slopes of the hill does not obscure the view.

The park at the summit, created by the Turkish Touring and Automobile Club *(see p175)* in 1980, is laid out with gardens, marble kiosks, and two 18th-century-style cafés.

Neighboring Küçük Çamlıca (Small Hill of Pines), located to the south, is somewhat less cultivated and consequently attracts fewer tourists to its little tea garden. It is another lovely place for a stroll, again with beautiful views.

### FLORENCE NIGHTINGALE

**A 19th-century painting of Florence Nightingale in Selimiye Barracks**

The British nurse Florence Nightingale (1820–1910) was a tireless campaigner for hospital, military, and social reform. During the Crimean War, in which Britain and France fought on the Ottoman side against the Russian Empire, she organized a party of 38 British nurses. They took charge of medical services at the Selimiye Barracks in Scutari (Üsküdar) in 1854. By the time she returned to Britain in 1856, at the end of the war, the mortality rate in the barracks had decreased from 20 to 2 percent, and the fundamental principles of modern nursing had been established. On her return home, Florence Nightingale opened a training school for nurses.

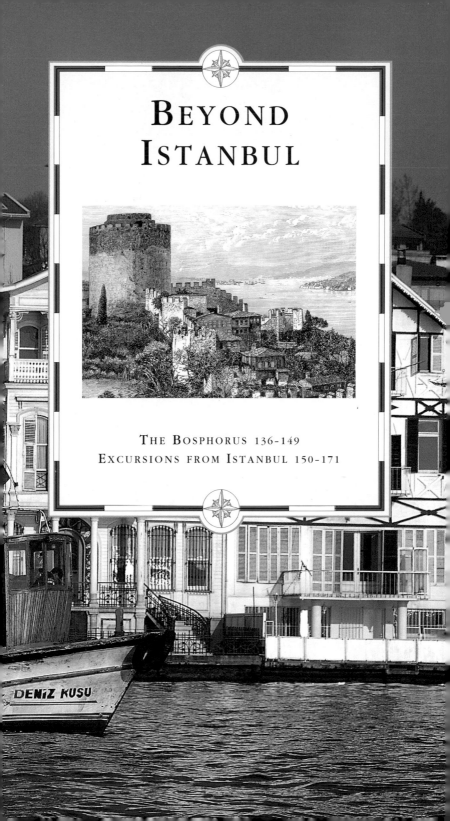

# BEYOND
# ISTANBUL

# THE BOSPHORUS

IF THE NOISE and bustle of the city are too harsh, a good antidote is a trip up the Bosphorus *(see pp144–9)*, the straits separating Europe and Asia that join the Black Sea and the Sea of Marmara. The easiest way to travel is by boat. An alternative is to explore the sights along the shores at your own pace. For much of their length, the shores are lined with handsome buildings: wooden waterside villas known as yalis, graceful mosques, and opulent, 19th-century palaces. The grander residences along the

**Sait Halim Paşa Yali on the Bosphorus**

Bosphorus have waterfront entrances. These date from the days when wooden caïques, boats powered by a strong team of oarsmen, were a popular form of transit along the straits among the city's wealthier inhabitants. Interspersed between the monumental architecture are former fishing villages, where you will find some of Istanbul's finest clubs and restaurants. The Bosphorus is especially popular in summer, when the cool breezes off the water provide welcome relief from the heat of the city.

## SIGHTS AT A GLANCE

**Museums and Palaces**
Aşiyan Museum **5**
Beylerbeyi Palace **2**
Khedive's Palace **10**
Küçüksu Palace **4**
Maslak Pavilion **9**
Sadberk Hanım Museum **12**

**Towns and Villages**
Bebek **3**
Beykoz **11**
Kanlıca **7**
Rumeli Kavağı **13**

**Historic Buildings**
Bosphorus Bridge **1**
Fortress of Europe **6**

**Parks**
Emirgan Park **8**

### KEY

| | |
|---|---|
| ◼ | Central Istanbul |
| ◻ | Greater Istanbul |
| ⛴ | Ferry stops on Bosphorus trip |
| ═ | Highway |
| ▬ | Main road |

0 kilometers          5
0 miles               5

### THE BOSPHORUS TRIP

This vital navigational channel is 33 km (20 miles) long and varies between 700 m (2,300 ft) and 3.6 km (2 miles) wide. The squares on this map indicate the three stages we have divided the trip into.

Black Sea
Kilyos
Rumeli Feneri
*See pp148–9*
*See pp146–7*
D016
O-2 (E80)
O-1(E5)
D020
O-3
O-2 (E80)
D020
D100
O-4 (E80)
*See pp144–5*
Sea of Marmara

◁ **Anadolu Hisarı, the Fortress of Asia, on the Asian shore of the Bosphorus**

The Bosphorus suspension bridge between Ortaköy and Beylerbeyi

# Bosphorus Bridge **❶**

Boğaziçi Köprüsü

Ortaköy and Beylerbeyi. **Map** 9 F2.
🚌 *200 (double decker, from Taksim).*

SPANNING the Bosphorus between the districts of Ortaköy and Beylerbeyi, this was the first bridge to be built across the straits that divide Istanbul. Known also as Atatürk Bridge, it was finished on October 29, 1973, the 50th anniversary of the inauguration of the Turkish Republic *(see p29)*. It is the world's sixth longest suspension bridge, at a length of 1,560 m (5,120 ft) and it reaches 64 m (210 ft) above water level.

# Beylerbeyi Palace **❷**

Beylerbeyi Sarayı

Çayırbaşı Cad, Asian side. 📞 *(0216) 321 93 20.* 🚌 *15 (from Üsküdar).*
🚢 *from Üsküdar.* 🕙 *9:30am–5pm Tue–Wed & Fri–Sun.* 📷 ✔

DESIGNED IN the Baroque style by Sarkis Balyan, Beylerbeyi Palace seems fairly restrained compared to the excesses of the earlier Dolmabahçe *(see pp128–9)* or Küçüksu *(see p140)* palaces. It was built by Sultan Abdül Aziz *(see p28)* in 1860–65 as a summer residence and a place to entertain visiting heads of state. Empress Eugénie of France visited Beylerbeyi on her way to the opening of the Suez Canal in 1869 and had her face slapped by the sultan's mother for daring to enter the palace on the arm of Abdül Aziz. Other visitors to the palace included the Duke and Duchess of Windsor.

The palace looks its most attractive from the Bosphorus, from where its two bathing pavilions – one for the harem and the other for the *selamlık* (the men's quarters) – can best be seen.

The most attractive room is the reception hall, which has a pool and fountain. Running water was popular in Ottoman houses for its pleasant sound and cooling effect in the heat. Egyptian straw matting covers the palace's floors as a form of insulation. The crystal chandeliers are mostly Bohemian and the carpets *(see pp210–11)* are from Hereke.

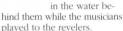

Detail of the gate of the Egyptian Consulate, Bebek

Ornate landing at the top of the stairs in Beylerbeyi Palace

Beylerbeyi impressed many visiting dignitaries, including the Empress Eugénie of France, who was so delighted by the palace that she had a copy of the window in the guest room made for her bedroom in Tuileries Palace, in Paris.

# Bebek **❸**

European side. 🚌 *25E, 40.*

BEBEK IS ONE OF the most fashionable villages along the Bosphorus. It is famous for its marzipan *(badem ezmesi, see p205)*, and for the cafés that line its waterfront. It was once a favorite location for summer residences and palaces of Ottoman aristocrats, and at the end of the 19th century, caïques *(see p126)* of evening revelers would set off on moonlit cruises from the bay, accompanied by a boat of musicians. The women in the party would trail pieces of velvet or satin, edged with silver fishes, in the water behind them while the musicians played to the revelers.

One of the hosts of these parties was the mother of the last Khedive of Egypt *(see p27)*, Abbas Hilmi II. Built in the late 19th century, the only remaining monumental architecture in Bebek is the Egyptian Consulate, which, like the Khedive's Palace *(see p142)*, was commissioned by Abbas Hilmi II. The steep, mansard roof of this yalı is reminiscent of 19th-century northern French architecture. There are lighter Art Nouveau touches including the railings draped with wrought-iron vines and a rising sun between the two turrets, symbolizing the beginning of the new century.

The khedive used the yalı as a summer palace until he was deposed by the British in 1914. From then to the present day it has been used as the Egyptian Consulate.

# Yalis on the Bosphorus

Aᴛ ᴛʜᴇ ᴇɴᴅ of the 17th
century, *paşas*, grand
viziers, and other distinguished citizens of Otto-
man Istanbul began to
build themselves elegant
villas – yalis – along the
shores of the Bosphorus.
These served as summer residences,
and the styles employed reflected their
owners' prestige. Since then, the yalis

**Old yali at Kandilli, Asian side**

that have been built have
become larger and more
elaborate, adopting
Baroque, Art Nouveau,
and contemporary styles
of architecture. Most of
them still conform to a
traditional plan, making
maximum use of the waterfront and,
inside, having a large living room
surrounded by bedrooms.

*Köprülü Amcazade Hüseyin Paşa Yali*
*(see p147), near Anadolu Hisarı, was built*
*in 1698 and is the oldest building on the*
*shores of the Bosphorus. Early yalis, like*
*this one, were built at the water's edge,*
*but in later years they were constructed*
*a little way inland.*

**A cumba,**
or bay window,
projects over
the water.

**Traditional wooden yalis**
were normally painted rust-
red, a color known as
"Ottoman rose."

**Later yalis**, built from
the 18th century, were
painted in pastel shades.

**A bracket** supports the
projecting upstairs rooms.

*Fethi Ahmet Paşa Yali (see p145), or Mocan Yali, at*
*Kuzguncuk, was built in the late 18th century. Among*
*the visitors were the composer Franz Liszt and the archi-*
*tect Le Corbusier (see p42). Famous as the "Pink*
*Yali," after its boldly decorated exterior,*
*the house is almost invisible from the land.*

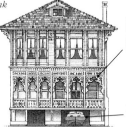

**Baroque influence**
is clearly visible in
the ornately carved
balcony.

*Ethem Pertev Yali (see p147), at Kanlıca, is*
*a prime example of the so-called "cosmopolitan*
*period" of yali building, between 1867 and*
*1908. It has a boathouse below and combines*
*intricate wood carving, a later development,*
*with the more traditional features of a yali.*

**Boathouse**
**under the yali**

*The Egyptian*
*Consulate (see p146)*
*at Bebek clearly shows*
*the influence of Art Nou-*
*veau, with its wrought*
*iron railings worked*
*into a leaf design. It was*
*commissioned by the*
*Khedive of Egypt (see*
*p138) in around 1900.*

**French-style**
**mansard roof**

**Ornamental details** were inspired
by Austrian Art Nouveau designs.

**A narrow dock** often
separates 19th-century
yalis from the shore.

## Küçüksu Palace ❹
### Küçüksu Kasrı

Küçüksu Cad, Asian side. ☎ (0216) 332 02 37. 🚌 15 (from Üsküdar) or 101 (from Beşiktaş). ⏱ 9:30am–5pm Tue, Wed & Fri–Sun.

**Küçüksu Palace, an ornate Bosphorus residence built in 1856**

MARBLE-FRONTED Küçüksu Palace has one of the prettiest facades on the shores of the Bosphorus. Particularly attractive is the curving double staircase that leads up to its main waterside entrance.

Sultan Abdül Mecit I *(see p28)* employed court architect Nikoğos Balyan *(see p128)* to build this palace to accommodate his entourage on their visits to the Sweet Waters of Asia, the romantic name that European visitors gave to the Küçüksu and Göksu rivers. For centuries the Ottoman nobility liked to indulge in picnics in the meadows between the streams.

On the completion of Küçüksu Palace in 1856, the sultan complained that it was too plain and demanded more ornamentation, including his monogram engraved on the facade. Later, in the reign of Abdül Aziz *(see p28)*, the facade was further embellished, with the result that it is hard to follow the lines of the original architecture.

The room arrangement is typically Ottoman, with a large central salon opening on to four corner rooms on each floor. The interior decor was carried out by Séchan, the decorator of the Paris Opera, soon after the palace was finished. The sumptuous carpets come from Hereke *(see pp210–11)* and the chandeliers are Bohemian crystal.

On the shore near Küçüksu Palace is the picturesque, turreted Fountain of the Valide Sultan Mihrişah. Dating from 1796, it is in the Baroque style.

Kıbrıslı Yalı, just south of the palace, was built in 1760. It is painted brilliant white, and at over 60 m (200 ft), its facade is the longest of any yalı *(see p139)* along the Bosphorus. A little farther south again is Kırmızı Yalı, the Red Yalı, so called for its distinctive crimson color. This yalı was constructed around 1790 for an aristocratic European family, the Ostrorogs.

## Aşiyan Museum ❺
### Aşiyan Müzesi

Aşiyan Yolu, Asian side. ☎ (0212) 263 69 86. 🚌 25E, 40. ⏱ 9am–5pm Tue, Wed & Fri–Sun.

AŞİYAN, OR BIRD'S NEST, is the former home of Tevfik Fikret (1867–1915), a teacher, utopian visionary, and one of Turkey's leading poets. The wooden mansion, built by Fikret himself in 1906, is an attractive example of Turkish vernacular architecture. The views from its upper-story balcony are stunning.

On show are the poet's possessions and *Sis* (Fog), a painting by Caliph Abdül Mecit (1922–24), inspired by Fikret's poem of that name.

## Fortress of Europe ❻
### Rumeli Hisarı

Yahya Kemal Cad, European side. ☎ (0212) 263 53 05. 🚌 25E, 40. ⏱ 9:30am–4:30pm Tue–Sun. 🧾

THIS FORTRESS was built by Mehmet the Conqueror in 1452 as his first step in the conquest of Constantinople *(see p24)*. Situated at the narrowest point of the Bosphorus, the fortress controlled a major Byzantine supply route. Across the straits are Anadolu Hisarı, or the Fortress of Asia, which was built in the 14th century by Beyazıt I.

The Fortress of Europe's design was planned by Mehmet himself. While his grand vizier

**The Fortress of Europe, built by Mehmet the Conqueror to enable him to capture Constantinople**

*(see p27)* and two other viziers were each responsible for the building of one of the three great towers, the sultan took charge of the walls. In the spirit of competition that evolved, the fortress was completed in four months.

The new fortress was soon nicknamed Boğazkesen, meaning both Throat- and Strait-cutter. It was garrisoned by a force of Janissaries *(see p127)*. These troops trained their cannons on the straits to prevent the passage of foreign ships. After they had sunk a Venetian vessel, this approach to Constantinople was cut off. Following the conquest of the city, the fortress lost its importance as a military base and was used as a prison, particularly for out-of-favor foreign envoys and prisoners-of-war.

The structure was restored in 1953. Open-air theater performances are now staged here during the Istanbul Music and Dance Festival *(see p45)*.

**Café serving the yogurt for which Kanlıca is famous**

## Kanlıca ❼

Asian side. 🚌 *15, 101.*

A DELICIOUS, creamy type of yogurt is Kanlıca's best known attraction. You will find this on the menu at cafés in the village square next to the ferry landing. The İskender Paşa Mosque, overlooking this square, is a minor work by Sinan *(see p91)*, built for Sultan Süleyman's vizier İskender Paşa in 1559–60. There have been changes to the original building: the wooden dome has been

replaced by a flat roof, and the porch was added later.

There are a number of yalis in and around Kanlıca, including the Köprülü Amcazade Hüseyin Paşa Yali *(see p139)*, the oldest surviving Bosphorus yali, just south of the village. This was built in 1698 by Mustafa II's grand vizier Hüseyin Paşa, the fourth grand vizier from the Köprülü family. The Treaty of Karlo-witz, in which the Ottomans acknow-ledged the loss of territory to Austria, Venice, Poland, and Russia, was signed here in 1699 *(see p25)*. All that remains of the yali, which is not open to visitors, is a T-shaped salon, its dome saved only by wooden props.

## Emirgan Park ❽

### Emirgan Parkı

Emirgan Sahil Yollu, European side.
📞 *(0212) 277 57 82.* 🚌 *25E, 40.*
🕐 *8am–8pm daily.*

E MIRGAN PARK IS the location of some famous tulip gardens that are at their finest for the annual Tulip Festival in April *(see p44)*. Tulips originally grew wild on the Asian steppes and were first propagated in large quantities in Holland. They were later reintroduced to Turkey by

**Pembe Köşk in Emirgan Park**

Mehmet IV (1648–87). The reign of his son Ahmet III is known as the Tulip Period *(see p25)* because of his fascination with the flowers.

In the late 19th century, Sultan Abdül Aziz gave the park to the Egyptian Khedive *(see p27)*, İsmail Paşa, and its three pavilions date from that era. They are known by their colors. The Sarı Köşk (Yellow Pavilion), built in the style of a Swiss chalet, suffered fire damage in 1954 and was re-built in concrete with a facade resembling the original. The Beyaz Köşk (White Pavilion) is a Neo-Classical-style mansion, while the Pembe Köşk (Pink Pavilion), whose terrace affords beautiful views of the Bosphorus, is in the style of a traditional Ottoman house. The pavilions have been renovated and are due to reopen shortly as cafés.

---

### BIRDS OF THE BOSPHORUS

In September and October, thousands of white storks and birds of prey fly over the Bosphorus on their way from their breeding grounds in eastern Europe to wintering regions in Africa. Large birds usually prefer to cross narrow straits like the Bosphorus, rather than fly over an expanse of open water such as the Mediterranean. Among birds of prey on this route, the lesser spotted eagle and the honey buzzard are visible. The birds also cross the straits in spring on their way to Europe, but before the breeding season, they are fewer in number.

**The white stork, which migrates over the straits**

Hothouse plants in the conservatory at Maslak Pavilions

# Maslak Pavilions ❾
## Maslak Kasırları

Büyükdere Cad, Maslak. **[** *(0212) 276 10 22.* 🚌 *40S (from Taksim).* 🕐 *9am–5pm Tue, Wed & Fri–Sun (closes at 4pm in winter).*

THIS SMALL GROUP of buildings was a royal hunting lodge and country residence, much prized for its leafy setting and glorious views. The pavilions were built in the early and mid-19th century, when the focus of Istanbul court life moved away from Topkapı Palace *(see pp54–9)*, in the center of the city, to the sultans' lavish estates along the shore of the Bosphorus. The buildings are thought to date mainly from the reign of Abdül Aziz (1861–76). He gave Maslak to his son Abdül Hamit in the hope that the crown prince would then stop sailing at Tarabya *(see p148)*, which his father regarded as unsafe.

The four main buildings are less ornate than other 19th-century pavilions in Istanbul. This is possibly due to the austere character of Abdül Hamit. He personally crafted the balustrades of the beautiful central staircase in the Kasr-ı Hümayun (the Pavilion of the Sultan) during his stay here. His initials in Western script – AH – can also be seen in the headpieces over the mirrors. The pavilion's lounge retains an Oriental feel, with a low sofa and a central, coal-burning brazier.

Behind the small but elegant Mabeyn-i Hümayun (the Private Apartments) is a large conservatory full of camellias, ferns, and banana plants. Nearby, at the edge of the forest, stands a tiny octagonal folly with an ornate balcony called the Çadır Köşkü, or Tent Pavilion, which now serves as a bookstore. The Paşalar Dairesi (the Apartments of the Paşa) are located at the other side of the complex.

# Khedive's Palace ❿
## Hıdiv Kasrı

Hıdiv Kasrı Yolu 32, Çubuklu. **[** *(0216) 425 06 03.* 🚌 *15 (from Üsküdar)* or *221 (from Taksim), then 30 mins walk.* 🕐 *9am–11pm daily.* 🖥

BUILT IN 1900 by the last khedive (the hereditary viceroy of Egypt, *see p27*), Abbas Hilmi II, this summer palace is one of the most striking buildings of its era in Istanbul. Its tower is an imposing landmark for those traveling up the Bosphorus.

The Italian architect Delfo Seminati based the design of the palace on an Italianate villa, throwing in Art Nouveau and vernacular Ottoman elements. Most impressive of all is the circular entrance hall. This is entered through Art Nouveau glass doors and features a stained glass skylight above a central fountain surrounded by eight pairs of elegant columns.

Renovated by the Turkish Touring Club (TTOK, *see p237*), the palace is now open to visitors as a luxury hotel and restaurant *(see p198)*.

# Beykoz ⓫

Asian shore. 🚌 *15 (from Üsküdar)* or *221 (from Taksim).*

BEYKOZ IS FAMOUS for its walnuts (*beykoz* means "prince's walnut") and for the glass produced here in the 19th century. The distinctive, mainly opaque, Beykoz glass *(see p205)*, with its rich colors

---

## JASON AND THE SYMPLEGADES

The upper Bosphorus features in the Greek myth of Jason's search for the Golden Fleece. The Argonauts, Jason's crew, helped a local king, Phineus, by ridding him of the harpies (female demons) sent by Zeus to torment him. In return, the king advised them on how to tackle the Symplegades, two rocks at the mouth of the Bosphorus that were reputed to clash together, making passage impossible. His advice was to send a dove in advance of the ship; if it went through safely, so would the ship. This the Argonauts duly did, and the rocks clipped the dove's tail feathers. The *Argo* then went through with only some damage to its stern.

Jason and the Argonauts making their way through the Symplegades

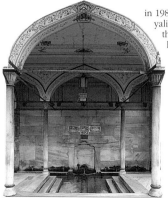

**Fountain in the village square at Beykoz**

and graceful designs, can be seen in museums all over Turkey. Today, the village's main attraction is its fish restaurants *(see pp192–3)*, which serve excellent turbot.

A fine 18th-century fountain stands in the central square. Built on the orders of Sultan Mahmut I *(see p31)*, it is called the İshak Ağa Çeşmesi, after the customs inspector who inaugurated it in 1746. It has a large domed and colonnaded loggia and 10 conduits spouting a constant stream of water.

Industrialization, particularly in the form of bottling and leather factories, has taken its toll on the village. Only a few buildings hint at its former splendor. The attractive 19th-century waterside mansion, Halil Ethem Yali, is an interesting mixture of Neo-Classical and Neo-Baroque styles. It stands on İbrahim Kelle Caddesi, south of the ferry landing.

## Sadberk Hanım Museum ⓬
Sadberk Hanım Müzesi

Piyasa Cad 25–29, Büyükdere,
📞 (0212) 242 38 13. 🚌 25E. 🕐 10:30am– 6pm Thu–Tue. 📷 🚫

Occupying two archetypal wooden Bosphorus yalis *(see p139)*, the Sadberk Hanım Museum was the first private museum to open in Turkey,

in 1981. The larger of these yalis, the Azaryan Yali, is the former summer house of the wealthy Koç family. A four-story mansion, it was built in 1911 and, like many buildings of the time, was inspired by European architecture. The distinctive crisscrossed wooden slats on its façade distinguish it from the neighboring buildings. It contains some fine ethnographic artifacts collected by Sadberk Hanım, wife of the industrialist Vehbi Koç, to whom the museum is dedicated. She found many of them in the Grand Bazaar *(see pp98–9)* and in Istanbul's other markets. A number of exhibits are laid out in tableaus depicting 19th-century Ottoman society. These include a henna party, at which the groom's female relatives would apply henna to the hands of his bride, and a circumcision bed, with a young boy dressed in traditional costume. Also worth seeking out in this section is a display of infinitely delicate *oya*, Turkish embroideries. These remarkably life-like pieces imitate garlands of flowers, such as carnations, roses, hyacinths, and lilies and were used to fringe scarves and petticoats. Some of the examples on display were made in palace harems in the 18th century.

**Attic vase, Sadberk Hanım Museum**

The neighboring building is called the Sevgi Gönül Wing. Also dating from the early 20th century, it was bought to house the archaeological collection of Hüseyin Kocabaş, a friend of the Koç family. Displays are ordered chronologically, ranging from the late Neolithic period (5400 BC) to the Ottoman era. Exhibits are changed from time to time, but typically include Assyrian cuneiform tablets dating from the second millennium BC, Phrygian metalwork, and Greek pottery from the late Geometric Period (750–680 BC). Among the other items usually on display are a large selection of Roman gold jewelry and Byzantine reliquary and pendent crosses.

## Rumeli Kavağı ⓭

European shore. 🚌 25A (from Beşiktaş). 🚢 Rumeli Kavağı.

This charming village has a broad selection of restaurants specializing in fish and fried mussels. They are clustered around the harbor from which there are views of the wild, rocky shores on the approach to the Black Sea. On the hill above Rumeli Kavağı are the scant remains of a castle, İmros Kalesi, built by Manuel I Comnenus *(see p19)* in the 12th century to guard his customs point.

Farther up the Bosphorus, the shore road leads from Rumeli Kavağı to Altın Kum beach. This small strip of sand backed by restaurants is popular with local people.

**The fishing village of Rumeli Kavağı, on the upper Bosphorus**

# The Bosphorus Trip

**Ceremonial gate,
Çırağan Palace**

ONE OF THE GREAT PLEASURES of a visit to Istanbul is a cruise up the Bosphorus. You can go on a prearranged guided tour or take one of the small boats that take passengers at Eminönü. But there is no better way to travel than on the official trip run by Turkish Maritime Lines (TDİ, *see pp234–5*), which is described on the following pages. Laden with sightseers, the TDİ ferry makes a round trip to the upper Bosphorus two or three times daily, stopping at six piers along the way, including a leisurely stop at Anadolu Kavağı for lunch. You can return to Eminönü on the same boat or make your way back to the city by bus, dolmuş, or taxi.

**LOCATOR MAP**

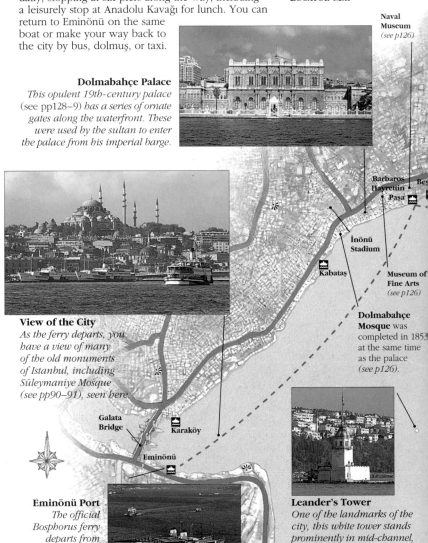

**Dolmabahçe Palace**
*This opulent 19th-century palace (see pp128–9) has a series of ornate gates along the waterfront. These were used by the sultan to enter the palace from his imperial barge.*

**Naval Museum**
*(see p126)*

**Barbaros Hayrettin Paşa**

**İnönü Stadium**

**Kabataş**

**Museum of Fine Arts**
*(see p126)*

**Dolmabahçe Mosque** was completed in 1853 at the same time as the palace *(see p126)*.

**View of the City**
*As the ferry departs, you have a view of many of the old monuments of Istanbul, including Süleymaniye Mosque (see pp90–91), seen here.*

**Galata Bridge**

**Karaköy**

**Eminönü**

**Eminönü Port**
*The official Bosphorus ferry departs from Istanbul's busiest ferry terminal.*

**Leander's Tower**
*One of the landmarks of the city, this white tower stands prominently in mid-channel, a short way off the Asian shore (see p130).*

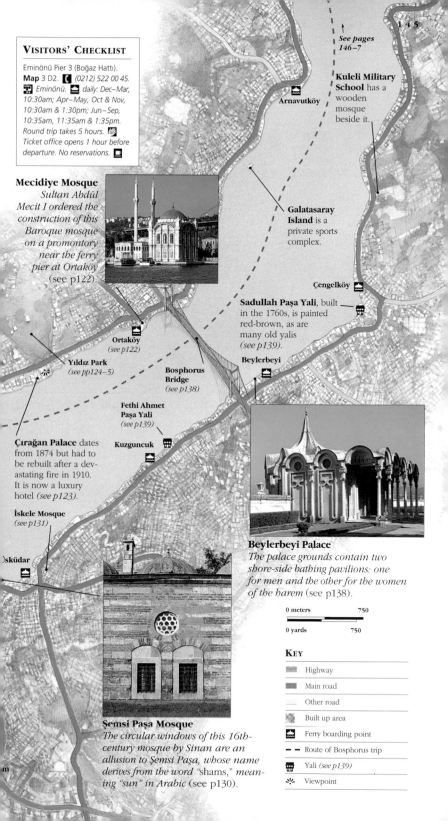

See pages
146–7

**Kuleli Military School** has a wooden mosque beside it.

**Arnavutköy**

## VISITORS' CHECKLIST

Eminönü Pier 3 (Boğaz Hattı).
**Map** 3 D2. (0212) 522 00 45.
Eminönü. daily: Dec–Mar, 10:30am; Apr–May, Oct & Nov, 10:30am & 1:30pm; Jun–Sep, 10:35am, 11:35am & 1:35pm. Round trip takes 5 hours. Ticket office opens 1 hour before departure. No reservations.

**Galatasaray Island** is a private sports complex.

**Çengelköy**

**Mecidiye Mosque**
*Sultan Abdül Mecit I ordered the construction of this Baroque mosque on a promontory near the ferry pier at Ortaköy (see p122).*

**Sadullah Paşa Yali**, built in the 1760s, is painted red-brown, as are many old yalis (see p139).

**Beylerbeyi**

**Ortaköy**
*(see p122)*

**Yıldız Park**
*(see pp124–5)*

**Bosphorus Bridge**
*(see p138)*

**Fethi Ahmet Paşa Yali**
*(see p139)*

**Kuzguncuk**

**Çırağan Palace** dates from 1874 but had to be rebuilt after a devastating fire in 1910. It is now a luxury hotel (see p123).

**İskele Mosque**
*(see p131)*

**Üsküdar**

**Beylerbeyi Palace**
*The palace grounds contain two shore-side bathing pavilions: one for men and the other for the women of the harem (see p138).*

| 0 meters | 750 |
|---|---|
| 0 yards | 750 |

### KEY

| | |
|---|---|
| ▬ | Highway |
| ▬ | Main road |
| — | Other road |
| ▧ | Built up area |
| ⚓ | Ferry boarding point |
| – – | Route of Bosphorus trip |
| ⌂ | Yali *(see p139)* |
| ☀ | Viewpoint |

**Şemsi Paşa Mosque**
*The circular windows of this 16th-century mosque by Sinan are an allusion to Şemsi Paşa, whose name derives from the word "shams," meaning "sun" in Arabic (see p130).*

# The Middle Bosphorus

LOCATOR MAP

Nᴏʀᴛʜ ᴏꜰ Aʀɴᴀᴠᴜᴛᴋöʏ, the outskirts of Istanbul give way to attractive towns and villages, such as Bebek with its popular bars and cafés. The Bosphorus flows fast and deep as the channel reaches its narrowest point – 700 m (2,300 ft) across – on the approach to the Fatih Sultan Mehmet suspension bridge. It was at this point that the Persian emperor Darius and his army crossed the Bosphorus on a pontoon bridge in 512 BC, on their way to fight the Scythians. Two famous old fortresses face each other across the water near here. Several elegant yalıs are also found in this part of the strait, particularly in the region known to Europeans as the Sweet Waters of Asia.

**Paşabahçe glass vase**

**İstinye Bay**
*This huge natural bay, the largest inlet on the Bosphorus, has been used as a dock for centuries. There is a fish market along the dock every morning.*

**Emirgan Park**
*Situated above the picturesque village of Emirgan, this park is famous for its tulips in spring (see p44). The grounds contain pleasant cafés and pavilions (see p141).*

**The Bosphorus University**, one of the most prestigious in Turkey, enjoys spectacular views. Almost all teaching here is in English.

**Fortress of Europe**
*Situated at the narrowest point on the Bosphorus, this fortress (see p140) was built by Mehmet II in 1452, as a prelude to his invasion of Constantinople (see p24).*

**Bebek**
*(see p138)*

**Egyptian Consulate**
*(see p138)*

**Kand**

**Arnavutköy**

*See pages 144–5*

See pages
148–9

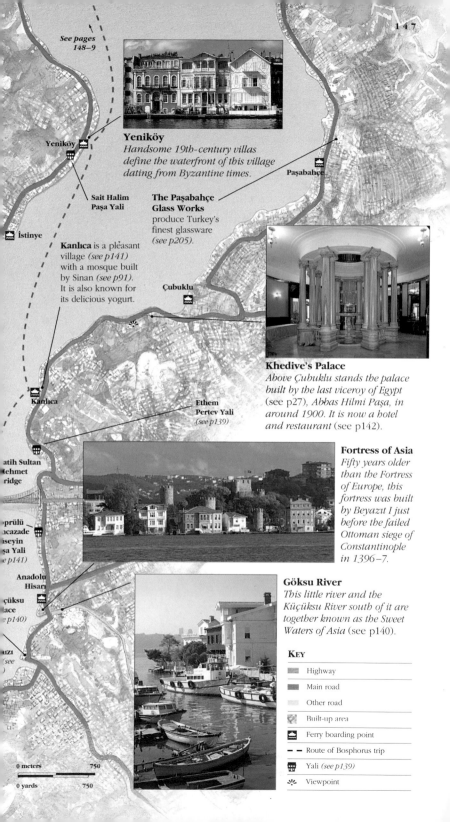

### Yeniköy
*Handsome 19th-century villas define the waterfront of this village dating from Byzantine times.*

Yeniköy

Paşabahçe

Sait Halim
Paşa Yali

**The Paşabahçe Glass Works**
produce Turkey's finest glassware *(see p205).*

İstinye

**Kanlıca** is a pleasant village *(see p141)* with a mosque built by Sinan *(see p91).* It is also known for its delicious yogurt.

Çubuklu

### Khedive's Palace
*Above Çubuklu stands the palace built by the last viceroy of Egypt (see p27), Abbas Hilmi Paşa, in around 1900. It is now a hotel and restaurant (see p142).*

Kanlıca

Ethem
Pertev Yali
*(see p139)*

atih Sultan
lehmet
ridge

### Fortress of Asia
*Fifty years older than the Fortress of Europe, this fortress was built by Beyazıt I just before the failed Ottoman siege of Constantinople in 1396–7.*

prülü
acazade
iseyin
şa Yali
*e p141)*

Anadolu
Hisarı

çüksu
lace
*p140)*

### Göksu River
*This little river and the Küçüksu River south of it are together known as the Sweet Waters of Asia (see p140).*

azı
*(see
)*

**KEY**

| | |
|---|---|
| | Highway |
| | Main road |
| | Other road |
| | Built-up area |
| | Ferry boarding point |
| - - | Route of Bosphorus trip |
| | Yali *(see p139)* |
| | Viewpoint |

0 meters          750

0 yards          750

# The Upper Bosphorus

**Black Sea mussels**

IN THE 19TH CENTURY ambassadors to Turkey built their summer retreats between Tarabya and Büyükdere, on the European side of the Bosphorus. As the hills fall more steeply toward the shore along the upper reaches of the straits, the built-up area peters out. The public ferry pauses for lunch at Anadolu Kavağı on the Asian side before heading back to Istanbul. You can also catch a bus or dolmuş back to the city. The Bosphorus itself continues for another 8 km (5 miles) or so to meet the Black Sea, but the land on both sides of this stretch is now under military control.

**LOCATOR MAP**

**Sadberk Hanım Museum**
*This museum, housed in two wooden yalis, has variety of interesting exhibits. These include antiquities from Greece and Rome, and Ottoman craftwork (see p143).*

**Sarıyer**

**Büyükdere**

**Tarabya Bay**
*The small village set within a lovely bay first attracted wealthy Greeks in the 18th century. The bay still thrives as an exclusive resort with upscale fish restaurants.*

**Huber Köşkü**
is a 19th century yalı owned by the Turkish president.

## FISHING ON THE BOSPHORUS

A multitude of fishing vessels ply the waters of the Bosphorus, ranging from large trawlers returning from the Black Sea to tiny rowboats from which a line is cast into the water. On the Bosphorus, you often see seine nets spread out in circles, suspended from floats on the surface. The main types of fish caught are mackerel, mullet, *hamsi* (similar to anchovy, *see p188*), and sardine. Much of the fish caught is sold at Istanbul's principal fish market in Kumkapı.

**Fishing boats at Sarıyer, the main fishing port on the Bosphorus**

**Rumeli Kavağı**
*This village is the
most northerly ferry
stop on the European side
(see p143). From here
the Bosphorus widens out
to meet the Black Sea.*

**Anadolu Kavağı**
*A short climb from this village – the last stop on
the trip – brings you to a ruined 14th-century
Byzantine fortress, the Genoese Castle, from
which there are great views of the straits.*

**Beykoz**
*Beykoz is the largest
fishing village along the
Asian shore. Close to its
village square, which
has this fountain
dating from 1746, are
several fish restaurants
that are very popular in
summer (see p142).*

Rumeli
Kavağı

Anadolu
Kavağı

Beykoz

0 meters       750

0 yards        750

Halil
Ethem Yali
*(see p143)*

See pages 146–7

**KEY**

| | |
|---|---|
| | Main road |
| | Other road |
| | Built-up area |
| | Ferry boarding point |
| – – | Route of Bosphorus trip |
| | Yali *(see p139)* |
| | Viewpoint |

# EXCURSIONS FROM ISTANBUL

S TANDING AT A NATURAL CROSSROADS, *Istanbul makes a good base for excursions into the neighboring areas of Thrace and Anatolia – European and Asian Turkey respectively. Whether you want to see great Islamic architecture, immerse yourself in a busy bazaar, relax on an island, or catch a glimpse of Turkey's rich birdlife, you will find a choice of destinations within easy reach of the city.*

On public holidays and weekends nearby resorts become crowded with Istanbul residents taking a break from the noisy city. For longer breaks, they head for the Mediterranean or Aegean, so summer is a good time to explore the Marmara and western Black Sea regions while they are quiet.

The country around Istanbul varies immensely from lush forests to open plains and, beyond them, impressive mountains. The Belgrade Forest is one of the closest green areas to the city if you want a short break. The Princes' Islands, where the pine forests and monasteries can be toured by a pleasant ride in a horse and carriage, are also just a short boat trip away from the city.

**Window, Selimiye Mosque, Edirne**

Farther away, through rolling fields of bright yellow sunflowers, is Edirne, the former Ottoman capital. The town stands on a site first settled in the 7th century BC. It is visited today for its fine mosques, especially the Selimiye.

South of the Sea of Marmara is the spa town of Bursa, originally a Greek city that was founded in 183 BC. Another early Ottoman capital, it has some fine architecture.

Near the mouth of the straits of the Dardanelles (which link the Sea of Marmara to the Aegean) lie the ruins of the legendary city of Troy, dating from as early as 3600 BC. North of the Dardanelles are cemeteries commemorating the battles that were fought over the Gallipoli peninsula during World War I.

**Boats in Burgaz Harbor on the Princes' Islands, a short ferry ride from Istanbul**

◁ **The Green Tomb of Mehmet I in Bursa, one of the city's best-known landmarks**

# Exploring Beyond Istanbul

WITHIN A RADIUS of 250 km (150 miles) of Istanbul there are many destinations worth visiting. To the northwest is Edirne, an attractive riverside town with several fine Ottoman mosques. South of Istanbul is Bursa, which lies at the foot of Uludağ, a mountain famed for its skiing. Closer to Istanbul are the Black Sea resorts of Şile and Kilyos, and the Princes' Islands, popular in summer, which are easily reached by ferry. The war cemeteries of the Dardanelles and the site of ancient Troy require a longer trip.

The 15th-century Beyazıt II
Mosque in Edirne

**KEY**

- Highway
- Main road
- Other road
- Scenic route
- River
- Vista

0 kilometers 25

0 miles 25

## SIGHTS AT A GLANCE

**One of the main ski runs in Uludağ National Park**

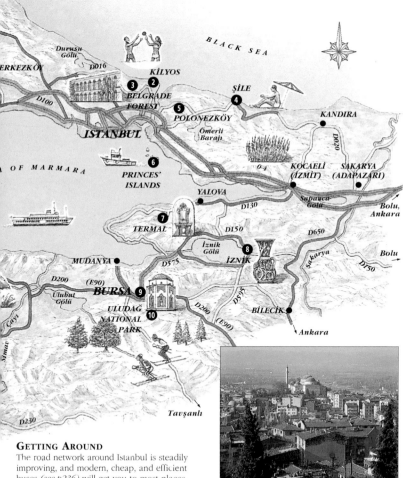

## GETTING AROUND

The road network around Istanbul is steadily improving, and modern, cheap, and efficient buses *(see p236)* will get you to most places. Ferries and sea buses *(see p236)* cross the Sea of Marmara to ports on its southern shore and reach both the Princes' and Marmara Islands.

**View over the picturesque city of Bursa**

# Edirne ❶

STANDING ON THE RIVER TUNCA near the border with Greece, Edirne is a provincial university town that boasts one of Turkey's star attractions, the Selimiye Mosque *(see pp156–7)*. As this huge monument attests, Edirne was historically of great importance. It dates back to AD 125, when the Roman Emperor Hadrian joined two small towns to form Hadrianopolis, or Adrianople. For nearly a century – from when Murat I *(see p23)* took the city in 1361 until Constantinople was conquered in 1453 *(see p24)* – Edirne was the Ottoman capital. The town has one other claim to fame – the annual grease wrestling championships in July.

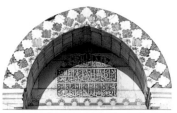
Entrance arch, Mosque of the Three Balconies

Entrance to Beyazıt II Mosque viewed from its inner courtyard

### 🄲 Beyazıt II Mosque
Beyazıt II Külliyesi
Yeni Maharet Cad. ⬜ *daily.* **Health Museum** 🄲 *(0284) 212 09 22.* ⬜ *8:30am–5:30pm daily.* 🄳 🄵

Beyazıt II Mosque stands in a peaceful location on the northern bank of the Tunca River, 1.5 km (1 mile) from the town center. It was built in 1484–8, soon after Beyazıt II *(see p30)* succeeded Mehmet the Conqueror *(see p24)* as sultan.

The mosque and its courtyards are open to the public. Of the surrounding buildings in the complex, the old hospital, which incorporated an asylum, has been converted into the **Health Museum**. Disturbed patients were treated in the asylum – a model of its time – with water, color, and flower therapies. The Turkish writer Evliya Çelebi (1611–84) reported that singers and instrumentalists would play soothing music here three times a week. Overuse of hashish was one of the commonest afflictions.

The colonnaded inner mosque courtyard, unlike most later examples, covers three times the area of the mosque itself. Inside, the mosque's impressive dome is supported on sweeping pendentives that arise just above head height.

### 🄲 Mosque of the Three Balconies
Üç Şerefeli Camii
Hükümet Cad. ⬜ *daily.* 🄵

Until the fall of Constantinople, this was the grandest building in the early Ottoman state. It was finished in 1447 and takes its name from the three balconies adorning its southeast minaret, at the time the tallest in existence. In an unusual touch, the other three minarets of the mosque are each of a different design and height. Unlike its predecessors in Bursa *(see pp162–8)*, the mosque has an open courtyard, setting a precedent for the great imperial mosques of Istanbul. The plan of its interior was also innovative. With minimal obstructions, the mihrab and *minbar* can both be seen from almost every corner of the prayer hall. Like the minarets, the dome, too, was the largest of its time.

### 🄲 Old Mosque
Eski Cami
Talat Paşa Asfaltı. ⬜ *daily.* 🄵

The oldest of Edirne's major mosques, this is a smaller version of the Great Mosque in Bursa *(see p164)*. The eldest son of Beyazıt I *(see p30)*, Süleyman, began the mosque in 1403, but it was his youngest son, Mehmet I, who completed it in 1414.

A perfect square, the mosque is divided by four massive piers into nine domed sections. On either side of the prayer hall entrance there are massive Arabic inscriptions proclaiming "Allah" and "Mohammed."

## GREASE WRESTLING

The Kırkpınar Grease Wrestling Championships take place annually in July, on the island of Sarayiçi in the Tunca River. The event is famed throughout Turkey and accompanied by a weeklong carnival. Before competing, the wrestlers dress in knee-length leather shorts *(kispet)* and grease themselves from head to toe in diluted olive oil. The master of ceremonies, the *cazgır*, then invites the competitors to take part in a high-stepping, arm-flinging parade across the field, accompanied by music played on a deep-toned drum *(davul)* and a single-reed oboe *(zurna)*. Wrestling bouts can last up to two hours and involve long periods of frozen, silent concentration interspersed by attempts to throw down the opponent.

Grease wrestlers parading before they fight

## ⛩ Rüstem Paşa Caravanserai

Rüstem Paşa Kervansarayı
Çilingirler Cad 57.
🄲 (0284) 212 61 19.
Sinan (see p91) designed this caravanserai for Süleyman's most powerful grand vizier, Rüstem Paşa (see p88), in 1560–61. It was constructed in two distinct parts. The larger courtyard, or han (see p96), which is now the Rüstem Paşa Kervansaray Hotel (see p184), was built for the merchants of Edirne, while the smaller courtyard, now a student hostel, was an inn for other travelers.

A short walk away, on the other side of Saraçlar Caddesi, is the Semiz Ali Paşa Bazaar, where Edirne's merchants still sell their wares. This is another work of Sinan, dating from 1589. It consists of a long, narrow street of vaulted stores.

## 🏛 Museum of Turkish and Islamic Arts

Türk ve İslam Eserleri Müzesi
Kıyık Cad. 🄲 (0284) 225 11 20.
🄲 8am–5pm Tue–Sun. 🖼
Edirne's small collection of Turkish and Islamic works of art is attractively located in the *medrese* of the Selimiye Mosque (see pp156–7).

The museum's first room is devoted to the local sport of grease wrestling. It includes enlarged reproductions of miniatures depicting 600 years of the sport. These show the wrestling stars resplendent in their leather shorts, their skin glistening with olive oil.

Other objects on display in the museum include the original doors of the Beyazıt II Mosque. There are also military exhibits. Among them are some beautiful 18th-century Ottoman shields, with woven silk exteriors, and paintings of military subjects.

**The tranquil 15th-century Muradiye Mosque**

## 🄲 Muradiye Mosque

Muradiye Camii
Küçükpazar Cad. ⬤ prayer times only. 🚫
This mosque was built as a *zaviye* (dervish hospice) in 1421 by Murat II (see p30), who dreamed that the great dervish leader Jelaleddin Rumi (see p104) asked him to build one in Edirne. Later converted into a mosque, its interior is notable for its massive inscriptions, similar to those in the Old Mosque, and for some early 15th-century İznik tiles (see p161).

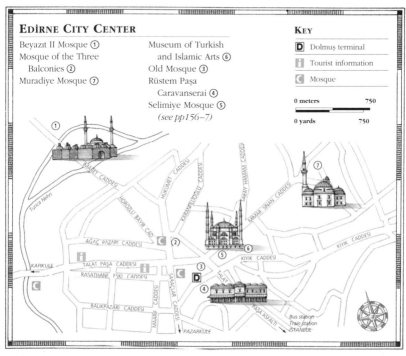

## EDİRNE CITY CENTER

Beyazıt II Mosque ①
Mosque of the Three Balconies ②
Muradiye Mosque ⑦
Museum of Turkish and Islamic Arts ⑥
Old Mosque ③
Rüstem Paşa Caravanserai ④
Selimiye Mosque ⑤ (see pp156–7)

### KEY

🄳 Dolmuş terminal
🄸 Tourist information
🄲 Mosque

0 meters     750
0 yards      750

# Edirne: Selimiye Mosque
## Selimiye Camii

T HE SELIMIYE IS THE GREATEST of all the Otto-man mosque complexes, the apogee of an art form and the culmination of a lifetime's ambition for its architect, Sinan *(see p91)*. Built on a slight hill, the mosque is a promi-nent landmark. Its complex includes a *medrese* *(see p36)*, now housing the Museum of Turkish and Islamic Arts *(see p155)*, a school, and the Kavaflar Arasta, a covered bazaar.

Selim II *(see p25)* commissioned the mosque. It was begun in 1569 and completed in 1575, a year after his death. The dome was Sinan's proudest achievement. In his memoirs, he wrote, "With the help of Allah and the favor of Sultan Selim Khan, I have succeeded in building a cupola six cubits wider and four cubits deeper than that of Hagia Sophia." In fact, the dome is of a diameter comparable to and slightly shallower than that of the building *(see pp72–5)* Sinan had so longed to surpass.

**★ Minarets**
*The mosque's four slender minarets tower to a height of 84 m (275 ft). Each one has three balconies. The two northern minarets contain three inter-twining staircases, each one leading to a differ-ent balcony.*

**Ablutions Fountain**
*Intricate, pierced carving decorates the top of the 16-sided open şadırvan (ablu-tions fountain), which stands in the center of the courtyard. The absence of a canopy helps to retain the open feel of the courtyard.*

## STAR FEATURES

★ **Minarets**

★ **Dome**

★ **Minbar**

**The columns** support-ing the arches of the courtyard are made of old marble, plundered from Byzantine architecture.

**Courtyard Portals**
*Alternating red and honey-colored slabs of stone were used to build the striking arches above the courtyard portals. This echoes the decoration of the magnificent arches running around the mosque courtyard itself.*

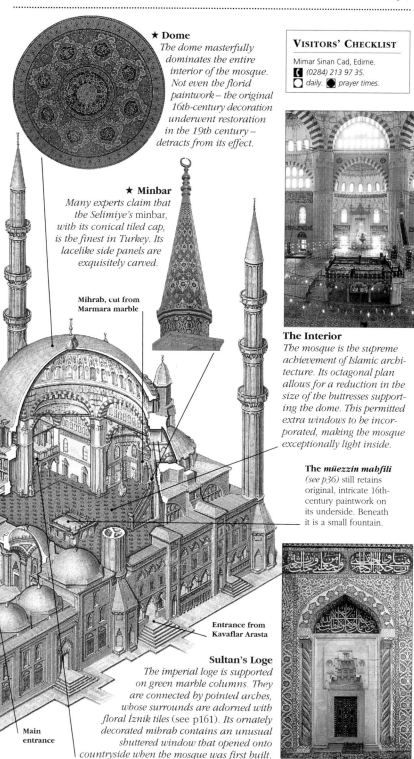

**★ Dome**
The dome masterfully dominates the entire interior of the mosque. Not even the florid paintwork – the original 16th-century decoration underwent restoration in the 19th century – detracts from its effect.

**★ Minbar**
Many experts claim that the Selimiye's minbar, with its conical tiled cap, is the finest in Turkey. Its lacelike side panels are exquisitely carved.

Mihrab, cut from Marmara marble

**The Interior**
The mosque is the supreme achievement of Islamic architecture. Its octagonal plan allows for a reduction in the size of the buttresses supporting the dome. This permitted extra windows to be incorporated, making the mosque exceptionally light inside.

**The *müezzin mahfili*** (see p36) still retains original, intricate 16th-century paintwork on its underside. Beneath it is a small fountain.

Entrance from Kavaflar Arasta

**Sultan's Loge**
The imperial loge is supported on green marble columns. They are connected by pointed arches, whose surrounds are adorned with floral İznik tiles (see p161). Its ornately decorated mihrab contains an unusual shuttered window that opened onto countryside when the mosque was first built.

Main entrance

## Kilyos ❷

27 km (17 miles) N of Istanbul.
🚶 1,665. 🚌 from Sarıyer.

KILYOS, on the shore of the Black Sea, is the closest seaside resort to Istanbul and very popular. It has a long, sandy beach and temptingly clear water, but visitors should not swim here in the absence of a lifeguard because there are dangerous currents beneath the calm surface.

A 14th-century Genoese castle perches on a cliff top overlooking the town but it is not open to visitors. The three ruined towers on the left of the main approach road into the village were formerly water control towers. They were part of the system that once brought water here from the Belgrade Forest.

## Belgrade Forest ❸
### Belgrad Ormanı

20 km (12 miles) N of Istanbul. 🚌 40S from Taksim to Çayırbaşı, then 42 to Bahçeköy. **Park** 📞 (0212) 226 23 35. ⭕ Apr–Oct: 6am–8:30pm daily; Nov–Mar: 8am–4pm daily. 🏛 ♿

ONE OF THE most popular escapes from the city, the Belgrade Forest is the only sizeable piece of woodland in the immediate vicinity of Istanbul. The forest is made up of pines, oaks, beeches, chestnuts, and poplars, beneath which an abundance of wildflowers grow in spring. Within it is a huge woodland park, best visited during the week, since it attracts hordes of picnickers on weekends. The main entrance to the park is near the village of Bahçeköy, and the popular Neşetsuyu picnic area is a half-hour stroll from this gate. Beautiful walks through the forest start here.

The park's other attractions are the relics of the dams, reservoirs, and aqueducts used for over 1,000 years to transport spring water in to Istanbul. The

**Büyük Bent, a Byzantine dam and reservoir in the Belgrade Forest**

oldest structure, Büyük Bent (Great Reservoir), dates back to the early Byzantine era. It is a pleasant half-hour walk from Neşetsuyu picnic area. Meanwhile, the Sultan Mahmut Dam, outside the park's gate, is a fine curve of marble that dates from 1839.

Eğri Kemer (Crooked Aqueduct) and Uzun Kemer (Long Aqueduct) are on the 016 road between Levent and Kısırmandıra and are best reached by taxi. Both have impressive rows of arches. The former probably dates from the 12th century, while Sinan *(see p91)* built the latter for Süleyman the Magnificent *(see p24)*.

## Şile ❹

72 km (45 miles) NE of Istanbul.
🚶 25,372. 🚌 from Üsküdar.

THE QUINTESSENTIAL Black Sea resort village of Şile has a number of sandy beaches and a black-and-white striped cliff-top lighthouse. In ancient

**The village of Şile, a vacation resort and center for cotton production**

times, the village, then known as Kalpe, was a port used by ships sailing east from the Bosphorus.

Şile's lighthouse, the largest in Turkey, was built by the French for Sultan Abdül Aziz *(see p28)* in 1858–9. It can be visited after dusk. Apart from tourism, the main industry is now the production of a coarse cotton that is made into clothing and sold in stores along Üsküdar Caddesi.

## Polonezköy ❺

25 km (16 miles) NE of Istanbul. 🚶 500. 🚌 221 from Taksim to Beykoz, then dolmuş. ℹ️ (0216) 432 31 61.

POLONEZKÖY WAS originally called Adampol, after the Polish Prince Adam Czartoryski who bought prime arable land here in 1842 for Polish emigrants settling in Turkey. Soon after, in 1853, the Poles formed a band of Cossack soldiers to fight for Abdül Mecit I *(see p28)* in the Crimea. After this he granted them the land as a tax-free haven.

Polonezköy's rustic charm is now big business, and a number of health spas and villas have sprung up. A couple of restaurants *(see p199)* still serve the pork for which the town was once famous.

The surrounding beech forest, which offers pleasant walks, has now been protected from further development. As part of this policy, the locals have even waived their rights to collect firewood.

# Princes' Islands ❻
## Kızıl Adalar

12 km (7 miles) SE of Istanbul. 🏛
*19,413.* ⛴ *from Sirkeci or Kabataş
(sea bus).* 🛈 *(0126) 382 70 71.*

THE PINE-FORESTED Princes'
Islands provide a welcome
break from the bustle of the
city and are just a short ferry
ride southeast from Istanbul.
Most ferries call in turn at the
four largest of the nine islands:
Kınalıada, Burgazada, Heybeliada, and finally Büyükada.

Easily visited on a day trip,
the islands take their name
from a royal palace built
by Justin II on Büyük-
ada, then known as
Prinkipo (Island of the
Prince) in 569. During
the Byzantine era the
islands became infa-
mous as a place of
exile. Members of the
royal family and public
figures were often
banished to the mon-
asteries here.

In the latter half of
the 19th century, with
the inauguration of
a steamboat service from
Istanbul, several wealthy ex-
patriates settled on the islands.
Among the foreign exiles to
live here was Leon Trotsky.
From 1929–33 he lived at 55
Çankaya Caddesi, one of the
finest mansions on Büyükada.

Büyükada is the largest
island and attracts the most
visitors with its sandy beaches,
ice creams, and *fin-de-siècle*
elegance. Its 19th-century
atmosphere is enhanced by

**Door to the
Monastery of
St George**

the omnipresence of horse-
drawn carriages. These quaint
carriages are in fact the only
form of public transportation
on Büyükada (and Heybeliada),
since motorized transportation
is banned. At the top of
Büyükada's wooded southern
hill, in a clearing, stands the
Monastery of St. George. It is
a 20th-century structure, built
on Byzantine foundations.

To the left of the ferry pier
on Heybeliada, the second
largest island, is the imposing
former Naval High School
(Deniz Harp Okulu), built
in 1942. The island's
northern hill is the
stunning location of
the Greek Orthodox
School of Theology
(built in 1841). The
school is now closed,
but its library, famous
among Orthodox
scholars, is still open.
The island also has a
pleasant beach on its
south coast at Çam
Limanı Köyü.

The smaller islands
of Kınalıada and
Burgazada are less
developed and are peaceful
places to stop off for a meal.

# Termal ❼

38 km (24 miles) SE of Istanbul.
🏛 *5,018.* ⛴ *from Kabataş to Yalova.*
🛈 *İskele Meyd 5, (0226) 814 21 08.*

THIS SMALL SPA buried deep
in a wooded valley has
been patronized by ruling
elites since the Roman era.

**Ornamental fountain at Atatürk's
former house at Termal**

Termal is situated 12 km (7
miles) from the port of Yalova.
Its popularity was revived by
Sultan Abdül Hamit II *(see p31)*
in the early 20th century, when
he refurbished the Kurşunlu
Baths, now part of the **Turban
Termal** complex. Comprising
four baths and a couple of
hotels, facilities include Turkish baths *(see p67),* a sauna,
and a swimming pool.

Atatürk enjoyed taking the
waters here. The small chalet-
style house he built at the
bottom of the valley, now the
**Atatürk Museum**, preserves
some of his possessions.

🕯 **Turban Termal**
Termal. 📞 *(0226) 675 74 00.*
○ *8:30am–5pm daily.*
🏛 **Atatürk Museum**
Atatürk Köşkü, Termal.
📞 *(0226) 675 70 28.*
○ *9:30am–5pm Tue, Wed, Fri–Sun.*

**The harbor of Burgazada, one of the relaxed and picturesque Princes' Islands near Istanbul**

# İznik ❽

87 km (54 miles) SE of Istanbul.
🏠 *17,200.* 🚌 *Yeni Mahalle, (0224)
757 25 83.* ℹ️ *Belediye İşhane,
Kılıçaslan Cad, (0224) 757 19 33.*
🚗 *Wed.* 🎭 *İznik Fair (Oct 5–10);
İznik Festival (late Nov).*

**Grand domed portico fronting the Archaeological Museum**

A CHARMING lakeside town,
İznik gives little clue now
of its former glory as – at one
point – the capital of the
Byzantine Empire. Its most important legacy dates, however,
from the 16th century, when
its kilns produced the finest
ceramics ever to be made in
the Ottoman world.

The town first reached
prominence in AD 325, when
it was known as Nicaea. In
that year, Constantine *(see
p18)* chose it as the location
of the first Ecumenical Council
of the Christian Church. At
this meeting, the Nicene Creed,
a statement of doctrine on the
nature of Christ in relation to
God, was formulated.

The Seljuks *(see p19)* took
Nicaea in 1081 and renamed
it İznik. It was wrested back
from them in 1097 by the First
Crusade on behalf of Emperor
Alexius I Comnenus. After the
capture of Constantinople in
1204 *(see p24)*, the
city was capital of
the "Empire of
Nicaea", a remain-
ing fragment of
the Byzantine
Empire, for half a
century. In 1331,
Orhan Gazi *(see
p30)* captured
İznik and incor-
porated it into the
Ottoman Empire.

İznik still retains its original
layout. Surrounded by the **city
walls**, its two main streets are
in the form of a cross, with
minor streets running out from
them on a grid plan. The walls
still more or less delineate the
town's boundaries. They were
built by the Greek Lysimachus,
then ruler of the town, in 300
BC, but they were frequently
repaired by both
the Byzantines
and later the
Ottomans. They
cover a total of
3 km (2 miles)
in circumference
and are punc-
tuated by huge
gateways. The
main one of
these, Istanbul
Gate (İstanbul
Kapısı), is at the city's northern limit. It is decorated with
a carved relief of fighting
horsemen and is flanked by
Byzantine towers.

One of the town's oldest
surviving monuments, the
ruined church of **Hagia
Sophia**, stands at the intersection of the main streets,
Atatürk Caddesi and

**Istanbul Gate from within
the city walls**

Kılıçaslan Caddesi. An earlier
version of the church was the
principal place of worship in
Byzantine Nicaea. The current
building was erected after an
earthquake in 1065. The remains of a fine mosaic floor,
and also of a Deësis, a fresco
that depicts Christ, the Virgin,
and John the Baptist, are protected from damage behind
glass screens.
Just off the east-
ern end of
Kılıçaslan Cad-
desi, the 14th-
century **Green
Mosque** (Yeşil
Cami) is named
after the tiles
covering its
minaret. Unfor-
tunately, the
originals have
been replaced by modern
copies of an inferior quality.

Opposite the mosque, the
Kitchen of Lady Nilüfer
(Nilüfer Hatun İmareti), one
of İznik's loveliest buildings,
now houses the town's
**Archaeological Museum**.
This *imaret* was set up in 1388
by Nilüfer Hatun, wife of
Orhan Gazi, and also served
as a hospice for wandering
dervishes. Entered through a
spacious five-domed portico,
the central domed area is
flanked by two further domed
rooms. The museum has displays of Roman antiquities
and glass as well as several
recently discovered examples
of Seljuk and Ottoman tiles.

🕌 **Hagia Sophia**
Atatürk Cad. 📞 *(0224) 757 10 24.*
🕐 *Tue–Sun.* 🎫
🕌 **Green Mosque**
Müze Sok. 🕐 *daily.*
🏛 **Archaeological Museum**
Müze Sok. 📞 *(0224) 757 10 27.*
🕐 *daily.* 🎫

**Green Mosque, İznik, named after the green tiles adorning its minaret**

# İznik Ceramics

TOWARD THE END of the 15th century, the town of İznik began to produce large quantities of ceramic bowls, jars, and later, tiles for the many palaces and mosques of Istanbul. Drawing on local deposits of fine clay and inspired by imported Chinese ceramics, the work of the craftsmen of İznik soon excelled both technically and aesthetically. İznik pottery is made from hard, white "fritware," which is

**16th-century İznik mosque lamp**

akin to porcelain. This style of pottery was invented in Egypt around the 12th century. It is covered by a bright, white slip (a creamy mixture of clay and water) and a transparent glaze. Early İznik pottery is brilliant blue and white. Later, other colors, including a vivid red, were added. The potteries of İznik reached their height in the late 16th and early 17th centuries but shortly after fell into decline.

*Chinese porcelain, which was imported into Turkey in the 14th century and of which there is a large collection in Topkapı Palace (see pp54–9), often inspired the designs used for İznik pottery. During the 16th century, İznik potters produced imitations of pieces of Chinese porcelain, such as this copy of a Ming dish.*

**Rock and wave border pattern**

*Damascus ware was the name erroneously given to ceramics produced at İznik during the first half of the 16th century, with fantastic floral designs in the new colors of turquoise, sage green, and manganese. When such tiles were discovered at Damascus, the similar İznik pots were wrongly assumed to have been made there.*

**Miniature depicting potters**

*Cobalt blue and white was the striking combination of colors used in early İznik pottery, produced between 1470 and 1520. The designs used were a mixture of Chinese and Arabesque, as seen on this tiled panel on the wall of the Circumcision Chamber in Topkapı Palace. Floral patterns and animal motifs were both popular at this time.*

*Armenian bole, an iron-rich red color, began to be used around 1550, as seen in this 16th-century tankard. New, realistic tulip and other floral designs were introduced, also during İznik's heyday, which lasted until around 1630.*

*Wall tiles were not made in any quantity until the reign of Süleyman the Magnificent (1520–66). Süleyman used İznik tiles to refurbish the Dome of the Rock in Jerusalem.*

*Some of the best examples are seen in Istanbul's mosques, notably in the Süleymaniye (see pp90–91), Rüstem Paşa Mosque (pp88–9), and here, in this example from the Blue Mosque (pp78–9).*

# Bursa ⑨

**Basin, Museum of Turkish and Islamic Arts**

BURSA EXTENDS in a swath along the northern foothills of Mount Uludağ *(see p169)*. A settlement known as Prusa was reputedly established here in the 3rd century BC by Prusias I of Bithynia. However, it was the Romans who first spotted the potential of Bursa's mineral springs; today there are an estimated 3,000 baths in the city. In 1326 Bursa became the first capital of the Ottoman Empire, following its capture by Osman Gazi *(see p23)*.

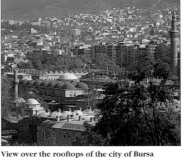

View over the rooftops of the city of Bursa

Today Bursa is a provincial capital whose status as one of Turkey's foremost centers of commerce and industry is evident in its broad boulevards and busy stores and bazaars. Apart from the central market area *(see pp164–5)*, the most frequented sightseeing area is Yeşil, on the eastern side of the Gök River, where the Green Mosque and Green Tomb are the main attractions.

### ◖ Yıldırım Beyazıt Mosque
Yıldırım Beyazıt Camii
Yıldırım Cad. ☐ daily.

This Mosque is named after Beyazıt I *(see p30)*, whose nickname was "Yıldırım," meaning "thunderbolt." This referred to the speed with which he reacted to his enemies. Built in 1389, just after Beyazıt became sultan, the mosque at first doubled as a lodge for Sufi dervishes *(see p104)*. It has a lovely portico with five domed bays.

Inside, the interior court – (a covered "courtyard" in Bursa mosques, which prefigures the open courtyards preferred by later Ottoman architects) – and prayer hall are divided by an impressive arch. This rises from two mihrablike niches. The walls of the prayer hall itself are adorned with several bold and attractive pieces of calligraphic design *(see p95)*.

### ◖ Green Tomb
Yeşil Türbe
Yeşil Cad. ☐ daily. 🖼 donation.

The tomb of Mehmet I *(see p30)*, which stands elevated above the mosque among tall cypress trees, is one of the city's most prominent landmarks. It was built between 1414 and 1421. The tomb is much closer to the Seljuk *(see p19)* style of architecture than Classical Ottoman. Its exterior is covered in green tiles, although these are mostly 19th-century replacements for the original faïence. However, a few older tiles remain around the entrance portal.

The interior, entered through a pair of superbly carved wooden doors, is simply dazzling. The space is small, and the ornamentation, covering a relatively large surface area, is breathtaking in its depth of color and detail. The mihrab has especially intricate tile panels, including a representation of a mosque lamp hanging from a gold chain between two candles.

The sultan's magnificent sarcophagus is covered in exquisite tiles and adorned by a long Koranic inscription. Nearby sarcophagi contain the remains of his sons, daughters, and nursemaid.

### ◖ Green Mosque
Yeşil Cami
Yeşil Cad. ☐ daily.

Bursa's most famous monument was commissioned by Mehmet I in 1412, but it remained unfinished at his death in 1421 and still lacks a portico. Nevertheless, it is the finest Ottoman mosque built before the conquest of Constantinople *(see p24)*.

The main portal is tall and elegant, with an intricately carved canopy. It opens into the entrance hall. Beyond this is an interior court, with a carved fountain at its center. A flight of three steps leads up from here into the prayer hall. On either side of the steps are niches where worshipers once left their shoes *(see p37)*. Above the entrance to the court is the sultan's loge, resplendent in richly patterned tiles created using the *cuerda seca* technique. They are in beautiful greens, blues, and yellows, with threads of gold that were added after firing.

The Green Tomb and Green Mosque, Bursa's most distinctive monuments

The tiling of the prayer hall was carried out by Ali Ibn İlyas Ali, who learned his art in Samarkand. It was the first time that tiles were used extensively in an Ottoman mosque and set a precedent for the later widespread use of İznik tiles (see p161). The tiles covering the walls of the prayer hall, which is well lit by floor-level windows, are simple, green, and hexagonal. Against this plain backdrop, the effect of the mihrab is especially glorious. Predominantly turquoise, deep blue,

and white, with touches of gold, the mihrab's tiles depict flowers, leaves, arabesques, and geometric patterns. The mosque's exterior was also once clad in tiles, but they have since disappeared.

### 🏛 Museum of Turkish and Islamic Arts

Türk ve İslam Eserleri Müzesi
Yeşil Cad. 📞 (0224) 327 76 79.
🕐 Tue–Sun. 🎟

This museum is housed in a fine Ottoman building, the former *medrese (see p36)* of the Green Mosque. A colon-

nade surrounds its courtyard on three sides, and the cells leading off from it, formerly used by the students, are now exhibition galleries. At the far end of the courtyard is the large, domed hall that was originally the main classroom.

Exhibits dating from the 12th–20th centuries include Seljuk and Ottoman ceramics, elaborately decorated Korans, and costumes ranging from linen dervish robes to ornate wedding gowns. A display on Turkish baths (see p67) features embroidered towels and exotic high-heeled silver bath clogs. There is also a recreated setting of a traditional circumcision room, complete with a four-poster bed.

**Façade of the Museum of Turkish and Islamic Arts**

## BURSA CITY CENTER

Alaeddin Mosque ⑦
Archaeological Museum ⑩
Green Mosque ③
Green Tomb ②
Hüsnü Züber House ⑨

Muradiye Mosque ⑧
Museum of Turkish
    and Islamic Arts ④
Osman Gazi Tomb ⑥
Tophane Citadel ⑤
Yıldırım Beyazıt Mosque ①

### KEY

Street-by-Street area
See pp164–5

🚌 Bus station

🅳 Dolmuş terminal

ℹ Tourist information

🅲 Mosque

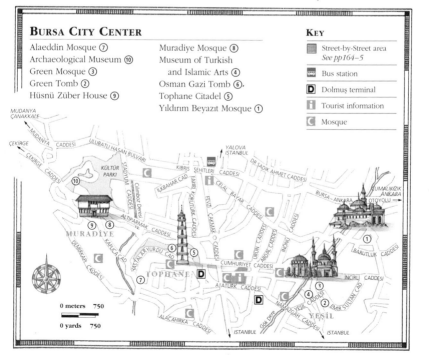

# Bursa: The Market Area

URSA'S CENTRAL MARKET AREA is a warren of streets and ancient Ottoman courtyards (hans). The area is still central to Bursa's commercial activity and is a good place to experience the life of the city. Here too you can buy the local fabrics for which the town is famous, particularly handmade lace, towels, and silk. The silkworm was introduced to the Byzantine Empire in the 6th century, and there is still a brisk trade in silk cocoons carried out in Koza Han in June and July. Among the many other items on sale today are the lovely hand-painted, camelskin Karagöz puppets *(see p168)*.

★ **Covered Bazaar**
*The great bazaar, built by Mehmet I in the 15th century, consists of a long hall with domed bays, with an adjoining high, vaulted hall. The Bedesten is home to jewelers' shops.*

★ **The Great Mosque**
*A three-tiered ablutions fountain stands beneath the central dome of this monumental mosque, which was erected in 1396–9.*

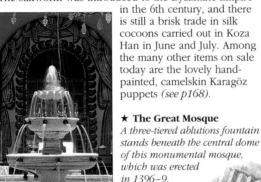

**Şengül Hamamı Turkish baths**

**Bey Han** (also called Emir Han) was built as part of the Orhan Gazi Mosque complex to provide revenue for the mosque's upkeep.

**Cafés**

**The Bey Hamamı** (1339) is the oldest Turkish baths building in the world. It now houses workshops.

**Koza Park**
*The gardens in front of Koza Han, with their fountains, benches, and shaded café tables, are a popular meeting place for locals and visitors throughout the day.*

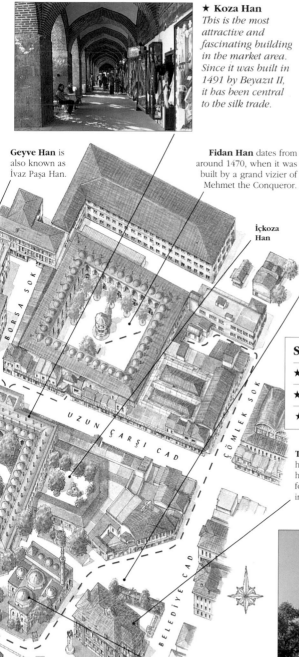

**★ Koza Han**
*This is the most attractive and fascinating building in the market area. Since it was built in 1491 by Beyazıt II, it has been central to the silk trade.*

**Geyve Han** is also known as İvaz Paşa Han.

**Fidan Han** dates from around 1470, when it was built by a grand vizier of Mehmet the Conqueror.

**İçkoza Han**

**Flower Market**
*The numerous bunches of flowers for sale in the streets around the town hall make a picturesque sight in the midst of Bursa's bustling market area.*

BORSA SOK

UZUN ÇARŞI CAD

SÖMLEK SOK

0 meters          40
0 yards           40

**STAR SIGHTS**

★ **Great Mosque**

★ **Covered Bazaar**

★ **Koza Han**

**The Belediye**, Bursa's town hall, is a Swiss chalet-style, half-timbered building that forms a surprising landmark in the center of the town.

BELEDİYE CAD

**Tourist information**

**KEY**

– – –   Suggested route

**Orhan Gazi Mosque**
*Built in 1339, just 13 years after the Ottoman conquest of Bursa, this mosque is the oldest of the city's imperial mosques.*

# Bursa: Tophane and Muradiye

**The clocktower in Tophane**

TOPHANE, the most ancient part of Bursa, is distinguished by its clocktower, which stands on top of a hill. This area was formerly the site of the citadel and is bounded by what remains of the original Byzantine walls. It is also known as *Hisar*, which means "fortress" in Turkish. If you continue westward for 2 km (1 mile), crossing the Cılımboz River, you come to the historic district of Muradiye. The 15th-century Muradiye Mosque, from which this suburb takes its name, is one of the most impressive royal mosque and tomb complexes in the city.

### Exploring Tophane

Tophane's northern limit is marked by the best-preserved section of the citadel walls, built onto an outcrop of rock. At the top is a pleasant, café-filled park, which also contains the imposing clocktower and the tombs of the founders of the Ottoman dynasty. From here you can look over the lower part of Tophane, where typical Ottoman houses still line many of the twisting streets. Pınarbaşı Kapısı, at Tophane's southern point, is the gate through which Orhan Gazi first entered Bursa in 1326 *(see p23)*.

### 🏛 Tophane Citadel
Hisar
Osman Gazi Cad. ⬤ *daily.* ♿
The citadel walls can be viewed from a set of steps that lead uphill from the intersection of Cemal Nadir Caddesi and Atatürk Caddesi. These steps end at the tea gardens above. The citadel fell into Turkish hands when

Orhan Gazi's troops broke through its walls. Later, he built a wooden palace inside the citadel and had the old Byzantine ramparts refortified. The walls had until this era delimited the entire circumference of the ancient city. However, Orhan began to encourage Bursa's expansion and developed the present-day commercial heart of the city farther to the east.

South of Hastalaryurdu Caddesi is an area notable for its old Ottoman houses *(see p61)*. Most of these have overhanging upper stories. They consist of a timber frame filled in with adobe, plastered over, and painted in bright colors. Kaleiçi Sokağı, which can be reached down Karadut Sokağı from Hastalaryurdu Caddesi, is one of the best streets of these houses.

### 🔲 Tombs of Osman and Orhan Gazi
Osman & Orhan Gazi Türbeleri
Ulu Cami Cad. ⬤ *daily.* 📷 *donation.*
Osman Gazi began the process of Ottoman expansion in the 13th century *(see p23)* and attempted to capture Bursa. But it was his son, Orhan, who took the city just before his father died. Orhan brought his father's body to be buried in the baptistry of a converted church, and he himself was later buried in the nave. The tombs that can be seen today date from 1868. They were rebuilt after the destruction of the church and the original tombs in an earthquake in 1855. Fragments of the church's mosaic floor survive inside the tomb of Orhan Gazi.

**Tomb of Osman Gazi, the first great Ottoman leader**

### 🔲 Alaeddin Mosque
Alaeddin Camii
Alaeddin Mahallesi. ⬤ *prayer times only.* 🚫
Further exploration in the Tophane area reveals the Alaeddin Mosque, the oldest in Bursa, built within 10 years of the city's conquest. It is in the form of a simple domed square, fronted by a portico of four Byzantine columns with capitals. The mosque was commissioned by Alaeddin Bey, brother of and vizier *(see p37)* to Orhan Gazi.

### Exploring Muradiye

Muradiye is a leafy, largely residential district. Close to the Muradiye Mosque are the Hüsnü Züber House and the Ottoman House, two fine examples of traditional Turkish homes. To the north is a park, whose attractions include a boating lake and the Archaeological Museum.

### 🔲 Muradiye Mosque
Muradiye Külliyesi
Murat II Cad. ⬤ *daily.* 📷 *donation.*
This mosque complex was built by Murat II, father of Mehmet the Conqueror *(see p24)*, in the early 15th century. The mosque itself is preceded by a graceful domed portico.

**Popular café in the park above the ancient citadel walls in Tophane**

**Octagonal tomb of Mustafa in the grounds of Muradiye Mosque**

Its wooden door is finely carved, and the interior is decorated with early İznik tiles *(see p161)*. The *medrese*, beside the mosque, is now a medical clinic. It is a perfectly square building, with rooms surrounding a central garden courtyard. Its *dershane*, or main classroom, is richly tiled and adorned with an ornate brickwork façade.

The mosque garden, with its cypresses, well-tended flower beds, and fountains, is one of Bursa's most tranquil retreats. Murat II was the last Ottoman sultan to be buried in Bursa, and his mausoleum, standing in the garden beside the mosque and *medrese*, was completed in 1437. His earth-filled sarcophagus lies beneath an opening in the roof. The eaves above the tomb's 16th-century porch still retain their original painted decoration.

There are 11 other tombs in the garden, several of which were built for murdered princes. One such is the tomb of Mustafa, a son of Süleyman the Magnificent, who was ruthlessly disposed of to clear the way for his younger brother, Selim II, "the Sot," to inherit the throne *(see p76)*. According to an inscription, Selim had the octagonal mausoleum built for his brother. The interior is decorated with some particularly beautiful İznik tile panels depicting carnations, tulips, and hyacinths. The tiles date from the best İznik period, the late 16th century.

### ♨ Hüsnü Züber House

Hüsnü Züber Evi
Uzunyol Sok 3, Muradiye. **(** *(0224) 221 35 42.* ☐ *Tue–Sun.* 🌐 🚫
**Ottoman House** *temporarily closed.*
Among the numerous well-preserved houses in the Muradiye district is the Hüsnü Züber House. This 150-year-old mansion has been opened as a museum by its present owner, the artist Hüsnü Züber. It was originally a guest house for visiting dignitaries, later becoming the Russian Consulate and, most recently, a private residence.

The house is an interesting example of vernacular architecture. The upper story projects over the street in the traditional manner of Ottoman houses *(see p63)*. Overlooking the interior courtyard, which has rooms arranged around it on sides, there is a loggia. Originally this would have been open, but it is now glassed in. Meanwhile, inside the house, the decorative wooden ceilings – some with hand-painted borders – are particularly attractive.

Hüsnü Züber's private collection of carved wooden objects is now displayed here. These include spoons, musical instruments, and even farming utensils. They are all decorated with Anatolian motifs by a unique technique of engraving by burning, known as pyrogravure.

The 18th-century **Ottoman House** (Osmanlı Evi) is located on the square in front of Muradiye Mosque. It is another fine house, but is closed to the public at present. The upper story is adorned with elaborately patterned brickwork. Shutters and grates hide the windows.

**Hüsnü Züber House, dating from the mid-19th century**

### 🏛 Archaeological Museum

Arkeoloji Müzesi
Inside Kültür Parkı. **(** *(0224) 234 49 18.* ☐ *Tue–Sun.* 🌐
Finds dating from the third millennium BC to the Ottoman conquest of Bursa are collected in this museum. In the first hall there are clasps, vessels, and an inscription from the Phrygian period. Other exhibits include Roman and Hellenistic jewelry and ceramics, a number of Roman statues of Cybele, goddess of nature, and a Roman bronze of the god Apollo with strange, lifelike eyes. There are also displays of Byzantine religious objects and coins.

**Muradiye Mosque, constructed by Murat II**

# Bursa: Çekirge

WITH A NAME THAT TRANSLATES literally as "Realm of the Cicadas," Çekirge still earns Bursa the tag of Yeşil, or "Green," by which it is known in Turkey. This leafy western spa suburb of the city has attracted visitors to its mineral springs since Roman times. In the 6th century the Emperor Justinian (see p18) built a bath-house here, and his wife Theodora later arrived with a retinue of 4,000. Çekirge is also the location of most of the city's finest hotels, and the area's hillside setting affords some spectacular views.

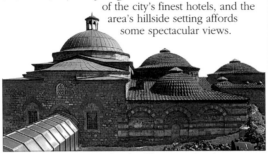

Çekirge's Old Spa, dating back to the 14th-century reign of Murat I

### 🅴 New Spa
Yeni Kaplıca
Yeni Kaplıca Cad 6, Osmangazi.
🅲 (0224) 236 69 68.
🅾 5am–11pm daily.
Despite their name, the New Spa baths have a substantial pedigree. They were rebuilt in 1522 by Rüstem Paşa, grand vizier (see p27) to Süleyman the Magnificent (see p24). The sultan is said to have ordered their rebuilding in gratitude for his recovery from gout while bathing in the Byzantine baths that stood on this site.
The present baths have a central pool surrounded with bays adorned with beautiful but damaged İznik tiles (see p161). They are not open to women. Within the same complex there are two other baths: the modern Kaynarca baths for women and the Karamustafa baths for couples.

### ♨ Çelik Palas Hotel
Çelik Palas Otel
Çekirge Cad 79.
🅲 (0224) 233 38 00.
This five-star hotel (see p185) stands on one of Bursa's main thoroughfares. Built in 1933, it is the city's oldest, most prestigious spa hotel. Atatürk (see pp28–9) frequented its baths. Open to both sexes, their centerpiece is an attractive circular pool in a domed marble room.

### 🅾 Old Spa
Eski Kaplıca
Çekirge Meydanı, Kervansaray.
🅲 (0224) 233 93 00.
🅾 7am–11pm daily.
The Old Spa baths were established by Murat I in the late 14th century and renovated in 1512 during the reign of Beyazıt II. Remnants of an earlier building, said to date from the reign of Emperor Justinian (see p18), are also visible. These include some Byzantine columns and capitals in the hararet (steam

room) of the men's section (see p67). You enter the baths through the new Kervansaray Termal Hotel. Spring water, said to cure skin diseases and rheumatism, bubbles into the central pool of both the men's and women's sections at 113 °F (45 °C). The women's baths are not as old or as grand but are still the most attractive women-only ones in Bursa.

### 🅲 Murat I Hüdavendigar Mosque
Murat I Hüdavendigar Camii
I. Murat Cad, Çekirge. 🅾 daily.
Bursa's most unusual mosque was built for Murat I, self-styled Hüdavendigar, meaning "Creator of the Universe," in 1385. It is unlike any other mosque in the Ottoman world: its prayer hall is on the ground floor, with the medrese built around a second level.
The façade looks more like that of a palace than a mosque, with a five-arched portico surmounted by a colonnade. This colonnade in turn has five sets of double-arched windows divided by Byzantine columns. Inside, the domed court and prayer hall rise through both stories. The upper-story colonnade leads to the cells of the medrese. On this level, passageways lead around both sides of the mosque to a mysterious room, located over the mihrab, whose original purpose is unknown.

## KARAGÖZ SHADOW PUPPETS

Suspended above Çekirge Caddesi is an imposing monument to the town's two famous scapegoats, Karagöz and Hacıvat. According to legend, these local clowns were executed in the 14th century for distracting their fellow workers while building the Orhan Gazi Mosque (see p165). It is said that Sultan Orhan (see p30) created a shadow play about them in remorse. In fact, shadow puppet theater arrived in Turkey later and is thought to have originated in Southeast Asia. Selim I is reported to have brought it back to Istanbul after his Egyptian campaign in 1517. The camel-skin puppets are 14–16 in (35–40 cm) high, brightly dyed and oiled to aid translucency. They are still made today and can be purchased in an antique shop in the Bedesten run by Şinasi Çelikkol, who also occasionally puts on shows.

Cadi, a witch in the Karagöz puppet shows

**Uludağ National Park, a popular ski resort in winter**

# Uludağ National Park ⑩

Uludağ Milli Parkı

100 km (60 miles) S of Istanbul.
📞 (0224) 271 51 68. 🚡 Teleferik to Sarıalan, then dolmuş. 🕐 daily. 🅿️ only for vehicles.

ONE OF A NUMBER of Turkish mountains to claim the title of Mount Olympus, Uludağ was believed by the Bithynians (of northwest Asia Minor) to be the home of the gods. In the Byzantine era, it was home to several monastic orders. After the Ottoman conquest of Bursa, Muslim dervishes (see p104) moved into their abandoned monasteries. Nowadays, however, no traces of Uludağ's former religious communities remain.

A visit to Uludağ National Park is especially enjoyable in spring or summer, when its alpine heights are relatively cool and it becomes a popular picnic area. The park includes 27,000 acres (67,000 hectares) of woodland. As you ascend, the deciduous beech, oak, and hazel gradually give way to juniper and aspen, and finally to dwarf junipers. In spring, hyacinths and crocuses blanket the wooded slopes.

In winter, Uludağ is transformed into Turkey's most fashionable ski resort. The industry centers on the Oteller region, which has good alpine-style hotels.

Osman Gazi (see p23) is supposed to have founded seven villages for his seven sons and their brides in the Bursa region. **Cumalıkızık**, on the lower slopes of Uludağ, is the most perfectly preserved of the five surviving villages and is now registered as a national monument. Among its houses are many 750-year-old half-timbered buildings. The village can be reached by minibus from Bursa.

# Bird Paradise National Park ⑪

Kuşcenneti Milli Parkı

115 km (70 miles) SW of Istanbul.
📞 (0266) 735 54 22. 🚌 from Bandırma. 🕐 8am till sunset daily. 🅿️ to park only.

AN ESTIMATED 255 species of birds visit Bird Paradise National Park at the edge of Kuş Gölü, the lake formerly known as Manyas Gölü. Located on the great migratory paths between Europe and Asia, the park is a combination of plant cover, reed beds, and a lake that supports at least 20 species of fish.

At the entrance to the park, there is a small museum with displays about various birds.

**Spoonbill wading in the lake at Bird Paradise National Park**

Binoculars are provided at the desk, and visitors make their way to an observation tower.

Two main groups of birds visit the lake – those that come here to breed (March–July) and those that pass by during migration, either heading south (November) or north (April–May). Among the numerous different birds that breed around the lake are the endangered Dalmatian pelican, the great crested grebe, cormorants, herons, bitterns, and spoonbills. The migratory birds, which can be seen in spring and autumn, include storks, cranes, pelicans, and birds of prey such as sparrowhawks and spotted eagles.

**Sandy beach on Avşa, the most popular of the Marmara Islands**

# Marmara Islands ⑫

Marmara Adaları

120 km (75 miles) SW of Istanbul.
⛴️ from Sirkeci. ℹ️ Neyire Cad 31/3, Erdek, (0266) 835 11 69.

THIS BEAUTIFUL archipelago in the Sea of Marmara is a popular destination with Turkish vacationers, particularly with residents of Istanbul.

The loveliest of the islands is Avşa, whose sandy beaches and regular summer ferry from Istanbul make it popular with Turks and, increasingly, foreign tourists. The ferry arrives at Türkeli on the west coast. Transportation to the most popular beach, at Maviköy, is by a tractor-pulled train.

Marmara, the largest island, has one beach, north of Marmara village at Çınarlı. It is famous for producing the prized Proconnesian marble.

# The Dardanelles ❸

Çanakkale Boğazı

200 km (125 miles) SW of Istanbul.
🚢 Çanakkale–Eceabat car ferry.
🚌 Çanakkale. ℹ️ Çanakkale İskele
Meydanı 67, (0286) 217 11 87.

Ⓝ AMED AFTER DARDANUS, an ancient king of Çanakkale, the Dardanelles are the straits that link the Aegean Sea to the Sea of Marmara and that separate European Turkey from Asia. Some 40 km (25 miles) long and narrowing to little more than a kilometer (half a mile) wide, they are steeped in legend and have been of strategic importance for thousands of years. In modern times they are probably best known as the setting for a disastrous Allied campaign during World War I.

The classical name for this channel of water was the Hellespont. According to legend, the Greek goddess Helle fell into the straits from the back of a golden winged ram. In another tale, the lovelorn Leander swam nightly across the Hellespont to meet his lover, Hero, until one night he drowned. The English Romantic poet Byron swam across the straits in 1810, in emulation of Leander, and remarked on the hazardous nature of the currents.

**Çanakkale**, the old town at the mouth of the Dardanelles, has two museums. The **Military and Naval Museum** is a short walk from the ferry docks. Its collection includes a pocket watch that saved the

**The Çanakkale Şehitleri Memorial, honoring the Turkish dead**

life of Atatürk (see pp28–9) when he was hit by shrapnel. The **Archaeological Museum**, south of the town center, has exhibits from ancient Troy.

To the west is the beautiful **Gallipoli** (Gelibolu) **Peninsula**. Part of this land is a national park, with an information center near Eceabat. The peninsula still bears the scars of the terrible battles that took place here in 1915. The objectives of the Allied forces' invasion of Gallipoli were to capture Istanbul, force Turkey into submission, and open a new supply route to Russia. The campaign began on April 25, 1915 with the landings of British and French troops at **Cape Helles**, and the Anzacs (Australian and New Zealand forces) at what they thought was the beach at Kabatepe. But currents had swept the Anzac force about 1.5 km (1 mile) to the north, to a place now known as **Anzac Cove**, near Arı Burnu. Here they were faced with unknown and tough terrain, including a cliff.

The Turks, led by Atatürk, managed to retain the high ground of **Chunuk Bair**. The battle here lasted three days, during which 28,000 men were killed. When the Allied

**Statue of Allied soldiers near Anzac Cove**

forces failed to make headway, more British troops landed at **Suvla Bay** on August 6. This new offensive might have been successful, but there was incompetence among the Allied commanders who continually underestimated the Turks and the difficult ground. The slaughter of deadlocked trench warfare continued until the Allies were finally evacuated on December 19. According to official estimates 160,000 Allied soldiers and 90,000 Turkish troops were killed at Gallipoli. Of the former, only 30,000 lie in marked graves. The whole peninsula is scattered with battlefield sites and war memorials.

The best place to begin a tour of the war memorials and cemeteries is at the **Kabatepe Visitors' Center**, which houses a large collection of memorabilia including weapons, uniforms, and soldiers' poignant letters home. North of here, near Anzac Cove, are several cemeteries and monuments. Chunuk Bair, now a peaceful pine grove above the beaches, has a memorial to the New Zealanders who died and some reconstructed Turkish trenches. The British Memorial is at Cape Helles, on the peninsula's tip.

Farther east along the coast stand both the French Memorial and the vast Çanakkale Şehitleri Memorial to the Turks who died defending Gallipoli.

🏛 **Military and Naval Museum**
Gimenlik Kalesi, Çanakkale.
📞 *(0286) 217 24 60.*
⭕ *Tue, Wed & Fri–Sun.* 📷
🏛 **Archaeological Museum**
Atatürk Cad, Çanakkale.
📞 *(0286) 217 32 52.* ⭕ *daily.* 📷
🅸 **National Park Information Center**
Near Eceabat. 📞 *(0286) 814 11 28.*
⭕ *daily.*
🅸 **Kabatepe Visitors' Center**
Near Kabatepe. 📞 *(0286) 814 12 97.*
⭕ *daily.* 📷

# Troy ⑭
Truva

350 km (220 miles) SW of Istanbul.
🚌 *from Çanakkale.*
⭕ *8am–5:30pm daily.* 📷

**Model of the legendary wooden horse at Troy**

IN THE ILIAD, Homer's epic poem from the 9th century BC, the city of Troy is besieged by the Greeks for ten long years. For hundreds of years Troy was assumed by many to be as mythical as Achilles, Hector, and the other heroes in the tale. But a handful of 19th-century archaeologists were convinced that Homer had based his story on a real city and that traces of it could be found by searching near the Dardanelles. In 1865 British Consul Frank Calvert began investigating some ruins in Hisarlık. This interested the German archaeologist Heinrich Schliemann who soon found evidence of an ancient city resembling Homer's Troy. Over the last hundred years, most historians have come to accept that this city must at least have inspired Homer and was possibly even called Troy and besieged at the time specified in the story.

The settlement mound in fact has nine distinct levels (labeled Troy I–IX) representing 3,000 years of habitation. Sadly, the remains are sparse, and it takes some imagination to evoke an image of a city. Many structures were made of mud bricks and obviously leveled before new settlements were built on top.

The city Homer refers to is probably Troy VI (1800–1250 BC), while the Greek and Roman levels, when the city was known as Ilion, are Troy VIII (700–300 BC) and Troy IX (300 BC–AD 1), respectively.

What has survived includes a defense wall, palaces, and houses from various periods, two sanctuaries (probably 8th century BC), and a Roman theater. The grandest dwelling is the Pillar House, near the southern gate. Some believe this is the Palace of King Priam mentioned in the *Iliad*.

More conspicuous is a re-creation of the wooden horse, inside which a small group of the Greeks supposedly hid as a way of tricking the Trojans into letting them into their city. There is also a visitors' center with a video and a scale model of the site.

## SCHLIEMANN'S SEARCH FOR ANCIENT TROY

Heinrich Schliemann used a fortune amassed in business to realize his lifelong dream of discovering ancient Troy. He began excavating some likely sites in the 1860s and started

**Schliemann's wife wearing some of the excavated treasure**

on the ruins at Hisarlık in 1870. An amateur, Schliemann drove a great trench through the mound, destroying some walls in his haste. He soon claimed to have found Troy, though he knew not all his findings pointed to this. His greatest find – a hoard of gold and silver jewelry that he smuggled to Germany, calling it "Priam's Treasure" *(see p64)* – predates Homer's Troy by 1,000 years. Some of the treasure disappeared after World War II only to reappear spectacularly in Moscow in August 1993.

# TRAVELERS' NEEDS

# WHERE TO STAY

HETHER YOU feel like staying in an Ottoman palace, taking a room in a restored mansion or traditional wooden house, or even spending a night in a converted prison, you will find the hotel of your choice in Istanbul. Following a recent boom in tourism, the city's hotels and guesthouses now cater to every taste, as well as all budgets. Hotels tend to be clustered around Istanbul's main sightseeing areas. Sultanahmet contains most of the city's historic hotels and guesthouses.

Beyoğlu, across the Golden Horn, is a good place to look for three- and four-star hotels, including the grand old hotels of the 19th century. Most of Istanbul's five-star hotels are located in the Taksim area, on the slopes above the Bosphorus. Use the chart on pages 178–9 to find a hotel in your preferred price range that has the facilities you need. Fuller details of each hotel are given on pages 180–85. Information on other types of accommodation can be found on pages 176–7.

*Doorman at Hilton (p184)*

## CHOOSING A HOTEL

MOST HOTELS in Istanbul are rated by the Ministry of Tourism according to a star system. They range from comfortable but basic one-star hotels to five-star luxury hotels. Other types of accommodations licensed by the Ministry of Tourism are the converted buildings known as Special License hotels and guesthouses *(pansiyons)*. There are also the nongraded accommodations licensed by the Greater Istanbul Municipality. These hotels provide spartan facilities, with communal toilets and washing facilities and shared rooms.

Accommodations are available in most central areas of the city. The Sultanahmet district is situated within walking distance of most of the city's major sights. Many of the Special License hotels in this area are tucked away on residential side streets. There are

Lounge of the Ceylan Inter-Continental Hotel in Taksim *(see p183)*

guesthouses along Divanyolu Caddesi, the main through road, and on the slopes leading down to the Sea of Marmara. There are also middle-range hotels in central Sultanahmet.

A short tram ride west from Sultanahmet are the Beyazıt, Laleli, and Aksaray districts, packed with one-, two-, and three-star hotels. The cheaper hotels here are used mostly by Central Asian and Russian traders, while many of the three-star hotels cater to package tour groups.

Beyoğlu and Taksim, the old European center of Istanbul, are within easy reach of the best sights in the city. Both have many cheap hotels that are comfortable and dependable, as well as international chain hotels.

The Asian side of Istanbul is a mainly residential area and has few hotels, most of them very basic. There are, however, better hotels in Kadıköy, used more by Turks than foreigners.

## LUXURY HOTELS

THERE HAS been a rapid growth in the number of luxury hotels in the city, and most international chains are now represented in Istanbul. Almost all five-star hotels boast spectacular Marmara or Bosphorus views, and between them they have some of the best international restaurants in the city. All the major hotels have swimming pools and health clubs, which are open to nonresidents for a fee. Many of them also have Turkish baths. Conference facilities are provided, and many hotels have casinos and extensive entertainment facilities. Most can also arrange tours of Istanbul and nearby places through local companies. Some of the largest hotels have floors where smoking is forbidden. They also provide facilities for the disabled and put on special activities for children *(see p176)*.

The luxurious Four Seasons Hotel, formerly a prison *(see p182)*

◁ **Freshly fried fish sandwiches being prepared on a boat in Eminönü** *(see p200)*

## SPECIAL LICENSE HOTELS

IN RECENT YEARS, a number of old buildings have been renovated and transformed into hotels. However, due to the nature of the buildings in which they are housed, most of these hotels cannot provide facilities such as elevators or air-conditioning and therefore do not meet the requirements of the official star-rating system. Instead, they belong to a separate category, the Special License hotel. Some are under private management, while others are owned and run by the Municipality.

The Special License hotels constitute some of Istanbul's most interesting and attractive hotels. They are often located in the residential streets of historic areas and range from small, modestly priced traditional wooden houses to luxury Ottoman mansions. Even though they lack some modern conveniences, Special License hotels, whether large or small, are generally of a high standard. The authentic period decor of many of them gives even the larger ones a warm atmosphere. Many Special License hotels exist only as a result of the efforts of the

**Latticed window of a Special License hotel**

Turkish Touring and Automobile Club (the TTOK, *see p237*). Led by its crusading director, Çelik Gülersoy, it has successfully preserved the Ottoman atmosphere of parts of the city by saving old buildings from demolition and restoring them. Its work can be seen particularly in the Special License hotels of Soğukçeşme Sokağı (*see p61*). The Club produces books, maps, and other publications in several languages on places of interest in Istanbul and on the history of the city. It also runs cafés and tea gardens at Büyük Çamlıca (*see p133*), in the park at Fenerbahçe on the Asian side (*see p130*), and at other locations.

**Hotel roof terrace overlooking Sultanahmet**

## CHEAPER HOTELS

ISTANBUL HAS many cheap, comfortable accommodations that meet the standards of the Turkish Ministry of Tourism. When choosing a cheaper hotel, however, do not base your decision on the façade or lobby, which may look brand new; it is always best to see a room.

One-star hotels provide the most basic facilities, but often have rooms with a private shower and toilet. Two- and three-star hotels have more comfortable rooms and usually a café or bar. Many three-star hotels offer rooms with a TV and minibar.

Guesthouses vary in terms of facilities. Most provide bed linen and towels, and the better ones will have rooms with bathrooms. All should have communal cooking

**Yeşil Ev (see p182), a Special License hotel**

facilities. While cheaper hotels usually have central heating, they are unlikely to have air-conditioning, but an electric fan may be provided. Some small hotels may not provide hot water 24 hours a day.

## WHAT TO EXPECT

ALL HOTELS listed in this book are comfortable, welcoming, and secure. Front desk staff usually speak English and will be able to give information on sights and travel.

Hotel rooms in Istanbul generally have two single beds and enough space to add a third one if need be. If you want a double bed you should make this clear when reserving or checking in.

Most hotels with three or more stories will have an elevator. There may not be a an elevator in a Special License hotel, however, because of the problems of installing one in an older building. Facilities for wheelchair users are usually found only in luxury hotels.

Noise can be a problem even in some upscale hotels, so in busy areas choose a room that does not face a main street. If you are not satisfied with your room, you can always ask for another.

Breakfast (*see p188*) is usually included in the price of the room and typically consists of fresh bread, butter, jelly, soft white cheese, tomatoes, and black olives, served with tea or instant coffee (not Turkish coffee). Four- and five-star hotels provide a much wider choice, including cold meats, fruits, cereals, and yogurt. Only larger hotels will have restaurants that serve buffet or à la carte meals other than breakfast.

Reception desk at the Istanbul Hilton *(see p184)*

## PRICES AND DISCOUNTS

HOTEL PRICES are usually quoted in US dollars, as exchange rates change daily. However, staff are always willing to quote in Turkish lira or any hard currency. All prices usually include breakfast and tax. Apart from first-class hotels, which have standard prices throughout the year, tariffs differ according to the season. The busy season, when hotel prices tend to be at their highest, is from April to the end of October. From the end of October until April prices fall by 40 percent or more.

Lounge area of the Empress Zoe *(see p180)*

During the brief Christmas and New Year period, the higher summer tariffs are applied. There are no single rooms, but all hotels offer a single room rate of slightly more than half the price of a double room.

You should always bargain with hotels, and expect to get a discount of at least 15 percent. For longer stays of a week or more you can easily get a larger reduction. The price of a room usually varies according to its location in the hotel. Do not expect a room with a view if you got it at a discount.

## RESERVING A ROOM

WHILE YOU will always be able to find a room of a reasonable standard, it is advisable to call in advance for the best hotels or those of your choice during the busy season. You can book any hotel listed in this guide directly, by telephone or fax. You will probably be asked to give your credit card details, which will guarantee your reservation. This does not necessarily mean that you will be able to pay by credit card when you check out. If you cannot find a place in any of the hotels that falls in your preferred price range, you could try reserving a room through one of the established travel companies based in Istanbul, such as **Meptur**, **Plan Tours** *(see p220)*, or **Vip Tourism**. If you arrive without having reserved a room, the tourist information offices *(see p221)* in the airport, Sirkeci Station, Sultanahmet Square, or Karaköy International Maritime Terminal will help you find a hotel, but they will not make a reservation for you.

## CHECKING OUT AND PAYING

GUESTS ARE expected to check out by noon, but hotels will usually keep luggage for collection later. Most hotels accept major credit cards as well as Turkish lira and hard currency cash (preferably US dollars) for payment. Some also accept Euro and traveler's checks. VAT and service are always included in the room price, although since junior staff and cleaners are usually underpaid, it is customary to tip them. Leave a few dollars, or its equivalent, in the room for the cleaner, or give a larger sum to the receptionist to be divided among the staff. Phone calls and minibar drinks can add to the size of your bill.

## CHILDREN

IN MOST hotels, children up to six years are not charged for accommodations, and many hotels offer a 50 percent discount for those between 12 and 15 years old staying in their parents' room. Some of the larger hotels have cribs for babies. A handful of hotels, including the Ceylan Intercontinental *(see p183)*, provide a baby-sitting service, usually hiring English-speaking sitters from agencies.

Some hotels arrange special entertainment for children. The Merit Antique *(see p182)* organizes Sunday brunches with children's menus, while the Swissôtel *(see p184)* offers a weekend package that includes complimentary museum and movie tickets.

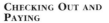

Double room in the Special License Kariye Hotel *(see p183)*

**Guests in the Yücelt Interyouth Hostel**

## HOSTELS

UNFORTUNATELY FOR those on a tight budget, Istanbul is short on decent youth hostels. The best known, in existence since the early 1970s, is the **Yücelt Interyouth Hostel** in Sultanahmet. On a peaceful, tree-lined street beside Hagia Sophia, Yücelt was often the first choice of travelers on the hippie trail in the 1970s. It is still a popular and friendly hostel, offering beds in dormitories, or in more expensive, but less crowded rooms. All rooms have heating. Yücelt is a member of the International Youth Hostel Federation (IYHF) and offers a discount for holders of an International Youth Hostel Card. The hostel has hot-water showers at certain hours of the day, a laundry, a safe, a luggage room, and a cafeteria. Nearby, in Çemberlitaş, the **Cordial** is a newer, more attractive youth hostel with better facilities.

The tour operator Gençtur (see p220) is also affiliated with the IYHF and can give further information on hostels.

## CAMPING

ONE OF Istanbul's main campsites, **Ataköy Tatil Köyü** (Ataköy Holiday Village), occupies a large site on the shore, not far from the airport and the Galleria shopping mall (see p203). It is open year round and has toilets, hot showers, and a communal cooking area. Other facilities include a bar, restaurant, swimming pool, and children's playground. The **Doğa Karavanı** company, on the grounds of Ataköy Tatil Köyü, rents comfortable, air-conditioned trailers for four or more, to use on or off the site. Nearby, **Londra Kamping** is also open all year. It has washing and cooking facilities, a fast-food restaurant, bar, pool table, and soccer field. It has two-room bungalows for rent. The **Kilyos Turban Tatil Köyü**, just behind the beach at Kilyos (see p158), is open in the summer months only and provides toilets and hot showers but no facilities for cooking. There is also a campsite at **Kumbaba Moteli**, 2 km (1.25 miles) outside Şile (see p158). Open between May and September, it has hot showers and cooking facilities.

**View of Dolmabahçe Mosque from the Swissôtel (see p184)**

## APARTMENT HOTELS

ISTANBUL HAS a number of apartment hotels located near central business and residential districts, providing furnished apartments for those who prefer them. The **Akmerkez Residence Apart Hotel**, which is used mostly by businessmen, is in the upscale Akmerkez shopping mall in Etiler (see p203). Its luxuriously decorated apartments have air-conditioning and all domestic appliances. The **Family House Apart Hotel**, near Taksim, rents three-room apartments. Meals can be provided upon request. The **Swissôtel** (see p184) also has fully serviced, luxury apartments.

Many travel agents can help to find apartments of all sizes for long or short stays.

### DIRECTORY

### TRAVEL AGENTS

**Meptur**
☎ (0212) 275 02 50.
FAX (0212) 275 40 09.

**Vip Tourism**
☎ (0212) 241 65 14.
FAX (0212) 230 64 25.

### YOUTH HOSTELS

**Cordial**
Peykhane Sok 29, Çemberlitaş.
**Map** 3 D4 (4 C4).
☎ (0212) 518 05 76.
FAX (0212) 516 41 08

**Yücelt Interyouth Hostel**
Caferiye Sok 6/1, Sultanahmet.
**Map** 3 E4 (5 E3).
☎ (0212) 513 61 50.
FAX (0212) 512 76 28.

### CAMPING

**Ataköy Tatil Köyü**
Ataköy Sahil Yolu, Ataköy.
☎ (0212) 559 60 00.

**Doğa Karavanı**
☎ (0212) 661 41 43.
FAX (0212) 661 41 44.

**Kilyos Turban Tatil Köyü**
Kilyos.
☎ (0212) 201 14 80.

**Kumbaba Moteli**
☎ (0216) 711 50 38.

**Londra Kamping**
Londra Asfaltı, Bakırköy.
☎ (0212) 560 42 00.

### APARTMENT HOTELS

**Akmerkez Residence**
Akmerkez Shopping & Business Center, Etiler.
☎ (0212) 282 01 20.
FAX (0212) 282 06 12.

**Family House**
Kutlu Sok 53, Gümüşsuyu, Taksim. **Map** 7 F4.
☎ (0212) 249 73 51.
FAX (0212) 249 96 67.

**Swissôtel Apartments**
Bayıldım Cad 2, Maçka.
**Map** 8 A4.
☎ (0212) 259 01 01.
FAX (0212) 259 01 05.

# Choosing a Hotel

THIS CHOOSING CHART is a quick reference to selected hotels in Istanbul, many of which have charming decor and surroundings, even in lower price categories. The hotels are described in more detail in the listings on the following pages. For information about other types of accommodation, see page 177.

| | Number of Rooms | Restaurant | Swimming Pool | Attractive Views | Quiet Location | Special License | Business Facilities |
|---|---|---|---|---|---|---|---|
| **SERAGLIO POINT** (see p180) | | | | | | | |
| Barut's Guesthouse ₺ | 22 | | | ● | ■ | | |
| Kybele ₺ | 16 | ● | | | ■ | ● | |
| Ayasofya Pansiyonları ₺₺ | 53 | ● | | ● | ■ | ● | |
| İshakpaşa Konağı ₺₺ | 18 | ● | | | ■ | ● | |
| Konuk Evi ₺₺ | 12 | ● | | ● | ■ | ● | |
| **SULTANAHMET** (see pp180–82) | | | | | | | |
| Karasu Green ₺ | 15 | ● | | | ■ | | |
| Nomade ₺ | 15 | | | | ■ | ● | |
| Şebnem ₺ | 7 | | | | ■ | | |
| Alzer ₺₺ | 21 | ● | | ● | ■ | ● | |
| Ayasofya ₺₺ | 21 | ● | | | ■ | ● | |
| Empress Zoe ₺₺ | 19 | | | | ■ | ● | |
| Historia ₺₺ | 27 | ● | | ● | ■ | ● | |
| İbrahim Paşa ₺₺ | 19 | | | | ■ | ● | |
| Pierre Loti ₺₺ | 35 | ● | | | | | |
| Sidera ₺₺ | 14 | ● | | | ■ | ● | |
| Antea ₺₺₺ | 45 | ● | | | ■ | | ■ |
| Armada ₺₺₺ | 110 | ● | | ● | ■ | ● | ■ |
| Avicenna ₺₺₺ | 49 | ● | | ● | ■ | ● | |
| Citadel ₺₺₺ | 29 | ● | | ● | | | |
| Festival ₺₺₺ | 113 | ● | ■ | | ■ | | |
| Obelisk ₺₺₺ | 41 | ● | | ● | ■ | ● | |
| Sarı Konak ₺₺₺ | 17 | ● | | | ■ | ● | |
| Sokullu Paşa ₺₺₺ | 37 | ● | | ● | ■ | ● | |
| Valide Sultan Konağı ₺₺₺ | 17 | ● | | ● | ■ | ● | |
| Kalyon ₺₺₺₺ | 103 | ● | | ● | | | ■ |
| Yeşil Ev ₺₺₺₺ | 18 | ● | | ● | ■ | | |
| Four Seasons ₺₺₺₺₺ | 65 | ● | | ● | ■ | ● | ■ |
| **THE BAZAAR QUARTER** (see p182) | | | | | | | |
| President ₺₺₺₺ | 204 | ● | ■ | ● | | | ■ |
| Merit Antique ₺₺₺₺ | 274 | ● | ■ | | | ● | ■ |
| **BEYOĞLU** (see pp182–3) | | | | | | | |
| Elan ₺ | 44 | ● | | | | | |
| Gezi ₺ | 50 | ● | | ● | | | |
| Plaza ₺ | 30 | ● | | ● | ■ | | |
| Büyük Londra ₺₺ | 54 | ● | | ● | | ● | |
| Vardar ₺₺ | 40 | ● | | | | ● | |
| Emperyal ₺₺₺ | 52 | ● | ■ | | | | ■ |
| Sed ₺₺₺ | 50 | ● | | ● | ■ | | |
| Dilson ₺₺₺₺ | 112 | ● | | | | | ■ |
| Mercure ₺₺₺₺ | 197 | ● | ■ | ● | | | ■ |
| Pera Palas ₺₺₺₺ | 144 | ● | | ● | | | ■ |
| Richmond ₺₺₺₺ | 109 | ● | | ● | | | ■ |
| Ceylan Inter-Continental ₺₺₺₺₺ | 335 | ● | ■ | ● | | | ■ |
| Marmara ₺₺₺₺₺ | 410 | ● | ■ | ● | | | ■ |

**ATTRACTIVE VIEWS**
Many hotels have beautiful views of the Bosphorus, while others have terraces overlooking the domes and rooftops of historic areas.

**QUIET LOCATION**
Noisy streets can be a problem in Istanbul. This column indicates a hotel on a side street or other location away from heavy traffic.

**SPECIAL LICENSE**
These are hotels housed in restored historic buildings (see p175). They range from luxurious establishments to simple guesthouses, and include some of Istanbul's most charming hotels.

**BUSINESS FACILITIES**
The hotel can provide at least a meeting or conference room with audiovisual equipment.

## GREATER ISTANBUL AND THE BOSPHORUS (see pp183–4)

| Hotel | Location | Price | Number of Rooms | Restaurant | Swimming Pool | Attractive Views | Quiet Location | Special License | Business Facilities |
|---|---|---|---|---|---|---|---|---|---|
| **Kariye** | Along the City Walls | ₺₺₺ | 27 | ● | | ● | ■ | ● | |
| **Lamartine** | Beyond Taksim | ₺₺₺ | 66 | ● | | | | | ■ |
| **Golden Age** | Beyond Taksim | ₺₺₺₺ | 180 | ● | ■ | | | | ■ |
| **Green Park** | Beyond Taksim | ₺₺₺₺ | 81 | ● | | | | | ■ |
| **Maçka** | Beyond Taksim | ₺₺₺₺ | 180 | ● | | ● | ■ | | ■ |
| **Çırağan Palace Hotel Kempinski** | Beyond Taksim | ₺₺₺₺₺ | 322 | ● | ■ | ● | ■ | | ■ |
| **Divan** | Beyond Taksim | ₺₺₺₺₺ | 180 | ● | | ● | | | ■ |
| **Istanbul Hilton** | Beyond Taksim | ₺₺₺₺₺ | 501 | ● | ■ | ● | ■ | | ■ |
| **Swissôtel** | Beyond Taksim | ₺₺₺₺₺ | 585 | ● | ■ | ● | ■ | | ■ |
| **Eysan** | The Asian Side | ₺₺ | 52 | ● | | ● | | | ■ |
| **Bebek** | The Bosphorus | ₺₺ | 30 | ● | | ● | | | |
| **Bosphorus Paşa** | The Bosphorus | ₺₺₺₺₺ | 14 | ● | | ● | ■ | ● | |

## OUTSIDE ISTANBUL (see pp184–5)

| Hotel | Location | Price | Number of Rooms | Restaurant | Swimming Pool | Attractive Views | Quiet Location | Special License | Business Facilities |
|---|---|---|---|---|---|---|---|---|---|
| **Rüstempaşa Kervansaray** | Edirne | ₺ | 79 | ● | | | | ● | |
| **Şile Resort** | Şile | ₺₺ | 52 | ● | ■ | ● | ● | | |
| **Polka Country** | Polonezköy | ₺₺₺ | 15 | ● | | ● | ■ | ● | |
| **Büyükada Princess** | Princes' Islands | ₺₺ | 24 | ● | ■ | ● | | ● | |
| **Splendid Palace** | Princes' Islands | ₺₺ | 70 | ● | ■ | ● | | ● | |
| **Halki Palace** | Princes' Islands | ₺₺₺ | 43 | ● | ■ | ● | ■ | | ■ |
| **Atlas Termal** | Bursa | ₺ | 26 | | | | | ● | |
| **Safran** | Bursa | ₺₺ | 10 | ● | | | | | |
| **Çelik Palas** | Bursa | ₺₺₺₺ | 173 | ● | | ● | ■ | | ■ |
| **En Ön** | Marmara Islands | ₺ | 30 | ● | | ● | | | |
| **Çınar** | Marmara Islands | ₺ | 52 | ● | | ● | | | |
| **Anzac** | The Dardanelles | ₺ | 27 | | | | | | |

---

## USING THE LISTINGS

The hotels on pages 180–85 are listed according to area and price category. These symbols summarize the facilities in each hotel.

- 🛁 bath or shower in all rooms
- 🛏 rooms for more than two people available
- 24 24-hour room service
- TV TV in all rooms
- 🍸 minibar in all rooms
- ▤ air-conditioning in all rooms
- 🏋 gym or fitness facilities in the hotel
- 🏊 swimming pool
- 🗄 business facilities available
- 🧒 caters to children (can provide at least a crib)
- ♿ wheelchair access
- 🛗 elevator
- 🅿 hotel parking available
- 🍸 bar
- 🍴 restaurant
- ♨ Turkish bath in the hotel
- 💳 credit cards accepted:
  *AE* American Express
  *DC* Diners Club
  *JCB* Japanese Credit Bureau
  *MC* MasterCard (Access)
  *V* VISA
- ◖ open (for hotels outside Istanbul that are only open in summer months)

**Price categories** for a standard double room per night, including breakfast, tax, and service:
₺ under $65
₺₺ $65–$95
₺₺₺ $95–$160
₺₺₺₺ $160–$240
₺₺₺₺₺ over $240

## SERAGLIO POINT

### Barut's Guesthouse

İshakpaşa Cad 8, Sultanahmet.
**Map** 3 E4 (5 F4). **(** *(0212) 517 68 41.* **FAX** *(0212) 516 29 44.* **Rooms:** *22.*
🛏 🖭 🗩 *MC, V.* 🗩

A short walk downhill from the entrance to Topkapı Palace, this popular guesthouse has plain but comfortable rooms. The manager, Hikmet Bey, is skilled in the art of making *ebru* (marbled paper and fabric). Examples of his work hang on the hotel walls and can be bought in the lobby.

### Kybele

Yerebatan Cad 35, Cağaloğlu.
**Map** 3 E4 (5 E3). **(** *(0212) 511 77 67.* **FAX** *(0212) 513 43 93.* **Rooms:** *16.*
🛏 🖭 🎰 📺 🗩 🗩 🍴 🗩 *AE, DC, MC, V.* 🗩

A tiny, family-run hotel, the Kybele is full of character, its public areas filled with Turkish antiques and crafts. The rooms are cozy and attractive, most with brass bedsteads. The little patio at the back, where breakfast is served in summer, is designed to resemble an Ottoman street. Advance booking is essential.

### Ayasofya Pansiyonları

Soğukçeşme Sok, Sultanahmet.
**Map** 3 E4 (5 F3). **(** *(0212) 513 36 60.* **FAX** *(0212) 514 02 13.* **Rooms:** *53.*
🛏 🖭 🎰 🗩 🍴 🗩 *AE, MC, V.*
🗩

The half-dozen pastel-colored wooden buildings on the cobbled street behind Hagia Sophia *(see pp72–5)* were among the first of the Special License hotels *(see p175)*. Ayasofya Pansiyonları is a now a row of quality guesthouses. It has elegant and peaceful rooms decorated with antiques in late-19th-century Turkish style. Some rooms are opulent, others understated and simple, but all are comfortable and full of character.

### İshakpaşa Konağı

İshakpaşa Cad 15, Sultanahmet.
**Map** 3 E4 (5 F4). **(** *(0212) 638 62 67.* **FAX** *(0212) 638 18 70.* **Rooms:** *18.*
🛏 🖭 🎰 📺 🗩 🗩 🍴 🗩 *V.*
🗩🗩

This reddish brown wooden building was opened as a Special License hotel in 1996. Its rooms are simply furnished, with iron bedsteads and white furniture. The garden, where you can have breakfast in summer, backs onto the high walls that surround Topkapı Palace *(see pp54–9)*.

### Konuk Evi

Soğukçeşme Sok, Sultanahmet.
**Map** 3 E4 (5 E3). **(** *(0212) 513 36 60.* **FAX** *(0212) 514 02 13.* **Rooms:** *12.*
🛏 🖭 🎰 🗩 🍴 🗩 *AE, MC, V.*
🗩🗩

The Konuk Evi hotel is a restored Ottoman mansion across the street from Ayasofya Pansiyonları. It, too, is under the management of the Turkish Touring and Automobile Club *(see p175)*. This handsome, white wooden building has large rooms, individually furnished in the luxurious Ottoman style. It also has a conservatory restaurant in an attractive garden, ideal for peaceful breakfasts.

## SULTANAHMET

### Karasu Green

Akbıyık Cad 5, Sultanahmet.
**Map** 3 E4 (5 F4). **(** *(0212) 638 66 01.* **FAX** *(0212) 638 66 02.* **Rooms:** *15.*
🛏 🖭 🎰 🍴 🗩 *V.* 🗩

The rooms in this friendly budget hotel are plainly furnished and airy. Like so many other hotels in the area, the Karasu Green has a large rooftop terrace with views of the waterways around the city and the major sights of Sultanahmet. Downstairs, there is a restaurant serving kebabs, *pide*, and *lahmacun* *(see p186)*. Although run by the hotel, it has a separate entrance.

### Nomade

Ticarethane Sok 15, Cağaloğlu.
**Map** 3 E4 (5 D3). **(** *(0212) 511 12 96.* **FAX** *(0212) 513 24 04.* **Rooms:** *15.*
🛏 🖭 🎰 🗩 🗩 🍴 🗩 *MC, V.* 🗩

Tucked away on a rather shabby sidestreet, Nomade comes as a refreshing surprise. The tiny lobby also serves as a sitting room. It is furnished with sofas covered in colorful ethnic textiles, and kilim-covered parquet floors surround the fireplace. The rooms are simple but charmingly decorated, with wooden wardrobes, Turkoman bedspreads, and iron bedsteads.

### Şebnem

Adliye Sok 1, Sultanahmet.
**Map** 3 E4 (5 F4). **(** *(0212) 517 66 23.* **FAX** *(0212) 638 10 56.* **Rooms:** *7.*
🛏 🗩 *AE, V.* 🗩

A tiny guesthouse, the Şebnem has a large rooftop terrace with exceptional sea views. The hotel's pretty little rooms are equipped with simple wooden furniture. All of them have central heating. In the small lobby you can find a cozy resting place to browse through a variety of foreign periodicals.

### Alzer

Atmeydanı Sok 72, Sultanahmet.
**Map** 3 D4 (5 D4). **(** *(0212) 516 62 62.* **FAX** *(0212) 516 00 00.* **Rooms:** *21.*
🛏 🖭 🎰 🗩 🗩 🍴 🗩 *AE, JCB, MC, V.* 🗩🗩

The Alzer is a friendly, busy hotel that could not be better situated. The front rooms look out over the monuments of the Hippodrome and the Blue Mosque. The hotel has a sidewalk café and restaurant for summer dining, and a covered, top-floor restaurant overlooking Sultanahmet.

### Ayasofya

Demirci Reşit Sok 28, Sultanahmet.
**Map** 3 D5 (4 C5). **(** *(0212) 516 94 46.* **FAX** *(0212) 518 07 00.* **Rooms:** *21.*
🛏 🖭 🎰 🗩 🍴 🗩 *AE, MC, V.*
🗩

This Special License hotel, not to be confused with the Ayasofya Pansiyonları, is a restored 19th-century wooden mansion. The floors of its comfortable rooms are covered with Turkish carpets. Some rooms have air-conditioning. The hotel has a small winter garden that serves as a café-bar. The Ayasofya's experienced staff is welcoming and gracious.

### Empress Zoe

Adliye Sok 10, Sultanahmet.
**Map** 3 E4 (5 F4). **(** *(0212) 518 25 04.* **FAX** *(0212) 518 56 99.* **Rooms:** *19.*
🛏 🖭 🗩 🗩 *MC, V.* 🗩🗩

Offering modest comforts in a compact space, the Empress Zoe is one of the most interesting and striking hotels in Istanbul. The hotel's reception is decorated with modern murals inspired by the mosaics of Hagia Sophia, and all the rooms are uniquely decorated. The beds, which include some four-posters, are covered with boldly colored Asiatic textiles. All the rooms, with the exception of two, are small. The hotel has a tiny garden and terrace.

### Historia

Amiral Tafdil Sok 23, Sultanahmet.
**Map** 3 E5 (5 F5). **(** *(0212) 517 74 72.* **FAX** *(0212) 516 81 69.* **Rooms:** *27.*
🛏 🖭 🎰 🗩 🗩 📺 🗩 🍴 🗩 *MC, V.* 🗩🗩

This is a pretty wooden hotel with beautiful views of the Sea of Marmara and its Asiatic shore in the distance. The rooms are plain but comfortably equipped. Ask for one of the three rooms with balconies that open onto the back gardens of the neighborhood. The Historia has a small, ivy-decked breakfast patio, which is open in the summer.

## İbrahim Paşa

Terzihane Sok 5, Sultanahmet.
**Map** 3 D4 (5 D4). **(** *(0212) 518 03
94.* **FAX** *(0212) 518 44 57.* **Rooms:** *19.*
*AE, DC, MC, V.*

The İbrahim Paşa is a charming
hotel housed in a small stone building. The individually decorated
rooms are uniquely stylish, with
furniture ranging from traditional
Turkish to Art Deco. Old family
photos hang in the breakfast room,
while a fireplace in the living
room warms winter evenings. The
tiny rooftop terrace is especially
pleasant after dark, when the
surrounding buildings of Sultanahmet are floodlit.

## Pierre Loti

Piyerloti Cad 5, Çemberlitaş.
**Map** 3 D4 (4 C4). **(** *(0212) 518 57
00.* **FAX** *(0212) 516 18 86.* **Rooms:** *35.*
*AE, MC, V.*

Named after the 19th-century novelist and lover of Istanbul *(see p42)*,
this is an attractive hotel in the
heart of the most historic part of
the city. Its summer garden is next
to the busy Divanyolu Caddesi,
where you can watch the trams and
people pass by. However, thanks
to a screen of green plants, it is
surprisingly peaceful. The rooms
are small and plainly furnished,
but modern and comfortable.

## Sidera

Dönüş Sok 14, Sultanahmet.
**Map** 3 D5 (4 B5). **(** *(0212) 638 34
60.* **FAX** *(0212) 518 72 62.* **Rooms:** *14.*
*AE, MC, V.*

A converted 19th-century wooden
house, the green-painted Sidera
feels like a family home. Although
it is small, it offers most hotel
facilities. Its location – in an old
residential area on a narrow street
lined with crooked wooden homes
– adds to its charm. Also, patch-
work-patterned bedspreads
brighten up the rooms.

## Antea

Piyerloti Cad 21, Çemberlitaş.
**Map** 3 D4 (4 C4). **(** *(0212) 638 11
21.* **FAX** *(0212) 517 79 49.* **Rooms:** *45.*
*DC, MC, V.*

Overlooking a small square shaded
by tall trees just off the main road
through Sultanahmet, the Antea is
a peaceful hotel housed in a plain
restored stone building. Its rooms
are modern and well furnished.
The spacious restaurant serves
Turkish and international dishes.

## Armada

Ahır Kapı Sok, Sultanahmet. **Map** 3
E5 (5 F5). **(** *(0212) 638 13 70.*
**FAX** *(0212) 518 50 60.* **Rooms:** *110.*
*AE, MC, V.*

This modern, atmospheric hotel is
distinguished by its luxury accommodations and dining facilities. It
is located just off the road along
the shore of the Sea of Marmara,
and some of the front rooms have
sea views. The hotel prides itself
on using environmentally friendly
products such as herbal soaps and
recycled paper. There is a large
glassed-in terrace with views of
Sultanahmet and the sea. The restaurant *(see p194)* and bar have a
convivial atmosphere.

## Avicenna

Amiral Tafdil Sok 31, Sultanahmet.
**Map** 3 E5 (5 E5). **(** *(0212) 517 05
53.* **FAX** *(0212) 516 65 55.* **Rooms:** *49.*
*AE, MC, V.*

Occupying two handsomely
renovated historic buildings, the
Avicenna is one of the more expensive Special License hotels. It has
luxurious interiors and parquet
floors covered with beautiful rugs.
The 13 rooms in the back building
are the largest and most elegant.
They also have air-conditioning, but
are right beside the railroad line
and can be noisy. The Avicenna
has several attic rooms with
private balconies, complete with
chaises lounges and umbrellas,
overlooking superb sea views.

## Citadel

Kennedy Cad, Sultanahmet.
**Map** 3 E5 (5 F5). **(** *(0212) 516 23
13.* **FAX** *(0212) 516 13 84.* **Rooms:** *29.*
*AE, MC, V.*

Located right on the busy coastal
road beneath Sultanahmet, the
Citadel is a pleasant hotel with
luxuriously comfortable rooms.
Those at the front of the building
have sea views. It has an attractive
restaurant and a nightclub that
features belly-dancing shows.

## Festival

Piyerloti Cad 62, Çemberlitaş.
**Map** 3 D4 (4 B4). **(** *(0212) 638 22
00.* **FAX** *(0212) 518 50 65.* **Rooms:**
*113.* *MC, V.*

Despite an unremarkable exterior,
the interior of the Festival is among
the prettiest to be found in this
area. The pleasant corner café on
the mezzanine floor, for example,
is a miniature version of the Fruit

Room *(see p58)* in the Harem of
Topkapı Palace. The bedrooms,
meanwhile, are elegantly furnished.
In the tiled lobby café, the wait-
resses wear Ottoman dress. There
is a tiny rooftop swimming pool.

## Obelisk

Amiral Tafdil Sok 17, Sultanahmet.
**Map** 3 E5 (5 F5). **(** *(0212) 517 71
73.* **FAX** *(0212) 517 68 61.* **Rooms:** *41.*
*AE, MC, V.*

The Obelisk is one of several
converted 19th-century wooden
mansions on this street. Its interior
is lavishly furnished in Ottoman
style. A number of rooms have
elegant brass bedsteads, and almost
all back rooms have spectacular
views of the Sea of Marmara, as
does the splendid terrace restaurant.

## Sarı Konak

Mimar Mehmet Ağa Cad 42–46,
Sultanahmet. **Map** 3 E5 (5 E5).
**(** *(0212) 638 62 58* **FAX** *(0212) 517
86 35.* **Rooms:** *17.*
*MC, V.*

This converted Ottoman mansion
is one of the most attractive hotels
in Sultanahmet. The Sarı Konak has
a lovely patio with a small marble
fountain, and an equally charming
roof terrace. Ask for one of the
three bay-windowed rooms, and lie
back on the sofa to watch the street
from behind latticed windows, just
as Ottoman women once did.

## Sokullu Paşa

Şehit Mehmet Paşa Sok 5–7, Sultanahmet. **Map** 3 D5 (4 C5). **(** *(0212)
518 17 90.* **FAX** *(0212) 518 17 93.*
**Rooms:** *37.*
*AE, DC, JCB, MC, V.*

What distinguishes the Sokullu Paşa
hotel is its intimate back garden
filled with plants, flowers, and small
antique fountains. Interior decoration is in Art Deco style, and some
of the rooms have views of the
Sea of Marmara. The Sokullu's
small tiled Turkish bath occupies
part of a wine cellar dating back
many centuries.

## Valide Sultan Konağı

Kutlugün Sok 1, Sultanahmet.
**Map** 3 E4 (5 F4). **(** *(0212) 638 06
00.* **FAX** *(0212) 638 14 60.* **Rooms:** *17.*
*AE, MC, V.*

Close to Topkapı Palace, the Valide
Sultan is a large corner building
with surprisingly few rooms. The
interior is lavishly decorated in the
style of late Ottoman mansions. It
has a rooftop restaurant *(see p194)*
and a summer terrace from which
there are panoramic views.

For key to symbols *see p179*

## Kalyon

Kennedy Cad, Sultanahmet.
**Map** 3 E5 (5 F5). 📞 *(0212) 517 44 00.* ᴀˣ *(0212) 638 11 11.*
*Rooms: 103.* 🛏 🎱 24 📺 🍴 🎿
🔒 🅿 🍷 🍽 🌊 *AE, MC, V.*
🔃🔃🔃🔃

The Kalyon, a large four-star hotel, which is a perennial favorite, is located on the main coastal road below Sultanahmet. The restaurant and bars are set in the hotel's green, spacious grounds and are popular with locals as well as guests.

## Yeşil Ev

Kabasakal Cad 5, Sultanahmet.
**Map** 3 E4 (5 E4). 📞 *(0212) 517 67 85.* ᴀˣ *(0212) 517 67 80. Rooms: 18.*
🛏 🎱 24 🍷 🍴 🌊 *AE, MC, V.*
🔃🔃🔃🔃

The pioneer of Special License hotels, Yeşil Ev (the "Green House") has been a favorite since its conversion in the early 1980s. Rooms are decorated in period style and service is attentive. Room 31, the Pasha Room, even has its own in-room Turkish bath. The tranquil rear garden is charming in every season with its birds, plants, and fountain. Advance booking is essential.

## Four Seasons

Tevfikhane Sok 1, Sultanahmet.
**Map** 3 E4 (5 F4). 📞 *(0212) 638 82 00.* ᴀˣ *(0212) 638 82 10. Rooms: 65.*
🛏 🎱 24 📺 🍷 🍴 🎿 🔒 🛁
🔂 🅿 🍷 🍽 🌊 *AE, DC, JCB, MC, V.* 🔃🔃🔃🔃🔃🔃

The only reminders that this luxury hotel was once a prison are a marble pillar with an inscription carved by a convict, dated 1935, and the iron grating on some windows. Neoclassical in style, it is the only five-star hotel in Sultanahmet. The rectangular building, with watchtowers on each corner, encloses an inner courtyard that has been turned into a beautiful garden with a conservatory restaurant. The impeccable rooms have spectacular marble bathrooms.

### • THE BAZAAR QUARTER

## President

Tiyatro Cad 25, Çarşıkapı. **Map** 2 C4 (4 A4). 📞 *(0212) 516 69 80.*
ᴀˣ *(0212) 516 69 98. Rooms: 204.*
🛏 🎱 24 📺 🍷 🍴 🌊 🛁 🔂
🅿 🍷 🍽 🌊 *AE, DC, MC, V.*
🔃🔃🔃🔃

The President is one of the few hotels worth mention in Beyazıt, an area busy with traders from the former Soviet Union and Eastern Europe. Most of the rooms in this large modern hotel have views of the Sea of Marmara, of the domes of mosques and ancient churches. The hotel has several restaurants and bars, a renowned belly-dance nightclub, Orient House *(see p213),* and an English pub. There is also a tiny rooftop pool and sunbathing deck, and an indoor pool.

## Merit Antique

Ordu Cad 226, Laleli. **Map** 2 B4.
📞 *(0212) 513 93 00.* ᴀˣ *(0212) 512 63 90. Rooms: 274.* 🛏 🎱 24 📺
🍷 📖 🎿 🛁 🔂 🍷 🍽 🌊 🔃🔃🔃🔃
*AE, DC, MC, V.* 🔃🔃🔃🔃

The four large buildings enclosing several courtyards that the Merit Antique occupies today were built in 1918. It is one of the most attractive examples of early 20th-century civil building in Istanbul. When it became a hotel in 1987, glass roofs were put over the courtyards, turning them into elegant lobbies and dining rooms, complete with birds, plants, marble fountains, and graceful chandeliers. Grand spiral staircases in every corner lead up to the rooms. The Merit Antique has gourmet Chinese and Turkish restaurants and the only Jewish kosher restaurant in the city. Rooms, however, tend to be small and dark. Ask for one overlooking the Tulip Mosque *(see p93).*

### BEYOĞLU

## Elan

Meşrutiyet Cad 213, Tepebaşı.
**Map** 7 D5. 📞 *(0212) 252 54 49.*
ᴀˣ *(0212) 252 61 17. Rooms: 44.*
🛏 24 📺 🍷 📖 🍷 🍽 🌊
*AE, DC, MC, V.* 🔃

The Elan is a modest but comfortable hotel for budget travelers, with small, well-furnished rooms. The upper front rooms have views of the Golden Horn. The small bar and the basement restaurant have decorative pools.

## Gezi

Mete Cad 42, Taksim. **Map** 7 F3.
📞 *(0212) 251 74 30.* ᴀˣ *(0212) 251 74 73. Rooms: 50.* 🛏 24 🔂 🍽
🌊 *AE, MC, V.* 🔃

Despite the shabby exterior of this downtown hotel, inside you will find comfortable rooms at budget prices, and attentive service. Above all, this hotel has exceptional views of the Bosphorus from all its back rooms and from the dining area. The view from the front rooms, overlooking Taksim Park, is equally pleasing. The Gezi is close to entertainment and shopping areas.

## Plaza

Arslanyatağı Sok 19–21, Beyoğlu.
**Map** 7 E4. 📞 *(0212) 245 32 73.*
ᴀˣ *(0212) 293 70 40. Rooms: 30.*
🎱 24 📺 🌊 🍷 🍽 🌊 *MC, V.* 🔃

This inexpensive hotel is an old apartment building on an atmospheric street in Cihangir, near central Taksim. It has excellent views of the Bosphorus and the Asian shore from its back rooms. Most rooms are rather spartan in style, and only 18 of them have connected showers.

## Büyük Londra

Meşrutiyet Cad 117, Tepebaşı.
**Map** 7 D5. 📞 *(0212) 245 06 70.*
ᴀˣ *(0212) 245 06 71. Rooms: 54.*
🛏 🎱 24 📺 🌊 🍷 🍽 🌊 *AE, JCB, MC, V.* 🔃🔃

Built in 1850 as the mansion of a wealthy Greek merchant family, this building was converted to the Grand Hotel de Londres in 1892. Since then, only the name of this museumlike building seems to have changed. It is full of dusty antique furniture but still impressive in its 19th-century grandeur. Ernest Hemingway *(see p42)* was one of the famous residents here after World War I, when he was a newspaper reporter. Sadly, although the rooms are large, the furniture and facilities are now worn out and shabby, but the Golden Horn view from the upper front rooms helps to compensate for this.

## Vardar

Sıraselviler Cad 54–56, Taksim.
**Map** 7 E4. 📞 *(0212) 252 28 88.*
ᴀˣ *(0212) 252 15 27. Rooms: 40.*
🛏 🎱 24 📺 🌊 🍷 🍽 🌊 *AE, MC, V.* 🔃🔃

A dignified-looking 19th-century stone building, the Vardar is situated in the heart of the city's entertainment district, close to Taksim Square. The rooms are comfortable, but those facing the main street can be noisy until well after midnight. Rooms at the back are quiet but rather dark.

## Emperyal

Meşrutiyet Cad 38, Tepebaşı.
**Map** 7 D4. 📞 *(0212) 293 39 55.*
ᴀˣ *(0212) 252 43 70. Rooms: 52.*
🛏 🎱 24 📺 🍷 📖 🌊 🛁 🔂
🍷 🍽 🌊 *AE, MC, V.* 🔃🔃🔃

This hotel stands on the site of the Grand Imperial Hotel, one of the great hotels of mid-19th-century Istanbul. It was destroyed by a fire at the end of the 19th century, but the façade of the present hotel was built in the style of the original. The Emperyal is a modern, comfortable hotel. The front rooms overlook a busy street, while the back rooms look out onto the attractive, peaceful garden of the British Consulate *(see p103)*.

## Sed

Beşaret Sok 14, Kabataş. **Map** 7 F4.
[C] *(0212) 252 27 10.* FAX *(0212) 252 42 74. Rooms: 50.* ⬛ ⬛ 24 TV
Y ⬛ ⬛ P Y 11 ⬛ *AE, MC, V.* ⓉⓁⓉⓁⓉⓁ

Tucked away in a peaceful residential street south of Taksim, the Sed has a familiar, domestic atmosphere despite of its size. But above all, most of the upper rooms offer delightful views of the Bosphorus. The hotel has a glass-roofed terrace that serves as a bar-restaurant.

## Dilson

Sıraselviler Cad 49, Taksim. **Map** 7 E4.
[C] *(0212) 252 96 00.* FAX *(0212) 249 70 77. Rooms: 112.* ⬛ ⬛ 24 TV
Y ⬛ ⬛ ⬛ Y 11 ⬛ *AE, DC, MC, V.* ⓉⓁⓉⓁⓉⓁ

A stone's throw from Taksim Square, on one of the busiest streets for nightlife, the Dilson is a large hotel that provides four-star facilities in spacious surroundings. Most of its upper back rooms have views of the sea and the Asian side of Istanbul.

## Mercure

Meşrutiyet Cad, Tepebaşı. **Map** 7 D5.
[C] *(0212) 251 46 46.* FAX *(0212) 249 80 33. Rooms: 197.* ⬛ ⬛ 24 TV
Y ⬛ ⬛ ⬛ Y 11 ⬛ *AE, DC, JCB, MC, V.* ⓉⓁⓉⓁⓉⓁ

Situated opposite the historic Pera Palas Hotel, the tall, modern Mercure is a strong contrast to it. Most of the rooms have breathtaking views over the rooftops of the Galata district, the Golden Horn, the old city, and the Sea of Marmara. The tiny swimming pool on the roof and the large breakfast salon also offer panoramic views. Café Opera in the lobby serves excellent Turkish and international food. There is also a patisserie there. Some of the rooms are reserved for nonsmokers. All are rather small, but comfortable.

## Pera Palas

Meşrutiyet Cad 98-100, Tepebaşı.
**Map** 7 D5 [C] *(0212) 251 45 60.*
FAX *(0212) 251 40 89. Rooms: 144.*
⬛ 24 TV Y ⬛ ⬛ ⬛ P Y
11 ⬛ *AE, DC, MC, V.* ⓉⓁⓉⓁⓉⓁ

Built in 1892 to accommodate the passengers of the Orient Express, the Pera Palas is the most famous hotel in Istanbul *(see p104)*. It has hosted celebrities from all over the world, but its fame is due mainly to Agatha Christie, who stayed here several times between 1924 and 1933. It is said that she wrote *Murder on the Orient Express* in Room 411, which is still available to visitors at no extra charge and is decorated with her books and pictures. The room Atatürk *(see pp28–9)* stayed in is preserved as a small museum. Today the Pera's faded beauty is still witness to its days of glory. Many of the fixtures are original, from the plumbing to the door handles, worn period furniture, and the shaky wood and wrought iron elevator. The salon, with its marble columns and lavish decorations, exudes a majestic atmosphere. The Pera's back rooms have enchanting views of the Golden Horn.

## Richmond

İstiklal Cad 445, Beyoğlu. **Map** 7 D5.
[C] *(0212) 252 54 60.* FAX *(0212) 252 97 07. Rooms: 109.* ⬛ ⬛ 24 TV
Y ⬛ ⬛ ⬛ Y 11 ⬛ *AE, MC, V.* ⓉⓁⓉⓁⓉⓁ

The Richmond offers a choice of views from its modern, comfortable rooms. Back rooms look out over the garden of the Russian Consulate, down to Seraglio Point and the Sea of Marmara. The front rooms face İstiklal Caddesi, with its colorful crowds and jingling red trams. When the hotel is not fully occupied, one floor is allocated to nonsmokers. Within the Richmond is one of the oldest cafés in Istanbul, the attractive, French-style Lebon *(see p201)*. There is also a Turkish restaurant that stages belly-dancing shows.

## Ceylan Inter-Continental

Asker Ocağı Cad 1, Taksim. **Map** 7 F3.
[C] *(0212) 231 21 21.* FAX *(0212) 231 21 80. Rooms: 335.* ⬛ ⬛ 24 TV
Y ⬛ ⬛ ⬛ ⬛ ⬛ P
Y 11 ⬛ *AE, DC, JCB, MC, V.*
ⓉⓁⓉⓁⓉⓁ

This landmark skyscraper, previously the Sheraton, is one of the top international hotels in the city. The imposing lobby is decorated in the style of a fairy-tale Arabian palace, with striking golden staircases, oversized chandeliers, and palm trees. The dining facilities and rooms are more sober. The Ceylan has one of the most beautiful and expansive views of Istanbul in all four directions, dazzling at any time of day. The top floor houses a French/Thai restaurant, Citronelle *(see p196)*; a quality Turkish restaurant, Safran; and the glitzy City Lights Bar. Amenities include an outdoor pool and a high-tech fitness center.

## Marmara

Taksim Meydanı, Taksim. **Map** 7 E4.
[C] *(0212) 251 46 96.* FAX *(0212) 244 05 09. Rooms: 410.* ⬛ ⬛ 24 TV
Y ⬛ ⬛ ⬛ ⬛ ⬛ P Y 11
⬛ *AE, DC, JCB, MC, V.*
ⓉⓁⓉⓁⓉⓁ

Few other hotels can beat the breathtaking views from the Marmara's rooftop restaurant and lounge bar. This towering luxury hotel in the middle of Taksim Square serves as the headquarters of the nearly 1,500 performers who appear in the International Istanbul Festival every summer *(see pp44–5)*. In the ground-level Café Marmara, which spills out onto the sidewalk in summer, you can have a late evening snack surrounded by the festival's celebrities. The Marmara's top-drawer facilities include a small terrace pool and the Brasserie Restaurant, which serves a variety of international dishes at its buffet lunches on Sundays.

# ALONG THE CITY WALLS

## Kariye

Kariye Camii Sok 18, Edirnekapı.
**Map** 1 B1. [C] *(0212) 534 84 14.*
FAX *(0212) 521 66 31. Rooms: 27.*
⬛ ⬛ Y P Y 11 ⬛ *AE, DC, MC, V.* ⓉⓁⓉⓁ

Set in the shadow of the Church of St. Savior in Chora *(see pp118–9)*, the Kariye is a wooden mansion, lovingly renovated by the Turkish Touring and Automobile Club *(see p175)*. The comfortable rooms are decorated in pale pastel colors, with wooden floors and latticed windows. Outside, there is a lovely, tree-shaded summer garden. The hotel has an atmospheric restaurant, Asitane *(see p196)*, that serves excellent Turkish food.

# BEYOND TAKSİM

## Lamartine

Lamartin Cad 25, Taksim.
**Map** 7 E3. [C] *(0212) 254 62 70.*
FAX *(0212) 256 27 76. Rooms: 66.*
⬛ ⬛ 24 TV Y ⬛ ⬛ ⬛ Y 11
⬛ *AE, MC, V.* ⓉⓁⓉⓁⓉⓁ

This is one of the numerous four-star hotels situated in Taksim, preferred for their convenient location close to the central shopping and entertainment areas of the city. The Lamartine's rooms are both comfortable and spacious. The Ming Garden Chinese Restaurant, located next door, is also run by the hotel.

## Golden Age

Topçu Cad 22, Taksim. **Map** 7 F3.
**(** (0212) 254 49 06. **FAX** (0212) 255
13 68. **Rooms:** 180. ▤ ♨ 24 TV
Y ▤ ▦ 5 ➡ P Y ▥
☒ AE, DC, MC, V. ⓣⓣⓣⓣ

A massive, modern hotel in one of
the busy side streets near Taksim
Square, the Golden Age has a large
roof terrace with a small swimming pool and panoramic views
of the city. Its spacious rooms are
comfortably furnished in pastel
shades, with wall-to-wall carpets.

## Green Park

Abdülhak Hamit Cad 50, Taksim.
**Map** 7 E3. **(** (0212) 238 05 05.
**FAX** (0212) 237 76 46. **Rooms:** 81.
▤ ♨ 24 TV Y ▤ 5 ♿ ▥
Y ▦ ☒ AE, DC, MC, V.
ⓣⓣⓣⓣ

Opened in 1996, the four-star Green
Park is one of the most pleasant
hotels in the area. It has comfortable, well-decorated rooms, and
several suites equipped with business facilities. The restaurant is
large and luxurious, and there is a
rooftop bar. The staff can arrange
car and boat rental, and city tours.

## Maçka

Eytam Cad 35, Maçka. **Map** 8 A3.
**(** (0212) 234 32 00. **FAX** (0212) 240
76 94. **Rooms:** 180. ▤ ♨ 24 TV
Y ▤ ▦ 5 ♿ P Y ▦ ☒
AE, DC, MC, V. ⓣⓣⓣⓣ

This large, well-established hotel,
close to the business and conven-
tion centers of uptown Istanbul, is
on a pleasant boulevard with little
traffic. The Maçka is also close to
the shopping districts of Nişantaşı
and Teşvikiye. Many of the rooms
have balconies overlooking Maçka
Park, one of the largest parks in
the city, and the Bosphorus. The
hotel facilities include a sauna.

## Çırağan Palace Hotel Kempinski

Çırağan Cad 84, Beşiktaş. **Map** 9 D3.
**(** (0212) 258 33 77. **FAX** (0212) 259
66 86. **Rooms:** 322. ▤ ♨ 24 TV
Y ▤ ▦ 🏊 5 ▥ P Y ▦
☒ AE, DC, MC, V. ⓣⓣⓣⓣⓣ

Originally an Ottoman palace on
the Bosphorus, the Çırağan Palace
(see p123) is now one of the most
luxurious hotels in Istanbul, and
probably the most enchanting. It
was restored and converted in the
early 1990s, when new buildings
were added. The dining and entertainment areas are decorated in
arabesque style, supposedly resembling that of the original palace.
The Çırağan has an exceptionally
good Ottoman-cuisine restaurant,

Tuğra, and an Italian restaurant.
It is also famous for its outdoor
swimming pool, located right at
the edge of the palatial garden,
giving one the impression of
swimming in the Bosphorus.

## Divan

Cumhuriyet Cad 2, Elmadağ.
**Map** 7 F3. **(** (0212) 231 41 00.
**FAX** (0212) 248 85 27. **Rooms:** 180.
▤ ♨ 24 TV Y ▤ ▦ 5 ♿
▥ P Y ▦ ☒ AE, DC, MC, V.
ⓣⓣⓣⓣ

Located on a tree-lined boulevard
a short walk from Taksim Square,
the Divan is one of the oldest five-
star hotels in the city. Opened in
1956, it is owned by the Koç family
(see p127), who head the biggest
industrial and commercial empire
in Turkey. Many of the rooms
overlook gardens. The front rooms
facing onto the street are noisy
when windows are open, but
otherwise well insulated. The hotel
has a good patisserie (see p200).

## Istanbul Hilton

Cumhuriyet Cad, Taksim. **Map** 7 F2.
**(** (0212) 231 46 50. **FAX** (0212) 240
41 65. **Rooms:** 501. ▤ ♨ 24 TV
Y ▤ ▦ 🏊 ▥ 5 ▥ P
Y ▦ 🔥 ☒ AE, DC, JCB, MC, V.
ⓣⓣⓣⓣ

All the rooms in the towering
Istanbul Hilton have balconies
offering marvelous sweeping
views of either the Bosphorus or
the spacious gardens in which the
hotel stands. Nonsmoking rooms
are available. Extensive leisure
facilities include squash and tennis
courts and a swimming pool. The
hotel also offers the most up-to-
date business services, such as
Internet access, and personal com-
puter connection in guest rooms.

## Swissôtel

Bayıldım Cad 2, Maçka. **Map** 8 A4.
**(** (0212) 259 01 01. **FAX** (0212) 259
01 05. **Rooms:** 585. ▤ ♨ 24 TV
Y ▤ ▦ 🏊 5 ♿ ▥ P
Y ▦ 🔥 ☒ AE, DC, JCB, MC, V.
ⓣⓣⓣⓣ

On a hill overlooking Dolmabahçe
Palace, the Swissôtel commands
expansive views that extend from
Seraglio Point along the Bosphorus. These can be enjoyed from
most of its rooms. Besides its
elegance and luxury, the Swissôtel
is noted for its variety of gourmet
restaurants (see p197), specializing
in Swiss, Turkish, Japanese, Chinese,
and French food. Outside, the
hotel has lush gardens and various
athletic facilities. For evening
entertainment there are several
bars and nightclubs. The Swissôtel
also has a nonsmoking floor.

## Eysan

Rıhtım Cad 26, Kadıköy. **(** (0216)
346 24 40. **FAX** (0216) 347 23 29.
**Rooms:** 52. ▤ ♨ 24 TV 5 ▥
P Y ▦ ☒ MC, V. ⓣⓣⓣ

Standing opposite Kadıköy pier,
the Eysan is one of the better hotels
clustered in this colorful area. The
front rooms have views of the Sea
of Marmara and Seraglio Point in
the distance, but can be noisy. The
hotel is conveniently located for
sights and shopping areas on the
Asian side, and for transportation
over to European Istanbul.

## Bebek

Cevdetpaşa Cad 113-115, Bebek,
European side. **(** (0212) 263 30 00.
**FAX** (0212) 263 26 36. **Rooms:** 30.
▤ ♨ 24 ▥ Y ▦ ☒ AE, DC,
MC, V. ⓣⓣ

Located right on the waterfront, the
Bebek is an unassuming but
charming hotel. Front rooms have
lovely views of Bebek Bay. The
first-floor terrace bar is a popular
spot to have an early evening
drink while listening to live jazz.

## Bosphorus Paşa

Yalıboyu Cad 64, Beylerbeyi, Asian
side. **(** (0216) 422 00 03.
**FAX** (0216) 422 00 12. **Rooms:** 14.
▤ ♨ 24 TV Y ▤ P Y ▦
☒ AE, DC, MC, V. ⓣⓣⓣⓣⓣ

The Bosphorus Paşa is a handsome
Special License hotel on the shores
of the Bosphorus. First built as a
yali (see p139) in 1890, it has been
carefully restored and retains its
original simple but elegant form.
The rooms are large, with high
ceilings, and are furnished with
period Italian pieces. In the basement there is a gourmet Italian
restaurant, Cecconi's, where waves
from the Bosphorus splash right
up against the windows.

## Rüstempaşa Kervansaray

Eski Camii Yanı, Edirne. **(** (0284)
212 61 18. **FAX** (0284) 212 04 62.
**Rooms:** 79. ▤ ♨ 24 TV P Y
▦ ☒ MC, V. ⓣ

An ancient caravanserai, built
by the architect Sinan in the 16th
century (see p155), houses the

oldest hotel in Edirne. It has been skilfully renovated to retain something of the atmosphere of the old inn. The bedrooms are thick-walled and small, with some of their original fixtures, like the fireplaces, but little furniture. Only half the caravanserai, the Büyük Han (Great Hall), is in use as a hotel; the other half, the Küçük Han (Small Hall), is a student hostel. In term time, the students congregate in the courtyard and pool hall below the hotel and practice their English on willing guests. The restaurant is open in summer only.

## ŞİLE

### Şile Resort

Uzunkum, Şile. 〔 *(0216) 711 36 27.* FAX *(0216) 711 40 03.* **Rooms:** *52.*

This brand-new hotel is the most luxurious in Şile. It is located 5 km (3 miles) out of town, but frequent dolmuşes connect it to Şile town center. The rooms are spacious and well furnished, with sea views from their balconies. The hotel has a private beach and an outdoor pool with a children's section. It also has a playroom. The price includes breakfast and an evening meal.

## POLONEZKÖY

### Polka Country

Cumhuriyet Yolu 36, Polonezköy. 〔 *(0216) 432 32 20.* FAX *(0216) 432 30 42.* **Rooms:** *15.* 🚗 🍴 ⓣⓛⓣⓛ

Standing in a lush green garden in the peaceful village of Polonezköy *(see p158),* the interior of the Polka Country is decorated with walnut furniture throughout. The rooms are very comfortable and the hotel also has a sauna for the use of its guests.

## THE PRINCES' ISLANDS

### Büyükada Princess

İskele Cad 2, Büyükada. 〔 *(0216) 382 16 28.* FAX *(0216) 382 19 49.* **Rooms:** *24.* 🚗 🍴 📺 🔌 ⓣⓛⓣⓛ

The Princess occupies an elegant neoclassical stone building in the town square on the largest of the Princes' Islands. Its rooms are comfortable, and some have balconies overlooking the sea. The hotel has an outdoor swimming pool and facilities for children, including a playground.

### Splendid Palace

Yirmiüç Nisan Cad 71, Büyükada. 〔 *(0216) 382 69 50.* FAX *(0216) 382 67 75.* **Rooms:** *70.* 🚗 🍴 📺 🔌 🍽 *AE, MC, V.* ☐ Apr–Oct. ⓣⓛⓣⓛ

Built in 1908, this wooden mansion set high on a hill is one of the most beautiful buildings on the island of Büyükada. The Splendid Palace has a large garden and an enticing outdoor swimming pool. Its balconied rooms have magnificent sea views. Sadly, the interiors have been somewhat neglected.

### Halki Palace

Refah Şehitleri Cad 88, Heybeliada. 〔 *(0216) 351 88 90.* FAX *(0216) 351 84 83.* **Rooms:** *43.* 🚗 🍴 📺 🔌 🍽 🍴 🍽 *MC, V.* ⓣⓛⓣⓛⓣⓛ

Set in a large, terraced garden, the Halki Palace was built in the mid-19th century. The interior of the white wooden building has been lavishly decorated with a combination of classic and modern furniture, glittering chandeliers, and antique pendulum clocks, one of which shows the ferry timetable from the island to the city. The Halki commands breathtaking views of the other islands and the Asian shore of Istanbul.

## BURSA

### Atlas Termal

Hamamlar Cad 35, Çekirge, Bursa. 〔 *(0224) 234 41 00.* FAX *(0224) 236 46 05.* **Rooms:** *26.* 🚗 🍴 📺 🔌 🍽 ⓣⓛ

The Atlas Termal is a small, intimate hotel with a pleasant open courtyard where breakfast is served. The interior is attractively decorated with modern stained glass, and a glass-walled elevator gives access to the upper floors. In the basement, as in many of the hotels in Çekirge, there are two well-kept marble Turkish baths, fed by natural hot spring water.

### Safran

Ortapazarı Cad, Arka Sok 4, Bursa. 〔 *(0224) 224 72 16.* FAX *(0224) 224 72 19.* **Rooms:** *10.* 🚗 🍴 📺 🔌 🍽 *AE, MC, V.* ⓣⓛⓣⓛ

This attractively renovated, half-timbered building is over one hundred years old. It is located in an atmospheric part of town renowned for its old buildings. The rooms are small and furnished in a disappointingly contemporary style, but the restaurant is excellent, serving a variety of hot and cold meat and vegetable dishes.

### Çelik Palas

Çekirge Cad 79, Çekirge, Bursa. 〔 *(0224) 233 38 00.* FAX *(0224) 236 19 10.* **Rooms:** *173.* 🚗 🍴 📺 📺 🔌 🍽 🍴 🍽 🔌 🍽 *AE, DC, MC, V.* ⓣⓛⓣⓛⓣⓛ

This renowned spa hotel *(see p168)* is situated high on the hillside above Bursa. From the front rooms there are spectacular views over Bursa, while back rooms look out toward the mountains that rise up behind the city. The hotel's luxurious Turkish bath is unusual in having a plunge pool (usually a feature of Roman baths) filled by a constant flow of hot spring water.

## MARMARA ISLANDS

### En Ön

En Ön Tatil Köyü, Marmara Island. 〔 *(0266) 885 50 32.* **Rooms:** *30.* 🚗 🍴 🔌 🍽 ☐ Jul–Sep. ⓣⓛ

There are few activities for tourists on Marmara Island. Instead, visitors come for its relaxed, village way of life. This small, family-run hotel is right on the beach, 20 minutes' walk from the town of Marmara. It has only simple facilities, but the inexpensive price includes full board. To liven things up there is a discotheque in the hotel every weekend.

### Çınar

Türkeli, Avşa Island. 〔 *(0266) 896 10 14.* FAX *(0266) 896 10 52.* **Rooms:** *52.* 🚗 🍴 🍴 🔌 🍽 🍽 *MC, V* ☐ Jun–Sep. ⓣⓛ

This popular family hotel is situated on the seafront of Türkeli, the main resort on Avşa Island, and has a private beach. The water-sports center next door offers reduced rates for guests. As well as two- and three-bed rooms, the Çınar has several larger family rooms. The price includes breakfast and an evening meal.

## THE DARDANELLES

### Anzac

Saat Kulesi Meydanı 8, Çanakkale. 〔 *(0286) 217 77 77.* FAX *(0286) 217 20 18.* **Rooms:** *27.* 🚗 🍴 📺 🍽 🔌 🍽 ⓣⓛ

In Çanakkale town center, the Anzac is extremely clean and well maintained, with comfortable, light, and spacious rooms and a rooftop terrace. The price is competitive compared with the larger, more conspicuous hotels around the ferry landing. The hotel has a laundry for its guests' use.

For key to symbols *see p179*

# RESTAURANTS, CAFÉS, AND BARS

ISTANBUL'S RESTAURANTS range from the informal *lokanta* and kebab house, which are found on almost every street corner, to the gourmet restaurants *(restoran)* of large hotels. There are also many international restaurants in the city, offering a choice of almost every other kind of cuisine, from French to Japanese. Pages 188–91 illustrate the most typical Turkish dishes, and the phrase book on pages 271–2 will help you tackle the menu. On page 191

*Simit* seller

you will find a guide to drinks available. The key features of the restaurants reviewed in the guide are summarized on pages 192–3 in the *Choosing a Restaurant* section, and a detailed description of each of the selected restaurants is provided on pages 194–9. These have been chosen from the best that Istanbul can offer, across all price ranges. Light meals and snacks sold by street vendors and served in cafés and bars are described on pages 200–1.

## WHERE TO LOOK

ISTANBUL'S MOST stylish and expensive restaurants are concentrated in the European parts of the city: in and around Taksim; in the chic shopping districts of Nişantaşı, Maçka, and Teşvikiye; and in the modern residential suburbs of Levent and Etiler, west of the Bosphorus. The best gourmet restaurants for both Western and Turkish food are usually in five-star hotels.

Beyoğlu district has several inexpensive restaurants, cafés, and fast-food establishments, particularly around İstiklal Caddesi *(see pp102–3)*, catering to a young, lively crowd.

Sultanahmet and the neighboring districts of Sirkeci, Eminönü, and Beyazıt are full of inexpensive restaurants geared to the local population. In recent years, however, restaurants with a cosmopolitan flair have also opened.

Farther afield, in areas such as Fatih, Fener, Balat, and Eyüp, there are plenty of inexpensive restaurants, cafés, and pudding shops *(see p200)*.

## TYPES OF RESTAURANT

THE MOST COMMON type of restaurant is the traditional *lokanta*. This is an ordinary restaurant offering a variety of dishes, often listed by the entrance. *Hazır yemek* (pre-cooked food) is usually served. This consists of hot meat and vegetable dishes displayed in steel containers. Other dishes on the menu may be *sulu yemek* (a broth or stew) and *et* (meat – meaning grilled meat and kebabs).

Equally ubiquitous is the Turkish kebab house *(kebapçı* or *ocakbaşı)*. As well as grilled meats, almost every kebab house serves *lahmacun*, a very thin dough base with ground meat, onions, and

**Pierre Loti café in Eyüp** *(see p200)*

tomato sauce on top *(see p188)*. Cheaper restaurants and kebab houses also serve *pide*, a flattened dough base, served with various toppings, such as eggs or lamb. There are also a few specialty *pide* restaurants *(pideci)*.

If you have had too much to drink you may welcome a tripe soup *(işkembe)*, a Turkish cure for a hangover, before going to bed. *İşkembe* restaurants stay open until the early hours of the morning.

## FISH RESTAURANTS AND MEYHANES

THE ATMOSPHERE is always informal and lively in Istanbul's innumerable fish restaurants *(balık lokantası)*. The best of these are located on the shores of the Bosphorus *(see pp198–9)* and in Kumkapı, on the Sea of Marmara, which is like one large open-air restaurant in summer. A typical fish restaurant will offer a large variety of mezes *(see p190)*.

**Körfez, a luxury restaurant overlooking the Bosphorus** *(see p199)*

**Diners eating at the Konyalı Restaurant in Topkapı Palace** *(see p194)*

before you order your main course from the day's catch. Baby tuna *(palamut)*, fresh sardines *(sardalye)*, and sea bass *(levrek)* are the most popular fish. They are served fried or grilled and often accompanied by a large plate of salad and a bottle of raki *(see p191)*. The majority of fish restaurants in these busy and popular areas will not accept reservations. However, if you cannot find a table at one restaurant, you will find one at another nearby.

*Meyhanes* (taverns) serve the same kind of food as fish restaurants. The difference is that in a *meyhane*, Turkish music is performed either by visiting musicians or by the customers themselves in an impromptu gathering.

In *meyhanes* and fish restaurants, you will seldom see a menu. Instead the waiters will bring a large tray of mezes to your table from which to make your choice. The day's fish will usually be displayed on large wooden trays. You can order your fish by pointing to it. The daily prices of fish, given per kilogram, should be displayed by the door. If not, simply ask the waiter to weigh the one you want. If you choose a small fish, ask how many fish there are in one portion. Bear in mind that even in the most modest restaurants, fish will always cost more than a meat dish, especially if you choose something out of the ordinary or not in season.

**A selection of pastries**

## OPENING HOURS

TURKS EAT LUNCH between 12:30 and 2pm and have dinner around 8pm. Ordinary restaurants and kebab houses are open from about 11am to 11pm, while fish restaurants serve all day but stay open later. International restaurants have strict opening hours, usually from noon to 3:30pm and 7:30pm to midnight. *Meyhanes* will be open from 7pm until well after midnight. Most restaurants are open seven days a week, but some are closed on either Sunday or Monday. During Ramazan *(see p47)*, when Muslims fast from sunrise to sunset, many restaurants are closed. Some close only during daylight hours and then serve special Ramazan meals, while others, especially in religious areas such as Fatih and Eyüp, will close altogether for the whole month. In sightseeing areas, however, you will always be able to find someplace open.

## WHAT TO EXPECT

FEW RESTAURANTS in Istanbul cater to special requirements such as vegetarian food or highchairs. However, staff are generally helpful, and with some ingenuity and good will a solution can often be found.

When choosing a place to eat, bear in mind that many cheaper restaurants and kebab houses do not serve alcoholic drinks. Only international hamburger and pizza chains, however, have a no-smoking section. No restaurant in the city is equipped for wheelchairs, but most are on the ground floor, making easy access possible. While vegetarian main courses are rare, most restaurants will have vegetable mezes, which can make a filling main course, and you can always ask for an omelette. In local Turkish restaurants, women should look for the *aile salonu* sign. This denotes a separate area for women and families, from which solitary men are barred. A single woman will be just as unwelcome in the main restaurant with the men.

No restaurant in Istanbul requires customers to wear jacket and tie, but in luxurious establishments it is more acceptable to be dressed up.

## SERVICE AND PAYING

IN SMALLER RESTAURANTS the waiter will recite the dishes from memory and possibly forget half your order instead of writing it down. Yet the friendliness of staff will make up for such shortcomings.

Major credit cards are widely accepted, except in kebab houses and cheaper restaurants. Tax and a service charge are included in the bill, but Turks always leave a 10% tip, regardless.

**Delicious fried and grilled mackerel sold on Eminönü quayside** *(see p200)*

# What to Eat in Istanbul

FOR ALMOST FIVE CENTURIES, the different cultures under Ottoman rule – territories ranging from the Balkans to North Africa – contributed to the sophisticated cuisine that was created in the kitchens of Topkapı Palace (*see pp54–9*). As well as drawing on this palace tradition, the food of Istanbul today includes diverse specialties from Anatolia (the Asian part of Turkey). Many of today's staple dishes originated in Central Asia and were brought by the nomadic Turks as they spread westward. Turkish food is sometimes ranked as one of the world's top three cuisines, along with French and Chinese.

***Breakfast** in Turkey consists of feta-type cheese, tomatoes, olives, and cucumber, as well as honey, jam, butter, and bread, all served with tea.*

**Yoğurt çorbası** *is a yogurt soup made with legumes or rice. Soups are eaten at any time of the day in Istanbul.*

**Palamut (Bonito)**

**Hamsi (Anchovies)**

**Uskumru (Mackerel)**

**Levrek (Sea bass)**

**Kalkan (Turbot)**

***Fish** is widely available in Istanbul, due to the city's proximity to the sea. During the winter months, oil-rich varieties of fish, such as bluefish and mackerel, are particularly plentiful in restaurants. The method of cooking can vary, but in most cases the fish is served either grilled or stewed.*

**Hamsi pilavı** *is a Black Sea dish made with a mixture of anchovies and rice. It is one of many Turkish rice dishes.*

**Levrek pilakisi** *is a stew made with a combination of sea bass, onions, and potatoes, flavored with garlic.*

## ANATOLIAN DISHES

The dishes of Anatolia are as varied as the regions they originate from. They are traditional and simple, but nonetheless often colorful and spicy in taste.

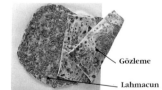

**Gözleme**

**Lahmacun**

**Lahmacun and gözleme** *are bread-based snacks. The first is a thin pizza-style snack. The second is folded over or rolled up.*

**Fırında mantı** *is a dish of noodle-dough dumplings filled with meat. Other mantı dishes use the same dough.*

**Karides güveç,** *shrimp with peppers and tomatoes topped with cheese, is just one of many kinds of güveç (stew).*

**Bamya bastısı** *is a popular okra and tomato stew that can be made with or without chunks of lamb.*

Doner
kebab

Şiş kebab

Adana
kebab

İskender
kebab

*Kebabs may be meat, fish, or vegetables. The most popular varieties are doner (sliced roast meat), şiş (cubes of meat grilled on a skewer), Adana (ground meat grilled on a skewer), and İskender, or Bursa kebab (doner meat on bread with a rich tomato sauce and yogurt).*

## PALACE SPECIALTIES

The cooks of the Topkapı Palace kitchens created elaborate dishes during the days of the Ottoman Empire. Vegetables were stuffed or cooked in olive oil. Meat was grilled or roasted, seasoned, and sometimes served with either a cream or tomato sauce.

**İmam bayıldı**, *literally "the imam fainted," is a dish of eggplants stuffed with tomatoes and onions.*

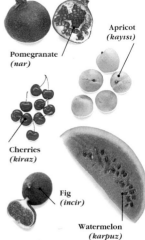

Pomegranate
(nar)

Apricot
(kayısı)

Cherries
(kiraz)

Fig
(incir)

Watermelon
(karpuz)

*Fresh fruit in season is the ideal way to round off a Turkish meal. Watermelons, figs, pomegranates, and apricots are among the most popular choices.*

**Hünkar beğendili köfte**
*is meatballs with "sultan's delight": a purée of smoked eggplant with cheese.*

**Karnıyarık** *is a dish of eggplants, split open and stuffed with ground lamb, pine nuts, and currants.*

## SWEETS

Sweets are eaten throughout the day in Turkey, not just after a meal. They are sold in stores, in stalls, and by street vendors. Some sweets are linked to religious feasts. Istanbul is renowned for its baklava.

Varieties of baklava

**Turkish pastries**
are sticky sweets made from various types of pastry, coated with syrup, and some-times filled with nuts.

Tulumba

**Tavuk göğsü kazandibi**
*is a milk pudding made with shredded chicken breasts.*

**Aşure**, *also known as "Noah's pudding," is made with a combination of dried fruit and beans.*

**Fırında sütlaç**, *an oven-baked rice pudding that is served cold, is popular in Istanbul.*

# Mezes

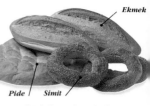

**M**OST TURKISH MEALS begin with mezes, Turkish appetizers, of which there are hundreds of different kinds, with new ones being created all the time. They range from simple combinations, such as plain white cheese with melon, to elaborately stuffed vegetables. Mezes are served in all Turkish restaurants and are often accompanied by raki. *Meyhane* restaurants *(see p187)* specialize in mezes from Anatolia and you may be offered a selection on a tray. Most mezes are served cold, and very few of them contain fish or meat, making them ideal for vegetarians.

*Ekmek*

*Pide*    *Simit*

*Turşu, pickles*

**Turkish bread** *includes* ekmek *(white loaves) and* pide *(flat bread), which is often served with kebabs and also eaten during religious festivals. Simit is a crisp, ring-shaped, savory bread covered with sesame seeds.*

Cigar-shaped
*Sigara böreği*

*Yalancı yaprak dolması* (stuffed grape leaves)

Triangular
*Muska böreği*

*Midye dolması* (mussel shells stuffed with rice)

## Böreks and Dolmas
*Anything that can be stuffed is made into a* dolma*. The most common are made with grape leaves, peppers, and mussels.* Börek *(or* böreği*), a filled pastry, deep fried and usually stuffed with meat, spinach, or cheese with herbs.*

## Circassian chicken
(Çerkez tavuğu) *is a cold dish consisting of strips of meat dressed in a creamy walnut and bread sauce.*

### COLD MEZES
Several mezes come in the form of purées and dips, often using yogurt as a base. They are served with fresh, warm bread. Some of the most popular include *patlıcan salatası* (smoked eggplant salad), *haydari* (mint, garlic, and yogurt) and *tarama* (fish roe).

*Patlıcan salatası* (smoked eggplant salad)

*Fava* (purée of broad beans)

*Tarama* (purée of fish roe)

*Haydari* (a dip made with mint and garlic)

*Çoban salatası* (tomato, onion, and cucumber salad)

**Lakerda**, *finely sliced smoked tuna served with lemon, is a popular fish meze from the Black Sea.*

**Fasulye piyazı** *is a salad of green beans with olive oil and lemon juice. It is sometimes topped with boiled egg.*

**Zeytinyağlı enginar**, *artichoke hearts, is one of many choice vegetable dishes cooked in olive oil.*

# What to Drink in Istanbul

THE MOST COMMON DRINK in Istanbul is tea *(çay)*, which is normally served black in small, tulip-shaped glasses. It is offered to you wherever you go, in shops and bazaars, and even in banks and offices. Breakfast is usually accompanied by tea, whereas small cups of strong Turkish coffee *(kahve)* are drunk mid-morning and also at the end of meals. Cold drinks include a variety of fresh fruit juices, such as orange and cherry, and refreshing, syrup-based sherbets. Although Turkey does produce its own wine and beer, the most popular alcoholic drink in Istanbul is raki, which is usually served to accompany mezes.

**Fruit juice seller**

## SOFT DRINKS

BOTTLED mineral water *(su)* is sold in corner stores and served in restaurants everywhere. If you are feeling adventurous, you may like to try a glass of *ayran*, salty liquid yogurt. *Boza*, made from bulgur wheat, is another local drink to sample *(see p92)*. There is always a variety of refreshing fruit and vegetable juices available. They include cherry juice *(vişne suyu)*, turnip juice *(şalgam suyu)*, and *şıra*, a juice made from fermented grapes.

**Vişne suyu**       **Ayran**

## COFFEE AND TEA

TURKISH COFFEE is dark and strong and is ordered according to the amount of sugar required: *az* (little), *orta* (medium), or *çok şekerli* (a lot). You may have to ask for it specially, as some restaurants may give you instant coffee. The ubiquitous daily drink is tea with sugar but without milk. It is often served from a samovar, a large metal urn. Alternatives include herb teas, such as linden *(ıhlamur)*. In winter, *sahlep*, a hot, milky drink, is a popular choice.

**Traditional samovar for tea**

## ALCOHOLIC DRINKS

THE NATIONAL alcoholic drink in Turkey is raki – "lion's milk" – a clear, anise-flavored spirit that turns cloudy when water is added. It is drunk with fish and mezes. The Turkish wine industry produces some good reds and whites, served in many restaurants. Doluca and Kavaklıdere are the leading brands. Wines from other countries are generally available only in the best foreign restaurants. Turkey's own Efes Pilsen beer is widely sold. Note that alcohol is not served in some of the cheaper restaurants and kebab houses.

**Raki**       **Beer**       **Red wine**       **White wine**

**Turkish coffee** is a very strong drink and an acquired taste for most people.

**Sahlep** is a hot, winter drink made from powdered orchid root.

**Apple tea**       **Linden tea**

# Choosing a Restaurant

THIS IS A QUICK reference chart to restaurants in Istanbul, highlighting the aspects that might influence your choice. They have been grouped according to the main type of food that each specializes in. More details are given on the following pages.

| | | Page Number | Outdoor Tables | Air-Conditioning | Vegetarian Food | Attractive Location | Alcohol not Served | Suitable for Children | Live Entertainment |
|---|---|---|---|---|---|---|---|---|---|
| **TURKISH RESTAURANTS** | | | | | | | | | |
| Bolkepçe | ₺ | 197 | | | ● | | | ■ | |
| Cennet | ₺ | 194 | | | | | | ■ | |
| Havuzlu | ₺ | 194 | | | ● | ■ | | ■ | |
| Sultanahmet Köftecisi | ₺ | 194 | | | | | | | |
| Birtat | ₺₺ | 199 | ● | | ● | ■ | | ■ | |
| Borsa | ₺₺ | 195 | | ■ | ● | | | ■ | |
| Çamlık Moteli | ₺₺ | 199 | ● | | ● | ■ | | | |
| Darüzziyafe | ₺₺ | 195 | ● | | ● | ■ | ● | ■ | |
| Hıdiv Kasrı | ₺₺ | 198 | ● | | ● | ■ | ● | | |
| Hünkar | ₺₺ | 196 | | ■ | ● | | | ■ | |
| Kanaat | ₺₺ | 198 | | ■ | ● | | ● | ■ | |
| Karaca | ₺₺ | 195 | ● | | ● | ■ | | | |
| Lades | ₺₺ | 195 | | ■ | ● | | ● | ■ | |
| Lalezar | ₺₺ | 199 | ● | | | ■ | | ■ | ● |
| Leonardo | ₺₺ | 199 | ● | | ● | ■ | | | |
| Moda Park | ₺₺ | 198 | ● | | ● | ■ | | | |
| Nature and Peace | ₺₺ | 195 | | ■ | ● | ■ | | ■ | |
| Safran Hotel Restaurant | ₺₺ | 199 | | ■ | ● | | | | |
| Şayan | ₺₺ | 198 | ● | ■ | ● | | | | |
| Sedef | ₺₺ | 196 | ● | ■ | | | | ● | |
| Subaşı | ₺₺ | 195 | ● | | | | | ● | |
| Sümengen | ₺₺ | 194 | ● | | ● | ■ | | | |
| A la Turka | ₺₺ | 197 | ● | | ● | ■ | ● | ■ | |
| Türkistan Aşevi | ₺₺ | 194 | ● | | ● | ■ | ● | ■ | |
| Ahırkapı | ₺₺₺ | 194 | ● | ■ | ● | | | ■ | ● |
| Asitane | ₺₺₺ | 197 | ● | ■ | ● | ■ | | ■ | ● |
| Çatı | ₺₺₺ | 196 | | ■ | ● | | | | ● |
| Hacı Baba | ₺₺₺ | 196 | ● | | ● | ■ | | | |
| Hasır Beykoz | ₺₺₺ | 198 | ● | ■ | | ■ | | ■ | ● |
| Huzur | ₺₺₺ | 198 | | | ● | ■ | | | |
| Kathisma | ₺₺₺ | 194 | ● | ■ | ● | ■ | | ■ | |
| Mercan | ₺₺₺ | 199 | ● | ■ | ● | ■ | | ■ | ● |
| Pandeli | ₺₺₺ | 195 | | | ● | ■ | | | |
| Rami | ₺₺₺ | 194 | | | ● | ■ | | | |
| Valide Sultan Konağı | ₺₺₺ | 194 | ● | ■ | ● | ■ | | | |
| Les Ambassadeurs | ₺₺₺₺ | 199 | | ■ | ● | ■ | | | |
| Four Seasons | ₺₺₺₺ | 196 | | ■ | | ■ | | | |
| Konyalı | ₺₺₺₺ | 194 | ● | | ● | ■ | | ■ | |
| Park Şamdan | ₺₺₺₺ | 197 | | ■ | ● | | | | |
| Şark Sofrası | ₺₺₺₺ | 197 | | | ● | ■ | | | ● |
| Divan | ₺₺₺₺₺ | 197 | | ■ | ● | | | ■ | |
| Körfez | ₺₺₺₺₺ | 199 | ● | | ● | ■ | | | |
| Panorama | ₺₺₺₺₺ | 196 | | ■ | ● | ■ | | | ● |
| Sarnıç | ₺₺₺₺₺ | 194 | | | ● | ■ | | | ● |
| **KEBAB HOUSES** | | | | | | | | | |
| Develi | ₺₺ | 196 | ● | ■ | | | | ■ | |
| Hacıbey | ₺₺ | 197 | | ■ | | | | ■ | |
| Kebab's Ocakbaşı | ₺₺ | 198 | | ■ | | ■ | | ■ | |
| He-De | ₺₺ | 198 | ● | ■ | | ■ | | ■ | |

**OUTDOOR TABLES**
The restaurant has outdoor tables, either on a terrace or the sidewalk.

**VEGETARIAN FOOD**
Restaurant serving either vegetarian dishes or a range of vegetable mezes *(see p190)* that can be eaten as a main course.

**ALCOHOL NOT SERVED**
Many Turkish restaurants, especially cheaper ones, do not serve alcohol.

**SUITABLE FOR CHILDREN**
This denotes a restaurant that will welcome parents with young children, and will not be too smoky or noisy.

| | Page Number | Outdoor Tables | Air-Conditioning | Vegetarian Food | Attractive Location | Alcohol not Served | Suitable for Children | Live Entertainment |
|---|---|---|---|---|---|---|---|---|
| **FISH RESTAURANTS** | | | | | | | | |
| Yakup 2 — ₺₺ | 195 | | | ● | | | | |
| Yedigül — ₺₺ | 198 | ● | | ● | ■ | | ■ | |
| Ali Baba — ₺₺₺ | 198 | ● | | ● | ■ | | ■ | |
| Façyo — ₺₺₺ | 198 | | | ● | ■ | | | |
| Karaca Han — ₺₺₺ | 198 | ● | | ● | ■ | | | |
| Pafuli — ₺₺₺ | 198 | ● | | ● | ■ | | | |
| Deniz Park — ₺₺₺₺ | 199 | ● | | ● | ■ | | ■ | |
| Karafaki — ₺₺₺₺ | 196 | | ■ | ● | | | | |
| Yeni Güneş — ₺₺₺₺ | 199 | ● | | ● | ■ | | ■ | |
| Pescatore — ₺₺₺₺₺ | 199 | ● | ■ | ● | ■ | | ■ | |
| **MEYHANES** | | | | | | | | |
| Bekriya — ₺₺ | 198 | | | | ■ | | | |
| Çiçek Pasajı — ₺₺ | 195 | ● | | ● | ■ | | | ● |
| Denizkızı — ₺₺ | 196 | ● | | ● | ■ | | | ● |
| Refik — ₺₺ | 195 | | | ● | | | | |
| Hasır — ₺₺₺ | 196 | | | ● | | | | ● |
| Ece Bar — ₺₺₺₺₺ | 199 | | | ● | ■ | | | ● |
| **INTERNATIONAL RESTAURANTS** | | | | | | | | |
| The China — ₺₺ | 197 | | ■ | ● | | | | |
| Fischer — ₺₺ | 195 | | ■ | | | | | |
| Rejans — ₺₺ | 195 | | | | | | | |
| Great Hong Kong — ₺₺₺ | 196 | | ■ | ● | | | ■ | |
| Mezzaluna — ₺₺₺ | 197 | | ■ | ● | | | | |
| Rock House Café — ₺₺₺ | 197 | | ■ | ● | | | ■ | ● |
| Dynasty Asian — ₺₺₺₺ | 195 | | ■ | ● | | | | |
| Yeşil Ev — ₺₺₺₺ | 194 | ● | | ● | ■ | | ■ | ● |
| Café du Levant — ₺₺₺₺₺ | 197 | | ■ | | | | ■ | |
| Citronelle — ₺₺₺₺₺ | 196 | | ■ | | ■ | | | |
| La Corne d'Or — ₺₺₺₺₺ | 197 | | ■ | | | | | ● |
| Miyako — ₺₺₺₺₺ | 197 | | ■ | ● | ■ | | | |
| Spasso — ₺₺₺₺ | 198 | | ■ | ● | ■ | | ■ | |
| Süreyya — ₺₺₺₺₺ | 199 | | | | ■ | | | |

## USING THE LISTINGS

The restaurants on pages 194–9 are listed according to area and price category. These symbols summarize the key features of each restaurant.

🍴₺ fixed-price menu
Ⓥ vegetarian dishes/mezes

🚼 suitable for children
♿ wheelchair access
❄ air-conditioning
🪑 outdoor tables
🎵 live entertainment, usually in the evening
🍷 recommended wine list
💳 credit cards accepted:
*AE* American Express
*DC* Diners Club
*JCB* Japanese Credit Bureau

*MC* MasterCard (Access)
*V* VISA

**Price categories** for a three-course meal for one, including tax and service:
₺ under US$8
₺₺ $8–15
₺₺₺ $15–25
₺₺₺₺ $25–35
₺₺₺₺₺ over $35

## SERAGLIO POINT

### Konyalı

Topkapı Palace, Sultanahmet.
**Map** 3 F3. **(** (0212) 513 96 96.
○ 9:30am–5pm Wed–Mon. **¶❶**
**V 🗔 🖿 🅔** AE, DC, MC, V.
**₺₺₺₺**

In business since 1897, Konyalı is a gastronomic landmark, serving various mezes and fish, as well as international dishes. It is extremely popular, not just for its outstanding food but also for its privileged setting in the grounds of Topkapı Palace, with splendid views of the Sea of Marmara. Because of its incomparable location, it can get crowded in summer.

### Sarnıç

Soğukçeşme Sok, Cağaloğlu.
**Map** 3 E4 (5 F3). **(** (0212) 512 42 91. ○ 8am–midnight. ● Mon and all of June. **V 🎵 ❢ 🅔** AE, MC, V. **₺₺₺₺₺**

Converted from a Byzantine cistern with lofty columns and a domed ceiling, Sarnıç is dimly lit by wrought-iron chandeliers, candles, and a fireplace. In the evening there is live piano music. The menu offers an assortment of options, but prices reflect the atmosphere rather than the quality of the food. Thanks to its underground setting, Sarnıç is always cool in summer and yet well heated in winter.

## SULTANAHMET

### Cennet

Divanyolu Cad 90, Çemberlitaş.
**Map** 3 D4 (5 C3). **(** (0212) 513 14 16. ○ 11am–10pm daily. ❢ 🖿
🅔 V. ₺

Cennet specializes in the cuisine of southeastern Turkey, such as mantı (meat-filled ravioli), gözleme (filled pancakes), and börek (see p190). Village women prepare pastry dishes in view of the guests, and the waiters wear embroidered Ottoman waistcoats and red hats.

### Sultanahmet Köftecisi

Divanyolu Cad 12, Sultanahmet.
**Map** 3 E4 (5 E4). **(** (0212) 513 14 38. ○ 11am–11pm daily. 🖿 ₺

Modest but highly recommended, this establishment is famous for its köfte (meatballs), piyaz (beans served with a vinegar dressing), and pilav (rice). This busy lokanta has become so popular that other restaurants on the street have taken its name, but this is the original one, in business since 1920.

### Sümengen

Amiral Tafdil Sok 21, Sultanahmet.
**Map** 3 E5 (5 F5). **(** (0212) 517 68 75. ○ 7am–11pm daily. ¶❶ V 🖿
🅔 AE, MC, V. ₺

The intimate restaurant of the pretty Sümengen hotel looks out over the Sea of Marmara. It serves an assortment of cold mezes, cheese and meat pastries, grilled meats, and a number of international dishes such as filet mignon, schnitzel, beef stroganoff, and chicken with curry sauce. In summer you can dine outdoors on the small terrace.

### Türkistan Aşevi

Tavukhane Sok 36, Sultanahmet.
**Map** 3 E5 (5 D5). **(** (0212) 638 65 25. ○ 11am–11pm daily. ¶❶ V
❢ 🖿 🅔 JCB, MC, V. ₺₺

A converted Ottoman house, Türkistan Aşevi is furnished with exquisite carpets and textiles, copper trays that serve as tables, and low, comfortable sofas. Guests are asked to take off their shoes and are given slippers. Central Asian-style mantı (ravioli), gözleme (see p188), and baklava dessert are some of the creations. The cold yogurt soup (made from chickpeas and peppermint) is refreshing. Alcoholic drinks are not served.

### Ahırkapı

Armada Hotel, Ahır Kapı Sok, Sultanahmet. **Map** 3 E5 (5 F5). **(** (0212) 638 13 70. ○ 7am–midnight daily. ¶❶ V ❢ 🖿 🎵 🅔 AE, MC, V. ₺₺₺

Aiming to recreate the atmosphere of a 1930s Turkish tavern, Ahırkapı has live fasıl music (see p213) performed by a female singer accompanied by lute, violin, and drums. The cuisine is strictly Turkish, with delicious mezes and main dishes, such as yoğurtlu yaprak dolması (ground meat in grape leaves with yogurt). From the rooftop terrace, you can see the illuminated monuments in Sultanahmet.

### Kathisma

Akbıyık Cad 26, Sultanahmet.
**Map** 3 E5 (5 F5). **(** (0212) 518 97 10. ○ 11:30am–midnight daily. ¶❶
V ❢ 🖿 🅔 MC, V. ₺₺₺

This stylish restaurant gets its name from the Byzantine emperor's loge that once overlooked the Hippodrome (see p80). Turkish dishes include mücver (fried zucchini), fırında kuzu (oven-cooked lamb), and traditional desserts, such as sakızlı sütlaç (rice pudding with resin liquor) and fig and apricot puddings. Some foreign food is also served. In summer, a guitarist may entertain diners on the terrace.

### Rami

Utangaç Sok 6, Sultanahmet.
**Map** 3 E4 (5 E4). **(** (0212) 517 65 93. ○ 11am–midnight daily.
V ❢ 🖿 🅔 MC, V. ₺₺₺

Dedicated to a 20th-century Impressionist painter, Rami Uluer, this romantic restaurant is owned by his son. It is housed in a restored wooden house and is arguably one of the prettiest restaurants in the area. Ottoman specialties include hünkar beğendi (meat with an eggplant sauce) and oven-cooked dishes served in terra-cotta terrines. Evening diners can hear the sound and light show at the Blue Mosque (see pp78–9) from the terrace.

### Valide Sultan Konağı

Kutlugün Sok 1, Sultanahmet.
**Map** 3 E4 (5 F4). **(** (0212) 638 06 00. ○ 11am–midnight daily. V ▤
🖿 🅔 AE, MC, V. ₺₺₺

The semicircular rooftop restaurant of the Valide Sultan Konağı Hotel (see p181) commands stunning views of the sea and the area's historic sights. The well-balanced menu of meat and vegetable dishes includes mezes, doner and şiş kebabs, eggplant stews, dolmas (vegetables stuffed with rice and meat), seafood, and pizza.

### Yeşil Ev

Kabasakal Cad 5, Sultanahmet.
**Map** 3 E4 (5 E4). **(** (0212) 517 67 86. ○ noon–3pm, 7–10:30pm daily.
V ❢ 🖿 🎵 🅔 AE, MC, V. ₺₺₺

An elegant and formal hotel and restaurant, Yeşil Ev is furnished with antiques in late-19th-century Ottoman style. The food it serves is both Turkish and international, including mezes, şiş kebabs, köfte (meatballs), steaks, a cheese platter, and desserts. Live piano and violin music add to the delightful atmosphere. In summer, meals are served in the shady garden.

## THE BAZAAR QUARTER

### Havuzlu

Gani Çelebi Sok 3, Grand Bazaar, Beyazıt. **Map** 3 C4 (4 B3). **(** (0212) 527 33 46. ○ noon–6pm Mon–Sat.
V ❢ 🅔 AE, MC, V. ₺

When hunger strikes on a shopping spree in the labyrinths of the Grand Bazaar, Havuzlu makes an excellent stop. Named after the Ottoman fountain in the middle of the restaurant, this is a simple, authentic lokanta that serves soups, dolmas, şiş kebab, and grilled meats.

## Borsa

Yalı Köşkü Cad, Yalı Köşkü Han 60–62, Sirkeci. **Map** 3 D2 (5 D1). ☏ *(0212) 527 23 50.* ◯ *7am–10pm daily.* 🍴 ♿ 🔊 ▤ ℡℡

This traditional Turkish *lokanta* has a self-service section, making it ideal for a quick lunch, as well as for more leisurely meals. Borsa has a varied menu, ranging from plain doner kebabs and grilled chicken to stews and traditional Turkish dishes such as *beğendili kebab* (meat with an eggplant sauce). All its dishes are of a consistently high quality.

## Darüzziyafe

Şifahane Cad 6, Beyazıt. **Map** 2 B2. ☏ *(0212) 511 84 14.* ◯ *noon–3pm, 6pm–11pm daily.* 🍴 ♿ 🎵 🍷 *AE, DC, MC, V.* ℡℡

The former kitchens of the 16th-century Süleymaniye Mosque *(see pp90–91)* have been converted into this stunning restaurant. In summer there is outdoor seating in a large courtyard with a fountain at its center. Darüzziyafe serves elaborate, Ottoman-inspired food, including Süleymaniye soup (with lentils, spinach, seasonal vegetables, and meatballs), *hünkar beğendi* (an eggplant and meat dish), *köfte* (meatballs), mezes, and desserts such as *keşkül* (custard with pistachios and almonds). Service can be rather slow. Darüzziyafe does not serve alcohol.

## Karaca

Gazi Sinan Paşa Sok 1/A, Cağaloğlu. **Map** 3 D4 (4 C3). ☏ *(0212) 512 90 94.* ◯ *11:30am–6pm Mon–Sat.* 🍴 ♿

This cavernous restaurant is part of an old caravanserai. The food is typically Turkish and includes *pazı dolması* (stuffed chard leaves with yogurt) and *islim kebabı* (lamb with eggplant). For dessert there is *sütlaç* (rice pudding) or *kabak tatlısı* (stewed pumpkin). In winter, fish is also served. Karaca is popular with local shopkeepers from the Grand Bazaar.

## Subaşı

Nuruosmaniye Cad 48, Çarşıkapı. **Map** 3 D4 (4 C3). ☏ *(0212) 522 47 62.* ◯ *10:30am–5pm Mon–Sat.* ♿ 🔊 ℡℡

Conveniently located near the Nuruosmaniye Gate of the Grand Bazaar, Subaşı is a simple restaurant on two floors. The menu, which changes daily, offers basic Turkish fare displayed in large steel containers at the entrance. With friendly and speedy service, Subaşı is a convenient lunch stop.

## Pandeli

Mısır Çarşısı 1, Eminönü. **Map** 3 D2 (4 C1). ☏ *(0212) 527 39 09.* ◯ *11:30am–4pm Mon–Sat.* 🍴 🍷 *AE, DC, MC, V.* ℡℡

Pandeli is one of Istanbul's oldest restaurants and something of an institution. Located in the Spice Bazaar, the restaurant's interior is decorated with blue Iznik-style tiles. It is popular with locals for its famous eggplant *börek* (stuffed pastry), *kağıtta levrek* (sea bass cooked in waxed paper), and *kılıç şiş* (swordfish on a skewer). Reservations are essential.

## Dynasty Asian

Hotel Merit Antique, Ordu Cad 226, Laleli. **Map** 2 B4. ☏ *(0212) 513 93 00.* ◯ *7–11pm Mon–Sat.* 🍴 🍷 ▤ *AE, DC, JCB, MC, V.* ℡℡℡℡

In the sumptuous setting of a five-star hotel, this Chinese restaurant is decorated with paper lanterns, giant fans, and dragons. Local gourmets agree that this is one of the best Chinese restaurants in Istanbul. The Peking duck, dressed with soy sauce and slices of orange, is highly recommended.

## BEYOĞLU

## Çiçek Pasajı

İstiklal Cad, Galatasaray. **Map** 7 D4. ◯ *11am–midnight daily.* 🍴 🍷 ♿ 🔊 🎵 🍷 ℡℡

This glassed-over alleyway *(see p103)* has numerous down-to-earth *meyhanes* along its length. They are all much the same and the street is renowned more for its lively, convivial atmosphere than for any one restaurant. However, two especially popular choices are Çınar and Mahzen. A typical meal begins with *kokoreç* (charcoal-grilled tripe) or *midye tava* (fried mussels) and continues with mezes, fish, and raki. Tables are nearly always available, so there is no need to book. Few restaurants here accept credit cards.

## Fischer

İnönü Cad 51/1, Taksim. **Map** 7 F4. ☏ *(0212) 245 25 76.* ◯ *noon–3pm, 7–10pm daily.* ▤ 🍷 *DC, MC, V.*

Since 1931 Fischer has been serving middle and eastern European specialties to a loyal clientele. The decoration is rather austere, but the food is of a consistently high quality. Among the staple items on the menu are borscht, an excellent Viennese schnitzel, and apple strudel for dessert.

## Lades

Ahuduhu Sok 14, Beyoğlu. **Map** 7 E4. ☏ *(0212) 251 32 03.* ◯ *11am–9:30pm daily.* 🍴 ♿ 🔊 ▤ ℡℡

Lades is an attractive little *lokanta* serving simple, tasty home-style food in a clean and cozy atmosphere. It is ideal for a quick lunch while sightseeing in Beyoğlu. There is a limited menu of meat dishes, but make sure you try the *lahana dolması* (stuffed cabbage), accompanied by homemade yogurt. Alcohol is not served.

## Nature and Peace

Büyükparmakkapı Sok 21, Beyoğlu. **Map** 7 E4. ☏ *(0212) 252 86 09.* ◯ *11am–midnight Mon–Sat.* 🍴 🍷 ▤ *MC, V.* ℡℡

Nature and Peace is one of the best health food restaurants in Istanbul, offering a selection of vegetable, chicken, and fish dishes but no red meat. Cakes and pastries are available all day, accompanied by delicious fruit juices.

## Refik

Sofyalı Sok 10–12, Tünel. **Map** 7 D5. ☏ *(0212) 243 28 34.* ◯ *noon–3pm, 6:30pm–midnight Mon–Sat.* 🍴

Refik is a cozy *meyhane*, named after its friendly owner whom the locals fondly call *baba* ("father"). This popular restaurant serves meat and vegetable dishes, including *karalahana dolması* (black cabbage stuffed with ground meat, served with homemade yogurt).

## Rejans

Emir Nevruz Sok 17, Beyoğlu. **Map** 7 D4. ☏ *(0212) 244 16 10.* ◯ *noon–3pm, 7–11pm Mon–Sat.* 🍷 *MC, V.* ℡℡

This is one of the oldest restaurants in Istanbul, established in the early 1920s by Russian immigrants. It is still popular among locals for its Russian specialties, such as beef stroganoff, *kievsky* (deep-fried chicken in breadcrumbs with garlic), *piroshki* (vegetables in pastry), and potent lemon vodka.

## Yakup 2

Asmalı Mescit Cad 35–7, Tünel. **Map** 7 D5. ☏ *(0212) 249 29 25.* ◯ *noon–2am daily.* 🍴 ♿ 🍷 🍷 *AE, MC, V.* ℡℡

The amiable owner of this restaurant, Yakup Aslan got his culinary education from his uncle Refik (who owns Refik, *see above*). This is a connoisseur's eating and drinking spot, with a friendly and informal atmosphere and a memorable selection of mezes and fish.

## Çatı

Orhan Apaydın Sok 20, Beyoğlu.
**Map** 7 D5. *(0212) 251 00 00.*
6pm–1am Mon–Sat.
MC, V.

Çatı is a popular rendezvous with local writers, poets, and actors, and its walls are covered with their caricatures, photographs, and paintings. Turkish and international dishes are available. There is piano music in the evenings and sometimes belly-dancing shows.

## Great Hong Kong

İnönü Cad 18, Taksim. **Map** 7 F4.
*(0212) 252 42 68.* noon–
3pm, 6–11:30pm daily.
AE, MC, V.

Decorated in rich reds with hanging lanterns and a pagoda-shaped door, the Great Hong Kong is one of Istanbul's best gourmet Chinese restaurants. The house specialties are its spicy Szechuan dishes, such as the excellent beef with pickles. The menu also includes tasty *goba* (fried rice) dishes eaten with seafood or beef sauce. Chinese wine is available by the glass to accompany meals.

## Hacı Baba

İstiklal Cad 49, Beyoğlu. **Map** 7 E4.
*(0212) 244 18 86.* noon–
11pm daily. AE, V.

This busy and popular *lokanta* serves traditional Turkish food such as mezes, kebabs, and other meat specialties. Recommended items on the menu include *hünkar beğendi* (meat with an eggplant sauce), *elbasan tava* (an oven-cooked meat dish), and *imam bayıldı (see p189)*. Customers choose their meal from a selection of dishes behind a glass counter. Hacı Baba's interior is somewhat characterless, but the terrace is charming and overlooks the courtyard of the Church of Aya Triada.

## Hasır

Kalyoncu Kulluk Cad 94, Beyoğlu.
**Map** 7 D4. *(0212) 250 05 57.*
1pm– midnight daily.

Although its official name has been changed to Asır, this smoky, convivial *meyhane* is still known as Hasır, a reference to its straw-matted walls. As well as fresh fish, Hasır serves over 50 mezes, some of which are no longer available elsewhere. Try *topik* (an Armenian delicacy made with chickpeas, chicken, and pistachios) or *bomba* (large kidney beans). Later in the evening musicians may stop by to perform *fasıl* music *(see p213)*.

## Four Seasons

İstiklal Cad 509, Beyoğlu. **Map** 7 D5.
*(0212) 293 39 41.* noon–
3pm, 6pm–midnight, Mon–Sat.
AE, DC, MC, V.

This highly acclaimed restaurant, run by a British woman, offers Turkish, French, and other international cuisines in a formal setting. It is a favorite with businessmen and staff from the nearby consulates. Chateaubriand and onion soup are two of its specialties. Its discreet and quiet atmosphere makes it an excellent locale for romantic evenings.

## Karafaki

Meşrutiyet Cad 100–102, Tepebaşı.
**Map** 7 D5. *(0212) 293 80 24.*
7–11pm Mon–Sat.
AE, DC, MC, V.

In the basement of the Pera Palas Hotel *(see p104)*, Karafaki is a hidden treasure trove of Turkish regional cuisine. The rather dim surroundings are brightened up by trompe l'oeil windows and candle-lit tables. The restaurant's cooking is innovative and original, taking the food of the Aegean region as its inspiration. The emphasis is on seafood (try the sushi-like raw fish), vegetables, and various different herbs. The dried fig dessert is especially recommended.

## Citronelle

Ceylan Inter-Continental Hotel, Taksim.
**Map** 7 F3. *(0212) 231 21 21.*
7–11pm Mon–Sat. AE, DC, JCB, MC, V.

Citronelle blends the subtle tastes of modern French cuisine with Thai flavors such as galingale, lemon grass, and delicious curries. All this is in a stylish setting with large modern paintings, red velvet chairs, and sweeping views of the city. A reservation is essential.

## Panorama

Marmara Hotel, Taksim Square.
**Map** 7 E4. *(0212) 251 46 96.*
6:30–11:30pm daily.
AE, DC, JCB, MC, V.

An elegant restaurant on the top floor of the high-rise Marmara hotel, Panorama has stunning views of the Bosphorus, the Sea of Marmara, and the Golden Horn, and serves a gourmet selection of Turkish, French, and Italian food. The rich decor is inspired by the Ottoman period: framed kilims blend with luxurious furnishings and candlelit tables. On Fridays and Saturdays a trio performs jazz, and dance music is played after 9:30pm.

## Denizkızı

Çakmaktaşı Sok 3/5, Kumkapı.
**Map** 2 C5 (4 A5). *(0212) 518 86 59.* 8pm–12.30am daily.
AE, DC, MC, V.

The cobbled streets of the old fishing neighbourhood of Kumkapı are full of simple but popular *meyhanes*. Denizkızı is just one of these lively restaurants, serving good fish meals, sometimes to musical accompaniment. In warm weather there are outdoor tables.

## Hünkar

Akdeniz Cad 21, Fatih. **Map** 1 C4.
*(0212) 525 77 18.* 11:30am–
11pm daily.

For decades this family-run restaurant has been a haven of tasty Turkish food. Decorated with jars of colorful, pickled fruits and a small fountain, Hünkar offers typical Ottoman dishes, such as *hamsili pilav* (rice with a fish similar to anchovy), *kadınbudu köftesi* (meatballs), grilled meats, *böreks*, and dolmas *(see p190)*. There is also an appetizing selection of sweets. Try the fig and apricot desserts.

## Sedef

Fevzipaşa Cad 19, Fatih. **Map** 1 C3.
*(0212) 532 82 33.* 11am–
midnight daily.

This bright and spacious restaurant specializes in meat dishes such as lamb stew, kebabs, grills, and hamburgers. The terrace with a fountain is perfect for outdoor dining. High chairs and small portions are provided for children. Alcoholic drinks are not served.

## Develi

Gümüşyüzük Sok 7, Samatya.
*(0212) 632 79 82.* noon–
midnight daily. AE, MC, V.

Develi devotes itself to the spicy meat specialties of southeastern Anatolia, such as kebabs with pistachios and the sharp-tasting loquat (*malta erik*, a yellow fruit). *Keme kebabı* (with mushrooms) and *patlıcan kebabı* (with eggplant) are also good. For dessert try the *künefe* (syrup-coated pastry filled with sweet cheese).

## Asitane

Kariye Hotel, Kariye Camii Sok 16, Edirnekapı. **Map** 1 B1. **[** *(0212) 534 84 14.* **[** *noon– 3pm, 7:30– 11pm daily.* **[]** **V** **[]** **[]** **[]** **[]**
**[]** **[** *AE, DC, M, V.* **[][][]**

Housed inside the Kariye Hotel *(see p183)*, Asitane offers Ottoman fare in a stylish setting. The menu consists of traditional dishes, such as *hünkar beğendi* (meat with an eggplant sauce), *sultan sarması* (a fillet steak), and a selection of kebab and fish specialties. The *kadırga pilavı* (rice with almonds, pistachios, and herbs) is excellent, as is the *incir tatlısı* dessert (figs with walnuts, cooked in syrup).

---

## BEYOND TAKSİM

## Bolkepçe

Muallim Naci Cad 41–9, Ortaköy. **Map** 9 F2. **[** *(0212) 259 82 61.* **[** *noon–2am daily.* **V** **[]** **[]**

This small, intimate *lokanta* serves excellent Turkish home cooking. The handmade curtains and rustic taste of the owner make it a warm and welcoming restaurant. The menu, which changes daily, includes soup of the day, cheese or meat *börek* (filled pastry), *tas kebabı* (meat stew), *hünkar beğendi* (meat with an eggplant sauce), *mantı* (ravioli), and *ayran* (a yogurt drink, *see p191*).

## The China

Lamartin Cad 17, Taksim. **Map** 7 E3. **[** *(0212) 250 62 63.* **[** *noon–3pm, 7–11pm Mon–Sat, 6–11pm Sun.* **[]** **V** **[]** **[]** **[** *AE, MC, V.* **[][]**

Opened in 1957, the China is still going strong despite all the other Chinese restaurants that have sprung up more recently. It has a light and unpretentious decor, albeit with the standard lanterns and fans found everywhere. İsa Wang, the friendly, multilingual owner, welcomes guests, while his mother is busy in the kitchen. The family grows its own beansprouts, makes its own soy sauce, and imports the spices from China.

## A la Turka

Hazine Sok 8, Ortaköy. **Map** 9 F3. **[** *(0212) 258 79 24.* **[** *noon–9pm daily.* **V** **[]** **[]** **[** *MC, V.* **[][]**

Tucked away on a side street near the Ortaköy mosque, A la Turka is a modest but attractive restaurant. It serves simple, well-cooked classic Turkish dishes, such as dolma (vegetables stuffed with meat), *köfte* (meatballs), and various types of filled pastries, such as *börek, mantı,* and *dürüm.*

## Hacıbey

Teşvikiye Cad 156/B, Teşvikiye. **Map** 8 A2. **[** *(0212) 231 71 34.* **[** *noon–10pm daily.* **[]** **[]**
**[]** **[** *AE, MC, V.* **[][]**

A bright and modern restaurant on two floors, Hacıbey caters to a chic crowd. Its specialty is an excellent Bursa kebab (served with butter, yogurt, and a tomato sauce, *see p189*). This is grilled over charcoal in the traditional manner, not under an electric grill as is now common. Try the red lentil soup and, for dessert, the *kemalpaşa* (a semolina and resin liquor sweet) from Bursa province.

## Mezzaluna

Abdi İpekçi Cad 38/1, Nişantaşı. **Map** 8 A3. **[** *(0212) 231 31 42.* **[** *noon– 3pm, 7–11:30pm Mon–Fri; noon– 3:30pm, 7pm–midnight Sat & Sun.* **V** **[]** **[]** **[]** **[** *AE, MC, V.* **[][][]**

Mezzaluna is a trendy American bistro with a well-known branch in California. It is a young and trendy place and gets busy during lunch hours. The food is hearty Italian fare, such as pizza and pasta. Try *cozze alla marinara* – a mussel dish topped with tomato sauce. Fiery grappa is also served.

## Rock House Café

Princess Hotel, Dereboyu Cad, Ortaköy. **Map** 9 F2. **[** *(0212) 227 60 10.* **[** *noon–3am daily.* **V** **[]**
**[]** **[]** **[** *AE, DC, JCB, MC, V.* **[][][]**

A successful imitation of the famous Hard Rock Café chain, this fashionable restaurant and bar is adorned with the gold records and guitars of famous rock stars. Rock House serves generous portions of hamburgers and ice cream, as well as Mexican, European, and Oriental dishes. During the day, the restaurant is popular with families with children. In the evening, the dance floor quickly fills up.

## Park Şamdan

Mim Kemal Öke Cad 18, Nişantaşı. **Map** 7 F1. **[** *(0212) 225 07 10.* **[** *noon–3:30pm, 7:30pm–midnight Mon–Sat; 7:30pm–midnight Sun.* **V**
**[]** **[][][]**

A stylish restaurant that serves excellent food, the Park Şamdan is where Istanbul's high society comes to be seen. The cuisine is a combination of Turkish and international fare. Some of the gourmet European dishes include lamb soup, grilled cutlets, steak, and chicken. Turkish specialties include *ekmek kadayıfı* (bread soaked in syrup with Devonshire cream).

## Şark Sofrası

Swissôtel, Maçka. **Map** 8 A4. **[** *(0212) 259 01 01.* **[** *7–11:30pm daily.* **[]** **V** **[]** **[]** **[]** **[** *AE, DC, JCB, MC, V.* **[][][]**

Şark Sofrası, a wooden building in the garden of Swissôtel *(see p184)*, is a top-class Turkish restaurant. The highly acclaimed specialties include *kuzu incik* (roast shin of lamb), *balık buğulama* (steamed fillet of fish with coriander and tomatoes), *manca* (fresh spinach in yogurt), and sumptuous desserts.

## Café du Levant

Hasköy Cad 27, Hasköy. **[** *(0212) 250 89 38.* **[** *noon–2:30pm, 7:30–10:30pm Tue–Sun.* **[]** **[]** **[]**
**[]** **[** *AE, DC, JCB, MC, V.* **[][][][]**

This stylish French bistro attracts gourmet diners and well-heeled Turkish families. Housed in the Rahmi Koç Museum *(see p127)*, it is decorated with 19th-century hats, bags, and posters.

## Divan

Cumhuriyet Cad 2, Elmadağ. **Map** 7 E2. **[** *(0212) 231 41 00.* **[** *noon– 3pm, 7–11pm Mon–Sat.* **V** **[]** **[]** **[** *AE, DC, JCB, MC, V.* **[][][][]**

Opened in 1956, Divan serves elaborate dishes based on traditional Turkish cuisine. The restaurant has a tranquil ambience, and the menu is extensive, ranging from simple olive-oil vegetable starters to extravagant meat specialties.

## La Corne d'Or

Swissôtel, Maçka. **Map** 8 A4. **[** *(0212) 259 01 01.* **[** *7–11:30pm Mon–Sat.* **[]** **[]** **[]** **[]**
**[** *AE, DC, JCB, MC, V.* **[][][][]**

La Corne d'Or (known as the Roof Garden in summer) is one of Istanbul's most authentic French restaurants, with stunning views of the city. The nouvelle cuisine dishes, prepared by a French chef, come in generous portions.

## Miyako

Swissôtel, Maçka. **Map** 8 A4. **[** *(0212) 259 01 01.* **[** *noon– 3pm, 7–11:30pm Tue–Sun.* **[]** **V**
**[]** **[]** **[]** **[** *AE, DC, JCB, MC, V.* **[][][][]**

This restaurant, decorated in minimalist style, serves an assortment of sushis, teriyaki grills, and deep-fried tempuras. The bright, well-ventilated dining area looks out onto a pretty miniature Japanese garden. This is one of the city's most expensive restaurants.

For key to symbols *see p193*

## Spasso

Hyatt Regency Hotel, Taşkışla Cad, Taksim. **Map** 7 F3. *(0212) 225 70 00.* noon–3pm, 7–11pm Mon– Sat. AE, DC, JCB, MC, V.

This fashionable Italian restaurant is decorated with black and white floor tiles, futuristic chairs, and abstract paintings. From the bar guests can watch the preparation of dishes like saffron risotto, spinach tortellini, and marinated salmon with mustard sauce.

## LEVENT AND ETİLER

## Şayan

Nispetiye Cad, Petrol Sitesi 8, Etiler. *(0212) 270 29 47.* noon–6am daily.

Open round the clock, Şayan is a welcoming restaurant opposite the Akmerkez shopping mall. Its menu includes *köfte* (meatballs), *mantı* (ravioli), *piyaz* (beans with vinegar dressing), and excellent soups.

## He-De

Nispetiye Cad 49, Etiler. *(0212) 263 67 74.* noon–midnight daily. AE, MC, V.

He-De rose to stardom when Hillary Clinton ate here in 1995. It was, nevertheless, popular before then, thanks to its excellent *adana* and *urfa* kebabs from southern Turkey, *lahmacun* (thin pizza, *see p188*), and various kebabs from the *ocakbaşı* grill bar.

## THE ASIAN SIDE

## Kanaat

Selmanıpak Cad 25, Üsküdar. **Map** 10 B2. *(0216) 333 37 91.* 10:30am–11:30pm daily.

A busy *lokanta* serving traditional dishes from *hünkar beğendi* (meat with an eggplant sauce) to liver dolma (stuffed peppers or eggplants). The restaurant has been run by the same family since 1933, and its *fasulye pilaki* (a bean dish) is said to be the best in town.

## Moda Park

Moda Cad 265, Moda. *(0216) 336 07 95.* noon–midnight daily.

This large restaurant in the suburb of Moda, near Kadıköy, boasts beautiful views of the Sea of Marmara. It is still widely known by its former name, Koço. The quality of its food, however, particularly its superb fish, never changes. The outdoor terrace is perfect for warm summer nights.

## Huzur

Salacak İskele Cad 18, Üsküdar. **Map** 10 A3. *(0216) 333 31 57.* noon–2am daily.

The view of Üsküdar and the good food make it worth the climb to this restaurant. Mezes are the main entree. Try the *barbunya pilaki* and *fava purée* (bean dishes with olive oil), and *kabak tatlısı* (stewed pumpkin with almonds).

## THE BOSPHORUS

## Bekriya

Birinci Cad 90, Arnavutköy, European side. *(0212) 257 04 69.* 7:30pm–12:30am Mon–Sat.

Decorated with rustic furniture and old photographs, Bekriya is a cozy *meyhane* with views over the Bosphorus. Balkan specialties are served including Macedonian, Bosnian, and Serbian dishes.

## Kebab's Ocakbaşı

Manolya Sok 2/1, Bebek, European side. *(0212) 257 71 41.* noon–11pm daily. AE, DC, MC, V.

This spacious and airy restaurant has various southeastern meat dishes on the menu, as well as mezes. Its large *ocakbaşı* (grill bar) is in the dining area itself in the proper Turkish fashion.

## Hıdiv Kasrı

Hıdiv Yolu 32, Çubuklu, Asian side. *(0216) 425 06 03.* 8:30–11am, noon– 10pm daily. AE, DC, MC, V.

Perched high on a hill on the Asian shore, this former summer palace *(see p142)* stands in a beautiful park. Its large, formal restaurant serves traditional Turkish food, while the terrace on the ground floor is open for buffet lunches on weekends. Alcohol is not served; instead, customers are encouraged to try sweet Ottoman sherbets.

## Yedigül

İskele Meydanı 4, Anadolu Kavağı, Asian side. *(0216) 320 21 80.* noon–10pm. AE, MC, V.

This is among the best of the many fish restaurants waiting for you as you disembark for lunch on a cruise up the Bosphorus. Yedigül serves delicious fish, salad, *köfte* (meatballs), and deep-fried mussels. If Yedigül is full, Yosun, also on the shore, is a reputable alternative choice.

## Ali Baba

Kireçburnu Cad 20, Tarabya, European side. *(0212) 262 08 89.* noon–midnight daily. MC, V.

This is a simple fish restaurant by the Bosphorus with a loyal clientele. Established in 1923, Ali Baba offers grilled and stewed fish, memorable mezes, and a delicious *ayva tatlısı* (quince dessert) served with Devonshire cream.

## Façyo

Kireçburnu Cad 13, Tarabya, European side. *(0212) 262 00 24.* noon–midnight daily. AE, DC, MC, V.

This unpretentious fish restaurant offers delicious seafood, which is complemented by a large variety of mezes. The *levrek buğulama* (steamed sea bass) and chocolate soufflé are especially good.

## Hasır Beykoz

Beykoz Korusu, Beykoz, Asian side. *(0216) 322 29 01.* noon–11pm daily. AE, DC, MC, V.

In a wooded area overlooking the Bosphorus, Hasır creates elaborate Ottoman fare, such as şiş kebab and chicken with soy sauce. But the *keşkek kebabı* (pounded wheat and meat), which is rarely available elsewhere, should not be missed.

## Karaca Han

Yahya Kemal Cad 10, Rumeli Hisarı, European side. *(0212) 265 29 68.* noon–midnight daily. AE, V.

This rustic restaurant serves fish and meze dishes in a lively, informal atmosphere. The terraces, which overlook the Bosphorus, are especially attractive on summer nights. Try *kiremitte balık* (fish cooked on an earthenware tile).

## Pafuli

Kuruçeşme Cad 116, Kuruçeşme, European side. *(0212) 263 66 38.* noon–10:30pm. MC, V.

This down-to-earth and lively restaurant specializes in *hamsi*, a Black Sea fish similar to an anchovy. An endless list of options has been devised using this inexpensive fish. It is served grilled, in bread, with *pilav* (rice), or as a börek. There is even a *hamsi* dessert.

## Les Ambassadeurs

Cevdet Paşa Cad 113–15, Bebek,
European side. **C** *(0212) 263 30 02.*
⊙ *noon–3pm, 7pm–midnight daily.*
**V 目 🔒 ⓔ** *AE, DC, MC, V.*
**℡℡℡℡**

This restaurant has a superb setting
right at the edge of the Bosphorus.
The fine menu includes *lakerda*
(pickled tunafish) and other
gourmet Turkish food, as well as
international dishes, including a
few Russian specialties. The
frozen vodka is very popular.

## Deniz Park

Daire Sok 9, Yeniköy, European side.
**C** *(0212) 262 04 15.* ⊙ *noon–*
*midnight daily.* **V 🔒 ⚷ 🛏**
**℡℡℡℡**

A firm favorite among the locals,
Deniz Park offers a good selection
of hot and cold mezes, including
shrimp stew, and fried squid with
a walnut dip. For the main course
there is excellent fish, accompanied by raki. The wooden terrace
affords fantastic sea views.

## Yeni Güneş

Cevdet Paşa Cad 73, Bebek, European
side. **C** *(0212) 263 38 23.* ⊙
*noon–midnight daily.* **V 🔒 ⚷ 🛏**
**℡℡℡℡**

Yeni Güneş is a simple seafood
restaurant in an excellent location
at the water's edge. A variety of
high-quality mezes and fresh fish
dishes are prepared. The door is in
an alleyway opposite the taxi
stand in Küçük Bebek Meydanı.

## Ece Bar

Tramvay Cad 104, Kuruçeşme, European side. **C** *(0212) 265 96 00.* ⊙
*7pm–1am daily.* ⬤ *Jul–Aug.* **V 🎵**
**ⓔ** *AE, V, MC.* **℡℡℡℡℡℡**

The owner of this restaurant uses
vegetables and herbs in simple,
healthy cooking. One unusual meze
creation combines wild chicory and
nettles. Covered with a myriad of
small mirrors, the restaurant is also
known as *Aynalı Meyhane* ("The
Mirrored Tavern"). The terrace has
views of the Bosphorus.

## Körfez

Körfez Cad 78, Kanlıca, Asian side.
**C** *(0216) 413 43 14.* ⊙ *noon–3pm,*
*7pm–midnight Tue–Sun.* **V 🛏 ⓔ**
*AE, MC, V.* **℡℡℡℡℡℡**

This elegant waterside restaurant,
housed in a luxurious villa, has
candlelit tables and a stunning
terrace. The house specialty of sea
bass is excellent, as are the mezes.
A private boat can be reserved to
carry guests over to Rumeli Hisar
on the European side.

## Pescatore

Kefeliköy Cad 29, Kireçburnu,
European side. **C** *(0212) 223 18 19.*
⊙ *noon–midnight daily.* **V 🔒 目**
**🛏 🎵 ⓔ** *AE, DC, MC, V.*
**℡℡℡℡℡**

Pescatore is a large restaurant
specializing in seafood. Fresh fish
is prepared in a wide variety of
ways. On the menu are fish balls,
grilled octopus, and seafood crêpes.
Pescatore's pride, however, is
*tuzda balık*: bream stuffed with
mushrooms, herbs, and spices.

## Süreyya

İstinye Cad 26, İstinye, European side.
**C** *(0212) 277 58 86.* ⊙ *noon–*
*2:30pm, 8pm–midnight, Mon–Sat.*
**目 🛏 ⓔ** *AE, DC, V.* **℡℡℡℡℡℡**

Originally established by a White
Russian immigrant, this restaurant
is one of the top-class culinary
landmarks of the Bosphorus, overlooking the bay of İstinye. The
staff still prepares some of the
recipes of its original chef, Süreyya
Usta. Caviar *blini*, chicken kiev,
beef stroganoff, and lemon vodka
are always on the menu. Süreyya
also serves Turkish and other
international dishes.

## EDIRNE

## Lalezar

Karaağaç Yolu, Edirne. **C** *(0284)*
*213 06 00.* ⊙ *11am–2am daily.*
**🍴 🔒 ⚷ 🛏 🎵 ⓔ** *AE, MC, V.*
**℡**

On the tree-lined bank of the
Meriç River, overlooking the
arched Meriç Bridge, Lalezar
serves mezes, kebabs, and fish.
The restaurant interior can get
rather lively (and smoky), but a
waterside table in the garden is
pleasant on summer evenings. To
get here, take the Karaağaç dolmuş
heading south out of the city.

## POLONEZKÖY

## Leonardo

Köyiçi Sok 32, Polonezköy. **C** *(0216)*
*432 30 82.* ⊙ *noon–10pm daily.* **V**
**🔒 🛏 ⓔ** *AE, MC, V.* **℡℡**

Leonardo is a pretty restaurant
located in a restored country
house in a charming Polish village
*(see p158).* A wide variety of
Turkish and European fare is
served as a buffet meal on weekends and as an à la carte menu
during the week. The restaurant's
large garden makes it a great
spot to spend a day away from
the city, and it is an ideal place to
go with children.

## THE PRINCES' ISLANDS

## Birtat

Gülistan Cad 10, Büyükada.
**C** *(0216) 382 68 41.* ⊙ *11am–*
*midnight daily.* **V 🔒 ⚷ 🛏 🍴 ⓔ**
*AE, DC, MC, V.* **℡℡**

Birtat is a long-established restaurant
whose menu offers fresh grilled
fish and meat, and also tasty
mezes. Leave room for the *künefe*
dessert (syrup-coated pastry filled
with sweet soft cheese). The
restaurant's outdoor seating is on
the main street of Büyükada, near
the lively ferry pier.

## İZNİK

## Çamlık Moteli

Sahil Yolu, İznik. **C** *(0224) 757 16*
*31.* ⊙ *8am–midnight daily.* **🍴 V**
**🔒 🛏 ⓔ** *MC, V.* **℡℡**

The lakeside restaurant of the
Çamlık Motel is an excellent place
to try the local specialties such as
*yayın* (catfish) or *inegöl köftesi*
(meatballs). This simple restaurant
has good views of the lake, İznik
Gölü, from the garden.

## BURSA

## Safran Hotel Restaurant

Safran Hotel, Arka Sok 4, Tophane.
**C** *(0224) 224 72 16.* ⊙ *10am–*
*midnight daily.* **V 🔒 目 🍴**
**ⓔ** *AE, MC, V.* **℡℡**

The rather shabby streets of the
Tophane district are an unlikely
location for this excellent restaurant within a comfortable hotel *(see
p185).* A wide selection of mezes
is offered, as well as *zeytinyağlılar*
(appetizers of vegetables in olive
oil), grilled meat, and casseroles.
For dessert the *kabak tatlısı* (stewed
pumpkin) is recommended.

## Mercan

Hotel Kervansaray Termal, Çekirge
Meydanı. **C** *(0224) 233 93 00.*
⊙ *8pm–midnight daily.* **V 🔒 目**
**🛏 🎵 🍴 ⓔ** *AE, DC, MC, V.*
**℡℡℡**

Dinner is served in the hotel's
elegant dining room or on the
rooftop terrace, from which there
are stunning views of the city and
surrounding countryside. The menu
includes international cuisine, as
well as Turkish regional specialties. Try *kağıtta pastırma* (pastrami
cooked in paper) or *güveçte sultan
mantısı* ("sultan's ravioli" cooked
in an earthenware pot).

For key to symbols *see p193*

# Light Meals and Snacks

Eating on the streets is very much a part of life in Istanbul. You cannot go far without coming across a café, street stall, or peddler selling snacks to appease the hunger of busy passersby. Snacks like kebabs, *lahmacun*, *pide*, and *börek* (*see pp186–91*) are eaten at any time of day, as are candies and puddings. On every street corner you will find a *büfe* (sandwich kiosk). If you want to sit down, try a traditional *kahve* or one of the increasing number of European-style cafés in the more affluent and cosmopolitan parts of Istanbul. There are also dozens of American-style restaurants in the city, selling hamburgers, pizzas, and other types of fast food.

## STREET FOOD

A common sight on the streets of Istanbul is the seller of *simits* – chewy bread rings coated with sesame. The traditional *simit*-seller (*simitçi*) carries his fare on his head on a wooden tray; better-off ones push a glass-fronted cart from which they also sell *poğaça* (flaky pastry filled with cheese or meat), *su böreği* (filled, layered pastry), *açma* (a fluffy *simit* shaped like a doughnut), and *çatal* (sweeter, eye-shaped *simits* without sesame seeds). They are all best eaten fresh.

During the summer, street vendors sell grilled or boiled corn on the cob (*mısır*), generously sprinkled with salt. In winter they sell roast chestnuts.

*Kağıt helvası*, a sweet pastry, is another summer snack. *Kağıt* means "paper," and the thin, crumbly layers of dough filled with sugar melt in your mouth.

## SANDWICH AND PASTRY SHOPS

Delicious sandwiches are on sale from small kiosks or *büfes*, usually near bus stops. They include inexpensive, thin, toasted sandwiches (*tost*) and hot dogs (*sosisli sandviç*) with pickles and ketchup.

The snack bars of Ortaköy (*see p122*) specialize in pastries from southern Turkey like *gözleme* and *dürüm*. Both consist of thin layers of bread, grilled on a hot sheet of iron and stuffed with meat, cheese, and vegetables. *Dürüm* bread is cooked first, then stuffed and rolled, while *gözleme* is cooked with the ingredients inside, then folded over in a triangle.

## FISH

Fish sandwich sellers offer delicious grilled or fried fresh fish inside a half or a quarter loaf of bread. Their small boats line the jetties in Eminönü to meet the passing ferry passengers. *Midye tava* (fried mussels), dressed with ground hazelnuts, garlic, and oil, are also served inside bread or on a stick.

Fish and mussel sandwiches are sold at the entrance to the Galatasaray Fish Market in Beyoğlu (*see p207*). Here you can also buy *midye dolma*, mussels stuffed with pine nuts, rice, and currants (*see p190*). Mussels sold on street stalls may not be very fresh and you should never eat a mussel that has not opened while it was cooked.

## KAHVEHANES

The typical Turkish café, *kahvehane* (or *kahve*), is a male-dominated local coffee shop. The original Ottoman name, *kıraathane*, means "a place to read," but such cafés are more a place where men play backgammon and cards, puff on a nargile (bubble pipe), and drink endless cups of coffee and tea. No alcoholic drinks or food are served.

In tourist areas like Beyazıt and Sultanahmet, female foreigners will be welcome in *kahves*, and although they may be stared at, they will not be disturbed. **Çorlulu Ali Paşa Medresesi** (*see p96*) is a *kahve* popular with artists and students. Another traditional *kahve* is **Pierre Loti Café** in Eyüp (*see p120*). Decorated with memorabilia and antique wall tiles, it serves good apple tea. The publicity material claims it was the home of Pierre Loti (*see p42*), but there is no evidence of this. **İsmail Ağa Café**, by the waterside in Kanlıca (*see p141*), is famous for delicious yogurt.

Next to the Bebek ferry jetty (*see p138*) and in the shadow of the mosque is **Bebek Kahvesi**. This café is a favorite with students and middle-class families who read their Sunday newspapers on the terrace while enjoying the breeze of the Bosphorus. Customers can buy *simit* and *poğaça* from street vendors. There are similar modest *kahves* beside the Bosphorus in Rumeli Hisarı (*see p140*), all with wonderful sea views.

## PATISSERIES AND PUDDING SHOPS

The best patisseries are in Beyoğlu, particularly in two hotels: the Divan (*see p184*) and Pera Palas (*see p104*). **Divan** is known for its chocolates. **Patisserie de Pera** retains its charm with period decor, classical music, and tasty cookies. It has a good selection of English teas. **İnci Patisserie** is famous for its excellent profiteroles and baklava. Despite its run-down appearance, it is always busy.

Next door to the Atatürk Cultural Center (*see p212*), **Patisserie Gezi** sells handmade desserts such as truffles and rich torte.

Pudding shops (*muhallebici*) sell traditional sweet milk puddings (*see p189*). **Sütiş Muhallebicisi** is a long-established chain.

## ICE CREAM SHOPS

Ice cream vendors are a common sight in residential districts in the summer. Turkish ice cream (*dondurma*) is thick and very sweet. It comes in milk chocolate and fruit varieties and is served in cones. One of the best places to eat ice cream is **Mado**, which has several shops. Also try **Mini Dondurma** in Bebek.

## EUROPEAN-STYLE CAFÉS

EUROPEAN-STYLE cafés serving light meals such as salads, croque monsieur, omelettes, and crepes are now common in Istanbul. Desserts usually include cheesecake, chocolate brownies, tiramisu, and, in summer, ice cream.

The best are around Taksim and İstiklal Caddesi in Beyoğlu (see pp102–3). The elegant, late 19th-century **Lebon** serves savory dishes such as vol-au-vent, and sumptuous Viennese cakes. **Gramofon** is a homey and relaxed café. Decorated with lace curtains and pictures of old Istanbul, it overlooks the square in Tünel.

Sultanahmet has a few chic designer cafés. **Rumeli** was created by the interior architect who designed the Empress Zoe Hotel (see p180). It is decorated in stone and brick. Jazz, cabaret, and classical music set the tone. **Sultan Pub** is a well-known café and restaurant with tables on the street in summer. The **Lale**

**Pudding Shop**, a hippie spot in the '70s, is now an inexpensive, self-service cafeteria restaurant serving casseroles and grilled chicken, as well as Turkish milk puddings.

**Zanzibar**, in the chic shopping district of Nişantaşı, is popular with a stylish young clientele. It serves dishes such as vegetable grill, Waldorf salad, and toast provençale.

The area around Ortaköy is a haven of street food and light snacks. **Myott** is popular with a trendy set for its fruit muesli, fresh coffee, and '60s furniture. In the early morning this tiny café fills with joggers.

On the shores of the upper Bosphorus, in Rumeli Hisarı, there is an exclusive English café called **Tea Room**. Decorated in a colonial style, Tea Room serves scones and a large variety of English teas.

Cafés are beginning to open on the Asian side as it begins to catch up with the booming trade on the European side. One of the most interesting is **Kadife Chalet** near Moda.

Housed in a 19th-century wooden building, it offers homemade cakes and dishes made with home-grown ingredients, and herbal teas.

## BARS

DESPITE THE ISLAMIC edict against alcohol, there are plenty of bars in Istanbul. The majority of the city's fashionable cafés turn into bars in the evening, signaled by a change of music from soft tunes to loud pop. It is possible just to sit with a drink, but for those who wish to have food, many serve pasta, steaks, grilled dishes, and salads at the bar. Even bars that are not cafés during the day serve snacks. A few hotel bars, such as **City Lights** at the Ceylan Inter-Continental Hotel (see p183), offer more elaborate dishes. Other bars, like **Ziya** and **Zihni's**, have restaurant sections. Many bars feature live bands playing rock or jazz music. For further details see page 213.

---

## DIRECTORY

### KAHVEHANES

**Bebek Kahvesi**
Cevdetpaşa Cad 137,
Bebek.
(0532) 261 98 69.

**Çorlulu Ali Paşa Medresesi**
Yeniçeriler Cad 36,
Çemberlitaş
**Map** 2 C4 (4 B3).
(0212) 528 37 85.

**İsmail Ağa Café**
Simavi Meydanı, Kanlıca.

**Pierre Loti Café**
Gümüşsuyu Balmumcu
Sok 5, Eyüp.
(0212) 581 26 96.

### PATISSERIES AND PUDDING SHOPS

**Divan**
Cumhuriyet Cad 2,
Elmadağ.
**Map** 7 F3.
(0212) 231 41 00.

**İnci Patisserie**
İstiklal Cad 124, Beyoğlu.
**Map** 7 E4.
(0212) 243 24 12.

**Patisserie Gezi**
İnönü Cad 5/1, Taksim.
**Map** 7 F4.
(0212) 251 74 30

**Patisserie de Pera**
Pera Palas Hotel,
Meşrutiyet Cad 98–100,
Tepebaşı. **Map** 7 D5.
(0212) 251 45 60.

**Sütiş Muhallebicisi**
Sıraselviler Cad 9/A, Taksim.
**Map** 7 E4.
(0212) 252 92 04.

### ICE CREAM SHOPS

**Mado**
Osmanzade Sok 26,
Ortaköy. **Map** 9 F3 .
(0212) 227 38 76.

**Mini Dondurma**
Cevdetpaşa Cad 107,
Bebek.
(0212) 257 10 70.

### EUROPEAN-STYLE CAFÉS

**Gramofon**
Tünel Meydanı 3, Beyoğlu.
**Map** 7 D5.
(0212) 293 07 86.

**Kadife Chalet**
Kadife Sok 29, Kadıköy.
(0216) 347 85 96.

**Lale Pudding Shop**
Divanyolu Cad 6,
Sultanahmet.
**Map** 3 E4 (5 E4).
(0212) 522 29 70.

**Lebon**
Richmond Hotel,
İstiklal Cad 445, Beyoğlu.
**Map** 7 D5.
(0212) 252 54 60.

**Myott**
İskele Sok 14, Ortaköy.
**Map** 9 F3.
(0212) 258 93 17.

**Rumeli**
Ticarethane Sok 8,
Sultanahmet.
**Map** 3 E4 (5 E4).
(0212) 512 00 08.

**Sultan Pub**
Divanyolu Cad 2,
Sultanahmet.
**Map** 3 E4 (5 E4).
(0212) 526 63 47.

**Tea Room**
Yahya Kemal Cad 36,
Rumeli Hisarı.
(0212) 257 25 80.

**Zanzibar**
Teşvikiye Cad 60,
Teşvikiye. **Map** 8 A2.
(0212) 233 80 46.

### BARS

**City Lights**
Ceylan Inter-Continental
Hotel, Asker Ocağı Cad 1,
Taksim. **Map** 7 F3.
(0212) 231 21 21.

**Zihni's**
Muallim Naci Cad 119,
Ortaköy. **Map** 9 F2.
(0212) 258 11 54.

**Ziya**
Muallim Naci Cad 109,
Ortaköy. **Map** 9 F2.
(0212) 261 60 05.

# SHOPPING IN ISTANBUL

ISTANBUL'S SHOPS and markets, crowded and noisy at most times of the day and year, sell a colorful mixture of goods from all over the world. The city's most famous shopping center is the Grand Bazaar, and there are many other bazaars and markets to browse around *(see pp206–7)*. Turkey is a center of textile production, and Istanbul has a wealth of carpet and fashion boutiques. If you prefer to do all

Contemporary
glass vase

your shopping under one roof, head for one of the city's shopping malls that offer a variety of international and Turkish brand goods. Wherever you shop, be wary of imitations of famous-brand products – even if they appear to be of a high standard and the salesman maintains that they are authentic. Be prepared to bargain where required; it is an important part of a shopping trip.

**Brightly decorated candle lanterns in the Grand Bazaar**

## OPENING HOURS

STORES ARE OPEN, in general, from 9am to 8pm Monday to Saturday; open-air markets from 8am onward. Large shops and department stores open slightly later in the morning. The Grand Bazaar and Spice Bazaar open their gates at 8:30am and close at 7pm. Big shopping malls open from 10am to 10pm seven days a

week. Stores do not close for lunch, although a few small shops may close briefly at prayer times, especially for the midday prayers on Fridays. Most stores close for the religious holidays of Şeker Bayramı and Kurban Bayramı, but remain open on national holidays *(see pp44–7)*.

## HOW TO PAY

ALMOST ALL STORES that do business with tourists are more than willing to accept foreign currencies (especially US dollars), as well as Turkish lira. When buying expensive goods, paying in cash, especially a hard foreign currency, may get you a considerable discount. The shopkeeper will check the exchange rate in the day's newspaper.

Most large stores and those near tourist sites accept major credit cards, although they may charge a 5% commission. Visa, MasterCard, and American Express are the most common cards. It is not usually possible

to pay with traveler's checks, although carpet shops and some stores in the Grand Bazaar may accept them.

## VAT EXEMPTION

VAT IS CHARGED on most items at a rate of 12–15% (8% for books). Foreign passport holders are entitled to a VAT refund on purchases made in Turkish lira from stores authorized for tax-free sales. These can be identified by stickers on their doors. To qualify for a refund, you must show your passport and obtain a special invoice *(özel fatura)* from the store at the time of purchase. The invoice should then be submitted to the customs officer at the airport on your departure. After you have returned home, the store will eventually refund the added tax, payable in your own country's currency. The procedure is time-consuming and not worth the effort for minor purchases. Shops may also offer a refund through a cash payment at the point and time of sale, or a bank check to be cashed in the customs area of the airport.

**Fezes for sale on a street stall**

## SIZES AND MEASURES

TURKEY USES continental European sizes for clothes and shoes. Food and drink are sold in metric measures. This book has a conversion chart on page 219.

**Turkish delight and boiled candies, sold by weight at market stands**

**Antique shop in Çukurcuma**

## BUYING ANTIQUES

EXPORTING RARE and antique local artifacts, including carpets, is strictly forbidden and carries severe penalties. There is, however, no official definition of the age of an antique, so an item that may be regarded as "antique" by the foreign visitor may not be classed as such in Turkey. In the case of antiques of European origin, permission must be obtained from the Directorate of Museums to take them out of the country. In spite of the restrictions, it is still worthwhile exploring Istanbul's antique shops (see p204). Reputable shopkeepers will advise you on whether you can export an item and help you with the necessary paperwork (which may take one or two days). **KÜSAV**, the Foundation for the Conservation and Promotion of Culture and Arts, is a source of expertise on the authenticity of antiques. KÜSAV also organizes auctions every other Sunday. Replicas of antique calligraphy, miniatures, ceramics, jewelry, etc., can be safely exported. Stores will provide a certificate to prove the item is a replica if needed.

## SHOPPING MALLS AND DEPARTMENT STORES

ISTANBUL'S MODERN shopping malls are popular with Turkish families and foreigners alike, for their entertainment as well as their shopping facilities. They have multiscreen theaters, food courts selling fast food, and chic cafés, as well as hundreds of stores.

**Akmerkez** in Etiler is an ultramodern skyscraper where, besides branches of almost all the leading Turkish fashion companies, outlets for famous international names can be found. **Galleria**, next to the yacht marina in Ataköy, also offers a wide range of well-known clothing stores. The complex contains a branch of the French department store, Printemps, as well as an ice rink (see p214). **Carousel**, close to Galleria, in Bakırköy, is a smaller mall that has branches of various foreign stores including Levi's and Benetton.

**International names alongside Turkish shops in Akmerkez**

## SEASONAL SALES

CLOTHING STORES are the main places for seasonal sales (indirim), although department stores and a number of specialty shops also have them. They begin in June or July and continue to the end of September. The winter sales start as soon as New Year shopping is over in early January and continue until mid-April. There are no sales in bazaars – every day of the year offers bargains depending on your haggling skills.

## HOW TO BARGAIN

In upscale stores in Istanbul, bargaining is rarely practiced. However, you will probably do most of your shopping in the Grand Bazaar and the shops located in or around the old city (Sultanahmet and Beyazıt). In these places, haggling is a necessity, otherwise you may be cheated. Elsewhere you can try making an offer but it may be refused.

Bazaar shopkeepers, characterized by their abrasive insistence, expect you to bargain. Always take your time and decide where to buy after visiting a few shops selling similar goods. The procedure is as follows:

• You will often be invited inside and offered a cup of tea. Feel free to accept, as this is the customary introduction to any kind of exchange and will not oblige you to buy.

• Do not feel pressured if the shopkeeper turns the store upside down to show you his stock – this is normal practice and most salesmen are proud of their goods.

• If you are seriously interested in any item, be brave enough to offer half the price you are asked.

• Take no notice if the shopkeeper looks offended and refuses, but raise the price slightly, aiming to pay a little more than half the original offer. If that price is really unacceptable to the owner, he will stop bargaining over the item and turn your attention to other goods in the shop.

**Haggling over the price of a rug**

# Where to Shop in Istanbul

**Caviar in the Spice Bazaar**

ISTANBUL IS HOME TO a vast range of shops and bazaars. Often, stores selling particular items are clustered together, competing for customers. The Grand Bazaar *(see pp98–9)* is a center for carpets and kilims, gold jewelry, and leather jackets, as well as many different crafts and souvenirs. Nişantaşı and İstiklal Caddesi on the European side, and Bağdat Caddesi on the Asian side, have a good range of clothes and shoe stores. The best choices for food are the Spice Bazaar *(see p88)* and the Galatasaray Fish Market *(see p207)*.

## CARPETS AND KILIMS

ONE OF the best places to buy rugs in Istanbul is in the Grand Bazaar *(see pp98–9)*, where **Şişko Osman** has a good range of carpets, and **Galeri Şirvan** specializes in Anatolian tribal kilims. The **Cavalry Bazaar** *(see p71)* has many kilim stores, and **Hazal**, in Ortaköy, stocks a fine collection of kilims. **Sümerbank**, in Beyoğlu, has a modestly priced but extensive collection of handmade carpets.

## FABRICS

AS WELL AS rugs, colorful fabrics in traditional designs from all over Turkey and Central Asia are widely sold. **Sivaslı Yazmacısı** sells village textiles, crocheted headscarves, and embroidered cloths. **Muhlis Günbattı** *(see p98)* has rare Central Asian textiles,

**Brightly colored Central Asian *suzani* wall hangings**

Uzbek and Turkmen *suzanis* (large hand-appliquéd cloths), silk ikats, and Ottoman kaftans, as well as carpets. The antique dealers **Aslı Günşiray** sell both original Ottoman and reproduction embroidered cloths.

## JEWELRY

ISTANBUL HAS A substantial gold market that centers on Kalpakçılar Caddesi in the Grand Bazaar. Here, gold jewelry is sold by weight, with a modest sum added for craftsmanship, which is generally of good quality. The daily price of gold is displayed in the store windows. Other stores in the Grand Bazaar sell silver jewelry and pieces inlaid with precious stones.

**Icons for sale in the Grand Bazaar**

**Urart** stocks collections of unique gold and silver jewelry inspired by the designs of ancient civilizations. **Antikart** specializes in restored antique silver jewelry made by Kurds and nomads in eastern Turkey.

## LEATHER

TURKISH LEATHERWEAR, while not always of the best quality hides, is durable, of good craftsmanship, and reasonably priced. The Grand Bazaar is full of shops selling leather goods. **B B Store**, for example, offers a good range of ready-to-wear and made-to-order garments.

**Derishow** is the top name in fashionable leatherwear, and **Desa** has a range of classic and fashionable designs.

## ANTIQUES

THE MOST INTERESTING area in which to browse for antiques is Çukurcuma *(see p107)*, a slightly shabby but fashionable neighborhood in the backstreets of Beyoğlu. Shops worth a visit are **Aslı Günşiray**, **Antikhane**, and **Antikarnas** for their Turkish, Islamic, and Western stock.

The antiquarian bookshops, such as **Librairie de Pera**, in and around Tünel *(see p102)* sell old postcards and prints.

## CRAFTS AND SOUVENIRS

MANY KINDS OF Turkish arts and crafts can be found in the Grand Bazaar. Possible gifts and souvenirs include embroidered hats, vests, and slippers, mother-of-pearl inlaid jewelry boxes, meerschaum pipes in the shape of heads, prayer beads made from semiprecious stones, alabaster ornaments, blue-eye charms to guard against the evil eye, nargiles (bubble pipes), and reproductions of icons. At the **Istanbul Crafts Center** *(see p76)* you can watch the traditional art of calligraphy being practiced. **Rölyef** in Beyoğlu, the **Book Bazaar** *(see p94)*, **Artrium**, and **Sofa** also sell antique and reproduction calligraphy as well as *ebru* (marbled paintings) and reproductions of Ottoman miniature paintings.

## POTTERY, METAL, AND GLASSWARE

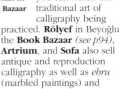

HUNDREDS OF STORES in the Grand Bazaar are stocked with traditional ceramics, including many pieces decorated with exquisite blue-and-white İznik designs *(see p161)*. Other types of pottery come from Kütahya – distinguished by its free style of decoration – and Çanakkale *(see p170)* – which uses more modern designs, often in yellows and greens. With its large and expertly selected stock of plates, bowls, Turkish coffee cups, and vases **May** is one of the best places in the Grand Bazaar. To purchase a modern piece of Kütahya ware, visit **Mudo Pera**, which stocks a collection by Sıtkı Usta, a master of Kütahya pottery. Most museum stores also have a good range of pottery for sale, including reproduction pieces.

The Grand Bazaar and the Cavalry Bazaar *(see p207)* are centers of the copper and brass trade and offer a huge selection to the browsing visitor. For glassware, **Paşabahçe**, the largest glass manufacturer

in Turkey, creates delicate *çeşmibülbül* vases (decorated with blue and gold stripes) and Beykoz-style ware (with gilded decoration).

## FOOD, DRINK, HERBS, AND SPICES

THE SPICE BAZAAR *(see p88)* is the place to buy nuts (especially pistachios) and dried fruits, herbs and spices, jellies, and the many types of herbal tea produced in Turkey. These include sage

*(adaçayı)*, linden *(ıhlamur)*, and camomile *(papatya)*. However, other foods can be bought here as well, including such luxuries as caviar. Another place with a wide variety of good quality herbs, jams, teas, and spices is the Galatasaray Fish Market.

Several shops specialize in particular foods. **Şekerci Hacı Bekir** is renowned for its delectable Turkish delight and baklava. Also popular is **Bebek Badem Ezmesi**, on the Bosphorus, widely acclaimed for its pistachio and almond candies. Over the course of more than a century in business, **Kurukahveci Mehmet Efendi** *(see p86)* has become the best-known producer of Turkish coffee. The quintessential Turkish spirit, raki *(see p191)*, can be bought in any grocery.

Pickled fruits and vegetables, sold in markets and on street stalls

## DIRECTORY

### SHOPPING MALLS

**Akmerkez**
Nispetiye Cad, Etiler.
( (0212) 282 01 70.

**Carousel**
Halit Ziya Uşaklıgil Cad 1, Bakırköy.
( (0212) 570 84 34.

**Galleria**
Sahil Yolu, Ataköy.
( (0212) 599 95 60.

### CARPETS AND KILIMS

**Galeri Şirvan**
Keseciler Cad 55–7, Grand Bazaar. **Map** 2 C4 (4 B3).
( (0212) 520 62 24.

**Hazal**
Mecidiyeköy Köprüsü Sok 27–9, Ortaköy. **Map** 9 F3.
( (0212) 261 72 33.

**Şişko Osman**
Halıcılar Cad 49, Grand Bazaar. **Map** 2 C4 (4 B3).
( (0212) 526 17 08.

**Sümerbank**
İstiklal Cad 302, Beyoğlu. **Map** 7 D5.
( (0212) 252 08 05.

### FABRICS

**Muhlis Günbattı**
Perdahçılar Sok 48, Grand Bazaar. **Map** 3 C4 (4 B3).
( (0212) 511 65 62.

**Sivaslı Yazmacısı**
Yağlıkçılar Sok 57, Grand Bazaar. **Map** 3 C4 (4 B3).
( (0212) 526 77 48.

### JEWELRY

**Antikart**
İstiklal Cad 207, Atlas Kuyumcular Çarşısı 32, Beyoğlu. **Map** 7 D4.
( (0212) 252 44 82.

**Urart**
Abdi İpekçi Cad 18/1, Nişantaşı. **Map** 7 F1.
( (0212) 246 71 94.

### LEATHER

**B B Store**
Gani Çelebi Sok 46, Grand Bazaar. **Map** 2 C4 (4 B3).
( (0212) 527 53 38.

**Derishow**
Vali Konağı Cad 85, Nişantaşı. **Map** 7 F1.
( (0212) 231 15 10.

**Desa**
İstiklal Cad 140, Beyoğlu. **Map** 7 D4.
( (0212) 243 37 86.

### ANTIQUES

**Antikarnas**
Faik Paşa Yok 41, Çukurcuma. **Map** 7 E4.
( (0212) 251 59 28.

**Antikhane**
Faik Paşa Yokuşu 41, Çukurcuma. **Map** 7 E4.
( (0212) 251 95 87.

**Aslı Günşiray**
Çukurcuma Cad 74, Çukurcuma. **Map** 7 E4.
( (0212) 252 59 86.

**KÜSAV**
Has Fırın Cad 305, Sinanpaşa İş Merkezi 3rd floor, Beşiktaş. **Map** 8 C3.
( (0212) 227 34 85

**Librairie de Pera**
Galip Dede Cad 22, Beyoğlu. **Map** 7 D5.
( (0212) 252 30 78.

### CRAFTS AND SOUVENIRS

**Artrium**
9th floor, Swissôtel, Maçka. **Map** 8 A4.
( (0212) 259 02 28.

**Rölyef**
Emir Nevruz Sok 16, Beyoğlu. **Map** 7 D4.
( (0212) 244 04 94.

### Sofa
Nuruosmaniye Cad 42, Cağaloğlu. **Map** 3 D4 (4 C3). ( (0212) 527 41 42.

### POTTERY, METAL, AND GLASSWARE

**May**
Koltuk Kazazlar Sok 10, Grand Bazaar.
**Map** 3 C4 (4 B3).
( (0212) 526 68 23.

**Mudo Pera**
İstiklal Cad 401, Beyoğlu.
**Map** 7 D5.
( (0212) 251 86 82.

**Paşabahçe**
İstiklal Cad 314, Beyoğlu.
**Map** 7 D5.
( (0212) 244 05 44.

### FOOD

**Bebek Badem Ezmesi**
Cevdetpaşa Cad 238/1, Bebek.
( (0212) 263 59 84.

**Kurukahveci Mehmet Efendi**
Tahmis Cad 66, Eminönü.
**Map** 3 D2.
( (0212) 511 42 62.

**Şekerci Hacı Bekir**
Hamidiye Cad 83, Eminönü. **Map** 3 D3.
( (0212) 522 06 66.

# Istanbul's Markets

**İznik-style plate,
Cavalry Bazaar**

WHETHER YOU WANT to lose your-self in the aromas of exotic spices, rummage for old prints and miniatures among secondhand books, hunt for souvenirs, or just shop for food, you will find a market or bazaar catering to your tastes somewhere in Istanbul. An obvious first stop is the Grand Bazaar, but several others are well worth visiting for their more specialized produce and atmospheric settings. Every neighborhood in Istanbul has its own open-air market on a specific day of the week. At these markets, crowded with budget-conscious housewives, you will find a huge variety of merchandise at the cheapest possible prices.

**Spice Bazaar**
*The Spice Bazaar is an exotic trading house for dried herbs, spices, and other foodstuffs (see p88).*

GOLDEN HORN

**Wednesday Street Market**
*One of Istanbul's colorful neighborhood markets, the Wednesday market is next to the Fatih Mosque (see p113) and sells everything from fresh produce and household goods to bulbs and seeds.*

THE BAZAAR
QUARTER

SULTANAH

**Book Bazaar**
*Next to the Grand Bazaar, the Book Bazaar (Sahaflar Çarşısı) offers a wealth of printed matter in various languages, from tourist guides to academic tomes and old magazines (see p94).*

**Grand Bazaar**
*The largest market in the world, the Grand Bazaar contains about 4,000 shops. In this roofed labyrinth of passages, you can find every commodity associated with Turkey, from costly jewelry to basic foodstuffs. It has operated for hundreds of years (see pp98–9).*

**Beşiktaş Square Market**
*A splendid array of fruits, vegetables, and fish is found in this interesting market near Dolmabahçe Palace (see pp128–9).*

**Ortaköy Flea Market**
*Every Sunday the main square of Ortaköy is filled with stalls selling souvenirs to suit every budget, from junk to fine jewelry and original Turkish handicrafts (see p122).*

BEYOĞLU

BOSPHORUS

**Galatasaray Fish Market**
*The best fish market in Istanbul runs along a historic alleyway. Constantly sprinkled with water to keep them cool, fresh fish from the Sea of Marmara and elsewhere lie waiting to be sold (see p103).*

THE ASIAN SIDE

**Kadıköy Street Market**
*The main market on the Asian side of the city fills the streets around Mahmut Baba Sokağı. Clothes are sold on Tuesdays and food on Fridays.*

AGLIO
OINT

**Cavalry Bazaar**
*Converted Ottoman stables are the setting for this bazaar below the Blue Mosque (see pp78–9). Carpets (see pp210–11) are the main items touted, but handicrafts and jewelry are also for sale (see p71).*

0 meters 500

0 yards 500

# What to Buy in Istanbul

**Turkish slippers**

W ITH ITS ENDLESS BAZAARS, markets, stores, and stalls, Istanbul is a souvenir hunter's paradise. If you are seeking a bargain, jewelry and leather can be worth investing in. For something typically Turkish, there is a wide selection of ceramics and copperware based on the designs of traditional Ottoman handicrafts and arts. The city's antique shops (see p204) are also worth a visit. Istanbul is possibly most famous for its carpets and kilims (see pp210–11), but check the quality before you buy.

## Copperware
*Antique copperware can be very expensive. Contemporary items are also available, at more affordable prices.*

**Copper goblets**

## Pipes
*Classic nargiles (bubble pipes) are still used by older Turkish men. They make attractive ornaments even if you do not smoke.*

## Jewelry
*Jewelry includes pendants made from gold, silver, semiprecious stones, and other materials. A simple blue glass eye is said to ward off evil.*

**Antique copper ewer**

**Blue glass-eye pendants**

## Ceramics
*Ceramics form a major part of Turkey's artistic tradition. The style varies according to the area of origin. Blue and white pottery is in the İznik style (see p161); other areas of production include Kütahya and Çanakkale (see p170).*

**Colorful Kütahya ware**

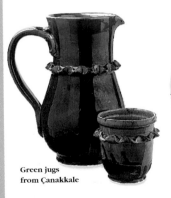

**Green jugs from Çanakkale**

**Blue and white decorated plate**

**İznik-style tile**

## Miniatures

Miniature from the Grand Bazaar

*Istanbul has a history of miniature painting, examples of which can be seen in the city's museums, especially Topkapı Palace (see p57). These tiny works of art, often depicting the sultan at court, were once bound in books. Those for sale are copies of originals.*

Box inlaid with mother-of-pearl

Box with painted scenes on bone inlay

## Crafts

*Jewelry boxes crafted from wood or bone, alabaster figurines, and other handmade ornaments make unusual souvenirs.*

## Textiles

*Handwoven cloths, including* ikat *work, where the cotton is dyed as it is woven, fine embroidery, and knits are just some of the range of textiles that can be bought.*

Embroidered scarves, known as *oyalı*

Cotton ikat work

## Glassware

*This elegant jug is an example of the blue and white striped glassware* çeşmibülbül, *made in the Paşabahçe works (see p147).*

Çeşmibülbül jug

## Local Delicacies

*Delicious sweets (see p189) such as halva, Turkish delight, and baklava are very popular. A huge range of fragrant spices, dried fruits, and nuts are sold loose by weight in the city's bazaars.*

Halva

Nuts in honey

Turkish delight

Dried red peppers and eggplant

Mulberries

Apricots

Sunflower and pumpkin seeds

Almonds

Chickpeas

Pistachio nuts

# Turkish Carpets and Kilims

THE ANCIENT SKILL of weaving rugs has been handed down from generation to generation in Turkey. Rugs were originally made for warmth and decoration in the home, as dowry items for brides, or as donations to mosques. There are two main kinds of rugs: carpets (*halı*), which are knotted, and kilims, which are flat-woven with vertical (warp) and horizontal (weft) threads. Many foreign rugs are sold in Istanbul, but those of Turkish origin come in a particularly wide range of attractive colors. Most of the carpets and kilims offered for sale will be new or almost new; antique rugs are rarer and far more expensive.

**A carpet** may be machine-made or handmade. Fold the face of the rug back on itself: if you can see the base of the knots and the pile cannot be pulled out, it means that it is handmade.

**Wool** is the usual material for making a rug, although some carpets are made with silk.

**Weaving a Carpet**
*Wool for rugs is washed, carded, spun, and dyed before it is woven. Weaving is a cottage industry in Turkey; the women weave in winter, leaving the summer months for farming duties.*

**CARPET**
This reproduction of a 16th-century Uşak carpet is known as a Bellini double entrance prayer rug.

## RUG-MAKING AREAS OF WESTERN TURKEY

The weaving industry in Turkey is concentrated into several areas of production, listed below. Rug designs are traditional to their tribal origins, resulting in a wide range of designs and enabling the skilled buyer to identify the area of origin.

### CARPETS

1. Hereke
2. Çanakkale
3. Ayvacık
4. Bergama
5. Yuntdağ
6. Balıkesir
7. Sındırgı
8. Milas
9. Antalya
10. Isparta

### KILIMS

11. Denizli
12. Uşak

### CARPETS AND KILIMS

13. Konya

**Indigo**

**Madder**

**Chamomile**

**Dyes**
*Before chemical dyes were introduced in 1863, plant extracts were used: madder roots for red; indigo for blue; and chamomile and other plants for yellow.*

The **"prayer design"** is inspired by a mihrab, the niche in a mosque that indicates the direction of Mecca *(see pp36–7)*.

The **tree of life** motif at the center of the kilim is symbolic of immortality.

## BUYING A RUG

Before you buy a rug, look at it by itself on the floor, to see that it lies straight – without waves or lumps. Check that the pattern is balanced, the borders are of the same dimensions, and the ends are roughly the same width. The colors should be clear and not bleeding into one another. Bargaining is essential *(see p203)*, as the first price given is likely to be at least 30% higher than the seller really expects.

Buying a good-quality old rug at a reasonable price, however, is a job for an expert. The age of a rug is ascertained from its color, the quality of the weaving, and the design. Check the pile to make sure that the surface has not been painted, and look for any repairs – they can easily be seen on the back of the rug. The restoration of an old carpet is acceptable, but the repair should not be too visible. Make sure the rug has a small lead seal attached to it, proving that it may be exported, and ask the shop for a receipt.

## KILIM

Kilims are usually made using the slit weave technique by which a vertical slit marks a color change.

The **width** of a rug is limited by the size of the loom. Most rugs are small because a large loom will not fit into a village house.

**Kilim pieces** are used to make a variety of smaller craft objects, also for sale in carpet shops.

**Burdock motif**

**Chest motif**

## Motifs

*The recurring motifs in rugs – some of them seemingly abstract, others more figurative often have a surprising origin. For instance, many are derived from marks that nomads and villagers used for branding animals.*

**Motif from wolf track, crab, or scorpion**

**Modern motif of a human figure**

# ENTERTAINMENT IN ISTANBUL

I STANBUL OFFERS A huge variety of leisure pursuits, ranging from arts festivals, folk music, and belly dancing to sports facilities and nightclubs. The most important event in the cultural calendar is the series of festivals organized by the Istanbul Foundation for Culture and the Arts *(see pp44–6)*. The festivals take place between March and November and have been drawing international performers and large audiences since 1973. Throughout the year, traditional Turkish music, opera, ballet, Western classical music, and plays are

**Belly dancer, Galata Tower**

performed at the Atatürk Cultural Center (AKM), the Cemal Reşit Rey Concert Hall (CRR), and other sites around the city. Beyoğlu is the main center for entertainment of all kinds. This area has the highest concentration of movie theaters in the city as well as several cultural centers, both Turkish and foreign. In the evening, the bars and cafés here play live music. Ortaköy, on the European shore of the Bosphorus, is another popular spot where, on summer nights, dining, music, and dancing continue until very late.

**Copies of *The Guide***

## ENTERTAINMENT GUIDES

I STANBUL HAS A bimonthly entertainment and listings magazine in English called *The Guide*. This publishes the programs of the AKM and CRR, and information on other cultural events, as well as bars and nightclubs around the city. *The Guide* is sold at the larger, central newsstands and bookstores. The English-language newspaper *Turkish Daily News*, available from newsstands, also has information on entertainment in Istanbul.

Lists of events taking place at individual theaters and cultural centers (including those attached to foreign consulates) can be obtained from tourist information offices *(see p221)*.

The Turkish Airlines in-flight magazine has details on major events in the city, and the daily Turkish newspaper *Hürriyet* has listings in Turkish.

## BOOKING TICKETS

T ICKETS FOR performances at the Atatürk Cultural Center and Cemal Reşit Rey Concert Hall can be purchased one week in advance from their box offices. Both offer a 50 percent discount for students and senior citizens, and a 20 percent discount for groups of 30 people or more. The information desks inside the **Vakkorama** department store and **Galleria**, **Akmerkez**, and **Capitol** shopping centers sell tickets for large pop and jazz concerts, and also for performances at the AKM and CRR. Payment is usually by cash.

## LATE-NIGHT TRAVEL

T HE LAST late-night buses and dolmuşes leave at midnight from Taksim, which is close to many entertainment locales. Taxis run throughout the night. During the music festivals in June and July there is a special bus service that runs between show locations and central parts of Istanbul.

## FESTIVALS

F IVE ARTS FESTIVALS, four annual and one biennial, are organized by the Istanbul Foundation for Culture and the Arts. The Film Festival runs from March to April every year, the Theater Festival is in May and June, the Music and Dance Festival – the original and biggest festival – is in June

and July, and the Jazz Festival is in July. The biennial Fine Arts Festival takes place in the autumn. Tickets for all these festivals can be bought over the phone from the **Istanbul Festival Committee**, which also has program details, and from the venues.

The Yapı Kredi Arts Festival, Akbank Jazz Festival, and Efes Pilsen Blues Festival are also in the autumn *(see p46)*.

## WESTERN CLASSICAL MUSIC AND DANCE

E VERY SEASON the Istanbul State Opera and Ballet companies, State Symphony Orchestra, and State Theater perform a wide repertoire of classical and modern works. The companies share the specially designed, 900-seat **Atatürk Cultural Center** in Taksim. Early reservations are essential for shows here. The **Cemal Reşit Rey Concert Hall** stages concerts of

**Classical concert in the church of Hagia Eirene *(see p60)***

Folk dancing at Kervansaray, an established performance space

Western classical music as well as hosting a wide variety of music and dance groups from all over the world. Concerts, operettas, and ballets are also performed at smaller sites throughout the city.

Laser disc screenings of opera, ballet, and classical music performances are held most days at 2pm and 6pm at the **Aksanat Cultural Center**. It also sometimes stages live plays and music recitals.

## ROCK MUSIC AND JAZZ

ISTANBUL HAS an increasing number of bars and clubs playing good live music. **Hayal Kahvesi** is a bar dedicated to jazz, rock, and blues by groups from Turkey and abroad. It also has an outdoor summer branch next to the Bosphorus in Çubuklu. The **Q Club**, located on the grounds

Musicians at the Jazz Festival

of the Çırağan Palace Hotel Kempinski (see p184), is an exclusive jazz bar that regularly invites well-known performers. Farther up the Bosphorus, in Ortaköy, the **Rock House Café** (see p197) is an imitation of the famous Hard Rock Café. It has live bands on certain nights of the week.

In the city center, **Kemancı** and **Roxy** feature live rock and heavy metal performers. In **Sappho** they play softer,

more sophisticated jazz and quality Turkish pop music. Other spots for Turkish pop are **Tribunal** and **Vivaldi**, while at **Beyoğlu Sanat Evi** they play Turkish pop with strong folk music influences.

## NIGHTCLUBS

THE LUXURIOUS, summer-only **Club 29** is probably the most glamorous nightclub in Istanbul. It has a restaurant, swimming pool, and torchlit garden with glorious views of the Bosphorus. Every half hour a boat ferries guests to and from İstinye on the European side. The bar becomes a disco after midnight. **Pasha**, also open in summer only, is the city's biggest nightspot, with a large dancefloor right beside the Bosphorus, as well as several bars and restaurants. **Majesty**, a chic bar and restaurant complex next to the Bosphorus, has a delightful outdoor balcony. Live bands play in the bar and there is dancing to Caribbean music. The restaurant features Turkish music and dance. The trendy club **DNA** plays house, garage, and techno music on Wednesday, Friday, and Saturday nights only.

Avoid the seedier-looking clubs in Beyoğlu, as these have been known to coerce people into paying extortionate bills.

## TRADITIONAL TURKISH MUSIC AND DANCE

TRADITIONAL Turkish music is regularly performed at the Cemal Reşit Rey Concert Hall. This includes Ottoman classical music, performed by an ensemble of singers and musicians, mystical Sufi music, and folk music from various regions of Turkey. In summer, recitals of Turkish music are occasionally organized in the Basilica Cistern (see p76), which has wonderful acoustics. The Sultanahmet Tourist Office (see p221) has details.

*Fasıl* is a popular form of traditional music best enjoyed live in *meyhanes* such as **Ece**, **Kallavi**, and **Hasır** (see p196). It is usually performed by gypsies on instruments that include the violin, *kanun* (zither), *tambur*, and *ut* (the last two similar to the lute).

Belly dancing is performed mostly in nightclubs. Although often underrated, the sensuous movements of the female dancers are considered an art. Many clubs and restaurants stage belly dancing together with Turkish folk music and dance. Dinner is often included in the show. Some of the best places for viewing belly dancing are the restaurant in the **Galata Tower** (see p105), **Kervansaray**, **Orient House**, and **Manzara**.

The Whirling Dervishes give a public performance of their extraordinary meditational dance at the Mevlevi Monastery (see p104) once a month.

The traditional *ut*, a lutelike instrument played in *fasıl* music

## MOVIE THEATERS

THE LATEST films are released in Istanbul at the same time as in other European countries. They are screened in their original languages with Turkish subtitles. Only a few movie theaters show films produced in Turkey.

The majority of the city's movie theaters are on İstiklal Caddesi. Of these, **Alkazar** and **Beyoğlu** tend to show art films. There are also numerous theaters in Kadıköy, on the Asian side, while all the main shopping centers have multiscreen theaters.

The first screening of the day is half price, and many theaters offer half-price tickets all day on Wednesdays. Students with a valid card are entitled to a discount for all showings. Films tend to stop about halfway through for an intermission.

## THEATER

PLAYS BY both Turkish and international playwrights are staged in Istanbul's theaters, but only in Turkish. One of the most popular companies is the Istanbul State Theater, which is based at the **AKM**. The theater season runs from September to June.

## HEALTH CLUBS AND ATHLETIC FACILITIES

THERE ARE a number of establishments with public sports facilities in and around Istanbul. All the main five-star hotels have good swimming pools and welcome nonresidents for a daily fee. Health clubs such as the **Vakkorama Gym** and the **Alkent Hillside Club**, can also be used by nonmembers for a daily fee.

At the edge of the Belgrade Forest, the **Kemer Country Riding and Golf Club** has stables and a 9-hole golf course. It also offers riding and golf lessons. The **Istanbul Golf Club** has an 18-hole course. **Enka Spor Tesisleri**, in Maslak, is a large complex with extensive facilities, including indoor and outdoor

pools and courts for tennis, basketball, and volleyball. For iceskaters, there is a rink in the **Galleria** shopping center *(see p203)* which is open to the public after 7pm. Rental skates are available.

## SPECTATOR SPORTS

SOCCER HAS a very large following in Turkey. The three Istanbul teams, **Beşiktaş**, **Fenerbahçe**, and **Galatasaray**, all compete internationally and play in Istanbul on most Sundays. Horse racing takes place at the **Veli Efendi** racecourse on Wednesdays and weekends. In the summer months, there are yacht regattas in the Sea of Marmara *(see p45)*. For an unusual spectator sport, head to Edirne at festival time to see the grease wrestling *(see p154)*.

**Galatasaray team logo** — 1905

## BEACHES

THE BEST PLACE to swim, water-ski, and windsurf in Istanbul is the Princes' Islands *(see p159)*. Yörükali Plajı, on Büyükada, is a public beach, but it is safe to swim anywhere around the islands. It is no longer possible to swim in the sea closer to Istanbul, however, due to heavy pollution.

There are large beaches at Kilyos *(see p158)* and Gümüşdere on the Black Sea, about 30 minutes' drive from central Istanbul, and Şile *(see p158)*. The Black Sea can be rough at times, with big waves, but all the beaches have watch-

towers, lifeguards, and lifeboats for emergencies. The Marmara Islands *(see p169)*, are also popular for their beaches.

## CHILDREN

LITTLE IN ISTANBUL has been designed with children in mind. Few neighborhoods have decent playgrounds, and there are not many large parks. Sidewalks are high, crowded, and often bumpy, making it difficult to use a stroller.

Socially, however, children are very welcome and will be made a fuss of almost everywhere they go. With a little thought you can discover lots of things for children to do. The State Opera and Ballet puts on children's musicals at the **AKM** every Saturday at 11am or 3pm.

Children are admitted free to the Archaeological Museum *(see pp62–5)*. It has a special children's section tracing the history of mankind, with a medieval castle and a Trojan horse to climb on.

There are big parks at Yıldız *(see pp124–5)* and Emirgan *(see p141)*. Another park near Emirgan, the **Park Orman**, is a family complex situated in woods, with picnic areas, a swimming pool, and a theater. On the Princes' Islands, there are no cars so children can bike safely or take a tour in a horse-drawn carriage or on a donkey. **Tatilya**, 35 km (22 miles) from Istanbul, is a theme park with roller coasters and other rides, a small lake, a simulation movie, and stores, all under a huge glass roof.

Roller-coaster ride at Tatilya, a theme park near Istanbul

## DIRECTORY

### RESERVING TICKETS

**Akmerkez**
Nispetiye Cad, Etiler.
*(0212) 282 01 70.*

**Capitol**
Tophanelioğlu Cad 1,
Altunizade. **Map** 10 C2.
*(0216) 391 18 34.*

**Galleria**
Sahil Yolu, Ataköy.
*(0212) 559 54 44.*

**Vakkorama**
Osmanlı Sok 13, Taksim.
**Map** 7 E4.
*(0212) 251 15 71.*

### ISTANBUL FESTIVAL COMMITTEE

*(0212) 293 31 33.*
FAX *(0212) 249 55 75.*

### WESTERN CLASSICAL MUSIC AND DANCE

**Aksanat Cultural Center**
Akbank Building, İstiklal
Cad, Zambak Sok 5,
Taksim. **Map** 7 E4.
*(0212) 252 35 00.*

**Atatürk Cultural Center (AKM)**
Taksim Meydanı, Taksim.
**Map** 7 F3.
*(0212) 251 56 00.*

**Cemal Reşit Rey Concert Hall (CRR)**
Darülbedayi Cad, Harbiye.
**Map** 7 F1.
*(0212) 231 51 03.*

### ROCK MUSIC AND JAZZ

**Beyoğlu Sanat Evi**
Abdullah Sok 22/1,
Beyoğlu. **Map** 7 E4.
*(0212) 252 61 96.*

**Hayal Kahvesi (Beyoğlu)**
Büyükparmakkapı Sok 19,
Taksim. **Map** 7 E4.
*(0212) 243 68 23.*

**Hayal Kahvesi (Çubuklu)**
Ağaçlı Mesire Yeri A Blok,
Burunbahçe, Çubuklu.
*(0216) 413 68 80.*

**Kemancı**
Sıraselviler Cad 69, Taksim.
**Map** 7 E4.
*(0212) 245 30 48.*

**Q Club**
Çırağan Palace Hotel
Kempinski, A Blok,
Beşiktaş. **Map** 9 D3.
*(0212) 236 24 89.*

**Rock House Café**
Princess Hotel, Dereboyu
Cad, Ortaköy.
**Map** 9 F2.
*(0212) 227 60 10.*

**Roxy**
Sıraselviler Cad, Arslan
Yatağı Sok 113, Taksim.
**Map** 7 E4.
*(0212) 249 48 39.*

**Sappho**
İstiklal Cad, Bekar Sok 14,
Beyoğlu. **Map** 7 E4.
*(0212) 245 06 68.*

**Tribunal**
Muammer Karaca
Çıkmazı 3, Beyoğlu.
**Map** 7 D5.
*(0212) 249 71 79.*

**Vivaldi**
Büyükparmakkapı Sok 29,
Taksim. **Map** 7 E4.
*(0212) 293 25 99.*

### NIGHTCLUBS

**Club 29**
Paşabahçe Yolu 24,
Paşabahçe.
*(0216) 322 28 29.*

**DNA**
Sıraselviler Cad 69/2,
Taksim. **Map** 7 E4.
*(0212) 293 67 99.*

**Majesty**
Muallim Naci Cad,
Salhane Sok 10, Ortaköy.
**Map** 9 F3.
*(0212) 236 57 57.*

**Pasha**
Muallim Naci Cad 142,
Ortaköy.
**Map** 9 F2.
*(0212) 259 70 61.*

### TRADITIONAL TURKISH MUSIC AND DANCE

**Ece**
Tramvay Cad 104,
Kuruçeşme.
*(0212) 265 96 00.*

**Galata Tower**
Büyükhendek Cad,
Galata.
**Map** 3 D1.
*(0212) 245 11 60.*

**Hasır**
Beykoz Korusu,
Beykoz.
*(0216) 322 29 01.*

**Kallavi**
Kallavi Sok 20, Beyoğlu.
**Map** 7 D4.
*(0212) 251 10 10.*

**Kervansaray**
Cumhuriyet Cad 30,
Elmadağ.
**Map** 7 F2.
*(0212) 247 16 30.*

**Manzara**
Conrad Hotel, Yıldız Cad,
Beşiktaş.
**Map** 8 C3.
*(0212) 227 30 00.*

**Orient House**
President Hotel, Tiyatro
Cad 27, Beyazıt.
**Map** 2 C4 (4 A4).
*(0212) 517 61 63.*

### MOVIE THEATERS

**Alkazar**
İstiklal Cad 179,
Beyoğlu.
**Map** 7 E4.
*(0212) 283 24 66.*

**Beyoğlu**
İstiklal Cad 140,
Halep Pasajı, Beyoğlu.
**Map** 7 E4.
*(0212) 251 32 40.*

### HEALTH CLUBS AND ATHLETIC FACILITIES

**Alkent Hillside Club**
Alkent Residential
Complex, Tepecik Yolu,
Etiler.
*(0212) 257 78 22.*

**Enka Spor Tesisleri**
Sadi Gülçelik Spor Sitesi,
İstinye.
*(0212) 276 50 84.*

**Istanbul Golf Club**
Büyükdere Cad,
Yeni Levent.
*(0212) 264 07 42.*

**Kemer Country Riding and Golf Club**
Göktürk Beldesi,
Uzun Kemer Mevkii,
Eyüp.
*(0212) 239 79 13.*

**Vakkorama Gym**
Osmanlı Sok 13,
Taksim.
**Map** 7 E4.
*(0212) 251 15 71.*

### SPECTATOR SPORTS

**Beşiktaş FC**
Spor Cad 92, Beşiktaş.
**Map** 8 A4.
*(0212) 227 87 80.*

**Fenerbahçe FC**
Fenerbahçe Spor Kulübü,
Kızıltoprak, Kadıköy.
*(0216) 345 09 40.*

**Galatasaray FC**
Galatasaray Spor Kulübü,
Hasnun Galip Sok 7,
Galatasaray.
**Map** 7 E4.
*(0212) 251 57 07.*

**Veli Efendi Hipodromu**
Londra Asfaltı,
Bakırköy.
*(0212) 543 70 96.*

### CHILDREN

**Park Orman**
Fatih Çocuk Ormanı,
Maslak Cad,
Maslak.
*(0212) 223 07 36.*

**Tatilya**
E5 Highway,
Beylikdüzü.
*(0212) 872 55 30.*

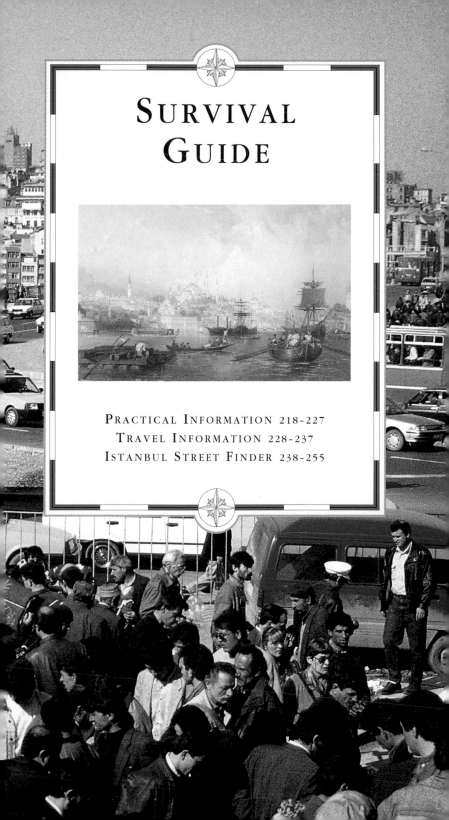

# SURVIVAL
# GUIDE

# PRACTICAL INFORMATION

IN RECENT YEARS Istanbul's infrastructure has greatly improved, and it now has the transportation, banking, and medical facilities of any large modern city. However, it is still worth taking a few precautionary measures, especially if you intend to explore the suburbs of the city. A few bus tickets, a phonecard, and at least one day's supply of hard currency or Turkish lira are a basic survival kit to carry at all times. Credit cards are still

**Official sign to a tourist sight**

not accepted everywhere, and it can be difficult to get cash outside bank opening hours away from the city center. Certain aspects of Turkish culture may seem strange to the foreign visitor, especially if you have never traveled in a Muslim country. It is not considered rude to stare, and foreigners are often objects of attention. In general, however, Turks are friendly and hospitable and will appreciate any effort to show respect for their traditions.

## VISAS

CITIZENS OF the US, the UK, and the Republic of Ireland require a visa. This is bought on arrival at the airport (or at land borders) and costs about $20, payable in cash. It is valid for three months. Canadians, Australians, and New Zealanders can enter Turkey without a visa and stay for up to three months. Requirements vary for other countries. French, German, and Greek nationals do not require visas, whereas Spanish passport holders must obtain a visa costing $30–40 from a Turkish consulate in Spain.

## CUSTOMS

IMPORT LIMITS INCLUDE 200 cigarettes (400 if bought from a Turkish duty-free shop), 7 oz pipe tobacco (18 oz if bought in Turkey), 25 oz alcohol, 35 oz chocolate, and 53 oz instant coffee. Details of cars and valuable electrical items will be entered in passports by customs officers to prevent their resale in Turkey.

There are strict rules on the export of antiquities (see p203). To export an antique carpet, you must have the receipt, and the carpet should have a small lead seal attached to it (check this when buying).

## LANGUAGE

AS A RULE, Turks will make every effort to communicate with foreigners, even if they have to resort to sign language. In areas frequented

by tourists, it is easy to find English spoken, although attempts to speak Turkish will be welcomed. Away from the main tourist circuit it can be harder to get your message across without some rudimentary grasp of the language. Useful vocabulary can be found in the phrase book on pages 271–2. There are several interpreting and translation agencies in Istanbul, including **Tercüme 80**, should you need one.

**No smoking sign**

## ETIQUETTE

TURKS TEND TO dress up on all social occasions and for work. In cities, Turkish women usually cover their arms and legs in public, and increasing numbers cover their heads. Men rarely wear shorts. Visitors are not expected to cover up in this way, but some Turks may be offended at exposed limbs in public

places. There are strict rules on dress in mosques (see p37).

Traditional rules of etiquette and hospitality are still an important aspect of Turkish society. Even though officials can often seem rude and the persistence of carpet salesmen can be annoying, always try to remain polite but firm. At all times show respect for Atatürk (see p29), whose picture you will see in offices, shops, and public places.

Intimate physical contact with a person of the opposite sex in public is likely to offend others. Turkish couples are rarely seen kissing, embracing, or even holding hands.

Smoking is common in Turkey. Most public places, and even offices, tend to be very smoky. Smoking is permitted on most intercity buses (see p236), but is forbidden on all local public transportation and internal flights.

**Fully veiled women, an increasingly common sight in Istanbul**

◁ **The area between the New Mosque and Galata Bridge in Eminönü, a hub of trade and transportation**

Newspaper stand where bus tickets and phone cards are also sold

## RESTROOMS

PUBLIC TOILETS are found all over Istanbul. These can sometimes be very unpleasant: dirty, squat toilets with no paper and the floor awash with water. Entrances are marked *Bay* for men and *Bayan* for women. The attendant sitting outside, whom you pay on exit (a sign shows the charge), may supply toilet paper, but it is a good idea to carry tissues with you. Toilet paper and tissues are widely available in groceries.

You may prefer to use the facilities in a good restaurant or hotel, which will have an American-style toilet. In most restrooms, public or otherwise, there will be a garbage can beside the toilet. This is for used toilet paper, since the plumbing system cannot cope with it. Nonflushing toilets should be flushed using the jug provided in the stall.

Sign for a public toilet

## TV, RADIO, AND NEWSPAPERS

THE STATE-OWNED TRT (Türk Radyo ve Televizyon) has four television channels and three radio stations. Of these, TRT2 television has news reports in English, French, and German at 7pm and 10pm. TRT3 radio (FM 88.2) broadcasts news in English, French, and German at 9am, 12pm, 5pm, 7pm, and 9pm.

Recent deregulation of the airwaves and the coming of satellite TV has meant a pro- liferation of private channels, from Turkey and abroad. Foreign channels that can be received include CNN, BBC Prime, and MTV. Some hotels only have Turkish television so check before checking in if you want foreign channels.

There is also a wide variety of private radio stations, playing western and Turkish pop, jazz, and classical music. Voice FM (FM 90.6) broadcasts Voice of America programs in Turkish and news in English at 3pm. The BBC World Service can be received on shortwave.

The only English language daily paper published in Turkey is the *Turkish Daily News*, but day-old foreign newspapers can be obtained in tourist areas of the city, as can *The Guide (see p212)*. This has good features on Istanbul and Turkish culture.

## CONVERSION CHART

### US Standard to Metric
1 inch = 2.54 centimeters
1 foot = 30 centimeters
1 mile = 1.6 kilometers
1 ounce = 28 grams
1 pound = 454 grams
1 US quart = 0.947 liters
1 US gallon = 3.6 liters

### Metric to US Standard
1 millimeter = 0.04 inch
1 centimeter = 0.4 inch
1 meter = 3 feet 3 inches
1 kilometer = 0.6 mile
1 gram = 0.04 ounce
1 kilogram = 2.2 pounds
1 liter = 1.1 US quarts

## ELECTRICITY

AS IN EUROPE, the electric current is 220V AC. Plugs have two round pins, and there are two diameters in use. The smaller one is more common. Adapters should be bought prior to departure.

## TIME

TURKEY IS SEVEN hours ahead of Eastern Standard Time (EST), eight hours ahead of Eastern Daylight Time.

## DIRECTORY

### CONSULATES AND EMBASSIES

**Canada**
Büyükdere Cad, Begün Han 107/3, Gayrettepe.
📞 *(0212) 272 51 74.*
Embassy in Ankara:
📞 *(0312) 436 12 75.*

**United States**
Meşrutiyet Cad 104–108, Tepebaşi.
📞 *(0212) 251 36 02.*
Embassy in Ankara:
📞 *(0312) 468 61 10.*

### INTERPRETERS

**Tercüme 80**
Dünya Sağlık Sok, Opera Han 15–18, Taksim. **Map** 7 F4.
📞 *(0212) 243 53 64.*

### RELIGIOUS SERVICES

**Anglican**
**Christ Church**
Serdar-ı Ekrem Sok, Tünel.
**Map** 7 D5. 📞 *(0212) 251 56 16.*

**Greek Orthodox**
**St. George's Cathedral**
Sadrazam Ali Paşa Cad 35, Fener.
📞 *(0212) 525 21 17.*

**Jewish**
**Neve Shalom Synagogue**
Büyük Hendek Cad 61, Azapkapı.
**Map** 6 C5. 📞 *(0212) 293 75 66.*

**Presbyterian**
**All Saints Church**
Yusuf Kemal Sok 8, Moda.
📞 *(0216) 449 39 74.*

**Roman Catholic**
**St. Anthony of Padua**
İstiklal Cad 325, Galatasaray.
**Map** 7 D4. 📞 *(0212) 244 09 35.*

# Tips for Tourists

T HE MAJOR MONUMENTS and museums of Istanbul are
state-owned and charge a moderate entrance fee.
Students and senior citizens are entitled to reduced or
free entry to most sights, and should always carry proof
of their status with them. In some museums there is a
separate charge for a special section within the building,
for example, the Harem in Topkapı Palace *(see pp58–9).*
Most sights are closed at least one day a week, usually
Monday or Tuesday. Exhibits in museums are generally
labeled in Turkish only, but some are labeled in English
as well. If you intend to visit mosques *(see pp36–7)*
remember that they close regularly for prayer, although
people may be worshiping in them at any time of day.

**Lining up for the Harem tour in
Topkapı Palace *(see pp58–9)***

**Sign for Sultanahmet tourist office**

## TOURIST INFORMATION

T HE SIGN FOR a tourist information office is a white "i"
on a light green background in
a white box. The offices themselves are named in English
and Turkish. They rarely have
much printed information to
give out, least of all public
transportation timetables, but
the main office in Sultanahmet Square, in particular,
will be able to answer ques-
tions on all aspects of your
stay in Istanbul. The Directorate of Tourism in Beyoğlu
does not give out information
to casual passersby, but if you
book an appointment with
them, they will help with
planning longer trips to places
outside Istanbul and with
mountaineering, walking, and
yachting expeditions. It is
open on weekdays only.
   Edirne, Bursa, İznik, and
Çanakkale all have tourist

offices near the town center. Most information offices
are open from 9am to 5pm,
Mon–Sat. Some stay open
later in summer, while the
one at the airport is open 24
hours every day of the year.

## OPENING HOURS

M USEUM OPENING times are
generally 8:30 or 9am to
5:30 or 6pm, with a break for
lunch in smaller establishments.
Private businesses are open
from 9am to 6pm,
and government
offices from 8am
to 5pm. Shops
open from 8:30
or 9am to 7 or
8pm *(see p202).*
Most banks are
open 8:30am to noon and
1:30 to 5pm, Monday to Friday,
while exchange offices *(döviz)*
are usually open until 8 or
9pm *(see p224).*
   Public offices are closed
on Saturdays and Sundays,
and most shops on Sundays,
although small grocers are
often open seven days a week.

## GUIDED TOURS

S EVERAL TOUR operators run
special-interest tours of
Istanbul, as well as general
guided tours of the city and
farther afield. **Plan Tours** has
a variety of tours, including
trips to Gallipoli, Troy, and
Bursa, Jewish heritage tours,
and private yacht cruises along
the Bosphorus *(see pp144–9).*
**Gençtur**, which does "green"
tours of Istanbul, offers discounts for young people.
Companies running city tours

**Sign showing opening hours**

include **Meptur** and **ITS
Tourism**. For more companies
offering trips to destinations
outside Istanbul see page 237.
   While sightseeing, you may
be approached by people
offering their services as tour
guides. Some of these will be
official guides licensed by the
Greater Istanbul Municipality,
others may not be. Before
you go anywhere with a guide,
make it clear
what you want
to see and agree
on the fee. If
you have little
time, or do not
wish to travel
by public trans-
portation, it is often worth
negotiating a private tour with
a taxi driver.

## WOMEN TRAVELERS

W OMEN TRAVELING in
Turkey may receive
unwelcome attention from
men but are rarely in danger
of physical attack. It is possible
to avoid harassment by dressing respectably and looking
purposeful when walking
around. Avoid being out alone
at night. Traditional cafés *(see
pp200–1)* tend to be male
preserves, but restaurants
often have a section reserved
for women *(see p187).*

## VISITING MOSQUES

A LTHOUGH LARGE mosques
are open all day, closing
after last prayers in the evening, smaller ones open only

**Entrance tickets for some of
Istanbul's public monuments**

five times daily, at prayer times *(namaz)*. At these mosques it may be difficult to gain entrance outside prayer times unless there is a caretaker around to open up for you. Non-Muslims should not enter any mosque during prayers. Instead, wait until most of the worshipers have left.

The times of prayer change throughout the year. They may be chalked up on a board outside the mosque, but they are always signaled by the call to prayer *(ezan)* from a loudspeaker attached to the minaret of the mosque.

When visiting a mosque, women and men should dress appropriately *(see p37)*. Some mosques can provide suitable attire at the door. Take your shoes off before entering and leave them outside or carry them in with you. Make as little noise as possible inside, and show consideration for anyone who is praying there.

**Attendant on duty outside the Blue Mosque *(see pp78–9)***

## Students

A FEDERATION OF International Youth Travel Organization (FIYTO) Card will usually allow free entry to sights, and an International Student Identity Card (ISIC) a 50% reduction. Reduced-price bus tickets are available only to those attending Turkish educational institutions, with a card to prove it. Non-Turkish students can get discounts on intercity trains with an ISIC card. Officially, there are no discounts on buses for non-Turkish students, but if you say you are a student when buying your ticket, you may be given a small reduction. Budget accommodations are easy to find. In July and August you can get a bed in a student dormitory through Sultanahmet tourist information office. There are also a few youth hostels *(see p177)*, and plenty of cheap hotels and guest houses in the city center *(see pp178–85)*.

**Student with local women**

## Disabled Visitors

ISTANBUL HAS FEW facilities for disabled people, and the poor state of the streets can make it difficult to get around. Most mosques will not allow wheelchairs in, and very few museums have disabled access. Toilets with special facilities are also very rare. Conversely, museum staff and the public will go to great lengths to assist with entry to buildings, and there are some low-height public telephones and special-access buses *(see p231)*.

The **Society for the Advancement of Travel for the Handicapped, Inc.** provides travel information for the disabled.

## Photography

MUSEUMS OFTEN CHARGE for the use of a video camera, and sometimes an extra fee is required even for the use of ordinary cameras. Be sure to check whether photography with cameras and flash attachments is allowed. To avoid disturbance to worshipers in mosques, flash cameras are often forbidden; however, discreet photography is usually permitted.

As extortionate prices are usually charged for camera film at tourist sights, you can avoid this by buying much more inexpensive film at neighborhood camera shops.

## Directory

### Tourist Information Offices

**Atatürk Airport**
International Arrivals Hall.
Tel *(0212) 663 07 93.*

**Directorate of Tourism**
Meşrutiyet Cad 57, Tepebaşı.
**Map** 7 D4. Tel *(0212) 243 37 31.*
FAX *(0212) 252 43 46.*

**Hilton Hotel Arcade**
Cumhuriyet Cad, Harbiye.
**Map** 7 F2. Tel *(0212) 233 05 92.*

**Karaköy**
International Maritime Passenger Terminal (Terminal 2). **Map** 3 E1.
Tel *(0212) 249 57 76.*

**Sirkeci Station**
Sirkeci İstasyon Cad, Sirkeci.
**Map** 3 E3 (5 E1).
Tel *(0212) 511 58 88.*

**Sultanahmet Square**
Divanyolu Cad 3, Sultanahmet.
**Map** 3 E4 (5 E4).
Tel *(0212) 518 18 02.*

**United States**
821 United Nation Plaza,
New York, NY 10017.
Tel *(212) 687-2194.*
FAX *(212) 599-7568.*

### Tour Operators

**Gençtur**
Prof Kazım İsmail Gürkan Cad 14/4, Cağaloğlu. **Map** 3 D4 (5 D3). Tel *(0212) 520 52 74.*

**ITS Tourism**
Kaya Aldoğan Sok 12/1, Zincirlikuyu. Tel *(0212) 275 18 70.*

**Meptur**
Büyükdere Cad 26/17, Mecidiyeköy. Tel *(0212) 258 25 89.*

**Plan Tours**
Cumhuriyet Cad 131/1, Harbiye.
**Map** 7 F3. Tel *(0212) 230 22 72.*

### Disabled Visitors

**Society for the Advancement of Travel for the Handicapped, Inc.**
347 Fifth Ave.,
New York, NY 10016.
Tel *(212) 447-7284.*

# Personal Security and Health

**Badge of the Turkish police**

ISTANBUL IS AS SAFE AS other European cities, and visitors rarely encounter violence or theft. However, lone travelers should avoid certain suburbs of the city, especially those bordering the city walls, and as in any city, particular care should be taken at night. At all times be alert for pickpockets in crowded areas. In the event of any trouble, contact the Tourist Police.

There are public and private health clinics all over the city (some with English-speaking doctors), and a number of excellent private hospitals. For minor complaints, pharmacists will be able to provide advice.

## POLICE

THERE ARE SEVERAL police forces in Turkey, distinguishable by their uniforms. The Security Police (*Emniyet Polisi*) is the main force in Istanbul. Its officers wear dark blue uniforms and caps, and pale blue shirts. The Tourist Police (*Turizm Polisi*) is a branch of the *Emniyet Polisi*. Most officers have some knowledge of one or two European languages. The Tourist Police station in Sultanahmet, opposite the Basilica Cistern (*see p76*), is open 24 hours a day, and has an English-Turkish translator available Monday to Friday, 8:30am to 5pm.

The Dolphin Police (*Yunus Polisi*) is a rapid-reaction branch of the *Emniyet Polisi*. Dolphin officers ride motor-

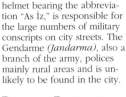

**Dolphin Motorbike Police badge**

bikes and wear black biking leathers with a red stripe.

The Traffic Police (*Trafik Polisi*) has the same blue uniform as the *Emniyet Polisi* but with white belt, hat, and gloves. You will see these officers patrolling the streets in black and white cars equipped with loudspeakers. The Falcon Police (*Şahin Polisi*) is the motorbike branch of the *Trafik Polisi*. Their black leather uniform is similar to that of the Dolphin Police but has a yellow stripe on the leathers instead of a red one.

The navy blue-uniformed Market Police (*Zabıta*) is a municipal police force that patrols bazaars and other areas of commerce.

The Military Police (*Askeri İnzibat*), distinguished by an army uniform and white helmet bearing the abbreviation "As İz," is responsible for the large numbers of military conscripts on city streets. The Gendarme (*Jandarma*), also a branch of the army, polices mainly rural areas and is unlikely to be found in the city.

## PERSONAL PROPERTY

ON THE WHOLE, Turks are very honest people and will go to great lengths to return lost property. It is always worth returning to the last place the item was seen, or going to the Tourist Police. Pickpockets, however, are numerous, and care should be taken in crowded areas. Property left on public transit can be reclaimed from the **Karaköy Gar** building.

## HEALTH PRECAUTIONS

VISITORS FROM from the US should check with their insurance carrier to be sure that they are covered. Be sure to get an itemized bill for your carrier. No vaccinations are legally required before entering Turkey, but your doctor may advise inoculation against hepatitis A (spread through contaminated food and water), hepatitis B, tetanus, and also typhoid.

**Bottled spring water**

Mosquitoes are more annoying than dangerous in Istanbul. Trucks run by the municipality spray the streets with repellent in the early evening, particularly in residential areas, but it is a good idea to bring some repellent lotion, spray, or gel from your home country. ESEM Mat machines, electric vaporizers that release an effective repellent into the atmosphere, are available in Turkey. You can buy the machine and spare tablets in pharmacies, supermarkets, and local groceries.

Many travelers to Turkey experience upset stomachs, diarrhea, and sometimes vomiting; this is often a result of mild food poisoning. It is

**Security policeman**

**Traffic policeman**

**Dolphin policeman**

**Turkish Security Police** *(Emniyet Polisi)* **patrol car**

**State ambulance in Istanbul**

have ambulances, but the hospitals mentioned here either have their own service or have a contract with a private company. The **Night Ambulance** is a private service that will take you to any hospital you request, while a state ambulance will take you only to the nearest state hospital.

---

## DIRECTORY

### EMERGENCY NUMBERS

**Ambulance**
📞 112.

**Night Ambulance**
📞 (0212) 247 07 81.

**Police**
📞 155.

### TOURIST POLICE

Yerebatan Cad 6, Sultanahmet.
**Map** 3 E4. 📞 (0212) 527 45 03 or 528 53 69.

### LOST PROPERTY

**Karaköy Gar**
Rıhtım Cad, Karaköy. **Map** 3 E1.
📞 (0212) 251 21 80.

### HOSPITALS

**American Admiral Bristol Hospital**
Güzelbahçe Sok 20, Nişantaşı.
**Map** 8 A2.
📞 (0212) 231 40 50.

**Cerrahpaşa Hospital**
Cerrahpaşa Cad, Cerrahpaşa.
**Map** 1 C5.
📞 (0212) 588 48 00.

**European (Avrupa) Hospital**
Mehmetçik Cad, Cahit Yalçın Sok 1, Mecidiyeköy. **Map** 8 A1.
📞 (0212) 212 88 11.

**German Hospital**
Sıraselviler Cad 119, Taksim.
**Map** 7 E4.
📞 (0212) 293 21 50.

**International Hospital**
İstanbul Cad 82,
Yeşilyurt.
📞 (0212) 663 30 00.

---

best to avoid drinking tap water altogether (bottled water is available everywhere), and some care should be taken when choosing restaurants and meals. Do not eat food that looks as if it might have been standing around, especially seafood. If you have a sensitive stomach, avoid half-cooked meats (usually grilled), salads, and milk products other than yogurt and *ayran (see p191)*.

## MEDICAL TREATMENT

**I**F YOU SUFFER from stomach troubles, remedies available from pharmacies include Lomotil, Ge-Oral (oral rehydration salts) and Buscopan. Drink lots of fluids – like bottled water, flat cola, weak black tea, or soda water – and stick to a bland diet, eating only bread, yogurt, and rice until you recover. More serious bouts will require antibiotics.

The first stop if you have a minor complaint should be a pharmacy *(eczane)*. Pharmacists are well trained, and many speak some English. If you need advice outside opening hours, look for a note in the window of a pharmacy giving the address of the local *nöbetçi eczane* (duty pharmacist).

There are excellent free public clinics *(poliklinik)* all over Istanbul, offering treatment for minor ailments. Private doctors often specialize in a particular branch of medicine, but there are general practitioners, called *tıbbi doktor*. Their clinics, located above stores in all the main shopping areas, are advertised by prominent signs outside.

Rabies poses a small threat in Turkey. If bitten or scratched by an animal, wash and cover the wound, and go straight to a hospital or health clinic.

**Şişli   Etfal Hastanesi**

**Sign for a state hospital in Şişli**

## HOSPITALS

**S**TATE HOSPITALS will take in non-Turkish nationals, but they are overcrowded, and treatment is not free. It is best to use private hospitals or university teaching hospitals such as **Cerrahpaşa**. Foreign private hospitals, such as the **American Admiral Bristol**, **European**, **German** (which also has a dental clinic), and **International**, treat anyone, regardless of nationality. Not all foreign hospitals

**Typical sign for a pharmacy in Istanbul**

# Banking and Currency

THERE IS NO LIMIT to the amount of foreign currency you can bring into Turkey. Most Turkish banks will change travelers' checks and Eurocheques as well as cash. Eurocheques are available only to travelers with European bank accounts. The best place to change cash is at a *döviz*, or foreign exchange office. It is also possible to change hard currency in gas stations, jewelers, and any other business dealing with large amounts of money.

Payment by credit card is becoming more widely accepted, and cash dispensers are found outside an increasing number of banks. Rates of exchange are far better in Turkey than outside, so it is better to change a minimal amount of money before traveling. Inflation is high, so change only a little money at a time.

**Cash dispenser with instructions in a range of languages**

## BANKS

MOST BANKS ARE open from 8:30am–midday and 1:30pm–5pm, Monday to Friday. However, the Garanti Bankası does not close for lunch and opens on Saturday mornings. There are branches in Sirkeci (Şehin Şah Pehlevi Caddesi), Sultanahmet (Divanyolu Caddesi), and Galatasaray (İstiklal Caddesi). The Vakıfbank at Esenler Coach Station is open daily 8:30am–11pm, and the Türkiye İş Bankası at the airport is open 24 hours.

There are many banks along Divanyolu Caddesi and İstiklal Caddesi. Nearly all banks have a foreign exchange desk, indicated by a sign in the window in several languages. Commission charges vary. Banks to look for that offer good exchange rates and low or no commission are Akbank, Garanti Bankası, Yapı Kredi, Türkiye İş Bankası, and Ziraat Bankası. A few foreign banks also have branches in Istanbul.

**Rates of exchange outside a *döviz***

## EXCHANGE OFFICES

FOREIGN EXCHANGE offices (*döviz*) are the best place to change foreign currency. They are efficient, open long hours (usually 8:30 or 9am to 8 or 9pm, Monday to Saturday), and give a better rate of exchange for cash than the banks. They do not charge commission on cash. Daily exchange rates will be clearly displayed. *Döviz* offices are found all over the city. Those on Divanyolu Caddesi in Sultanahmet, however, give poor rates of exchange and should be avoided if possible. Instead use offices such as **Para Döviz** in the Grand Bazaar, **Ye-Ye Döviz** in Beyoğlu, and **Bamka Döviz** and **Çetin Döviz** in Taksim.

## TRAVELERS' CHECKS AND CREDIT CARDS

TRAVELERS' CHECKS and Eurocheques should be cashed in banks or post offices. Many of the large banks, such as Garanti Bankası, do not charge commission on checks. Post offices always charge commission but give a better rate of exchange. *Döviz* offices, stores, and hotels rarely accept travelers' checks.

To cash either Eurocheques or travelers' checks, you will need your passport, which will be photocopied with the check. You will also need a Eurocheque card for Eurocheques. You must then collect your money from the cashier. It is advisable to check the amount you receive against your receipt.

The major credit cards, such as VISA, American Express, MasterCard (Access), and Diners Club, are accepted in increasing numbers of hotels, gas stations, stores, and restaurants. Credit cards and bank cards with PIN numbers can now also be used in the 24-hour cash dispensers of many banks, including Yapı Kredi Bankası, Garanti Bankası, and Türkiye İş Bankası. They dispense Turkish lira.

Even if you have a credit card or travelers' checks, it is a good idea to take some foreign currency with you into Turkey. Hard currency is in great demand, and you will often be able to use dollars, British pounds, or German marks to pay for larger items.

## CURRENCY

THE CURRENCY of Turkey is the Turkish lira, abbreviated to TL. There are no smaller units. The lira has one of the lowest unit values in the world, with inflation sometimes reaching 2% per week. It may be useful to carry a small calculator as you will be dealing with millions of lira at a time. High-denomination bills cannot always be changed in smaller stores, so try to carry a range of bills. Small change is so worthless that taxi drivers and sales assistants will often waive a few thousand lira in a transaction.

You can take up to US$5,000 worth of lira out of Turkey, but the rapid devaluation means that you will get a very poor rate if you exchange lira back for your own currency, so try to use up what you have left.

## Bills

*Turkish bills come in denominations ranging from 50,000TL to 5 millionTL. You may see red 20,000TL bills. These are no longer being printed but are still officially legal tender, although you may have difficulty getting some stores to accept them. Be aware that the higher-denomination bills are similar in color to each other and can easily be confused.*

50,000 lira

100,000 lira

250,000 lira

500,000 lira

1,000,000 lira

5,000,000 lira

## Coins

*The coins shown here (at their actual sizes) range in denomination from 500TL to 50,000TL. As with the bills, the head of Atatürk appears on one side of all coins. The 500TL and 1,000TL coins are of very little value.*

500 lira

1,000 lira

2,500 lira

5,000 lira

10,000 lira

25,000 lira

50,000 lira

# Telephone and Postal Services

**PTT sign on a street letter box**

POST OFFICES ARE identified by the letters PTT (Post, Telephone, and Telecommunications) in black on a yellow sign. Most post offices are open for general business between 9am and 5pm, Monday to Saturday. If you wish to just buy stamps or mail letters, stamp divisions in post offices are open from 8am to 8pm, and the telephone divisions are open every day until midnight. In the main tourist areas you can also buy stamps and mail letters at PTT kiosks. Particularly useful is the kiosk in Sultanahmet Square.

The Turkish telephone network has been privatized and is now run by a company called Türk Telekom. Public telephones, which are mostly blue although you may see older yellow or orange ones, are found throughout the city. There is a variety of methods for paying for calls: with a *jeton* (token), a phonecard, by credit card, or at post offices, in cash for a metered call. Hotels generally add high surcharges to phone calls.

**Small, independent kiosk selling phonecards and telephone tokens**

## USING A CARD PHONE

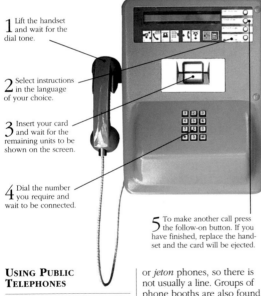

1 Lift the handset and wait for the dial tone.

2 Select instructions in the language of your choice.

3 Insert your card and wait for the remaining units to be shown on the screen.

4 Dial the number you require and wait to be connected.

5 To make another call press the follow-on button. If you have finished, replace the handset and the card will be ejected.

## USING PUBLIC TELEPHONES

THE BEST PLACE to make a call from a public phone is at a post office. There is usually a row of phones, taking either phonecards or tokens, outside the office. Inside the office is an area reserved for *kontürlü* (controlled or metered) phones, for which you pay after making your call. Rates are slightly higher than for card

or *jeton* phones, so there is not usually a line. Groups of phone booths are also found in busy areas, such as mass transit terminals.

You can often find phones for making local calls in cafés, newsstands, and grocers. Calls from such places are charged at slightly higher rates than those from post offices. You may need to buy special tokens at the counter, or you may be billed a flat fee or by a meter after your call.

## CARD PHONES

CARD PHONES CAN now be found all over Istanbul. Phonecards *(telefon kartı)*, available at post offices and from street vendors and kiosks, come in units of 30, 60, 100, 120, and 180. Instructions on the phones are in English, French, German, and Turkish.

Phonecards are the most economical method of making both international and local calls. Card phones are also considered more reliable than the older *jeton* phones. The disadvantages are that there are often long lines for them, and you can be cut off with little warning, especially if you forget to press the "Card Change" button, labeled in English, when changing cards. Cheap rate is from 6pm to 8am on weekdays and all day on weekends and holidays.

**Phonecards depicting scenes of Turkey on the reverse side**

## REACHING THE RIGHT NUMBER

• Istanbul is divided into two area codes:
0212 (European side)
0216 (Asian side).
• To call a number in the same area, do not use the code. For another area, dial the code first.
• To call another city in Turkey, use the appropriate area code. For example, 0224 for Bursa.
• To call Turkey from the US, dial 011 90 followed by the last three digits of the area code.
• To make an international call from Turkey, dial 00 followed by the code for the country, e.g.:
US and Canada: 1.
Australia: 61.
New Zealand: 64.

## OPERATOR SERVICES

**Directory Inquiries**
[ 118.

**Intercity Operator**
[ 131.

**International Operator**
[ 115.

**Wake-Up Call Service**
[ 135.

*Note: only international operators are guaranteed to speak English.*

## JETON PHONES

SINCE THE LINES FOR *jeton* phones are usually shorter than those for card phones, it is worth carrying a few tokens as well as a phonecard. They can be bought in post offices, at newspaper kiosks, and from vendors near groups of phone booths. Tokens come in two sizes: small *(küçük)* for local calls and medium *(orta)* for long-distance calls. However, it is better to use a card or metered phone for nonlocal calls. The slots on the phone for the tokens are usually labeled in English, but other instructions

**Medium and small telephone tokens**

appear in Turkish. To make a call, pick up the receiver and insert one *jeton*, or several if phoning abroad. When the red light goes out you will hear a tone. If you are making a local call, dial the number; otherwise dial 0 for an intercity call and 00 for an international call. When you hear the long-distance tone, dial the code and the number. If the red light comes on and beeps during your call, insert more tokens.

## CREDIT CARD PHONES

THERE ARE A FEW credit card phones in the central districts of Istanbul, at the airport, and in some five-star hotels. They have comprehensive instructions in English on the front of the telephone.

**Row of public telephone booths in Taksim Square**

## SENDING LETTERS

STAMPS ARE available only from post offices and PTT kiosks. These kiosks, found in tourist areas, also sell tokens, phonecards, and will change travelers' checks. Post offices are found throughout Istanbul. There are large branches, with a full range of postal services, in Sirkeci (Şehin Şah Pehlevi Caddesi), Taksim (Taksim

Square), and Beyoğlu (İstiklal Cad 192). These are marked on the Street Finder *(see pp238–48)*. Letters and postcards can be handed over the counter at post offices or put in mail boxes, which are yellow and labeled PTT. Common signs indicating which box or slot to put your letter in are: *Şehiriçi* (local), *Yurtiçi* (domestic), and *Yurtdışı* (international).

## POSTAL SERVICES

IT IS BEST TO USE airmail *(uçak ile)* when sending letters and parcels to another country, as surface mail is very slow. If you want to send a package by surface mail, use registered *(kayıtlı)* mail. The contents of a package must be inspected at the post office, so take tape to seal your package at the counter. Folding boxes *(kutu)* are supplied free in larger post offices. You may be asked to show a receipt to prove you are not sending antiquities.

**International mail box**

The express *Acele Posta Servisi* (APS) competes with private courier companies to provide a fast and efficient service. It costs more than airmail, but delivery is promised within three days.

## GENERAL DELIVERY

GENERAL DELIVERY mail should be sent to the central post office in Sirkeci. Mail should be addressed with the recipient's name, then: poste restante, Büyük Postane, Büyük Postane Caddesi, Sirkeci, Istanbul, Turkey. A nominal fee is payable on collection.

**Stamps in 10,000 and 50,000 lira denominations**

# TRAVEL INFORMATION

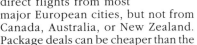

THE EASIEST WAY to get to Istanbul is to fly directly to the city's international airport, Atatürk Airport. There are regular, nonstop flights, both scheduled and chartered, from Chicago and New York. There are also direct flights from most major European cities, but not from Canada, Australia, or New Zealand. Package deals can be cheaper than the cost of a scheduled flight and may include hotel accommodations. Buses and trains run from many European countries to Istanbul, but any saving on the airfare may not be enough to make a much longer trip worthwhile. There are no direct ferry sailings from Europe, although cruises of the Aegean and Mediterranean usually include a one-day stopover in Istanbul.

Turkish Airlines (THY) airplane

---

### ARRIVING BY AIR

TURKEY'S MAIN international airline, **Turkish Airlines** (THY), has direct flights to Istanbul from Chicago and New York. **Delta Airlines** also has regular flights from New York. It is always worth asking about discounted offers when buying a ticket for a scheduled flight. Various travel companies arrange chartered flights, at much cheaper prices, throughout the summer months. The flying time between Chicago and Istanbul is approximately ten hours; it is about two hours less from New York.

Another Turkish airline, **Istanbul Airlines**, has flights from most European countries. **British Airways** has regular flights from London if you want to fly to Europe first.

**Passengers in the baggage hall of Atatürk Airport**

### ATATÜRK AIRPORT

ISTANBUL HAS ONE airport, **Atatürk Airport** (Atatürk Hava Limanı), with separate international *(dışhatları)* and domestic *(içhatları)* terminals. It is 25 km (16 miles) west of the city center, in Yeşilköy.

Services provided in the international terminal include duty-free shops open 24 hours daily. On arrival as well as departure, you can buy perfume, cigarettes, alcoholic drinks, candy, personal stereos, watches, and cosmetics. There are also gift shops, a café, a restaurant, a post office, 24-hour banking facilities, car rental centers, a tourist information office, and a hotel reservation desk.

Leave plenty of time – at least 2 hours – to check in for departures from Istanbul, particularly during the summer; there are often long lines to get through security checks at the terminal building.

**Sign giving details of the Havaş airport buses**

### TRANSPORTATION FROM THE AIRPORT

TAXIS *(see p230)* are easy to find at the large rank just outside the arrival hall of the international terminal. They are the most convenient means of reaching the city center from the airport.

The airport bus is an efficient, cheaper way of getting to the city center. Buses depart approximately every half-hour between 6am and 11pm. The bus stop is marked '**Havaş**' (the name of the operating company) and is situated outside the main doors of the arrival hall. The service into Istanbul makes one scheduled stop, on Mustafa Kemal Paşa Bulvarı in Aksaray, from where you can take a tram or taxi to Sultanahmet and Eminönü. It terminates in Taksim Square *(see p107)*. If you wish to get off somewhere else along the route, tell the driver before boarding.

Alternatively, there is a train connection to the city center from Yeşilköy, or you can take the Metro from Yenibosna as far as Zeytinburnu, and change onto the Tramway *(see pp232–3)*. Both Yeşilköy and Yenibosna are some distance from the airport, however, and far less convenient than taking the bus.

### PACKAGE TOURS

A NUMBER OF travel companies organize package deals to Istanbul. These offer substantial savings on a stay in some of the city's top hotels, as well as the reassurance of having a company rep on hand to deal with any problems. Among the companies in the US that offer package deals to Istanbul are **Big Apple Tours**, **International Tours and Cruises**, and for ages 18–35, **Contiki Holidays**.

**Sirkeci Station in Eminönü, where trains from Europe arrive**

## ARRIVING BY TRAIN

THE ORIENT EXPRESS *(see p66)* no longer runs as far as Istanbul, and there has been a decline in train travel east through Europe since the break up of the former Yugoslavia. At present, the only direct route is from Thessaloniki, in Greece. The main overland route is from Munich via Salzburg, Vienna, and Budapest, a journey lasting two and a half days. Passengers traveling from London can book the full trip through **British Rail International**.

Istanbul has two main-line stations: Sirkeci on the European side of the Bosphorus, and Haydarpaşa on the Asian side. Trains from Europe arrive at Sirkeci Station *(see p66)*. Trains from Anatolia and Asian cities arrive at Haydarpaşa Station *(see p133)*, from where you can get a ferry across to the European side.

**Highway sign showing Turkish and European road numbers**

## ARRIVING BY BUS

THE LEADING TURKISH bus companies **Ulusoy** and **Varan** operate direct services from several European cities to Istanbul. Ulusoy buses run from Paris, Vienna, Munich, Milan, and Athens. Varan runs from cities in Austria only, including Vienna and Salzburg.

Traveling by bus, you will arrive at Esenler bus station *(otogar)*, 10 km (6 miles) northwest of Istanbul city center. Esenler is also the main terminal for domestic connections *(see p236)*. Your bus company will probably take you into town in a courtesy minibus. If not, take the Metro *(see pp232–3)* from the station in the center of the *otogar*, getting on at the platform marked Aksaray. The 83E and 91 buses also go to the city center.

## ARRIVING BY CAR

DRIVERS TAKING CARS into Turkey are asked to show registration documents and a valid driver's license at the port of entry. You will be given a certificate by the Turkish customs authorities and this should be carried at all times, together with your driver's license and passport. You must also have the appropriate insurance, which you can obtain through your car-rental company. The car should be equipped with a fire extinguisher, a first-aid kit, and two hazard warning triangles, for breakdowns.

Foreign drivers may find driving in Istanbul difficult and time-consuming, since local traffic may be at a standstill in a traffic jam or traveling at dangerously high speeds. There are public parking lots, although it can be difficult to get a space. Your hotel may have its own parking facilities.

---

## DIRECTORY

### AIRLINES

**Delta Airlines**
[ (800) 221-1212.

**Istanbul Airlines**
[ (0212) 509 21 21 (Istanbul).

**Turkish Airlines (THY)**
[ (0212) 663 63 63 (Istanbul).
[ (212) 339-9650 (New York).
[ (312) 943-7858 (Chicago).

### AIRPORT

**Atatürk Airport**
[ (0212) 663 64 00.

**Havaş**
[ (0212) 663 68 50.

### PACKAGE TOURS

**Big Apple Tours**
1423 55th Street,
Brooklyn, NY 11219.
[ (718) 438-8747.

**Contiki Holidays**
300 Plaza Alicante, Suite 900,
Garden Grove, CA 92840.
[ (800) CON-TIKI.

**International Tours and Cruises**
184 Fifth Avenue, 4th floor,
New York, NY 10010.
[ (800) BUY-TRAVEL.

### TRAIN TRAVEL

**British Rail International**
[ 0990 848 848 (UK).

### INTERNATIONAL BUS SERVICES

**Ulusoy**
Esenler Bus Station,
[ (0212) 658 30 00.

**Varan**
Esenler Bus Station.
[ (0212) 658 02 70.

**Buses parked in front of their company offices at Esenler**

# GETTING AROUND ISTANBUL

IT IS POSSIBLE TO WALK between most major sights in Istanbul, and central areas are well served by an expanding system of metro and tram lines. Buses and dolmuşes provide city-wide transportation, but take care to avoid traveling by road at rush hour times, when the main roads in and out of the city are congested with traffic.

**Street sign at a junction in central Sultanahmet**

Since there are many types of public transportation, it is often very confusing trying to figure out the best means

of transit for any one trip. Still, the system is interconnected, so you can always get where you want to go, somehow. See the map inside the back cover for more information. Each type of transit has an individual ticket system, but there is also a travel pass, AKBİL *(see p233)*, which can be useful whatever the length of your stay. If time is short take a taxi. Istanbul's yellow cabs are relatively cheap, and their drivers can usually find a fairly traffic-free route.

## ISTANBUL ON FOOT

THE DEVELOPMENT of pedestrian areas, such as İstiklal Caddesi and central Sultanahmet, has made it possible to walk with ease around some parts of Istanbul. This can be particularly pleasant in spring and autumn, when the weather is mild. It is also possible to walk around the city's quieter backstreets – like the area around the antique shops of Çukurcuma, near Galatasaray, or Eyüp *(see pp120–21)* – without encountering much traffic. For specialized tour companies that offer various walking tours around the city, see page 221.

**Sign for a pedestrian underpass**

Wherever you walk, bear in mind that traffic stops only at pedestrian crossings controlled by lights, and always make use of pedestrian overpasses and underpasses on main roads.

Istanbul, like any city, has parts that should be avoided. If you are planning to walk in areas off the usual tourist track seek local advice, take extra care, and try not to walk in unfamiliar streets after dark.

## TAXIS

TAXICABS ARE ubiquitous in Istanbul, and fares are cheap in relation to other major European cities. Taxis operate day and night and can be

hailed in the street or found at taxi stands *(see pp238–48)*. Hotel and restaurant staff can always phone for a taxi.

Cabs are bright yellow, with the word "taksi" on a sign on the roof. They take up to four passengers. In all licensed taxis the fare is charged according to a meter. The daytime *(gündüz)* fare is applied between 6am and midnight; the nighttime *(gece)* rate is 50 percent higher. If you cross the Bosphorus Bridge in either direction, the toll will be added to the fare at the end of your ride. The driver will not expect a sizable tip unless he has helped you load luggage. The normal procedure for tipping is just to round up the fare to the nearest convenient figure.

**Old-style dolmuş, still in use on some routes in the city**

Most taxi drivers do not speak much English, if any. You may also find that some drivers are not familiar with routes to lesser-known sights, so it is a good idea to know which part of the city you want

to go to and to carry a map with you. It may also help to have the name and address of your destination written down.

## DOLMUŞES

DOLMUŞES ARE a useful means of transit outside the city center. These shared taxis with fixed routes are cheaper than regular taxis and more frequent than buses. In Turkish the word *dolmuş* means "full," and drivers usually wait until every seat is taken before moving off.

Four types of vehicle are used. The most distinctive are the large American cars made in the '50s, which are yellow or black and have two rows of seats in the back. These are gradually being phased out and replaced with new, yellow diesel minibuses. There are also old-style minibuses, often blue, known either as *minibüs* or *dolmuş*. Finally, some yellow taxis operate as dolmuşes and are

**Licensed Istanbul taxicab with its registration number on the side**

## USEFUL DOLMUŞ ROUTES

**Taksim – Ataköy**
*(from Şehit Muhtar Bey Caddesi)*
**Taksim – Eminönü**
*(from Lamartin Caddesi)*
**Taksim – Kadıköy**
*(from Lamartin Caddesi)*
**Taksim – Topkapı**
*(from Abdülhak Hamit Caddesi)*
**Beşiktaş – Taksim**
*(from Beşiktaş Caddesi)*
**Eminönü – Topkapı**
*(from Sobacılar Caddesi)*
**Kadıköy – Üsküdar**
*(from Haydarpaşa Rıhtım Caddesi)*
**Kadıköy – Bostancı**
*(from Kumluk Meydanı)*
**Üsküdar – Beykoz**
*(from Paşa Limanı Caddesi)*
**Beşiktaş – Sarıyer**
*(from Barbaros Bulvarı)*
**Yedikulc – Edirnekapı**
*(along the city walls, changing at Topkapı Gate)*

distinguishable from taxis only by the sign with their destination in the front window. Dolmuşes run throughout the day until midevening, and later on busy routes, such as those starting from Taksim.

Points of origin and final destinations are displayed in the front windows of all dolmuşes, and passengers can get in and out anywhere en route. The fare depends on the length of your ride. State your destination, then hand your money to the driver or another passenger to pass forward. Any change will be returned. To stop the vehicle, simply say to the driver *"inecek* (pronounced eenejek) *var"* ("somebody wants to get out") and he will stop at the first opportunity.

Dolmuş stands are marked by a blue sign with a black "D" on a white background. A main center for dolmuşes is Taksim. Dolmuşes from here cross Bosphorus Bridge but, unlike taxis, do not charge passengers the bridge toll.

## GETTING AROUND BY BUS

LOCAL BUSES ARE either run by the municipality or rented out to private operators. The most common buses are **Belediye Otobüsü**, which are

owned and operated by the municipality. Tickets must be bought before boarding and you need one per ride, regardless of how far you are going. You can buy tickets at kiosks in bus stations, at newspaper stands near bus stops, and (conveniently, but at a slightly higher price) from private vendors who set up small stalls near bus stops and telephone kiosks. On boarding, deposit your ticket in the metal box near the driver.

An Özel Halk city bus, on which you pay a conductor after boarding

Recent deregulation of advertising has resulted in an array of brightly decorated buses, but the standard colors are red with an indigo stripe on the sides and front. A few Belediye buses run on natural gas. They are painted green and run mostly on the Asian side. There are also a few double-decker Belediye buses, on which all passengers are seated. They require two or three tickets depending on the trip. Some routes are served by special buses with lifts and wider doorways, to facilitate wheelchair

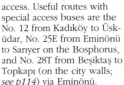
**Full-fare and student tickets for Belediye buses**

access. Useful routes with special access buses are the No. 12 from Kadıköy to Üsküdar, No. 25E from Eminönü to Sarıyer on the Bosphorus, and No. 28T from Beşiktaş to Topkapı (on the city walls; *see p114*) via Eminönü.

Some older Belediye buses are orange with a cream roof,

but most of these are now rented out to private operators. They are known as **Özel Halk Otobüsü** ("private buses of the people") and have this or "ÖHO" written on the side. On Özel Halk buses you do not buy a ticket in advance. A conductor will come round to collect your fare, which costs the same as a Belediye bus ticket. A few green double-decker buses are also privately leased.

On all buses, major destinations and bus numbers are shown on the front; there is sometimes a list of stops in the front window. Always get on through the front door. To stop the bus, press the button above the rear or middle doors before reaching your stop. There are big local bus stations in Taksim, Beşiktaş, Eminönü, Kadıköy, and Üsküdar.

Most buses run between 6 or 7am and 9 or 10pm, although some run until midnight. There are no night buses.

**Belediye bus advertising a brand of tomato paste**

# Getting Around by Metro, Tram, and Train

T HE MODERN TRAM and metro systems are invaluable to both locals and visitors. Trams combine a congestion-free ride on popular routes, with easy access and a comparatively comfortable journey, while the Metro provides an efficient means of linking the center with the European suburbs and Esenler bus station. Greater Istanbul Municipality intends eventually to integrate the tram, metro, and train systems into a more comprehensive network covering the whole city, with a tunnel under the Bosphorus linking the European and Asian sides.

Modern tram in Sultanahmet

**Full-fare and student Tramway tickets, valid for one trip**

## THE MODERN TRAMWAY

T HE TRAMWAY *(Tramvay)* is a useful service on which you will probably travel more than once during the course of your stay. The line runs from Eminönü, passing all the main sights in Sultanahmet, to Yusuf-paşa, which is close to Aksaray – the first station on the Metro line. It then goes out past the city walls into the suburbs, ending at Zeytinburnu.

Trams travel on the right-hand side of the street, so be sure to stand on the correct platform. To board a tram, buy a flat-fare ticket from the booth *(gişe)* near the platform and put it into the receptacle at the top of the platform steps. Trams are frequent, running every 5 minutes between 5am and midnight, but get crowded during rush hour.

Metro sign

## THE METRO

I STANBUL'S METRO system has only recently come into operation, with much of it still under construction and still more at the planning stage. The existing Metro runs from Aksaray out to Esenler bus station (Otogar). There it divides, with one line going to the suburb of Esenler and the other continuing to Ataköy and Yenibosna. Running both above and below ground, the

## TRAM AND METRO ROUTE MAP

Metro lines shown here as planned or under construction should be open by the year 2000. There are also plans to extend the metro line past Yenibosna to the airport.

**KEY**

— Metro

- - Metro planned or under construction

— Tünel

— Tramway

- - Tramway planned or under construction

— Old tram

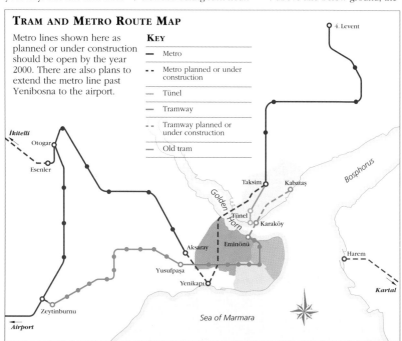

Istanbul Metro is known locally by a variety of other names. These include Hızlı Tramvay (High Speed Tram), Hafif Metro (Light Metro), and LRT (Light Railway).

Trains run every 10–15 minutes seven days a week, starting at 5:40am and ending at 11:15pm. To board a train, buy a flat-fare ticket from the booth marked "Gişe" and feed it into the turnstile under the sign "Tek Geçiş." The final destination of each route is clearly indicated on the platform.

**Turkish Railways sign on the side of a train**

The Metro route will eventually extend across the Golden Horn to link the airport to the suburb of 4. Levent, with potential to go even farther in the future. There are also plans to construct more overland Metro lines on the Asian side.

## THE TÜNEL

INAUGURATED IN 1875, this French-built underground railway climbs steeply uphill for a distance of 500 m (550 yards) from Karaköy to Tünel Square in Beyoğlu, from which you can get the old tram up İstiklal Caddesi. The Karaköy station is set back from the main road just off the Galata Bridge (see p101). The best way to get to it is through the underpass at the end of the bridge. Watch for the exit marked "Tünel." To board it at either station, you need to buy a token (jeton) from the booth and drop it into the turnstile at the entrance to the platform.

## THE OLD TRAM

THE OLD TRAM (or Nostaljik Tramvay) runs just over 1 km (0.75 mile) along İstiklal Caddesi from Tünel to Taksim Square. The trams are the original, early-20th-century vehicles, taken out of service in 1966 but revived in 1989 for their historical value. The ticket collectors wear period costume. Tickets can be purchased from kiosks at either end of the line.

## SUBURBAN TRAINS

SUBURBAN TRAINS (banliyö) run beside the Sea of Marmara between Sirkeci and Halkalı (on the European side), and Haydarpaşa and Gebze (on the Asian side). The service is slow, and stations are generally not close enough to tourist sights to be of much use to visitors. Exceptions are Yedikule (for Yedikule Museum, see p115), Ataköy (near Galleria shopping mall, see p203), and Yeşilköy (the airport station, see p228). On the Asian side, Bostancı is one of the ferry piers for the Princes' Islands.

A train ticket costs the same flat rate as a bus ticket and should be retained for the whole trip. Suburban trains start daily at 6am and stop at 11:30pm. For further information on the rail network, see the map inside the back cover.

## THE AKBİL TRAVEL PASS

THE AKBİL is a type of travel pass that can be used on almost all forms of public transportation in Istanbul. Short for akıllı bilet, or "intelligent ticket," this metal token can be purchased from main

DIRECTORY

**METRO AND TRAMWAY INFORMATION**

(0212) 568 99 70.

**TRAIN INFORMATION**

Haydarpaşa Station
(0216) 336 04 75.

Sirkeci Station
(0212) 527 00 51.

bus stations and other public transit ticket offices. It can be used on the Metro, the Tramway, the Tünel, ferries and sea buses, and most city buses.

When purchasing an AKBİL, you pay for a number of units in advance and also a deposit, which is refundable, for the token itself. More units can be added to the token at any time. The distinctive orange-colored AKBİL machines are located at the entrances to stations and on buses. To use the AKBİL, place the metal token in the socket on the front of the machine, near the display panel. The fare will then be deducted in units.

**AKBİL passes**

**Old tram traveling along İstiklal Caddesi in Beyoğlu**

# Getting Around by Boat

**Token (jeton)
for TDİ ferry**

PERHAPS THE MOST pleasant and relaxing means of getting around Istanbul is by the innumerable water-borne craft that ply the Bosphorus between the European and Asian sides. These range from small, privately operated motorboats to a fleet of high-speed catamarans. Traveling by boat, you will avoid the traffic jams and tolls of the Bosphorus road bridges. As well as being a relatively fast way to get around, a boat will also provide some great views of the city.

**Old ferries at Karaköy**

## FERRIES

A CONSTANT TRAFFIC of ferries crosses the Bosphorus and the Golden Horn. Called *vapur*, they belong to the state-run TDİ (Turkish Maritime Lines).

The principal ferry terminus on the European side is at Eminönü *(see p87)*. Each of the six piers here has a boarding area, with the destination written in large black letters on the outside. The three main piers are numbered. Pier 1 serves Üsküdar; pier 2 serves Kadıköy; and pier 3, labeled "Boğaz Hattı," is for all ferries traveling up the Bosphorus, including the special cruise. The other three piers are a short distance from Eminönü proper. On the west side of the Galata Bridge is the pier

**Passengers boarding a ferry**

for ferries up the Golden Horn (Haliç Hattı). To the east of pier 1, at Sirkeci, across the road from the station, is the departure point for car ferries to Harem. Farther along from this, at Sarayburnu, is the final pier, labeled "Adalar," from which long-distance ferries depart. This is the pier for ferries to the Princes' Islands.

Another main terminal is Karaköy, opposite Eminönü, from which ferries run to Haydarpaşa and Kadıköy.

## FERRY AND SEA BUS ROUTE MAP

There are numerous ferry and sea bus services departing daily from Eminönü and the other ports. In addition, a number of smaller, privately operated motorboats serve the same destinations as the state-run ferries.

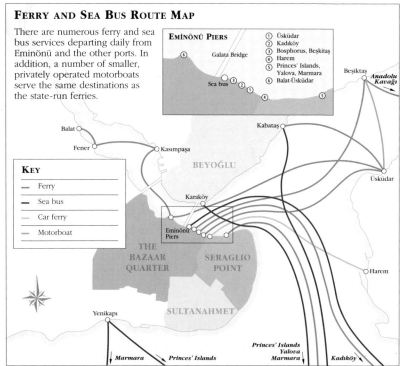

**EMİNÖNÜ PIERS**

Galata Bridge

Sea bus

① Üsküdar
② Kadıköy
③ Bosphorus, Beşiktaş
④ Harem
⑤ Princes' Islands, Yalova, Marmara
⑥ Balat-Üsküdar

Beşiktaş
*Anadolu Kavağı*

Kabataş

Balat

Fener

Kasımpaşa

BEYOĞLU

Üsküdar

**KEY**

— Ferry

— Sea bus

— Car ferry

— Motorboat

Karaköy

Eminönü Piers

THE BAZAAR QUARTER

SERAGLIO POINT

Harem

Yenikapı

SULTANAHMET

↓ Marmara   ↘ Princes' Islands

Princes' Islands
Yalova
Marmara

↘ Kadıköy ◂

The international dock, where cruise liners berth, is also here.

There are ferries from Eminönü to Kadıköy between 7:30am and 9pm, and from Eminönü to Üsküdar between 6am and 11:30pm, every 15 minutes (20 minutes at weekends). Other services are less frequent. If you want to use the ferry system more extensively, especially to hop between the villages along the Bosphorus, you will need to arm yourself with a timetable.

## MOTORBOATS

A NUMBER OF privately run craft cross the Bosphorus and Golden Horn at various points and run up the Bosphorus. These routes are also served by TDİ ferries, but private motorboats are more frequent, although slightly more expensive. A conductor will collect your fare after the boat leaves the pier.

## SEA BUSES

T HE MODERN, Swedish-built catamarans that are known as sea buses *(deniz otobüsleri)* are run by İDO, a municipal company. Their interiors resemble aircraft cabins, with long rows of comfortable, reclining seats, piped-in music, and air-conditioning. Sea buses are considerably faster and more comfortable than ferries, but cost two or three times as much.

The most useful routes are Eminönü to Kadıköy (half-hourly from 7:40am to 7pm Monday to Friday, and 8:15am to 6:10pm at weekends); and Bakırköy to Bostancı (hourly between 8:15am and 10pm). In the summer, sea buses run

**Ferry for Kadıköy, docked at Eminönü's pier 2**

from Kabataş and Bostancı to Büyükada on the Princes' Islands. For destinations outside Istanbul, see pages 236–7.

## THE BOSPHORUS TRIP

T URKISH MARITIME LINES runs daily excursions up the Bosphorus *(see pp136–49).* These are normal ferries on which light refreshments are served (at inflated prices) but no meals. They get crowded in the summer months, especially on weekends, so it is a good idea to arrive early to ensure a deck seat with a view. You should retain your ticket during the trip, as you must show it when boarding for the return trip. You

**Sea bus timetable**

can disembark at any pier along the way, boarding the next ferry that comes along with the same ticket; but if you make a second stop you will need to buy a new ticket. TDİ also has a trip from Kadıköy in summer on weekends only.

There are alternatives to the official Bosphorus trip. The small private boats that leave Eminönü just after the TDİ ferry sails in the summer months go only halfway up the straits and do not stop along the way. If you decide to book a private cruise with a tour company, be sure to choose a reputable company, such as **Hatsail Tourism.**

## BUYING BOAT TICKETS

F OR FERRIES AND sea buses, you need to buy a flat-fare *jeton* from the booth *(gişe)* at the pier or from one of the unofficial street vendors who sit nearby and sell them at slightly higher prices. These *jetons* can be used for all local trips. For ferries to the Princes' Islands or for the Bosphorus trip, you still need to buy a *jeton* that will cover the outward and return trips, but it is more expensive than the normal TDİ fare.

To enter the pier, put the *jeton* into the slot beside the turnstile, and then wait in the boarding area for a boat.

A schedule of sailing times hangs in each pier, and a copy of the timetable *(tarife)* can usually be bought at the ticket booth.

---

### DIRECTORY

**FERRY INFORMATION**

📞 (0212) 244 42 33.

**SEA BUSES**

📞 (0216) 362 04 44.

**PRIVATE CRUISES**

**Hatsail Tourism**
📞 (0212) 258 99 83.

---

**A sea bus catamaran, Istanbul's fastest form of water transit**

# Traveling Beyond Istanbul

THE BEST WAY of getting from Istanbul to other towns and cities is by long-distance bus. A bewildering number of companies offer services to every conceivable destination in Turkey, with several companies serving any one intercity route. It is worth paying a bit extra to travel with a reputable company, to ensure a safe and comfortable journey.

**Courtesy minibus to and from the bus station**

The train network is much more limited than the bus network. Trains go to only a limited number of cities in Turkey, and the service is less efficient. Even express trains take longer than the same journey by bus. For destinations across the Sea of Marmara, ferries and sea buses are a relaxing means of transportation.

## INTERCITY BUSES

THE MAIN BUS station (*otogar*) for all domestic and international destinations is at Esenler, 10 km (6 miles) northwest of the city center. It is served by the Metro. Facilities in the bus station include two banks, one of which is open until 11pm. There is another bus station in Harem, on the Asian side of Istanbul. Most buses stopping here will be on their way to or from Esenler.

**One of the many intercity buses from Esenler**

Bus tickets can be bought from travel agents or bus company offices in the city center, or direct from offices in the bus station. If you buy your bus ticket from a travel agency they will provide a service vehicle from their office to the bus station.

At first sight, Esenler bus station can seem daunting. The central courtyard is surrounded by over 150 ticket offices, their destinations displayed on signs. Company representatives walk around the station calling out destinations of buses about to depart. If you cannot find the company or destination you want, there is an information office next to the Metro station, or you can ask any company representative, who will take you to the most suitable office.

**Kamil Koç** (Bay 144), **Uludağ** (Bay 99), and **Hakiki Koç** (Bay 7) have services to Bursa. The trip takes about four hours. Kamil Koç also goes to Çanakkale, taking six hours, and Gallipoli (about five hours). **Edirne Birlik** (Bay 109) has a service to Edirne, which takes three hours. Smoking is generally permitted on buses, but some companies now provide nonsmoking (*sigarasız*) seats, so that at least the person next to you will not be smoking. A few companies have totally nonsmoking services. Single passengers will usually be seated next to someone of the same sex. Couples can sit together. Mineral water, and sometimes other refreshments, are available on board free of charge. There will also be frequent rest and meal stops at service stations. On most buses, the attendant will come around at regular intervals with a bottle of cologne that passengers are invited to use.

## LONG-DISTANCE FERRIES

FERRIES AND SEA BUSES are a convenient means of traveling long distances from a city surrounded by water. TDİ ferries (*see p234*) are a good value, and cars are carried on many lines. Few concessions are made to comfort, however; seating is often rudimentary and the food service is overpriced and poorly equipped.

The trip to Bursa can be made by a combination of sea bus or ferry, and bus. The fastest route is to take one of four daily sea buses from Kabataş to Yalova, just an hour away. Ferries also sail from Sarayburnu, in Eminönü, to Yalova. The port of Mudanya is even closer to Bursa, but boats are much less frequent. Sea buses go there from Yenikapı, ferries from Sarayburnu. Frequent buses meet incoming boats at Yalova and Mudanya.

In the summer, sea buses go from Yenikapı to Marmara. TDİ also has ferries to the Marmara Islands. Departing from Sarayburnu, they take 5 hours to reach Marmara and another 45 minutes to reach Avşa.

**Sea bus for Yalova about to depart from Kabataş on the Bosphorus**

## FLIGHTS TO BURSA

SÖNMEZ AIRLINES fly between Istanbul and Bursa twice daily, Monday to Friday at 9:30am and 6pm. The flight lasts one hour. Bursa airport is approximately 15 minutes' drive from the city center.

## TRAINS TO EDİRNE

THERE IS a daily train to Edirne from Sirkeci Station *(see p66)*. The trip takes six hours, twice the length of the bus trip. Reservations can be made at the stations in either city, or in certain travel agencies displaying the TCDD (Turkish State Railways) sign. Bursa is not on the rail network.

## CAR RENTAL

TURKEY'S comprehensive intercity bus network means that a car is not necessary for traveling to other cities. If you do wish to drive, car-rental companies such as **Avis** and **Hertz** have offices in the airport, as well as in the city center. Make sure that you take out adequate insurance with your car-rental agency. You do not need an international driver's license; a normal license from your own country will suffice.

All roads in Turkey, both in and outside cities, are hazardous; extreme caution is recommended. Traffic drives on and yields to the right, even on

**Car-rental office in the arcade of the Hilton Hotel, Taksim**

traffic circles. The Turkish Touring and Automobile Club (Türkiye Turing ve Otomobil Kurumu, or **TTOK**, *see p175*), based in Istanbul, gives motorists advice on driving in Turkey, as well as offering assistance with breakdowns, accidents and insurance.

## DAY TRIP TOURS

A NUMBER of companies offer day trips from Istanbul to the Princes' Islands, the Dardanelles, Bursa, and villages on the Black Sea. Recommended tour operators are **She Tours**, **Türk Express**, and **Plan Tours** *(see p221)*. **Arnica** specializes in trips to the countryside around Istanbul. Edirne is not usually included on tour company itineraries, although some will organize special tours there on request.

## LOCAL TRANPORTATION OUTSIDE ISTANBUL

THE MAIN means of public transportation in both Bursa and Edirne is the dolmuş *(see pp230–31)*, with the destination displayed on a sign on the roof. If you stay in the center of either city and are moderately fit, you will find that all of the major sights are within easy walking distance.

In Bursa city center, Heykel, at the eastern end of Atatürk Caddesi, is the main dolmuş station. From there you can get dolmuşes to most other parts of the city. There is also an efficient bus service.

Edirne is much smaller than Bursa, and the public transit system is not as comprehensive. To get from the bus station to the town center, a distance of 2 km (1 mile), take a Merkez–Garaj minibus dolmuş or a taxi.

There are no motor vehicles on the Princes' Islands. On Büyükada and Heybeliada there are horse-drawn carriages; otherwise you have to get around the islands on foot or by bicycle.

**Horse-drawn carriage on Büyükada**

# STREET FINDER

THE MAP REFERENCES that are given throughout this guide refer to the maps on the following pages. Some small streets with references may not be named on the map. References are also given for hotels *(see pp174–85)*, restaurants *(see pp186–201)*, stores *(see pp202–11),* and entertainment venues *(see pp212–15)*. The

**Visitor to Istanbul consulting a map**

map below shows the area covered by the ten maps and the key lists the symbols used. The first figure of the reference tells you which map page to turn to; the letter and number indicate the grid reference. For an overview of Greater Istanbul, see pages 108–9. The map on the inside back cover shows public transit routes.

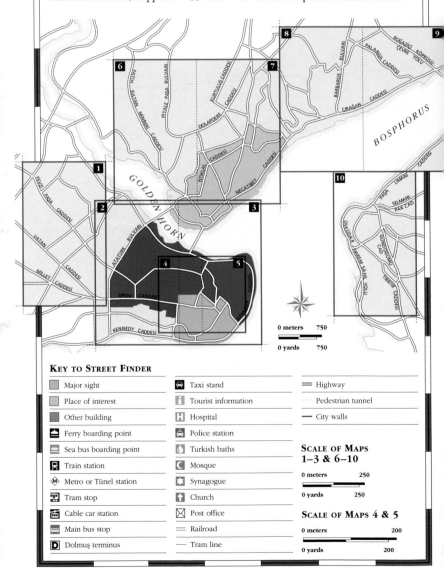

## KEY TO STREET FINDER

| | |
|---|---|
| ■ | Major sight |
| ■ | Place of interest |
| ■ | Other building |
| ⛴ | Ferry boarding point |
| 🚤 | Sea bus boarding point |
| 🚉 | Train station |
| Ⓜ | Metro or Tünel station |
| 🚊 | Tram stop |
| 🚡 | Cable car station |
| 🚌 | Main bus stop |
| D | Dolmuş terminus |

| | |
|---|---|
| 🚕 | Taxi stand |
| ℹ | Tourist information |
| H | Hospital |
| 🚓 | Police station |
| 🛁 | Turkish baths |
| C | Mosque |
| ✡ | Synagogue |
| ✝ | Church |
| ⊠ | Post office |
| ═ | Railroad |
| — | Tram line |

| | |
|---|---|
| ═ | Highway |
| ·· | Pedestrian tunnel |
| — | City walls |

**SCALE OF MAPS 1–3 & 6–10**

0 meters     250
0 yards      250

**SCALE OF MAPS 4 & 5**

0 meters     200
0 yards      200

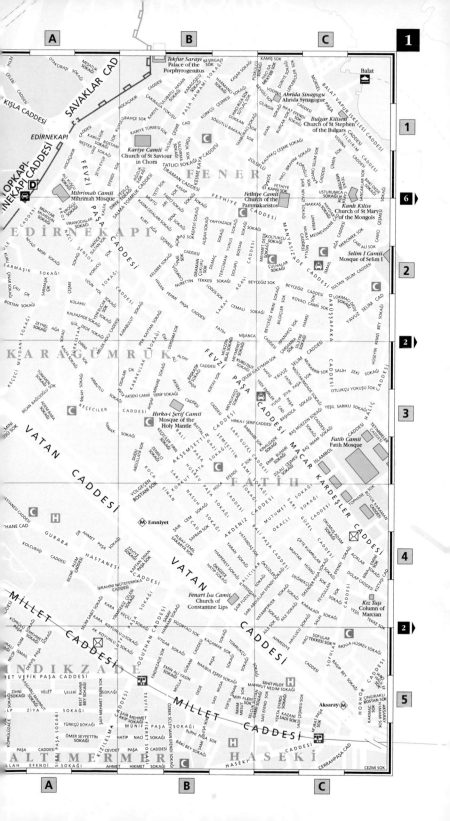

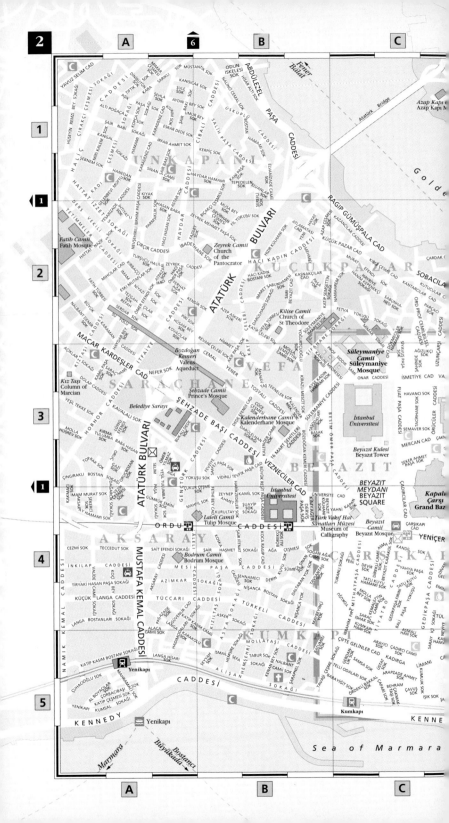

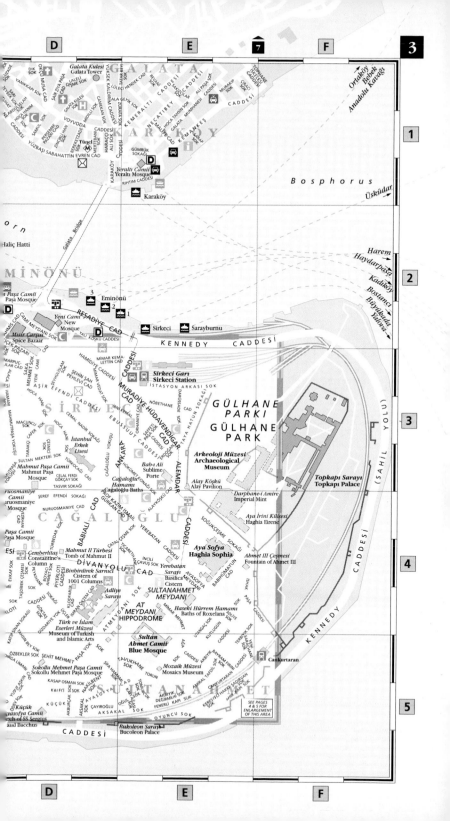

**GALATA**

Galata Kulesi
Galata Tower

YÜKSEK KALDIRIM CAD

KEMERALTI   CADDESİ

REVANİ

SAKIZ ÇIKMAZI

HOCA TAHSİN SOK

ALİ PAŞA SOK

TOPHANE CADDESİ

**KARAKÖY**

VOYVODA

Tünel

**Ortaköy
Bebek
Anadolu Kavağı**

**Üsküdar**

**B o s p h o r u s**

GÜMRÜK
SOKAĞI

Yeraltı Camii
Yeraltı Mosque
RIHTIM CADDESİ

Karaköy

**Haliç Hatti**

**1**

**MİNÖNÜ**

Paşa Camii
Paşa Mosque

3
Eminönü
2
1

**Harem
Haydarpaşa
Kadıköy
Bostancı
Büyükada
Yalova**

**2**

Yeni Camii
New
Mosque

REŞADİYE   CAD

Sirkeci
Sarayburnu

Mısır Çarşısı
Spice Bazaar

ÇİÇEK PAZARI

KÖŞKÜ CADDESİ

**KENNEDY   CADDESİ**

MARPUÇ
LAR SOK

SAKA
MEHMET SOK

ŞEİH MEHMET
PEHLEVİ CAD

HAMİDİYE CADDESİ

MİMAR KEMA-
LETTİN CAD

Sirkeci Garı
Sirkeci Station
İSTASYON ARKASI SOK

MURADİYE HÜDAVENDİGAR
CAD

NÖBETHANE

TAYA HATUN SOKAĞI

**GÜLHANE
PARKI
GÜLHANE
PARK**

**SİRKE**

İBN KEMAL

ORHANİYE CAD

Arkeoloji Müzesi
Archaeological
Museum

İstanbul
Erkek
Lisesi

Mahmut Paşa Camii
Mahmut Paşa
Mosque

SULTAN MEKTEBİ

TÜRKOCAĞI

CELAL FERDİ
GÖKÇAY SOK

TASVİR SOKAĞI

Bab-ı Ali
Sublime
Porte

Alay Köşkü
Alay Pavilion

Topkapı Sarayı
Topkapı Palace

**3**

ruosmaniye
Camii
ruosmaniye
Mosque

ŞEREF   EFENDİ SOKAĞI

NURUOSMANİYE CAD

Çağaloğlu
Hamamı
Çağaloğlu Baths

MAHMUT PAŞA İSMAİL
GÜRKAN CAD

Darphane-i Amire
Imperial Mint

(SAHİL   YOLU)

**CAĞALOĞLU**

Paşa Camii
Paşa Mosque

BABIALİ

CATALÇEŞME SOK

CAĞALOĞLU   CADDESİ

SOĞUKÇEŞME   SOKAĞI

Aya İrini Kilisesi
Haghia Eirene

**ESİ**

Çemberlitaş
Constantine's
Column

Mahmut II Türbesi
Tomb of Mahmut II

DİVANYOLU   CAD

TİCARETHANE SOKAĞI

İNCİLİ
ÇAVUŞ SOK

Aya Sofya
Haghia Sophia

Ahmet III Çeşmesi
Fountain of Ahmet III

BAHÇEKAPI

CADDESİ

**4**

EVKAF SOK

Binbirdirek Sarnıcı
Cistern of
1001 Columns

Yerebatan
Sarayı
Basilica
Cistern

AYASOFYA

BABIHÜMAYUN

Adliye
Sarayı

**SULTANAHMET
MEYDANI**

ADLİYE

A
T
MEYDANI
HIPPODROME

Türk ve İslam
Eserleri Müzesi
Museum of Turkish
and Islamic Arts

Haseki Hürrem Hamamı
Baths of Roxelana

MİMAR MEHMET

KUTLUGÜN

TEVKİFHANE SOK

KENNEDY

Sultan
Ahmet Camii
Blue Mosque

CADDESİ

AMİRAL TAFDİL SOK

Cankurtaran

**5**

ÖZBEKLER SOK
ŞEHİT MEHMET

Sokollu Mehmet Paşa Camii
Sokollu Mehmet Paşa Mosque

Mozaik Müzesi
Mosaics Museum

KASAP OSMAN SOK

TORUN

KABASAKAL SOK

KALFA

AKSAKAL SOK

ÇAYIROĞLU

AKSAKAL SOK

AKBIYIK

DEĞİRMENLİK SOK

FENERLİ MESCİT

OYUNCU SOK

AMİRAL TAFDİL SOK

KÖRFES HASAN PAŞA SOKAĞI

**SULTANAHMET**

Küçük
yasofya Camii
rch of SS Sergius
and Bacchus

**CADDESİ**

Bukoleon Sarayı
Bucoleon Palace

SEE PAGES
4 & 5 FOR
ENLARGEMENT
OF THIS AREA

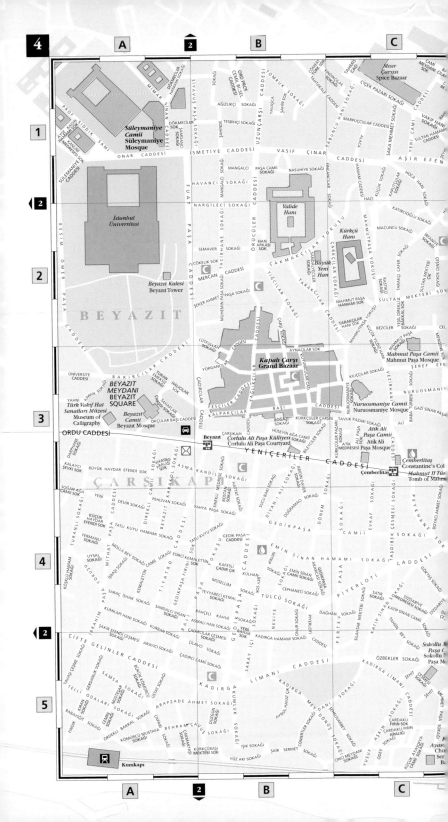

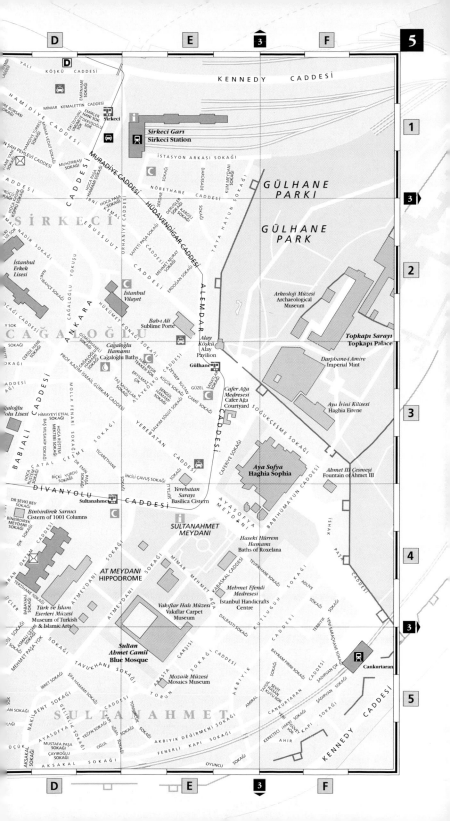

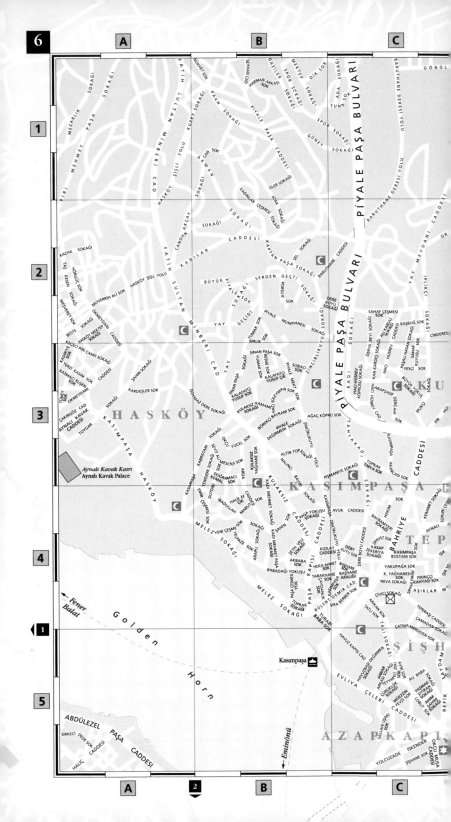

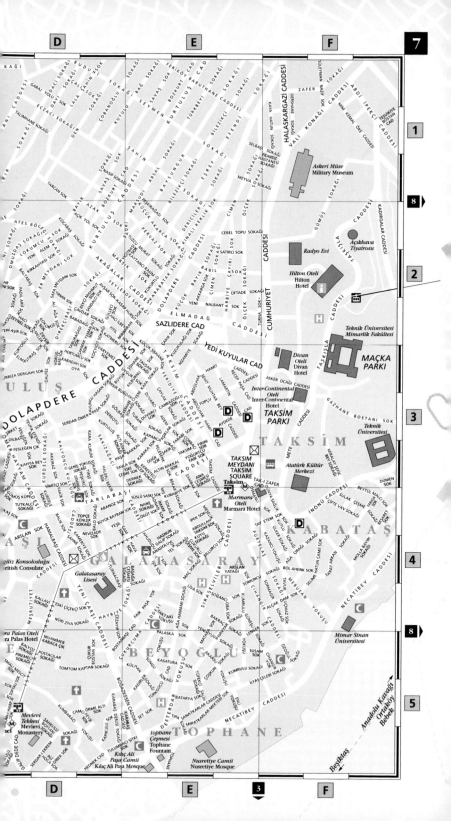

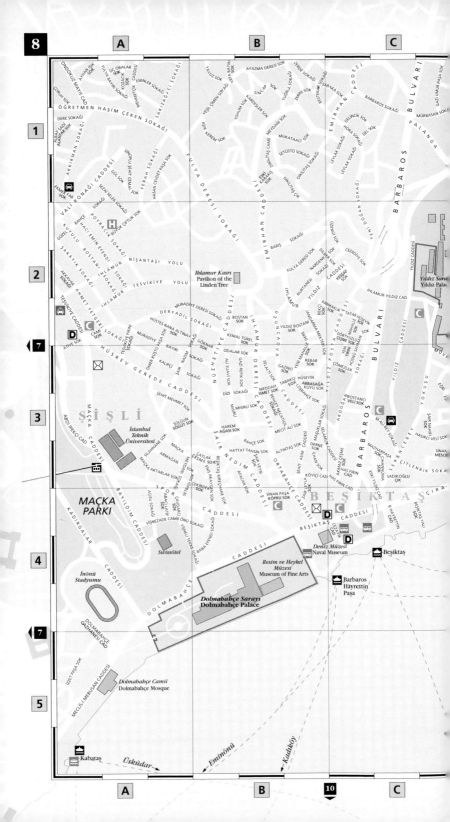

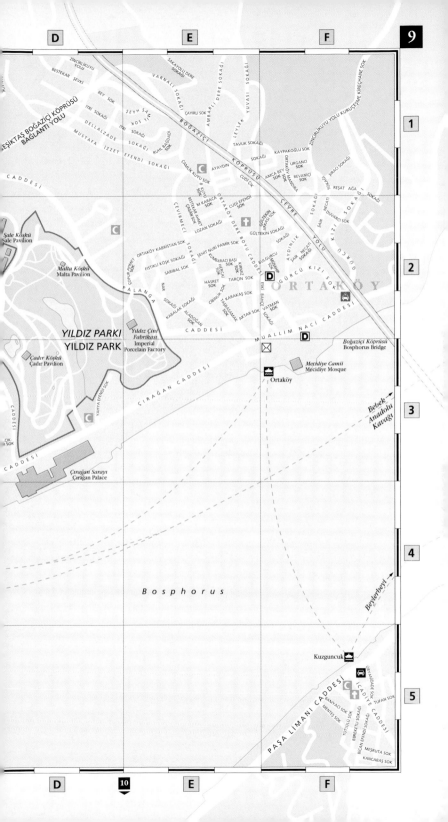

ZINCIRLIKUYU YOLU
BESTEKAR ŞEVKİ
BEY SOK
İTRİ SOKAĞI
ŞEYH ŞAM
İTRİ SOKAĞI
DELLALZADE
MUSTAFA İZZET EFENDİ SOKAĞI
RUHL BAĞDADI SOK
ÇAMLIK KUYU SOK
AYAYDIN
CUDİ ÇIK
C
M KARACA SOK
BETTEKAR AHMET ÇIKAN SOK
ÇEVİRMECİ SOKAĞI
ORTAKÖY KABRİSTAN SOK
ÇÖPÜR AHMET SOKAĞI
FISTIKU KÖŞK SOKAĞI
SARIBAL SOKAĞI
ŞEHİT NURİ PAMİR SOK
KUMBARACI BAŞI SOK
HASRET SOK
TARÇIN SOK
NAR SOKAĞI
KABALAK SOKAĞI
ALADOĞAN SOK
CIBINLIK SOK
KARAKAŞ SOK
PAŞACAMAK SOK
AKTAR SOK
HERCAI
PALANGA
CADDESİ

GEŞİKTAŞ BOĞAZİÇİ KÖPRÜSÜ BAĞLANTI YOLU
CADDESİ

BOĞAZİÇİ KÖPRÜSÜ ÇEVRE YOLU

VARNALI SOKAĞI
SARAYOLU DERE
ÇAYIRLI SOK
AMBARLI DERE SOKAĞI
LEYLEK YUVASI SOKAĞI
TAVUK SOKAĞI
KAYPAKOĞLU SOK
ORTAKÖY MANDIRA
AMCA BEY SOKAĞI
URGANCI SOK
REVANİÇİ SOK
ZİNCİRLİKUYU YOLU KURUÇEŞME KİREÇHANE SOK
SİRACI SOKAĞI
REŞAT AĞA SOKAĞI
ŞAİR NECATİ
DUVARCI SOK
GÜRCÜ KIZI SOKAĞI
YOLU

*Şale Köşkü*
*Şale Pavilion*
C

*Malta Köşkü*
*Malta Pavilion*

YILDIZ PARKI
YILDIZ PARK

*Çadır Köşkü*
*Çadır Pavilion*

*Yıldız Çini Fabrikası*
Imperial Porcelain Factory

GÜLTEKİN ARAÇ SOK
GÜLTEKİN SOKAĞI
LOZAN SOKAĞI
KIRMIZ SOK
VATMAN SOKAĞI
ESKİ
BAHÇE
BULGURCU
AYDINLIK SOKAĞI
ŞAİR NECATİ SOKAĞI

O R T A K Ö Y

MUALLİM NACİ CADDESİ

YAHYA EFENDİ SOK
C

ÇIRAĞAN CADDESİ

CADDESİ
CIK SOK
CADDESİ

D
D
D

⊠

*Boğaziçi Köprüsü*
Bosphorus Bridge

*Mecidiye Camii*
Mecidiye Mosque

Ortaköy

*Çırağan Sarayı*
Çırağan Palace

Bebek
Anadolu
Kavağı

Beylerbeyi

B o s p h o r u s

Kuzguncuk
ORTABAHÇE SOK
ÇADİYE CADDESİ
TUFAN SOK
C
BAMYACI SOK
MENTEŞ SOK
TUTULU SOK
BİREKTLİ SOKAĞI
BİCAN EFENDİ SOKAĞI
MEŞRUTA SOK
KANCABAŞ SOK
PAŞA LİMANI CADDESİ

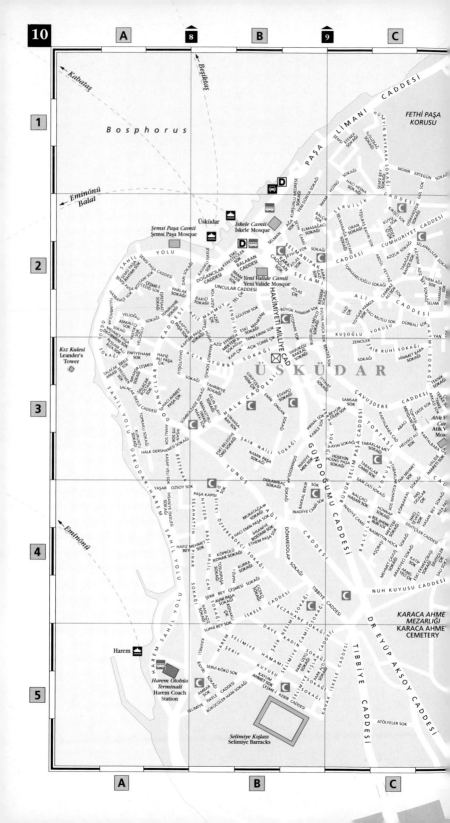

# Street Finder Index

IN TURKISH, Ç, Ğ, İ, Ö, Ş and Ü are listed as separate letters in the alphabet, coming after C, G, I, O, S and U respectively. In this book, however, Ç is treated as C for the purposes of alphabetization and so on with the other letters. Hence Çiçek follows Cibinlik as if both names began with C. Following standard Turkish practice we have abbreviated Sokağı to Sok and Caddesi to Cad. References in brackets refer to the enlarged section of the Street Finder (maps 4 and 5).

# General Index

# Acknowledgments

DORLING KINDERSLEY would like to thank the following people whose assistance contributed to the preparation of this book:

**MAIN CONTRIBUTORS**

ROSIE AYLIFFE lived in Turkey for three years, during which time she worked as a freelance writer in Istanbul for the English-language weekly *Dateline Turkey* and as a tour guide traveling all over western Turkey. She is one of the authors of the *Rough Guide to Turkey*, and has also contributed to the *Rough Guide to France* and to Time Out's London guides.

ROSE BARING is a travel writer who has spent many months exploring Istanbul. She is the co-author of *Essential Istanbul* (AA) and has also contributed to guides to Tunisia, and Moscow and St. Petersburg.

BARNABY ROGERSON has travelled, written and lectured extensively in the countries of the eastern Mediterranean. He is, with Rose Baring, co-author of *Essential Istanbul* (AA), and has contributed to several other AA and Cadogan guides. He is the author of *A Traveller's History of North Africa*.

CANAN SILAY worked for many years as the editor-in-chief of the English-language magazine *Istanbul, The Guide*. Previously, she had worked as a journalist with the Turkish daily newspaper *Hürriyet*. She has contributed to several books on Turkey, including Insight guides to Istanbul, Turkey, and the Turkish coast.

**ADDITIONAL CONTRIBUTORS**

Ghillie Başan, Krysia Bereday Burnham, Professor Anthony A M Bryer, Jim Crow, José Luczyc-Wyhowska, Colin Nicholson, Venetia Porter, Dott. A Ricci, Professor J M Rogers.

**ADDITIONAL CARTOGRAPHY**

Robert Funnell, Lee Rowe (ESR Cartography Ltd).

**DESIGN AND EDITORIAL ASSISTANCE**

Gillian Andrews, Gary Cross, Mehmet Erdemgil, Sally Hibbard, Francesca Machiavelli, Ella Milroy, Marianne Petrou, Nicola Rodway, Anna Streiffert, Rosalyn Thiro, P. Todd-Naylor, Dutjapun Williams, Veronica Wood.

**PROOFREADER**

Stewart Wild.

**INDEXER**

Hilary Bird.

**ADDITIONAL PHOTOGRAPHY**

DK Studio/Steve Gorton, John Heseltine, Dave King, Ian O'Leary, Clive Streeter.

**ARTWORK REFERENCE**

Kadir Kir, Remy Sow.

**SPECIAL ASSISTANCE**

THE PUBLISHER would like to thank staff at museums, mosques, churches, local government departments, shops, hotels, restaurants, and other organizations in Istanbul for their invaluable help. Particular thanks are also due to: Feride Alpe; Halil Özek, Archaeological Museum, Istanbul; Hamdi Arabacıoğlu, Association of Mevlevis, Istanbul; Veli Yenisoğancı (Director), Aya Sofya Museum, Istanbul; Nicholas Barnard; Ahmet Kazokoğlu, Bel Bim A.Ş., Istanbul; Poppy Body; Banu Akkaya, British Consulate, Istanbul; Vatan Ercan and Mine Kaner, Bursa Tourist Office; Hanife Yenilmez, Central Bank of the Republic of Turkey, London; Reverend Father Ian Sherwood, Christ Church, Istanbul; Father Lorenzo, Church of SS. Peter and Paul, Istanbul; Münevver Ek and Muazzez Pervan, Economic and Social History Foundation of Turkey, Istanbul; Edirne

Müze Müdürlüğü; Emin Yıldız, Edirne Tourist Office; Tokay Gözütok, Eminönü Belediyesi, Istanbul; Mohammet Taşbent, Eminönü Zabıta Müdürlüğü, Istanbul; Orhan Gencer, Protocol Department, First Army HQ, Istanbul; Robert Graham; Cengiz Güngör, Şevki Sırma and Mustafa Taşkan, Greater Istanbul Municipality; Hikmet Öztürk, İETT Genel Müdürlüğü, Istanbul; Bashir Ibrahim-Khan, Islamic Cultural Centre, London; İsmet Yalçın, İstanbul Balık Müstahsilleri Derneği; Nedim Akıner, İstanbul Koruma Kurulu; Süheila Etürk Akdoğan and all staff of the Istanbul Tourist Offices; Abdurrahman Gündoğdu and Ömer Yıldız, İstanbul Ulaşım A.Ş.; İznik Tourist Office; Mark Jackson; Sibel Koyluoğlu; Semra Karakaşlı, Milli Saraylar Daire Başkanlığı, Istanbul; Akın Bavur and Recep Öztop, Cultural Department, Ministry of Foreign Affairs, Ankara; staff at the Edirne Müftülüğü and Eyüp Müftülüğü; Mehmet Sağlam and staff at the İstanbul Müftülüğü; Professor Kemal İskender, Museum of Painting and Sculpture, Istanbul; Öcal Özerek, Museum of Turkish and Islamic Arts, Bursa; Dilek Elçin and Dr Celia Kerslake, Oriental Institute, Oxford University; Kadri Özen; Dr İffet Özgönül; Cevdat Bayındır, Public Relations Department, Pera Palas Hotel; Chris Harbard, RSPB; Rosamund Saunders; John Scott; Huseyin Özer, Sofra; Ahmet Mertez and Gülgün Tunç, Topkapı Palace, Istanbul; Doctor Tüncer, Marmara Island; Mr U Kenan İpek (First Secretary), Turkish Embassy, London; Orhan Türker (Director of International Relations), Turkish Touring and Automobile Club, Istanbul; Peter Espley (Public Relations Counsellor) and all staff at the Turkish Tourist Office, London; Mustafa Coşkan, Türkiye Sakatlar Derneği, Istanbul; Dr Beyhan Erçağ, Vakıflar Bölge Müdürlüğü, Istanbul; Yalova Tourist Office; Zeynep Demir and Sabahattin Türkoğlu, Yıldız Palace, Istanbul.

**PHOTOGRAPHY PERMISSIONS**

DORLING KINDERSLEY would like to thank the following for their kind permission to photograph at their establishments: the General Directorate of Monuments and Museums, the Ministry of Culture, the Ministry for Religious Affairs, İstanbul Valiliği İl Kültür Müdürlüğü, İstanbul Valiliği İl Müftülüğü, the Milli Saraylar Daire Başkanlığı and Edirne Valiliği İl Müftülüğü; also the many churches, restaurants, hotels, shops, transport services, and other sights and establishments too numerous to thank individually.

**PICTURE CREDITS**

t = top; tl = top left; tlc = top left center; tc = top center; trc = top right center; tr = top right; cla = center left above; ca = center above; cra = center right above; cl = center left; c = center; cr = center right; clb = center right below; cb = center below; crb = center right below; bl = bottom left; b = bottom; bc = bottom center; bcl = bottom center left; br = bottom right; d = detail

The publisher would like to thank the following individuals, companies, and picture libraries for their kind permission to reproduce their photographs:

A TURİZM YAYINLARI: 158b; Archaeological Museum 40b, 62b, 63tr, 64tr, 65t/c; *Aya Sofia from Fossart Album* 74tr; Topkapı Palace 56b; ABC BASIN AJANSI A.Ş.: 44t, 47c/b, 207cr; THE ADVERTISING ARCHIVES: 102t; AISA ARCHIVO ICONGRAFICO, S.A., Barcelona: 17, 18c, 22c, 30tr, 31br, 119t, 171t; Louvre Museum 19c; Topkapı Palace 55bl, 57c; AKG, London: 29tl; Erich Lessing 28t, Erich Lessing/Kunsthistoriches Museum, Vienna 30c; *Der Schriftsteller Pierre Loti*, Henri Rousseau (1910) 42cl; ANCIENT ART AND ARCHITECTURE COLLECTION LTD: 18tr, 21tr; AQUILA PHOTOGRAPHICS: Hanneand Jens Eriksen 169b; ARCHIVE PHOTOS: 173 inset; TAHSİN AYDOĞMUŞ. 4t, 15b, 19b, 20tl, 41b, 71ca, 72t, 75b, 78t, 86tl, 86u, 119ca, 144b, 170b.

BEL BİM İSTANBUL BELEDİYELERİ BİLGİ İŞLEM SAN VE TİC A.Ş: 233c; BENAKI MUSEUM, Athens: 23t; BRIDGEMAN ART LIBRARY, London: British Library *A Portrait of Süleyman the Magnificent* (1494–1566), Persian 30br; Roy Miles Gallery,

29 Bruton Street, London W1, *Lord Byron reposing in the house of a fisherman having swum the Hellespont*, Sir William Allan (1782–1850) 42t; National Maritime Museum, London *Battle of Lepanto, 7th October, 1571*, Anonymous 25t; Private Collection *Constantine the Great (c.274–337 AD, Roman Emperor 306–337AD)*, *gold aureus* 18tl; Sheffield Art Gallery, *Lady Wortley Montagu*, Jonathon Richardson (1665–1745) 43b; Stapleton Collection *Ibrahim from a Series of Portraits of the Emperors of Turkey, 1808*, John Young (1755–1825) 31tl; Victoria and Albert Museum, London *Sultan Mahmud II: Procession*, Anonymous 31tc, 161cbl/cbr; © THE TRUSTEES OF THE BRITISH MUSEUM: 161cla; DIRECTORATE OF MUSEUMS, BURSA: 162tl.

ÇALIKOĞLU REKLAM TURİZM VE TICARET LTD.: 212b; CAMERA PRESS LTD, London: 42br; MG/Jacobs 42bl, MG/Johnson 43clb; JEAN LOUP CHARMET: 27t, 31cr; MANUEL ÇITAK: 46b, 103c, 141t, 162b; BRUCE COLEMAN COLLECTION: 141b.

C.M DIXON PHOTO RESOURCES: 62tr.

ET ARCHIVE, London; 16; Bibliotheque de L'Arsenal, Paris 22t; Greater London Record Office 43crb; National Gallery 30bl; MARY EVANS PICTURE LIBRARY: 142b, 171b, 217 inset; ES Collection/Vatican Library 21tl.

FIRST ARMY HQ, ISTANBUL: 133b.

GETTY IMAGES: 9 inset, 28c, 30tl, 42cr, 49 inset; PHOTOGRAPHIE GIRAUDON, Paris: 24c, 43t; Bibliotheque Nationale, Paris 31bl; Bridgeman Art Library *Portrait de Guillame I de Hohenzollern (1797–1888), roi de Prusse (1861–1888), empereur d'Allemagne (1871–1888)* Gottlieb Biermann (1824–1908) 43cra; Lauros 27bl; Topkapı Palace 24b, 25c, 26c, 26–7, 30tc; ARA GÜLER: 21bl, 24tl, 33br, 87b, 128c, 211tr, 216–7; Mosaics Museum 77c; Topkapı Palace 1, 57t/b, 81t, 95bl, 161bl; ŞEMSI GÜNER: 41t, 129ca, 140t, 158t.

SONIA HALLIDAY PHOTOGRAPHS: 27br, 127b; engraved by Thomas Allom, painted by Laura Lushington 21c, 26br, 59tr; Bibliotheque Nationale, Madrid 19t; drawn by Miss Pardoe, painted by Laura Lushington 104c; Topkapı Palace 31tr, 76b; ROBERT HARDING PICTURE LIBRARY: Robert Francis 33cla; David Holden 150; Michael Jenner 3 inset,

55br; Odyssey, Chicago/Robert Frerck 38br, 168b; JHC Wilson 129cb; Adam Woolfitt 37cl, 91tr, 202b.

ISTANBUL FOUNDATION FOR CULTURE AND THE ARTS: 213b; ISTANBUL HILTON: 176t; ISTANBUL HISTORY FOUNDATION: 28br; ISTANBUL LIBRARY: 66b, 95tl.

GÜROL KARA: 2–3, 98c, 115b, 146ca, 153t, 169t; İZZET KERİBAR: 5b,14tr, 47t, 48–9, 50, 52ca, 118tl, 128tr, 134–5, 138b, 139t, 146cb, 206br.

JOSÉ LUCZYC-WYHOWSKA: 210tr, 211cl/cr/bl/blc/brc/br.

MAGNUM PHOTOS LTD.: Topkapı Palace/Ara Güler 8–9, 26bl, 31cl, 39b, 55t, 56t; MILITARY MUSEUM, Istanbul: 127t.

NOUR FOUNDATION, London: The Nassar D. Khalili Collection of Islamic Art Ferman (MSS801) 95tr, Mahmud II (CAL 334) 95cr, Leaf (CAL 165) 95cl; Burnisher (SC1210) 95bra, Knife (SC1297) 95brb.

GÜNGÖR ÖZSOY: 60t, 70b, 157t/cr, 170c.

PAŞABAHÇE GLASSWORKS: 146t; PICTURES COLOUR LIBRARY: 44b, 206tr, 210cl; PRIVATE COLLECTION: 135 inset.

SCIENCE PHOTO LIBRARY: CNES, 1993 Distribution SPOT image 10t; NEIL SETCHFIELD: 84; ANTONY SOUTER: 53b; REMY SOW: 174c; SPECTRUM COLOUR LIBRARY: 153b; THE STOCKMARKET: 130t.

TATILYA: 214b; TRAVEL INK: Abbie Enock 33bc; TRIP PHOTOGRAPHIC LIBRARY: 154b; Marc Dubin 45t; TURKISH AIRLINES: 228t; TURKISH INFORMATION OFFICE: Ozan Sadık 45b.

PETER WILSON: 56c, 75t/c, 79tl, 118c.

ERDAL YAZICI: 32, 44c, 167r, 169c.

Front endpaper: all special photography except ROBERT HARDING PICTURE LIBRARY: David Holden tc; İZZET KERİBAR: c; NEIL SETCHFIELD: cl.

Jacket: all special photography except PETER WILSON: front bl.

# Phrase Book

## PRONUNCIATION

Turkish uses a Roman alphabet. It has 29 letters: 8 vowels and
21 consonants. Letters that differ from the English alphabet are:
**c**, pronounced "j" as in "jolly"; **ç**, pronounced "ch" as in "church";
**ğ**, which lengthens the preceding vowel and is not pronounced;
**ı**, pronounced "uh"; **ö**, pronounced "ur" (like the sound in
"further"); **ş**, pronounced "sh" as in "ship"; **ü**, pronounced
"ew" as in "few."

## IN AN EMERGENCY

| | | |
|---|---|---|
| Help! | **İmdat!** | *eem-dat* |
| Stop! | **Dur!** | *door* |
| Call a doctor! | **Bir doktor çağrın!** | *beer dok-tor chah-ruhn* |
| Call an ambulance! | **Bir ambulans çağrın!** | *beer am-boo-lans chah-ruhn* |
| Call the police! | **Polis çağrın!** | *po-lees chah-ruhn* |
| Fire! | **Yangın!** | *yan-guhn* |
| Where is the nearest telephone? | **En yakın telefon nerede?** | *en ya-kuhn teh-leh-fon neh-reh-deh* |
| Where is the nearest hospital? | **En yakın hastane nerede?** | *en ya-kuhn has-ta-neh neh-reh-deh* |

## COMMUNICATION ESSENTIALS

| | | |
|---|---|---|
| Yes | **Evet** | *eh-vet* |
| No | **Hayır** | *h-'eye'-uhr* |
| Thank you | **Teşekkür ederim** | *teh-shek-kewr eh-deh-reem* |
| Please | **Lütfen** | *lewt-fen* |
| Excuse me | **Affedersiniz** | *af-feh-der-see-neez* |
| Hello | **Merhaba** | *mer-ha-ba* |
| Goodbye | **Hoşça kalın** | *hosh-cha ka-luhn* |
| Good morning | **Günaydın** | *geun-'eye'-duhn* |
| Good evening | **İyi akşamlar** | *ee-yee ak-sham-lar* |
| Morning | **Sabah** | *sa-bah* |
| Afternoon | **Öğleden sonra** | *ur-leh-den son-ra* |
| Evening | **Akşam** | *ak-sham* |
| Yesterday | **Dün** | *deun* |
| Today | **Bugün** | *boo-geun* |
| Tomorrow | **Yarın** | *ya-ruhn* |
| Here | **Burada** | *boo-ra-da* |
| There | **Şurada** | *shoo-ra-da* |
| Over there | **Orada** | *o-ra-da* |
| What? | **Ne?** | *neh* |
| When? | **Ne zaman?** | *neh za-man* |
| Why? | **Neden** | *neh-den* |
| Where? | **Nerede** | *neh-reh-deh* |

## USEFUL PHRASES

| | | |
|---|---|---|
| How are you? | **Nasılsınız?** | *na-suhl-suh-nuhz* |
| I'm fine | **İyiyim** | *ee-yee-yeem* |
| Pleased to meet you | **Memnun oldum** | *mem-noon ol-doom* |
| See you soon | **Görüşmek üzere** | *gur-reush-mek ew-zeh-reh* |
| That's fine | **Tamam** | *ta-mam* |
| Where is/are ...? | **... nerede?** | *... neh-reh-deh* |
| How far is it to ...? | **... ne kadar uzakta?** | *... neh ka-dar oo-zak-ta* |
| I want to go to ... | **... a/e gitmek istiyorum** | *... a/eh geet-mek ees-tee-yo-room* |
| Do you speak English? | **İngilizce biliyor musunuz?** | *een-gee-leez-jeh bee-lee-yor moo-soo-nooz?* |
| I don't understand | **Anlamıyorum** | *an-la-muh-yo-room* |
| Can you help me? | **Bana yardım edebilir misiniz?** | *ba-na yar-duhm eh-deh-bee-leer mee-see-neez?* |

## USEFUL WORDS

| | | |
|---|---|---|
| big | **büyük** | *bew-yewk* |
| small | **küçük** | *kew-chewk* |
| hot | **sıcak** | *suh-jak* |
| cold | **soğuk** | *sob-ook* |
| good/well | **iyi** | *ee-yee* |
| bad | **kötü** | *kur-tew* |
| enough | **yeter** | *yeh ter* |
| open | **açık** | *a-chuhk* |
| closed | **kapalı** | *ka-pa-luh* |
| left | **sol** | *sol* |
| right | **sağ** | *saa* |
| straight ahead | **doğru** | *doh-roo* |

| | | |
|---|---|---|
| near | **yakın** | *ya-kuhn* |
| far | **uzak** | *oo-zak* |
| up | **yukarı** | *yoo-ka-ruh* |
| down | **aşağı** | *a-shah-uh* |
| early | **erken** | *er-ken* |
| late | **geç** | *gech* |
| entrance | **giriş** | *gee-reesh* |
| exit | **çıkış** | *chuh-kuhsh* |
| toilets | **tuvaletler** | *too-va-let-ler* |
| push | **itiniz** | *ee-tee-neez* |
| pull | **çekiniz** | *cheh-kee-neez* |
| more | **daha fazla** | *da-ha faz-la* |
| less | **daha az** | *da-ha az* |
| very | **çok** | *chok* |

## SHOPPING

| | | |
|---|---|---|
| How much is this? | **Bu kaç lira?** | *boo kach lee-ra* |
| I would like ... | **... istiyorum** | *... ees-tee-yo-room* |
| Do you have ...? | **... var mı?** | *... var muh?* |
| Do you take credit cards? | **Kredi kartı kabul ediyor musunuz?** | *kreh-dee kar-tuh ka-bool eh-dee-yor moo-soo-nooz?* |
| What time do you open/close? | **Saat kaçta açılıyor/ kapanıyor?** | *Sa-at kach-ta a-chuh-luh-yor/ ka-pa-nuh-yor* |
| this one | **bunu** | *boo-noo* |
| that one | **şunu** | *shoo-noo* |
| expensive | **pahalı** | *pa-ha-luh* |
| cheap | **ucuz** | *oo-jooz* |
| size (clothes) | **beden** | *beh-den* |
| size (shoes) | **numara** | *noo-ma-ra* |
| white | **beyaz** | *bay-yaz* |
| black | **siyah** | *see-yah* |
| red | **kırmızı** | *kuhr-muh-zuh* |
| yellow | **sarı** | *sa-ruh* |
| green | **yeşil** | *yeh-sheel* |
| blue | **mavi** | *ma-vee* |
| brown | **kahverengi** | *kah-veh-ren-gee* |
| shop | **dükkan** | *dewk-kan* |
| till | **kasa** | *ka-sa* |
| bargaining | **pazarlık** | *pa-zar-luhk* |
| That's my last offer | **Daha fazla veremem** | *da-ha faz-la veh-reh-mem* |

## TYPES OF SHOP

| | | |
|---|---|---|
| antique shop | **antikacı** | *an-tee-ka-juh* |
| bakery | **fırın** | *fuh-ruhn* |
| bank | **banka** | *ban-ka* |
| bookstore | **kitapçı** | *kee-tap-chuh* |
| butcher's | **kasap** | *ka-sap* |
| cake shop | **pastane** | *pas-ta-neh* |
| drugstore/ pharmacy | **eczane** | *ej-za-neh* |
| fish store | **balıkçı** | *ba-luhk-chuh* |
| greengrocer's | **manav** | *ma-nav* |
| grocery | **bakkal** | *bak-kal* |
| hairdresser's (ladies) | **kuaför** | *kwaf-fur* |
| (mens) | **berber** | *ber-ber* |
| leather shop | **derici** | *deh-ree-jee* |
| market/bazaar | **çarşı/pazar** | *char-shuh/pa-zar* |
| newsstand | **gazeteci** | *ga-zeh-teh-jee* |
| post office | **postane** | *pos-ta-neh* |
| shoe shop | **ayakkabıcı** | *'eye'-yak-ka-buh-juh* |
| stationer's | **kırtasiyeci** | *kuhr-ta-see-yeh-jee* |
| supermarket | **süpermarket** | *sew-per-mar-ket* |
| tailor | **terzi** | *ter-zee* |
| travel agency | **seyahat acentesi** | *say-ya-hat a-jen-teh-see* |

## SIGHTSEEING

| | | |
|---|---|---|
| castle | **hisar** | *hee-sar* |
| church | **kilise** | *kee-lee-seh* |
| island | **ada** | *a-da* |
| mosque | **cami** | *ja-mee* |
| museum | **müze** | *mew-zeh* |
| palace | **saray** | *sar-'eye'* |
| park | **park** | *park* |
| square | **meydan** | *may-dan* |
| theological college | **medrese** | *med-reh-seh* |
| tomb | **türbe** | *tewr-beh* |
| tourist information office | **turizm danışma bürosu** | *too-reezm da-nuhsh-mah bew-ro-soo* |
| tower | **kule** | *koo-leh* |
| town hall | **belediye sarayı** | *beh-leh-dee-yeh sar-'eye'-uh* |
| Turkish bath | **hamam** | *ha-mam* |

## TRANSPORTATION

| | | |
|---|---|---|
| airport | **havalimanı** | *ha-va-lee-ma-nuh* |
| bus/coach | **otobüs** | *o-to-bewss* |
| bus stop | **otobüs durağı** | *o-to-bewss doo-ra-uh* |
| coach station | **otogar** | *o-to-gar* |
| dolmuş | **dolmuş** | *dol-moosh* |
| fare | **ücret** | *ewj-ret* |
| ferry | **vapur** | *va-poor* |
| sea bus | **deniz otobüsü** | *deh-neez o-to-bew-sew* |
| station | **istasyon** | *ees-tas-yon* |
| taxi | **taksi** | *tak-see* |
| ticket | **bilet** | *bee-let* |
| ticket office | **bilet gişesi** | *bee-let gee-sheh-see* |
| timetable | **tarife** | *ta-ree-feh* |

## STAYING IN A HOTEL

| | | |
|---|---|---|
| Do you have a vacant room? | **Boş odanız var mı?** | *bosh o-da-nuhz var muh?* |
| double room | **iki kişilik bir oda** | *ee-kee kee-shee-leek beer o-da* |
| room with a double bed | **çift kişilik yataklı bir oda** | *cheeft kee-shee-leek ya-tak-luh beer o-da* |
| twin room | **çift yataklı bir oda** | *cheeft ya-tak-luh beer o-da* |
| for one person | **tek kişilik** | *tek kee-shee-leek* |
| room with a bath | **banyolu bir oda** | *ban-yo-loo beer o-da* |
| shower | **duş** | *doosh* |
| porter | **komi** | *ko-mee* |
| key | **anahtar** | *a-nah-tar* |
| room service | **oda servisi** | *o-da ser-vee-see* |
| I have a reservation | **Rezervasyonum var** | *reh-zer-vas-yo-noom var* |
| Does the price include breakfast? | **Fiyata kahvaltı dahil mi?** | *fee-ya-ta kah-val-tuh da-heel mee?* |

## EATING OUT

| | | |
|---|---|---|
| A table for ... please | **... kişilik bir masa lütfen** | *... kee-shee-leek beer ma-sa lewt-fen* |
| I want to reserve a table | **Bir masa ayırtmak istiyorum** | *beer ma-sa 'eye'-uhrt-mak ees-tee-yo-room* |
| The bill please | **Hesap lütfen** | *heh-sap lewt-fen* |
| I am a vegetarian | **Et yemiyorum** | *et yeh-mee-yo-room* |
| restaurant | **lokanta** | *lo-kan-ta* |
| waiter | **garson** | *gar-son* |
| menu | **yemek listesi** | *ye-mek lees-teh-see* |
| fixed-price menu | **fiks menü** | *feeks meh-new* |
| wine list | **şarap listesi** | *sha-rap lees-teh-see* |
| breakfast | **kahvaltı** | *kah-val-tuh* |
| lunch | **öğle yemeği** | *ur-leh yeh-meh-ee* |
| dinner | **akşam yemeği** | *ak-sham yeh-meh-ee* |
| appetizer | **meze** | *meh-zeh* |
| main course | **ana yemek** | *a-na yeh-mek* |
| dish of the day | **günün yemeği** | *gewn-ewn yeh-meh-ee* |
| dessert | **tatlı** | *tat-luh* |
| rare | **az pişmiş** | *az peesh-meesh* |
| well done | **iyi pişmiş** | *ee-yee peesh-meesh* |
| glass | **bardak** | *bar-dak* |
| bottle | **şişe** | *shee-sheh* |
| knife | **bıçak** | *buh-chak* |
| fork | **çatal** | *cha-tal* |
| spoon | **kaşık** | *ka-shuhk* |

## MENU DECODER

| | | |
|---|---|---|
| **badem** | *ba-dem* | almond |
| **bal** | *bal* | honey |
| **balık** | *ba-luhk* | fish |
| **bira** | *bee-ra* | beer |
| **bonfile** | *bon-fee-leh* | steak |
| **buz** | *booz* | ice |
| **çay** | *ch-'eye'* | tea |
| **çilek** | *chee-lek* | strawberry |
| **çorba** | *chor-ba* | soup |
| **dana eti** | *da-na eh-tee* | veal |
| **dondurma** | *don-door-ma* | ice cream |
| **ekmek** | *ek-mek* | bread |
| **elma** | *el-ma* | apple |
| **et** | *et* | meat |
| **fasulye** | *fa-sool-yeh* | beans |
| **fırında** | *fuh-ruhn-da* | roast |
| **fıstık** | *fuhs-tuhk* | pistachio nuts |
| **gazoz** | *ga-zoz* | fizzy drink |
| **hurma** | *hoor-ma* | dates |
| **içki** | *eech-kee* | alcohol |
| **incir** | *een-jeer* | figs |
| **ızgara** | *uhz-ga-ra* | charcoal grilled |

| | | |
|---|---|---|
| **kahve** | *kah-veh* | coffee |
| **kara biber** | *ka-ra bee-ber* | black pepper |
| **karışık** | *ka-ruh-shuhk* | mixed |
| **karpuz** | *kar-pooz* | watermelon |
| **kavun** | *ka-voon* | melon |
| **kayısı** | *k-'eye'-uh-suh* | apricots |
| **kaymak** | *k-'eye'-mak* | cream |
| **kıyma** | *kuhy-ma* | chopped meat |
| **kızartma** | *kuh-zart-ma* | fried |
| **köfte** | *kurf-teh* | meatballs |
| **kuru** | *koo-roo* | dried |
| **kuzu eti** | *koo-zoo eh-tee* | lamb |
| **lokum** | *lo-koom* | Turkish delight |
| **maden suyu** | *ma-den soo-yoo* | mineral water (fizzy) |
| **meyve suyu** | *may-veh soo-yoo* | fruit juice |
| **midye** | *meed-yeh* | mussels |
| **muz** | *mooz* | banana |
| **patlıcan** | *pat-luh-jan* | eggplant |
| **peynir** | *pay-neer* | cheese |
| **pilav** | *pee-lav* | rice |
| **piliç** | *pee-leech* | roast chicken |
| **şarap** | *sha-rap* | wine |
| **sebze** | *seb-zeh* | vegetables |
| **şeftali** | *shef-ta-lee* | peach |
| **şeker** | *sheh-ker* | sugar |
| **su** | *soo* | water |
| **süt** | *sewt* | milk |
| **sütlü** | *sewt-lew* | with milk |
| **tavuk** | *ta-vook* | chicken |
| **tereyağı** | *teh-reh-yah-uh* | butter |
| **tuz** | *tooz* | salt |
| **üzüm** | *eu-zewm* | grapes |
| **vişne** | *veesh-neh* | sour cherry |
| **yoğurt** | *yoh-urt* | yogurt |
| **yumurta** | *yoo-moor-ta* | egg |
| **zeytin** | *zay-teen* | olives |
| **zeytinyağı** | *zay-teen-yah-uh* | olive oil |

## NUMBERS

| | | |
|---|---|---|
| 0 | **sıfır** | *suh-fuhr* |
| 1 | **bir** | *beer* |
| 2 | **iki** | *ee-kee* |
| 3 | **üç** | *ewch* |
| 4 | **dört** | *durt* |
| 5 | **beş** | *besh* |
| 6 | **altı** | *al-tuh* |
| 7 | **yedi** | *yeh-dee* |
| 8 | **sekiz** | *seh-keez* |
| 9 | **dokuz** | *doh-kooz* |
| 10 | **on** | *on* |
| 11 | **on bir** | *on beer* |
| 12 | **on iki** | *on ee-kee* |
| 13 | **on üç** | *on ewch* |
| 14 | **on dört** | *on durt* |
| 15 | **on beş** | *on besh* |
| 16 | **on altı** | *on al-tuh* |
| 17 | **on yedi** | *on yeh-dee* |
| 18 | **on sekiz** | *on seh-keez* |
| 19 | **on dokuz** | *on doh-kooz* |
| 20 | **yirmi** | *yeer-mee* |
| 21 | **yirmi bir** | *yeer-mee beer* |
| 30 | **otuz** | *o-tooz* |
| 40 | **kırk** | *kuhrk* |
| 50 | **elli** | *eh-lee* |
| 60 | **altmış** | *alt-muhsh* |
| 70 | **yetmiş** | *yet-meesh* |
| 80 | **seksen** | *sek-sen* |
| 90 | **doksan** | *dok-san* |
| 100 | **yüz** | *yewz* |
| 110 | **yüz on** | *yewz on* |
| 200 | **iki yüz** | *ee-kee yewz* |
| 1,000 | **bin** | *been* |
| 100,000 | **yüz bin** | *yewz been* |
| 1,000,000 | **bir milyon** | *beer meel-yon* |

## TIME

| | | |
|---|---|---|
| one minute | **bir dakika** | *beer da-kee-ka* |
| one hour | **bir saat** | *beer sa-at* |
| half an hour | **yarım saat** | *ya-ruhm sa-at* |
| day | **gün** | *gewn* |
| week | **hafta** | *haf-ta* |
| month | **ay** | *'eye'* |
| year | **yıl** | *yuhl* |
| Sunday | **pazar** | *pa-zar* |
| Monday | **pazartesi** | *pa-zar-teh-see* |
| Tuesday | **salı** | *sa-luh* |
| Wednesday | **çarşamba** | *char-sham-ba* |
| Thursday | **perşembe** | *per-shem-beh* |
| Friday | **cuma** | *joo-ma* |
| Saturday | **cumartesi** | *joo-mar-teh-see* |

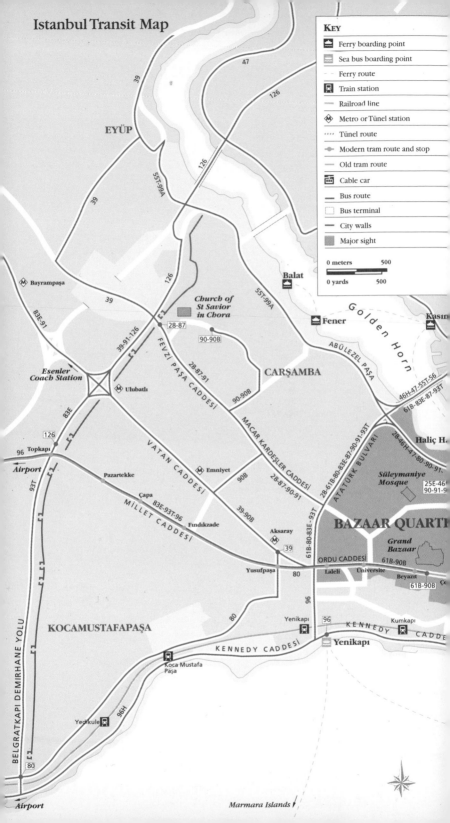